Speech
Communication

D1315901

Ernest G. Bormann & Nancy C. Bormann

University of Minnesota

Normandale Community College

Speech
Second Edition

Communication

A COMPREHENSIVE APPROACH

Harper & Row, Publishers
New York / Hagerstown / San Francisco / London

Sponsoring Editor: Larry Sifford
Project Editor: Renee E. Beach
Designer: Emily Harste
Production Supervisor: Kewal K. Sharma
Photo Researcher: Myra Schachne
Compositor: Progressive Typographers, Inc.
Printer and Binder: The Murray Printing Company
Art Studio: J&R Technical Services Inc.

SPEECH COMMUNICATION
A Comprehensive Approach
Second Edition

Copyright © 1972, 1977 by Ernest G. Bormann and Nancy C. Bormann

All rights reserved. Printed in the United States of America. No part of this book may be used or reproduced in any manner whatsoever without written permission except in the case of brief quotations embodied in critical articles and reviews. For information address Harper & Row, Publishers, Inc., 10 East 53rd Street, New York, N.Y. 10022.

Library of Congress Cataloging in Publication Data

Bormann, Ernest G
    Speech communication.

    Includes bibliographical references and index.
    1. Oral communication. 2. Communication.
I. Bormann, Nancy C., joint author. II. Title.
PN4121.B578 1977   808.5   76-6163
ISBN 0-06-040859-6

CONTENTS

PN4121
.B578
cop.2

PREFACE

In the preface to the first edition we noted that "the first course in speech communication has been undergoing an important change which reflects a growing student demand for pertinent information as well as skills related to life experiences." Since we wrote this, the trend for meaningful communication skills has accelerated, and student interest in education which is useful for professional and career interests has grown.

This second edition is entitled *Speech Communication: A Comprehensive Approach*. The word *comprehensive* has been used instead of the word *interpersonal*, as in the first edition, because while we have in this edition expanded the concepts from humanistic psychology and the human potential movement which led to the interest in interpersonal communication, we feel that a first course in speech communication must be more comprehensive. There are three basic styles of communication being used and studied in America now, and a college student taking perhaps a first and, unfortunately, very often a last, in-depth look at the process of communication should become conversant with all three styles: public-speaking communication, message communication, and relationship communication. Although some instructors will be, because of their particular backgrounds and preferences, interested in one style more than others, the student needs to know the history the theory and the criteria of all three, as well as to receive expert advice about how to practice them all. Everyone uses all three styles at one time or another in a busy lifetime; understanding how the styles differ, how they are alike, and what good communication is in all three styles is what we feel a good basic course in speech communication should be at this time. That is why the second part of the title of the book has become *A Comprehensive Approach.*

We have presented the communication theory which undergirds the public-speaking style of communication, the oldest of the three styles. Beginning with the formation of the Association of Academic Teachers of Public Speaking in the early decades of the twentieth century, this style is still an important one in our society and one which few can practice comfortably or effectively without help.

The message communication style is of more recent origin; it developed largely after World War II and owes much of its theory to the development of information processing systems and the rise of cybernetics. Most of the task-oriented communication in interviews, work situations, and small group meetings is in the message communication style. The enormous amount of research carried on to check the fidelity of message communication transactions attests to the importance of the student's need to understand the basic concepts involved, plus the need to have practical advice in how to make his or her own message communication more effective.

Relationship communication is the most recent style of communication to be studied in depth by researchers in this field, as well as by psychologists, psychiatrists, and many others. Modern living has fractured old family units; alienation in an urban society has led many people to feel that their skills for forming supportive and nourishing interrelationships with others need study and insights and improvement. The familiar statement, "What it all came down to was a problem of communication," attests to the need for understanding what goes into good relationship communication, and we have included the results of the most recent research and the best advice that has come out of the humanistic search for better understanding of this very personal aspect of communication.

From the moment the student leaves the basic speech course classroom, he or she should know, at the very least, of the existence of material pertinent to all three styles of communication. Facts are forgotten, but the key concepts that connect and separate the styles will be remembered. If, after the first year on the job, the former student is asked to make a short report to the newest members of the firm explaining what the year has been like, she or he will appreciate the basic public speaking information and skills learned in class.

If students find themselves in a job situation where verbal orders from an immediate superior tend to be incomplete, difficult to follow, or worse, somewhat contradictory, they may be able to attend to the problems in the message communication with which they are dealing, rather than assuming that their superiors are going to be impossible to work for. They will be able to look at message communication as an entity and will at least know where to start in trying to improve it.

If students realize, while studying relationship communication, that they have been involved in game playing with someone and have not been honest about their feelings in a particular relationship, they may well put the knowledge to work immediately and begin the slow, two-steps-forward, one-step-back work that is involved when two human beings work to build better interrelationships through improved practices in relationship communication. It is the possibility of immediate application of these principles that often appeals to the beginning student of communication, but the importance of the message and public speaking communication styles must not be neglected merely because their usefulness may not be as obvious at the moment of study

Speech Communication: A Comprehensive Approach, Second Edition, is a teaching textbook. An instructor may begin using exercises in any of the three communication styles from the beginning of the course. The theory relating to all three styles is presented early in the book and is interwoven throughout while we deal with such topics as non-verbal communication, the use of language, techniques of persuasion, listening, and informal and formal contexts of communication. As in the previous edition, we discuss the nature of dialects and the social effects of minority and ethnic group uses of language from a psycholinguistic perspective. The general principles of clarifying ideas and the use of evidence and reasoning are included, as is theoretical information about ethos, source credibility, and physical attractiveness. The role of persuasion and propaganda and the media are treated in detail, and much new research on mass media and political and social movement campaigns is included. Two-person and small group communication are included, as is communication in the organizational context. We have added an entirely new chapter on criticizing communication, with special emphasis on rhetorical criticism, its function and practice.

Our new theoretical emphasis has meant that we have had to add more technical terminology in this revised edition. We have incorporated definitions into the text and have footnoted studies previously alluded to, and have added extensive new research bases as well. Foremost in our minds, however, has been to keep the readability of the first edition. As before, we have tried to "stress solid information that the student can use throughout life," and we have kept the book as practical as possible.

Ernest G. Bormann
Nancy C. Bormann

Chapter 1

THE ROLE OF COMMUNICATION IN THE MODERN WORLD

The Spoken Word: Man's Common Means of Communication

The television speaker makes a shocking statement; he tells us 7 million adult Americans are functionally illiterate. Yet every day these 7 million communicate, with speech. They cannot read or write adequately, but they speak. They listen. They get along. But the point of the television announcement is that these functional illiterates could get along a lot better if they learned to read and write sufficiently well to get better jobs, to say nothing of the personal satisfactions they could derive from reading for pleasure and writing to friends.

When, however, does anyone say much about the everyday oral "illiteracy" that plagues many Americans as well? What of the people who cannot seem to say what they mean? What of the people who go through life unable to assert themselves sufficiently or to express enough warmth to form satisfactory relationships through their communication with others? Aren't these people equally handicapped, equally uneducated?

Before the invention of the printing press, nearly all mankind lived in a speech-oriented world. Only a very few could read or write. There are still cultures in the world where speaking is the prime method of communication, and although illiteracy is decreasing, much of the world's day-to-day business is conducted orally.

With the increasing literacy in western Europe after the invention of the printing press, written messages became more important. Marshall McLuhan has argued with considerable wit that printing after Gutenberg became one of the most important shaping forces in society. The alphabet, reading, writing, and the print media, according to McLuhan, taught people to break things into parts, to specialize in narrow ways, and to be detached from the stuff of experience—that is, to symbolize and exchange meanings other than those drawn from experiences which two people have shared firsthand and can point to, talk about, and agree upon.

TECHNOLOGY'S IMPACT ON COMMUNICATION IN MODERN SOCIETY

Since World War II, however, the technology that emphasizes the spoken word has grown with great rapidity. The inven-

tion of the telephone and the radio had led the way; after the war, the development and acceptance of television, communication satellites, and worldwide electronic communication followed in rapid succession. Written records are time-consuming to prepare, to retrieve, and to store. We found ourselves, after the war, almost buried under a blizzard of paper memos, forms, reports, abstracts, prospectuses, and letters. The reaction soon set in, encouraged by the development of ways to talk together across distances, such as the efficient telephone systems that allow conference calls among several people in different cities so that business meetings can be held immediately, without the difficulties of letter writing. Many observers, McLuhan being perhaps the most popular, found the growing importance of speech communication profoundly significant.

Television, information retrieval systems, and all the technology of spoken communication create a new way of thinking and give us new perceptions of the entire world. Events around the globe pour in upon everyone's living room. A natural disaster in Pakistan is as close as a tornado in a neighboring state. The typical American is washed in oral messages for several hours every day. We live in the age of information, which is to say we live in an age of communication in which the basic quality of life and of consciousness is largely a function of communication skills. A brilliant atomic physicist from Chile who lived for a year in the United States while studying at Oak Ridge, Tennessee, once remarked that be-

cause of his lack of skill in speaking English, he had lived an intellectually poor life during his stay here. In Chile he led a life of rich cultural complexity; he experienced and discussed classical music, the fine arts, politics, philosophy, and religion. In the United States, his limited language ability caused him to lead an inner life largely confined to the "give-me-a-cup-of-coffee" level of existence. What he could not talk about, he could not fully experience.

We live in an age in which we sometimes get messages from someone standing in front of us giving a speech, but in which we also get messages while being hammered by rock music as we watch light shows and look at images projected on a screen. The communication events of today are frequently aimed at mass audiences; messages are brief and polished, and usually have to compete for our attention with hundreds of other messages. This fight for attention leads communicators to use every avenue of the senses to reach us, hold our attention, and persuade us to buy a particular car, adopt a new hemline, or vote for a certain candidate. Perhaps most effective of all modern persuasion devices is the television commercial—using music, slogans, dance, drama, still pictures, moving pictures, animated cartoons, poetry, and argument—all orchestrated into a tight, smooth sales pitch, crammed into 60 seconds or less.

Much occurs, however, on the television set, on the motion picture screen, and over the radio waves, that is unintentional; yet we take it in even as we pay attention to other things. Are the long-haired characters the good guys or the bad guys? Are the hippies the heroes or the villains? Are the drug users we see in the movies or on TV cool and admirable or sad and bewildered? Do you gradually get the impression that the mayor is a fool as you watch him answer reporters on a news show? Do you begin to wonder if marines are great guys or if the cops are the good guys? Much of what we believe and much of how we act derives from those sometimes unintended impressions gained from radio, television, and film—impressions which are reinforced when we talk with our family and friends.

YOUR PERSONAL INVOLVEMENT IN SPEECH COMMUNICATION

Talking and listening are among the most important things we do; yet we do them so easily and naturally, for the most part, that we often think there is nothing difficult about communicating effectively. Actually, sometimes the hardest thing we have to do is to talk to someone or to a group of people. Usually those moments when we cannot talk easily are the very times we want most to talk smoothly, clearly, interestingly, and convincingly. Why do we feel tense or excited when we try to communicate with some people? Tension comes when much is at stake, when we feel failure will be unpleasant, perhaps even punishing, to us, and success will be pleasant and rewarding. The body alerts itself for verbal battle or for flight.

A good way to understand how vital speech communication is to you personally is to sit down for a few minutes and recall your own feelings over the last couple of days. Did you get churned up in an argument with a friend, with a date, with your wife or husband? Did you feel nervous and excited in a class because you wanted to say something but were afraid of what others would think of you? Were you ill at ease at a party where you did not know anybody? Did your turn your face away and avoid having to talk to somebody because you felt that particular conversation might be uncomfortable?

Before we get any further into the ways we are all involved in communication, you should realize two things: If you are shy and find it difficult to talk to people, you are not necessarily a poor communicator; if you talk easily with anybody and everybody, you are not necessarily a good communicator. The shy person can be compassionate and understanding and convey more with a quiet "Yes, I understand" than the person who talks on and on. Both extremes of people need to work toward the goal of give-and-take communication.

THE THREE COMMUNICATION STYLES

What's more, you need to develop a sophistication about speech communication because of three "traditions," or schools, or, as we will call them, *styles of communication* that are being used and taught and studied today, sometimes separately, sometimes in an overlapping format, and sometimes without a definite understanding as to their distinctiveness. Because a style of communication develops certain unique characteristics, people who are attempting to communicate in one style, but who unconsciously bring in elements of another style, may find themselves confusing their listeners unintentionally. They will wonder why they are ineffective, or why their listeners are not responding as they had expected. There are basic textbooks in speech communication which contain chapters that are 99 percent "let it all hang out" in emphasis, teaching students the importance of building trustful relationships through self-disclosure, but which then throw in a chapter on persuasion. Now persuasion is very purposive: Persuasion is often unapologetically manipulative communication, and such persuasion is the antithesis of trusting communication. Such texts do not distinguish sufficiently between the different styles of communication, and might lead the student to use a confusing mixture of self-disclosure and manipulation in his communications.

In the real world, a used car salesman can be a successful businessman, can have a very trusting, supportive relationship with his wife, and can be a loyal member of the city council, working for the common good. Whether he is aware of it or not, however, he is communicating in each of these three instances in three fairly distinct communication styles, each useful, each necessary, each sharing some elements with the other two, yet each worth studying as a distinct type of speech communication.

First of all, we use practical, day-to-day *message communication*, the kind of communication we all have to use to get along. In message communication we tell somebody something for a reason, and we have to find out if we are understood.

Secondly, we are all involved at times, if not all the time (as some would claim) in *relationship communication.* In this kind of communication we are less concerned with "getting a job done" than with enhancing our lives or the lives of others, with the growth of understanding and support from one person to another, or several others.

And thirdly, nearly every educated person, at one time or another in his or her life, must stand up and describe, define, plead for, or argue against, an idea or person. This is the *public speaking communication* style, and because public speaking style differs from the relationship communication style and from the style of message communication, each style should be understood for what it is, and for what it isn't.

We will define these three styles in much more detail in Chapter 2. It will be useful first to take a look at the various ways in which all of us use (and consume) spoken and unspoken communication.

The Economic Importance of Communication

Most college students have already come in contact with the communication difficulties and special needs every person finds when he moves outside the home and school and into the world of work. Suddenly you present yourself as a person and as a commodity at the same time; you are a particular person, but you are trying to sell your skills to somebody who needs those skills. You have, in other words, your first job interview.

Face to face with a prospective employer, we all become acutely aware of the importance of basic communication skills in getting and holding a job. But while the job interview may be a particularly graphic example of the importance of communication in business, industry, government, education, and the professions, every work situation demands a wide variety of speaking abilities.

ON-THE-JOB COMMUNICATION
Every job in today's complex urban culture brings us in contact with other people. Often we must cooperate with others as part of a team working to reach some objective. We have to get along comfortably with other people as we work together.

We often must be able to explain things to others so they can carry out their part of a job or join with us, if the job requires coordinated efforts.

People in management positions discover that most of what they do in their jobs is communication. After all, a supervisor seldom moves a subordinate around physically. Management requires the ability to organize, coordinate, delegate duties and responsibilities, and integrate the efforts of the group. A manager must also gain the willing cooperation of the workers. All managerial tasks require the ability to communicate clearly and persuasively with subordinates.

No matter what sort of job one has, many decisions are made in meetings of several people. Much important work is thus done in small group discussions, and the ability to communicate effectively in group meetings is basic to success on the job. Much research has been done about how groups work, and this book will give you tested and proven advice about how to work more effectively in group situations.

We need communication skills to live successfully and happily and to work effectively; we need them also to help us move through what is popularly called the maze of governmental red tape, with which all of us come in contact at one time or another. Government agencies related to city, county, state, and nation have an important dollars-and-cents effect upon us. We have to learn how to talk with people responsible for income tax problems, housing, licensing, and social welfare; we may have to help our parents fill out intricate Medicare forms.

SELLING AND CONSUMING: THE USES OF PERSUASION

Frequently we find ourselves in positions where we must meet the public either as part of a service industry or in some sales capacity. Meeting the public requires skill in opening conversations and giving clear directions or providing information quickly and in an interesting fashion. To be a successful salesman, one needs a high level of speaking ability. Selling requires the ability to meet people and to explain ideas clearly. Selling also requires skill in the use of techniques of persuasion. Persuasion is one of the most challenging, interesting, and exciting dimensions of communication, and we have devoted Chapters 11 through 13 to it.

Communication ability is vital in a final economic sense when we spend the money we have earned on the job. Wherever we go, we are encouraged to buy something. Billboards, television and radio commercials, newspaper and magazine ads tell us how to spend our money. Persuasive messages are everywhere. We need to know about persuasion not only to be more influential in our own lives, but also to be able to spot a phony ad, an illogical argument, or an appeal to our emotions rather than to our logical consideration.

When we buy something really important, such as an automobile or a house, or even when we make a sizable purchase such as a refrigerator, color television set, or boat, we find ourselves involved in an important communication event. Skillful persuaders try to sell us their particular product. If a person does not listen carefully and critically, a salesman will give him, in addition to the information he needs in order to compare products, much additional suggestion aimed at persuading him to buy the salesman's product. Salesmen sometimes seem to work at keeping the customer from making careful comparisons; with other, similar products on the market. As we stand there, knowing we are listening to a hard sell, we nonetheless want the basic information about his product, and we try to sift facts from suggestion. Most of us find it far easier to turn off a television commercial than to resist the efforts of a face-to-face salesman.

As you learn more about communication techniques, particularly about persuasion, you will become much more aware of the techniques used to make you consume this or that particular product or idea.

Communication and Individual Fulfillment

Man has a basic urge to symbolize—to communicate—but more than that, to generate words and images for the pure joy of playing with language and with ideas. Even when we are resting, our minds think up symbols. When people find themselves thrown together by accident or for purely social reasons, they feel the urge to talk to one another. Idle chitchat can be playful and great fun. A rich fantasy life can make a lonely existence bearable. Wordplay and small talk provide pleasant moments for all of us, and such communication should not be considered trivial, for the same tendency reaches into such important and fulfilling activities as theater, painting, the writing of fiction, and sculpture. Religion, too, is deeply symbolic and an expression of man's basic need to share his most intense experiences.

Most people gain satisfaction from creating something,

from discovering a new idea or product or way to do something from writing a poem or a good letter, from concocting a new recipe, or even from finding a new way to get from one place to another. If we are lucky enough to have a job that allows us to be creative, to figure out solutions to important and difficult problems, we gain much satisfaction from this and find our work rewarding. If we cannot get achievement rewards from our work, we say it is dull, routine, and boring, and our lives are not enriched by our work even if our pocketbooks are sufficiently filled. People with uncreative jobs usually seek individual fulfillment in other activities related to hobbies, volunteer work for the public welfare, or social contacts that enable them to feel important as individuals, not just like cogs in a machine.

We talk to people to be creative as well as to get some job done or to make social contacts. Often we do not know the outcome of our communication. We try out ideas in a tentative way with people who have similar interests and abilities. We "brainstorm" or "kick ideas around" or try out wild and far-out notions on close friends. Playing with words and ideas in a nonthreatening communication situation not only helps us do creative things and solve problems, but the act of communication itself becomes fun.

Finally, some of the highest and most satisfying moments for a human being come when two people transcend their self-centeredness and reach a high level of understanding. One of the warmest rewards in life is to really know another, to achieve what the theologian Martin Buber called the I-thou relationship. In the search for identity and fulfillment, the ability to communicate at the highest level is a basic requirement.

Maybe you can remember a time when feelings or thoughts welled up inside you to the point where you felt you had to share them with somebody else. Artur Rubinstein, classical pianist and world citizen, was in his forties when he met and married his wife Aniela; Rubinstein had traveled the world over from the time he was a boy, giving concerts in major cities and for heads of government. He had been wined and dined in the best restaurants in the world, had met and talked with many of the world's leading figures in politics and the arts; yet after he had been married a short while, he literally began his career all over again. Everything was new now that he had someone to share it with, he felt, and he gave no public concerts for two years while he worked diligently, relearning many of the pieces he had played for years, determined to be absolutely the best pianist he could be, for Aniela. He wanted to share the best of himself, and he has continued to do so for another 45 years.

Most people look for a deep personal relationship with one or two people in their lives, and building it is as much a creative act as the painting of a picture or the building of a highway. Communication can be an act of creativeness in a relationship.

The Social Importance of Communication

Man is a social animal. Loneliness is punishing, and friendships are rewarding. We all have to get along with people every day. If we live in a family, we have to get along with parents, brothers, sisters, other relatives, and most importantly, when married, with husbands, and wives and children.

Most young men and women are anxious to be able to talk easily and well with other young people, to make friends, enjoy dates, and come to know prospective mates. With so much evidence around us that communication problems cause unhappiness, even divorce, most of us are eager to do a better job of communicating than, perhaps, our parents or grandparents. If you were fortunate enough to grow up in an atmosphere of free and open and supportive communication, you will have less trouble talking with others than someone who was raised in a family that did not discuss family problems, family skeletons, or socially or politically sensitive matters. Unfortunately, much that passes for communication within the family is repetitive chatter that covers up thoughts and feelings rather than shares them.

Most of us are drawn to people outside the family, particularly to others in our peer group, people our own general age and stage in life, those with similar interests, people with whom we feel we have a lot in common. Sometimes, though, we find ourselves drawn to people who are quite different from us, people who strike us as being unusual, novel, and exciting, perhaps largely because they do differ from us. Communicating with people who are quite different from us poses additional problems of insight and understanding and requires a higher level of communicating ability.

Much of the misunderstanding that plagues us in our social relationships, both with those who are close to us and who are much like us and with those who are quite different from us, comes from bad habits of communication. If we look at our communication habits honestly and objectively and make conscious, supervised efforts to improve ourselves, we can form better habits.

Group Learning

The search for identity, community, and fulfillment through communication has resulted in the growth of learning and human-potential groups. The group dynamics movement developed in the 1960s into the T-group or sensitivity group approach. The main source of group dynamics work has been the National Training Laboratory at Bethel, Maine. Sensitivity groups are training devices to make participants aware of the importance and the dynamics of groups and to make individuals more sensitive to how they come across in a communication situation. Sensitivity groups have been used to train management personnel, to improve organizational communication, and to institute individual and organizational change. Business and industrial training programs, church groups, educational organizations, and charitable institutions all have sponsored sensitivity programs in attempts to bridge the various communication gaps between generations, religions, and economic and racial groups, and to increase individual potential.

Somewhat analogous to the sensitivity approach but centered more on the West Coast at such places as the Esalen Institute and the Western Behavioral Sciences Laboratory is the human-potential movement, which utilizes encounter groups. The encounter group is an intensive emotional experience in group communication. The professional trainer or facilitator who organizes and supervises the encounter group usually stresses authentic, sincere communication. The facilitator often uses nonverbal techniques which encourage the participants to touch fingers, feel faces, and hug one another.

The search for authenticity of communication through group techniques, no matter what its origin or the details of its practice, reflects the needs of contemporary society for new and better communication skills. The philosophy underlying the group search for solutions (sometimes referred to as "group grope") emphasizes the fight against fragmentation, isolation, alienation, and loneliness. Man is once again battling to conquer his environment, but this time, instead of the wilderness, he is trying to deal with an urban social scene.

From time to time we all feel misinterpreted. We feel that

people do not understand us or do not take into consideration the reasons for our reactions and statements. Sensitivity and encounter groups probe these actions and reactions, statements and responses, always trying to help the individual become more aware of how he affects others as well as how he allows others to affect him. At best, sensitivity and encounter groups can lead people toward increased awareness of their own needs and the needs of others. At worst, they can be punishing, painful experiences, similar to a "truth" session in junior high school when your "best friends" tell you all your faults "for your own sake."

Obviously, the mysticism, the drama, and the possibility of an intensely exciting and rewarding experience of genuine group feeling or belonging, of sharing and brotherhood, of acceptance, even if only temporary, make sensitivity and encounter groups appealing. You should be aware, however, of the possible dangers of participating in such groups; what starts out as a lark or a whim to get in on something exciting may turn out to be a valuable growth experience or it may turn out to be a painful, destructive exercise producing few new insights. A long talk with the leader of any sensitivity or encounter group with which you plan to involve yourself would be worth your time. You must be completely aware of what you are getting into.

The fact that such groups as those described above are so common—in churches and organizations, in business, and in schools and universities—says much about our society at this stage in its development. We need contact. We need communication. We need interplay and interaction with other human beings. The more our lives become surrounded by the unfamiliar and the uncaring, the more we need the strengths of good relationships with a few—or at least one—other persons.

Communication and Citizenship

THE LINK BETWEEN COMMUNICATION AND DEMOCRACY

Huey Long, a colorful southern politician in the 1930s, gained a large following during the Depression with his slogan, "Every Man a King." In a very real sense, every citizen is a ruler in a representative democracy such as the one in the United States. The basic assumption of our government is that with freedom of speech, of press, and of assembly, all points of view will be given an opportunity to be heard and the people, once they have heard the competing positions debated, will have the wisdom to choose the best policy and the best representatives.

The leaders in a democracy must be skilled debaters and persuasive speakers. Democracy has always encouraged the study and practice of real communication. Our earliest and still some of our most sophisticated ideas about communication were first developed in the Greek states several thousand years ago; they received their greatest development in the democracy of Athens and were further refined in Rome during the days when the Roman senate was a power. Totalitarian governments discourage the study of communication skills by all citizens and try to keep such skills in the hands of those working for the power structure. Controlled communication can be a powerful propagandistic tool. Open communication in which everyone is expected to participate is doubtless one of the best methods we, as private citizens, have to maintain a free and open society.

CITIZEN RESPONSIBILITY

Every citizen must be skilled in debate and discussion of public issues to be a participant in the democratic processes. Informal discussions in the home or on the job about various candidates and political programs are important to intelligent voting. A citizen in a democracy has to be more responsible, more politically knowledgeable and active, than a citizen in any other form of society. Citizens have to become as wary of political candidates and campaign techniques as consumers are of sales pitches. *As* wary? Far more so.

We should be aware that candidates often hire ghostwriters to help them prepare messages for the public. At best the ghostwriter helps the candidate frame his ideas in more effective language; at worst the ghostwriter provides both ideas and language and may fool the public into thinking a poor candidate is a good one. Some candidates have teams of ghostwriters, and several persons contribute to the preparation of a single speech. Most politicians running for important public office now use the latest persuasive techniques developed by advertising agencies and public-relations firms to produce their television programs. How can a person know for whom he is voting under such circumstances? Are the policies the candidate's or did they spring from other brains? Will the candidate be able to cope with the pressure of office? Will he be able to deal with the problems he must face? If we have been conned by human merchandising, our elected officials may be inadequate for effective government.

POSITIVE POLITICAL USES OF TELEVISION

Fortunately television not only encourages a candidate to use advertising agencies, short commercial announcements, and ghostwriters, but also forces politicians to appear on shows such as "Meet the Press" and "Face the Nation." On such programs, skilled newsmen and political analysts ask probing questions, and the candidate cannot rely on other people to answer for him. Indeed, on the better public-affairs programs, the issues receive a fuller airing and more intensive probing than is the case with the typical political address or rally speech delivered in person by a candidate before an audience. As these probing question sessions continue, the public soon gets to know the genuine articles from the phonies. Television gives us the best tool yet to take the measure of political candidates and policies. The cold fish eventually comes across as a cold fish, and an involved, concerned, effective human being projects his personality as well. You cannot fool the public long if what it sees is an unedited close-up of a person working in an unrehearsed communication event.

In summary, to be a citizen in a democracy, a person needs to know how to analyze political persuasion, how to test the validity of an argument, the truthfulness of evidence, and the wisdom of policy. All citizens also need to have basic communication skills to support the positions in which they believe and to bring their points of view into public discussion. The Greek philosopher Aristotle wrote one of the ancient world's famous books on communication. In his *Rhetoric*, Aristotle argued that the truth has a basic advantage over error, and if truth fails to win out in public debate, it is because the defenders of the truth are inept, lacking in persuasive skill. He therefore urged the development of communication skills to assure that truth would always have able defenders. To avoid a horrible world such as the one George Orwell envisioned in *1984*, where all our thinking is done for us, we would do well to remember Aristotle's 2300-year-old advice. It is still valid.

Multimedia Communication

Today the old emphasis on reading and writing as the basic avenues for effective communication is outdated. The most important messages tend to use all the resources of film, drama, dance, music, poetry, speech, and technology to make their point. As we have said earlier, the television commercial is a prime example. Brief persuasive messages costing thousands of dollars per minute to plan and produce are broadcast over television every hour. Many talented people and much money have combined over the years to develop the necessary technology to produce effective messages. The same tendency is reflected in the use by business, government, and the professions of the *presentation,* in which important messages are developed using visual aids, videotape recorders, films, music, and all the modern communication technology.

Although teachers have not been in the forefront of the multimedia revolution, more and more instructors are using modern technology in developing new ways of teaching. In the early 1970s a popular television program for preschool children, "Sesame Street," proved the popularity and effectiveness of teaching basic information by means of a great variety of visual approaches together with music and dramatic presentations.

Communication in the world of tomorrow will continue the trend toward greater use of multimedia approaches and technology. The electronic music and light shows of today's entertainment and the artistry of today's television commercial are but clues to the information culture and speech communication of the future.

The Basic Course in Speech Communication

The search for a solution to the needs of the future is evident also in the growth of the discipline of speech communication in our high schools, colleges, and universities. More and more schools are developing programs in the research and teaching of communication theory and skills relevant to the world of the future.

THE PURPOSE OF THIS BOOK

This first course in speech communication is designed to help you appreciate the universality of the need to communicate. This book is also designed to help you develop a keen awareness of the varying styles of communication used in different settings and for different functions in our society. An effective communicator does not have *a* style; he has several, and he knows when to use which. He works toward flexibility.

This book examines how we all, to some degree, appreciate positive communication from others and are upset by negative communication. Marriages fail because one partner is not able to fulfill the ego needs of the other. Communication within marriage and the family is now a big part of most family education courses. When young people talk of forming a meaningful relationship with someone, they have a good idea of what this means and of what is needed to achieve and sustain such a relationship.

More formal communication settings which remain important in many fields of endeavor are examined in this book. Preachers, priests, and rabbis still deliver sermons. Politicians still give rally speeches. Formal occasions still require formal addresses. Teachers still lecture to inform. The speech to inspire, to inform, or to persuade is still an important form of communication, and as students of interpersonal communication we need to study public speaking. But the public speech is only one of the ways in which people communicate, and it is becoming a less important way. The increasing use of small groups to achieve religious conversion and mystical experience, and the use of small groups of Students for a Democratic Society, Gay Liberation, Women's Liberation, and Black Power movements to make converts to political radicalism, testify that the persuasive revival speech is but one form of persuasive communication. The heavy reliance on political persuasion via television since 1948 and the increasing importance of interviews, conferences, business meetings, rap sessions, discussions, and public-affairs question-and-answer shows also indicate that the student of modern communication preparing for the future needs a much broader introduction to communication theory and practice than is provided by a course in public or platform speaking only.

This book, therefore, discusses communication attitudes, theories, and skills in relation to interviews, conferences, and group communications, as well as the preparation of materials and the performance skills needed for public speaking. We will also give you tools for becoming a more knowledgeable consumer of communication, especially that directed at you by the mass media. The emphasis will be upon theory and techniques, so you can understand communication well enough both to improve your own abilities and to listen critically to others. This book should help you to participate more effectively in your personal life and work, to be a more aware consumer, and to be a more capable citizen.

Chapter 1

THE KEY IDEAS

We live in an age of information, which is to say we live in an age of communication.

Television creates a new way of thinking and gives us a new perception of the world.

The fight for our attention leads professional communicators to use every avenue of the senses to reach us.

Much of what we believe comes from unintended impressions gained from radio, television, and film.

Sometimes the hardest thing we have to do is to talk to someone.

If you talk easily with anybody and everybody you are not necessarily a good communicator.

The three basic communication styles important in contemporary society are the public speaking style, the message communication style, and the relationship communication style.

Management is largely communication.

The ability to communicate effectively in group meetings is basic to success on most jobs.

THE IMPORTANCE OF THIS COURSE

Since each instructor tells you how important the subject he or she teaches is, you may naturally say, "Sure, from where *you* stand, but not from where *I* stand." Or, as the talk-show people on television sometimes say to one another when too much manufactured enthusiasm has been called for, "Who cares?" We have spent many hours trying to help people who have considered their formal education long over, who have risen to positions of importance in their business and professions; these same people now have information others need, and they do not have the skills to give out this information effectively. They have been promoted to positions in management, and they are having trouble communicating with people. Time and time again they say to us, "If only I had had some training in communication years ago." In the world of the future, an understanding of, and an ability to com-

The ability to communicate is vital for all jobs which require a person to meet the public.

The ability to listen, to understand, and to critically evaluate persuasion is economically important when we become consumers.

Man has a basic urge to symbolize.

We often talk just for the fun of it.

The highest and most satisfying moments of human communication come when we transcend ourselves to reach a high level of understanding.

Much that passes for communication within the family is repetitive chatter that covers up thoughts and feelings.

Much of the misunderstanding that plagues us comes from bad communication habits that can be changed.

The search for real communication through group methods reflects society's need for better communication skills.

The more our lives become surrounded by the unfamiliar and uncaring, the more we need authentic communication with a few people significant to us.

Democracy has always encouraged the study and practice of real communication.

A citizen in a democracy has to be more responsible, more politically knowledgeable, and more skillful in communicating than a citizen in any other form of society.

On the better public-affairs television programs, political issues get a fuller airing than in the typical rally speech.

Television gives more of us the best tool yet to measure a political candidate and his policies.

If the truth loses in public debate, the fault lies with its defenders.

Today's important messages use all the resources of film, drama, dance, music, poetry, and speech to make their points.

The first course in speech communication grew out of the need for developing communication skills appropriate to our complex contemporary society.

municate with, the spoken word will be essential to any person's individual quality of life. We can give you only a glimpse of the complexities that the in-depth study of communication includes, problems that have long fascinated serious students of modern culture. Our purpose in this book and in this course is to give you an appreciation of the importance of communication and practical suggestions for increasing your own communication skills.

SUGGESTED PROJECTS

1 Think of some person you know who, in your judgment, communicates exceptionally well with others. Pick a personal acquaintance, not a public figure. What qualities does this person have that contribute to his or her skill in communication? What sorts of things does this person do that others seldom do? After

providing a thorough description of this "unusually good communicator," compare yourself with this person. Be frank and candid. Make a list of the qualities you already possess that help you as a communicator; make another list of the things you should work on to improve your ability. Do you feel you have any habits that you particularly need to work on and change in order to improve your ability to communicate?

2 This project is designed to help class members become better acquainted with one another. First think of some appropriate method of name identification. (We take a wide roll of white adding-machine tape, cut it into pieces long enough to be taped or pinned from shoulder to shoulder, and print the student's name on each piece in huge letters that can be read across the room.) The instructor divides the class into pairs. The pairs are given five minutes during which one person interviews the other and takes notes so that he or she can tell the class about the other person for two or three minutes. The student who has been described to the class then has a few moments to add to or amend the comments of the introductory speech given by the interviewer if he wants to. If time permits, the students in each pair may then switch roles.

3 Estimate how much time in a typical day you spend reading, writing, speaking, and listening. Keep a personal log of these communication experiences for one 24-hour period. Further, classify your communication within this period as to its type — social conversation, business communication, school related communication, communication related to self-fulfillment, and multimedia communication. Keep the log with you and record your communication each hour; be accurate and complete. Afterwards, make a percentage scale approximation of your typical daily communication interaction. What percentage of your day do you spend reading, writing, speaking, and listening? Were you aware of any times during the 24-hour period when you consciously avoided a communication situation? If so, be specific as to what and why.

SUGGESTED READINGS

Bormann, Ernest G., William S. Howell, Ralph G. Nichols, and George L. Shapiro. *Interpersonal Communication in the Modern Organization*. Englewood Cliffs, N.J.: Prentice-Hall, 1969. "The Spoken Word in the Modern World," pp. 3–18; "Epilogue," pp. 296–306.

Brooks, Keith (ed.). *The Communicative Arts and Sciences of Speech*. Columbus, Ohio: Merrill, 1967.

McLuhan, Marshall, and Quentin Fiore. *The Medium Is the Massage: An Inventory of Effects*. New York: Bantam Books, 1967.

Reid, Ronald F. (ed.). *An Introduction to the Field of Speech*. Glenview, Ill.: Scott, Foresman, 1965.

Chapter 2

COMMUNICATION THEORY

Scientific and Artistic Aspects of Communication Theory

Communication theory is a particularly confusing field of study, because experts have sometimes used *theory* in the scientific sense and sometimes in the artistic sense, often not differentiating between the two. *Theory* in the scientific sense refers to verified laws which explain all events within a significantly large class. For example, the phenomenon described by the scientific *law of gravity* is always present (except in such unusual instances as the orbiting of a spaceship, and a person can account for such exceptions easily.) If we have a scientific theory we can plan things. We can account for the effects of gravity on a bridge, for instance, and design the structure so it will not fall down of its own weight. The confusion comes from the fact that experts sometimes use *theory* in the artistic sense (that is as organized principles and methods, in contrast to scientific laws and mathematical applications) and expect the practice of these theories to re-

theory *In science, a coherent, verified explanation for a class of events. In art, a particular conception or view of something to be done or method of doing it; a system of rules or principles.*
communication style *A distinctive or characteristic mode of verbal and nonverbal communication common to a group or community.*

sult in the same prediction and control of events as does the application of scientific theories. Artistic theories do not allow for prediction and control as do scientific ones. Sometimes artistic theories work out beautifully; sometimes we end up having to say, "Well, it was all right in theory, but . . . ," and have to admit that the practice did not prove the theory in a given instance.

Consider the *theory of music.* Using good principles of music theory, a composer may plan a composition, but only his listeners can tell him whether or not it "works," if they find it interesting and pleasing. His musical theory has not worked for him in the same way as the engineer's scientific theory of gravity has, invariably, aided him in designing his bridge.

There are experts in the field of speech communication today who often use the term **communication theory** in the sense of a particular view or vision of how communication should take place, or the methods which communicators ought to use. Because of the dependability of scientific laws, these experts seem to try to use their communication theories in the scientific sense, when in truth, useful and well documented as they are, they are artistic theories: they have limitations of acceptance, individual preference and taste, and viability; and they are subject to change.

We are going to be discussing various communication theories throughout the book, and we need to share an understanding of the important meanings for the term **communication theory,** so that in the chapters which follow we can make it clear whether we are providing scientific explanations or whether we are stating general principles and methods relating to the practice of the art of communication.

Communication Styles: Learned Behavior

We will use the idea of *communication style* to explain the ways in which theory is often a mixture of scientific laws and artistic views of good communication. As human beings go about their daily affairs talking to one another, they create ways of communicating which, when they become widespread, become communication styles. We are using the word **style** in this instance to refer to a manner of communicating which is common to a large number of people. Although some individuals often have more talent and skill in prac-

ticing any particular communication style, we are not referring to those individuals who are particularly distinctive or
unusually adept or elegant in the practice of the style; we
refer to the general, overall style of the group.

In this sense, a communication style is always *learned*.
You are not born with a certain communication style; you
must be taught to appreciate and practice it. Furthermore, you
may learn one communication style as a child, learn another
as you mature and become a member of a particular work
community or social community, and learn several other
communication styles as you live. An "uninitiated" newcomer at a planning session in a computer firm may well be
confused and upset by the way the members conduct the
meeting. The computer firm people use many shorthand
labels to refer to things which the newcomer does not understand. They may use numbers or initials instead of longer
words; they prefer talking in a no-nonsense manner, pushing
for efficiency, always aware of time limits. These are "machine" engineers, and they live in a community whose communication style reflects their work to a great extent.

Contrast this with the communication style in a sensitivity session where the computer expert is the newcomer and
comes expecting the group to "get something done," only to
find that there are long periods of silence, great acceptance—even encouragement—of highly charged emotional
statements, a general preoccupation with feelings, and little
sense of time, no specified goals or projects. Interminable
amounts of time may be spent going over the same materials,
and no one says impatiently, "We've gone over that already!
Let's get on with it." The sensitivity group is using a very different communication style than is the planning group in the
computer firm.

DIFFERENT RULES FOR DIFFERENT STYLES
Can one communication theory cover both kinds of communication styles? Not and remain consistent, although in
some instances stretching a theory will allow partial explanations. The reason styles differ is because they follow different
rules and standards, and these rules and standards are an important part of the separate theories. Once you have learned a
style you are able to communicate according to its rules. As
you practice, depending upon your talent and how much you
practice, you may become a fair, good, or excellent communicator in the style. If you go further and learn the communication theory related to the style and become competent

to criticize or judge communication according to the standards established in the theory, you will become a *connoisseur.*

THE ARTISTIC COMPONENT OF COMMUNICATION THEORY

You may become a **connoisseur** in a large variety of human activities related to art or taste. You might, say, become a dog breeder, a pigeon fancier, a rose enthusiast, or an opera buff. Take the case of the **gourmet,** who must undergo a period of study and practice in some style of cooking and wine tasting, to develop his or her palate to a state that makes him a judge and critic of good food and drink, according to gourmet tastes. Sometimes, untrained people find gourmet food untempting, even unpleasant, to the taste. Many good peasants (like ourselves!) just might prefer roast chicken, baked potatoes, and a slice of watermelon to creamed sweetbreads (a calf pancreas), steamed artichokes, and a wedge of Camembert. Certainly the person untrained in French wine-making and tasting will be unable to tell a "good" wine from a "really great one." Human beings have been taking natural foodstuffs and artfully changing them by baking, basting, boiling, broiling, seasoning, mixing, and decorating for thousands of years. In the process, different styles of cooking have emerged, just as in the process of communication, human beings have artfully created distinctive communication styles.

Without the artificial dressing-up of foodstuffs there would be no need for, and indeed no point in, criticism, beyond the judgment "I like the way this tastes" or "I don't like this." There would be no need for a theory of cooking, in the sense of principles and methods as opposed to practice. What connoisseurs do is set standards on the basis of tastes that are sometimes not even naturally attractive, so that it will not be possible for an unschooled person to make critical judgments. The people who set standards need models of excellence and ways to criticize practice. The dog breeder must have a model of the ideal dog in mind in order to select an individual animal to train for dog shows, where the judges will hopefully have a similar ideal type in mind in making their decision. The models of what is good and bad and the critical standards related to the models come to be an important part of the theory of the art of breeding show dogs, or of gourmet cooking, or any other "artful" enterprise. When a person teaches others to become a gourmet, much of the instruction relates to explaining models of excellence and training the students in methods of criticism. Cooking, functional in origin, becomes, for the gourmet, an art.

There are obvious functional bases for communication. Communication helps individuals and groups accomplish tasks, as well as providing the joys of "breaking the silence" and making contact with others. Cooking can simply provide nourishment; communication can be largely functional. Cooking can be an expression of artful excellence, and communication can often exist purely as an end in itself. Styles of communication often differ in the extent to which their practioners stress communication as a means to an end, or an end in itself.

THE SCIENTIFIC COMPONENT OF COMMUNICATION THEORY

There are scientific theories that relate to cooking. Investigators can use scientific laws to explain the effect of heat upon certain chemicals in food, to discover the presence or absence of various vitamins in food before and after different kinds of preparation; they can measure the number of energy units, or calories, in any given amount of food. Scientific theories also provide an explanation of the effect of vitamins and calories on the health and growth of the human organism.

Similarly the laws of nutrition set some limits for the art of cooking. No matter what style of food preparation people prefer, they are not likely to adopt a practice which, if used, will make those who eat the food ill. Even if they might make a dish out of certain mushrooms once, they would not likely do so again if the mushrooms proved poisonous. Still, within the limits of foods which are safe to eat, cooks may well choose to create dishes that are more tasty and attractive than nutritious.

There are also scientific theories that relate to communication. The energy in a sound wave can be measured, and the effect of the amount of energy on the human ear can be explained scientifically. A community is not likely to develop a style of communication which restricts the amount of power in a sound wave to the point where people cannot hear one another when communicating face to face. Before the invention of electronic amplifying equipment, speakers talking to large groups of people often develop styles of communication which included a careful, slow formation of consonant sounds and the bellowing of vowels. Often these speakers spoke very slowly to increase the likelihood of being heard and understood. The eighteenth-century British

scientific method *Systematic investigation of a problem, based upon observation, induction, and deduction: A hypothesis is formulated from data gathered and is tested by observation.*

evangelist George Whitefield, for example, spoke to thousands in the open air and developed a style of clear articulation and great physical force in projecting his voice to his listeners.[1] He was so dramatically effective that many preachers took him as their model and began to imitate him.

THE CONFUSION BETWEEN TYPES OF THEORY

Researchers in communication have had trouble distinguishing between the scientific components of theory and the artistic parts. The **scientific method** assumes that there is a regular pattern to events which can be found and generalized to a large class of happenings. The person who understands the scientific component of cooking can discover the caloric content of foods whether they are prepared in French or Japanese style of cooking. Questions for study may grow out of either the scientific or the artistic elements of a theory. The question What effect does the amount of chili pepper have upon the way people evaluate the food? is an artistic consideration; it is not a scientific question. The results of a study to determine the effect of the amount of chili pepper on the eater's evaluation of the food will vary depending on the style of cooking the eater happens to prefer. Rather than such variable artistic judgments, the scientist searches for answers which cut across styles, such as answers concerning the effect of varying amounts of vitamin B on the human organism.

The communication researcher, too, must find out what features of communication are measurable and constant across styles. If investigators ask questions which are a function of the artistic side of the theory and apply the assumptions of science and the scientific method to the answering of those questions, they may well confuse art and science, and think they have made a discovery which will generalize over time to include a wide range of communication events, when what they have actually discovered is something about a style limited to a few people in a given period of time.

THE EXAMPLE OF FEAR—AROUSAL RESEARCH

One of the early topics of investigation by people who wished to expand the scientific theory relating to communication was the effectiveness of communicating with people in a way

---

[1] See, for example, C. Harold King, "George Whitefield: Dramatic Evangelist," *The Quarterly Journal of Speech,* 19 (1933), 165–175; Eugene White, "The Preaching of George Whitefield During the Great Awakening," *Speech Monographs,* 15 (1948), 33–43.

which made them afraid, in order to change their attitudes and behavior. Basically they wondered, Can a speaker scare listeners into thinking or acting differently? The question about how much fear arousal will cause the listener to change behavior is like the question about how much chili pepper will cause the diner to like the dish. We will explain why.

Early communication researchers at Yale University first asked the questions about the effect of fear arousal in the 1950s, and discovered that their subjects, including some students at Yale at the time, were not as likely to change their attitudes when subjected to high-fear-arousal messages as they were under conditions of less fear arousal.[2] Apparently the style of communication that many students at Yale preferred in the 1950s was one that did not involve highly emotional messages or overt emotional responses. The college generation of the 1950s had the reputation of being a cool and introverted group. Consider Yale two hundred years before, however. Had the researchers conducted their studies at Yale in the 1740s, when a powerful religious revival swept across the American colonies, including Yale College, they probably would have gotten a different answer to their question. During the revival, high-fear-arousal sermons designed to put the fear of God into their listeners proved very successful in changing attitudes and behavior. Jonathan Edwards, himself a graduate of Yale College, delivered a famous sermon called "Sinners in the Hands of an Angry God," which is a classical example of high fear arousal. In part he said:

> The God that holds you over the pit of hell, much as one holds a spider, or some loathsome insect over the fire, abhors you, and is dreadfully provoked: his wrath towards you burns like fire; he looks upon you as worthy of nothing else, but to be cast into the fire; he is of purer eyes than to bear to have you in his sight; you are ten thousand times more abominable in his eyes, than the most hateful venomous serpent is in ours.[3]

Apparently the style of the revival of the 1740s would no longer have been appreciated by the Yale students of the 1950s. Interestingly enough, other communication researchers attempted to repeat the same studies in the 1960s

[2] An important study revealing resistance to high fear arousal was I. L. Janis and S. Feshback, "Effects of Fear-arousing Communications," *Journal of Abnormal and Social Psychology*, 48 (1953), 78–92. A number of other studies from the 1950s supported the Janis and Feshback discoveries; see, for instance, J. C. Nunnally and H. M. Bobren, "Variables Influencing the Willingness to Receive Communications on Mental Health," *Journal of Personality*, 27 (1959), 38–46.

[3] Wayland Parrish and Marie Hochmuth, *American Speeches*, New York: McKay, 1954, p. 82.

and found that the results contradicted the discoveries in the 1950s.[4] The antiwar, civil rights generation of the 1960s participated in a style of communication which celebrated higher levels of emotion than did that of the students in the 1950s.

Other communication researchers have raised questions relating to the effectiveness of emotional arguments compared to logical arguments, of climactic order of arguments compared to anticlimactic order, of one-sided versus two-sided arguments.[5] All of these questions relate to features of communication styles which change from style to style, rather than to scientific theories related to communication which remain constant throughout varying styles.

THE IMPORTANCE OF BOTH COMPONENTS OF COMMUNICATION THEORY

Throughout this book we will indicate the material for which verification in the scientific sense is available and the material which is essentially part of a given communication style. We ought not, however, make value judgments that the scientific component of our theories is better than or worse than the artistic component. You might find the science of nutrition a dull matter even though you become very excited about cooking and eating fancy dishes. You would thus be tempted to emphasize the artistic and put down the scientific, but you would be neglecting an important factor. Or you might feel that the scientific component is more reliable and valid and useful in predicting and controlling health and nutrition, and thus has more value; but anyone who has had to eat hospital or other institutional food knows that the addition of art to basic nutrition has a great deal to do with our total response to what is served. To become a student of the culinary arts you must understand both the scientific and the artistic parts of the theory.

In communication theory the scientific part is important because it undergirds and limits the stylistic developments. The artistic component is equally important, because it enables a person to learn to communicate effectively, understand the standards of the style, and develop critical evaluation and an educated appreciation of a human activity as im-

[4] See, for example, Howard Leventhal, "Findings and Theory in the Study of Fear Communications," in L. Berkowitz, ed., *Advances in Experimental Social Psychology*, vol. 5, New York: Academic Press, 1970, pp. 119–189.

[5] For surveys of such studies see Elliott Aronson, *The Social Animal*, San Francisco: Freeman, 1972, pp. 47–87; and C. David Mortensen, *Communication: The Study of Human Interaction*, New York: McGraw-Hill, 1972, pp. 184–204.

public-speaking communication style *The style used in the preparation, delivery, and evaluation of speeches before audiences assembled for an occasion.*

message communication style *The style used where communication is goal-oriented information processing.*

relationship communication *The open, trusting style used when communication is viewed as a means to achieve individual growth and establish meaningful relationships.*

rhetoric *The study of persuasive communication.*

public address *Communication by a speaker to a group, in a face-to-face audience situation or over the electronic media. Some would include printed addresses to the public.*

portant, widespread, and essential to life as is eating. In this book we will present the theory relating to the most important and widespread communication styles practiced in North America. From time to time we will comment upon intercultural communication and the growing need for all of us to become more knowledgeable in communication with people from cultures different from our own, both right here in our country and in countries all over the world. The main focus of our attention, however, will be upon the styles most of you are using or are likely to use in your daily lives.

THE THREE COMMUNICATION STYLES WE WILL STUDY

Three distinct speech communication styles are currently receiving attention from scholars and are in widespread use throughout the American public. These were listed in Chapter one as **message communication, relationship communication,** and **public-speaking communication.** We will change the order here because the styles developed in a different chronological order, and we will describe each as it developed historically. We will also show how each is a current and important communication style in the American culture. If we understand how each came into being as a distinct style, hopefully we will be able to keep the three separate in our minds and thus avoid some of the confusion that results from unwittingly mixing the styles in our everyday communication.

First to receive much attention from scholars was the style of *public-speaking communication.* The public speaking style has a long tradition, kept alive by scholars in colleges and universities and going back at least to the classical cultures of Greece and Rome. The theory associated with the communication style is often called rhetorical. Aristotle defined *rhetoric* as the art of finding the available means of persuasion. Many definitions have been provided after Aristotle, but most are essentially variations on the theme of intentional persuasive communication. Teachers who participate in the style and can teach you to criticize and participate in it are often called specialists in **rhetoric** and **public address.**

The second style, *message communication,* has a much shorter tradition, as it goes back largely to the development of experimental research in communication and to the beginnings of "thinking" machines in the twentieth century. Teachers who participate in the style and can teach you to appreciate and practice the approach are often called specialists in *communication.*

interpersonal communication *The practice of communication in the relationship style.*

The third style, most recent of the three, we will call *relationship communication*. Relationship communication as a style and as a study goes back to the rise of humanistic psychology, the human potential movement, and the impulse against science of the 1960s. Teachers who participate in the relationship style and can teach you to appreciate and practice the approach are often called specialists in **interpersonal communication.**

The Public-Speaking Communication Style

The current public-speaking communication style emerged in the early part of the twentieth century. The style was a result of the development of interest in the study of oral communication on the part of a number of teachers in departments of English. The study of rhetoric had been an important part of liberal arts college training in the 1800s. For centuries, examinations in colleges had been oral, and a graduate often had to demonstrate his ability to handle discourse while giving an exposition of his knowledge, during platform examinations before his professors. By the beginning of the 1900s, however, more and more departments of English were concentrating on the study of literature, and the lack of attention to rhetoric caused a number of instructors who were primarily interested in oral communication to break away and found their own departments, which were often called departments of speech.[6]

DEVELOPMENTS SINCE 1915
Although advanced work in the new departments often included the study of works on rhetoric, oratory, and eloquence from ancient times to the present, the public-speaking style itself was supported by a theory developed largely in the basic public-speaking course and in the textbooks written for that course, beginning around 1915.

Any communication style begins when a number of people start to practice a new and different way of communicating. As the practice becomes imitated and more people begin to use the style it may reach a point where it begins to spread rapidly. Once a style becomes widespread, the usual human

[6] For the history of these developments see Karl Wallace, ed., *History of Speech Education in America*, Englewood Cliffs, N.J.: Prentice-Hall, 1954.

desire to make informal critical comments becomes more organized. The rapid spread of any activity requires instruction to newcomers and systematic criticism. The pressure for instruction also results in the development of manuals or textbooks which provide advice on how to communicate properly and how to evaluate communication. The textbooks provide the theory for the style. A fully mature communication style thus involves practice, criticism, and theory—all interrelated.

Our current public-speaking style is supported by criticism and theory that have evolved gradually over the last sixty years. An early and important textbook containing the theory was written by James A. Winans in 1915, and is entitled *Public Speaking.*[7] By the time Winans wrote his book, the practice and criticism of the communication style had reached a point where he could provide a model of the ideal communication events and include detailed discussion for the student who wanted to approximate the ideal in practice.

THE BASIC MODEL
The basic model of the public-speaking style is essentially a situation in which the central character is *the speaker.* Other parts of the communication situation include *an audience*

[7] Englewood Cliffs, N.J.: Prentice-Hall, 1915.

and *an occasion.* The occasion is something which the speaker must take into account in planning the speech. An audience is also an important part of the event, but the speaker sets the action in motion, and the audience then responds. The speaker may be free to select *the topic* (another basic element of the situation), or the topic may be part of the given situation. In any case, the focus is upon the speaker, center stage, who has studied the audience carefully, has skillfully adapted the topic and supporting ideas to the audience and the occasion. The final part of the model is *the speech,* which results from the dynamic interplay of the other parts of the speaking situation: The audience is not passive but tends to respond positively or negatively to the speech and may provide complications which cause the speaker problems as the speech unfolds. If the audience is hostile to the speaker or the topic or both at the beginning, the suspense and drama is heightened. Not only that, but a speech which succeeds against high odds is evaluated as a better speech than one which achieves the speaker's objective with little trouble. The speaker is alert to the response of the audience: He reads the nonverbal cues as well as the shouts, questions, and other verbal responses, and adjusts to the unfolding situation. In the final analysis, the speaker succeeds or fails on the basis of native ability, trained artistry, and the capacity to take initiative and act in such a way that he or she can achieve consciously thought-out objectives.

THE IDEAL PUBLIC-SPEAKING COMMUNICATION EVENT

A good public-speaking communication event is one in which a skillful speaker with a clear purpose analyzes the audience and occasion carefully and wisely, selects a suitable topic, preplans the organization and content of the message, delivers the speech with appropriate nonverbal gestures and vocal intonations, phrases the ideas in suitable language for the hearers, carefully reads the audience's response, accommodates the ideas to the audience both in the planning and delivery of the speech, and achieves his purpose by gaining the suitable audience response.

The theory associated with a good public-speaking communication event is related to the basic parts of the model. The theory deals with the occasions for public speeches, for example: Some occasions call for humor, others for solemnity; some call for argument, others for emotion; some call for information; others for moving the listener to action;

some call for celebrating the community and its values; others call for attacking enemies and wrongdoers. The theory also deals with those elements of the speaker's character which serve as means of persuasion: What is it about the personality and ability of the speaker that makes the audience believe, trust, and accept the information and advice in the speech? The theory also deals with the audience: What are the natures of audiences composed of people of various ages, socioeconomic and educational backgrounds, interests, and attitudes?

Since the speech itself is perhaps the most important feature of the public-speaking model, the theory deals with many of its aspects. Much of the theory is devoted to detailed analysis regarding selecting the general topic and inventing the supporting material for the speech; organizing the material to adapt it to the audience; phrasing the ideas in suitable language; and using nonverbal communication to support the objectives of the speaker. Often the invention or discovery of supporting material is examined in terms of ways that speakers may include material that will bolster their personal authority with the audience, of ways that speakers may include material that will make a convincing case to support their argument, and ways that speakers may include material which will arouse suitable emotional responses in the audience, promote the proper attitudes and values, and cause the proper behavioral results.

The Message Communication Style

While the liberal arts and humanities traditions were providing a hospitable environment for the growth and practice of the public-speaking style, engineers were applying scientific methods to the study of communication, particularly to sending messages by telephone, radio, and television. Out of their practice grew a new way of criticizing communication events. In the 1940s they produced the message communication theory, which rounded out another style of communication. By the 1940s engineers working at such places as the Bell Telephone Laboratories and the Massachusetts Institute of Technology were also beginning to develop electronic thinking machines. They tended to blueprint their plans for electronic circuits for radios, telephones, television sets, and computers. One of the first important descriptions of the ideal communication event in the new style was a model presented in the form of an electronic blueprint by Shannon and Weaver in their study, *The Mathematical Theory of Communication*.[8] Shramm, who was more interested in mass communication than in electronic transmission, modified the Shannon and Weaver model, and Berlo made further modifications, which resulted in a description of the ideal message communication event which was abstract and broad enough to cover much human as well as machine communication.[9]

Berlo's model of communication was complete, explicit, and widely accepted as the basis for the new style. To be sure, others criticized and modified the basic description, but most of the subsequent changes dealt with minor details and were designed to solve puzzles within the agreed-upon rules and assumptions of the style. Theorists in the message communication style have been preoccupied with the schematic representation of the ideal communication event.[10] They have experimented with various alternative schematic and graphic blueprinting to explain their models. Whereas the model of the ideal event in the public speaking style was dramatic and emphasized human characters in action—people meeting obstacles and overcoming audience resistance to win out and achieve their objectives—the ideal communication event in the message communication style was blueprinted like a

---

[8] Urbana, Ill.: University of Illinois Press, 1949.

[9] Schramm presented his model in "How Communication Works," in W. L. Schramm, ed., *The Processes and Effects of Communication*, Urbana, Ill.: University of Illinois Press, 1954, pp. 3–26. Berlo developed his model in David K. Berlo, *The Process of Communication*, New York: Holt, Rinehart & Winston, 1960.

[10] For a survey of some typical models see Mortensen, pp. 29–45.

radio circuit. The model emphasized the engineers' world of electronic components, wires, and the application of scientific principles of electricity. Using the analogy of the electronic circuit to describe human communication sometimes misled people into believing that the communication models of the message communication style were part of a scientific theory rather than an artistic one. Both the message communication model and the public speaking model are descriptions of ideal communication events according to the assumptions of either style.

THE IDEAL: MAN TALKING TO MACHINE
The basic ideal communication event of the message communication style comes from the model of man talking to machine. Assume that we want to talk to a computer. The first step is to decide what we want the machine to do. We then plan a message to reach our goal, put the message into symbols the computer can understand, and taking care that each sentence is in the correct form and that no information is left out, we punch the message onto cards and feed it into the computer. The computer reads the cards until it comes to a sentence with a mistake in it. Perhaps we have forgotten to put in a necessary comma. The computer stops and prints out a sentence that explains there is an error. We then go back to the card that caused the trouble, check the sentence, discover the mistake, put in the comma, and replace the card in the computer. Now the computer understands; it keeps on communicating with us, either understanding completely or stopping and asking for a correction or for new information. Thus we work together with the machine to achieve understanding.

When the computer indicates it does not understand a message, it lets the programmer know about the problem. When programmers found ways to teach the machine to indicate the source of a communication problem they made a major breakthrough in developing computer technology. The machine's ability to indicate the nature of a communication difficulty lead to the discovery of a very powerful principle. The engineers needed to term for the principle and picked one that was common to the study of electronics, *feedback.*

THE PRINCIPLE OF FEEDBACK
Cybernetics, the study of the way humans set goals and control behavior to achieve those goals and the way in which machines can come to serve the same functions, is based

feedback *The process wherein a machine continuously gives information about its output to an automatic control device so that errors can be corrected. Knowledge about the results of an action or message which influences further messages in a communication event.*
cybernetics *The study of human control functions, especially as it relates to messages, and to ways in which machines can replace them.*

upon the ability of organisms and machines to provide and use feedback. The principle of feedback is most easily illustrated by the furnace thermostat in most homes. The homeowner selects a temperature level as a goal and sets the thermostat control to that temperature. The thermostat contains a sensing mechanism that measures the actual temperature level of the air surrounding it. When the actual level departs from the desired level (the goal) the thermostat sends out an electrical message to the furnace which either turns it on, thus giving more heat to bring the level up to the goal, or, once the goal is reached, cuts off the furnace to allow the house to remain at the desired level of heat.

The term feedback refers to the data about the output of a machine which the machine continuously feeds to an automatic control device so that errors can be corrected and performance controlled. The principle of feedback, of course, is a part of the goal-seeking behavior of all organisms, including human beings. Although the principle has always operated in goal-directed behavior, it had not drawn much attention nor been analyzed much until the development of automation and computers elevated the principle to a key position in the theory of the message communication style.

Because of the importance of feedback in the theory of message communication, which is the basis for many sections of the book, we will explain the principle in greater detail. We will use the letters *I G M* as the key to the description of the ideal operation of feedback. The *I* refers to an *initiator*, a person or thing, who/that does something to reach a *goal* (*G*). The *M* indicates the *monitor* built into the initiator to provide information on what the *I* is doing so the *I* can correct mistaken attempts to reach the goal; the monitor is thus part of the "automatic control system" for the initiator.

Let us say you see a pencil on the desk and decide to pick it up. You stretch your hand out toward the pencil and as you watch your hand, you see that you are going to overreach the pencil, so you tighten certain muscles in your arm and shoulder and slow down the movement. You keep watching your hand, and now you see that you have slowed down too much and your hand will fall short, so again you adjust the push you give your hand, until your fingers land on target and you pick up the pencil. One action loops back and causes another.

Does the situation of picking up the pencil contain the necessary parts of a feedback loop? You are the *initiator* (person or thing) with the *goal* (of picking up the pencil), and you

Figure 1

THE CONCEPT OF FEEDBACK (IGM)

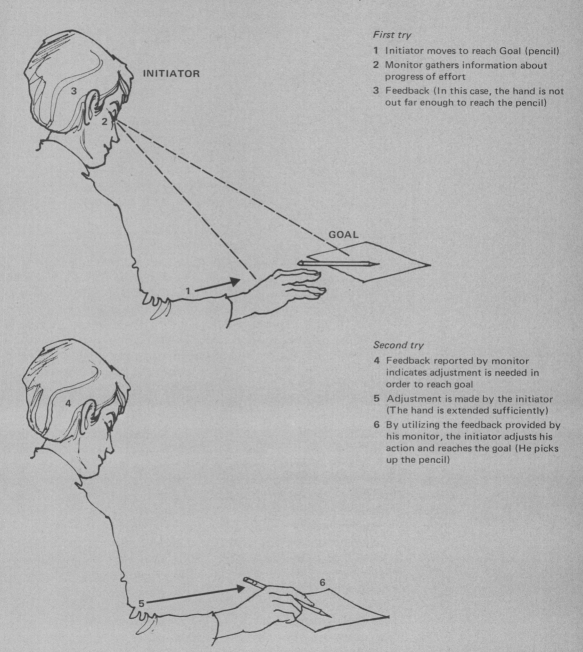

INITIATOR

GOAL

First try

1 Initiator moves to reach Goal (pencil)
2 Monitor gathers information about progress of effort
3 Feedback (In this case, the hand is not out far enough to reach the pencil)

Second try

4 Feedback reported by monitor indicates adjustment is needed in order to reach goal
5 Adjustment is made by the initiator (The hand is extended sufficiently)
6 By utilizing the feedback provided by his monitor, the initiator adjusts his action and reaches the goal (He picks up the pencil)

fidelity *The ability of a communication system to produce information output which accurately reflects the information input.*
noise *Disturbance in a communication system which interferes with transmission of information.*
redundancy *Message elements which add no new information.*

sense through your eyes (the monitor) continuous information about how your arm is moving in comparison with where it ought to be if you are to reach your goal. Using the information you get from watching the path of your hand, you change your reach to hit directly on target. The situation illustrates all the parts, *I G M*, of the ideal feedback loop, as presented in Figure 1.

One important feature of the feedback loop is that only one person or thing has the goal. The pencil does not have a goal; the computer does not set up a different goal and fight the programmer over what they ought to do as a team. (We are all familiar with certain science-fiction dramas based on the idea that our machines will begin to have goals of their own and start to take over the world; but up to now such stories remain fiction, thank goodness!) In the ideal situation, feedback is information about behavior that enables the initiator to modify behavior to achieve the goal.

THE IDEAL OF THE MESSAGE COMMUNICATION STYLE

The communication theory that relates to the message communication style developed a set of critical standards as well as a rationale for practice. One of the earmarks of good communication according to this theory is **fidelity.** The concept of fidelity refers to how much of the message is transmitted without distortion or loss. High-fidelity tape or record players give the listener a more accurate reproduction of sound than do low-fidelity systems. **Noise** in a communication system cuts down on fidelity, and to combat noise (such as static) engineers at one point used the practice of repeating messages until the machines could decipher the appropriate information. They called such repeating of messages **redundancy.** As the engineers continued to work with electronic communication they discovered that redundancy (repeating things) was costly in terms of time and energy, and this led the cost-conscious engineers to come up with two more features of good communication: efficiency and low cost. The theorists of the new style suggested that good communication results from a balancing of the relationships among noise, redundancy, and fidelity. The ideal situation is one in which noise is minimized and the redundancy level is adjusted to a rate which results in the appropriate degree of fidelity with no unnecessary repetitiveness.

S M C R: THE ELEMENTS OF MESSAGE COMMUNICATION

Figure 2 presents a typical schematic description of the elements in an ideal event in the message communication style.

Figure 2
ELEMENTS OF THE MESSAGE COMMUNICATION EVENT

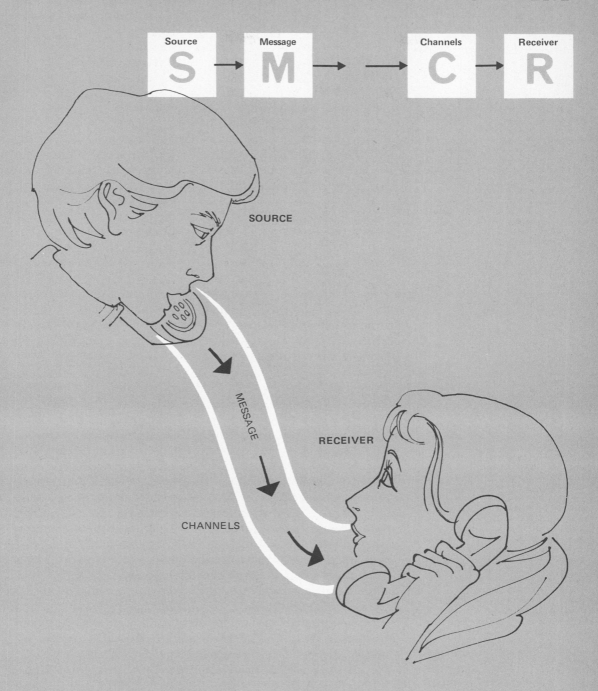

Our model is essentially the same as the one Berlo described. The *S* in the model stands for *source.* The source is the person or group who decides to communicate with some other person, persons, or machines. If you meet someone in the hall and say "Good morning," you are the source of the communication.

The *M* stands for *message.* In our example, the message is the words *good* and *morning,* plus the way you gesture and emphasize the words to indicate "I really mean it is a pleasant morning," or "I am glad to see you again," or "I am saying these words because I always say these words, even if the day is lousy and I feel terrible."

The *C* stands for *channel,* or channels, through which the message moves. Television messages come through channels, as you know. Each person, unless handicapped, receives messages through the channels of the senses of sight, hearing, smell, taste, and touch. Light and sound waves travel through the air and over electric wires. In the case of television, the message travels through several channels at the same time, and the viewer both sees a picture and hears the sound. The most popular sense communication channels are the eyes and ears.

The final *R* stands for *receiver.* The listener or viewer is the receiver of the message. When you greet someone in the hall you are the *source;* the words and the way you say them are the *message;* the message goes through the *channels* of sound (hearing) and light (sight) to the *receiver.*

THE MESSAGE COMMUNICATION PROCESS

Figure 3 represents a model of the ideal process in the message communication style. Note that the message source has an end in view and sends out messages to achieve that goal. The communication process is a step-by-step, give-and-take interaction between source and receiver by which the source reaches the desired goal. The idea of feedback includes the notion that the source receives information and can thus correct those attempts to reach the goal which fail. The programmer gets error statements from the computer and can rephrase the program in light of the feedback provided by the error statements until the computer understands the program. The computer is willing to take the programmer's directives and accepts the programmer's goal without question. When the target for the message is another human being, however, the receiver often is not willing to be controlled and does not accept the objective of the source.

THE HUMAN ELEMENT

What often happens in conversation between people is that after a first attempt by one person to be the source of messages in a communication event, the other person tries to be the source also. When both try to be the source, neither gives the other feedback. The result is a battle over who will control the situation and whose ends will be achieved by the talk.

Even when a person willingly accepts the listener's role and tries to achieve understanding, the response of a human being is much more complex than that of a machine. A person who listens to a message must, like the machine, receive the sentences in understandable form, made up of words within the individual's vocabulary. If you understand computer language you can always tell when somebody has made a mistake in writing a sentence, because the machine only accepts messages put in precisely the right form. A message for a computer is like an arithmetic or geometry problem, in that you can tell whether the message can be understood simply by checking its form. But people can often understand messages whether or not they are expressed in proper grammar. Of course we cannot put together just any bunch of English words and expect people to understand them. Within limits, our grammar must be correct to be understood.

Even when communication does not at first appear to make sense, people will try to find out its meaning, be it grunts, one-word exclamations, unstructured poetry, or ideas expressed in improper grammar. In that respect, people are much different from computers, and while the difference can be helpful, because it enables people to talk about complicated ideas and complex feelings, it can also be a disadvantage. For while the computer never proceeds until it understands a message completely and thus fulfills one of the important requirements for good communication in the message communication style, people often plunge deeper and deeper into misunderstandings.

Like the computer, human beings can feed back error statements and thus indicate when they do not understand the message. As a matter of fact, people *ought* to be much better than machines at giving feedback, because they can explain in greater detail exactly what they do not understand or in what ways they are confused. In practice, however, people are often much worse than a machine at providing a speaker with feedback. People often hear only a few words of a message and get the idea that they know what it is all about, without listening to the rest. ("I know, I know, I've heard it a hundred times,"

Figure 3

A MODEL OF THE PROCESS OF MESSAGE COMMUNICATION

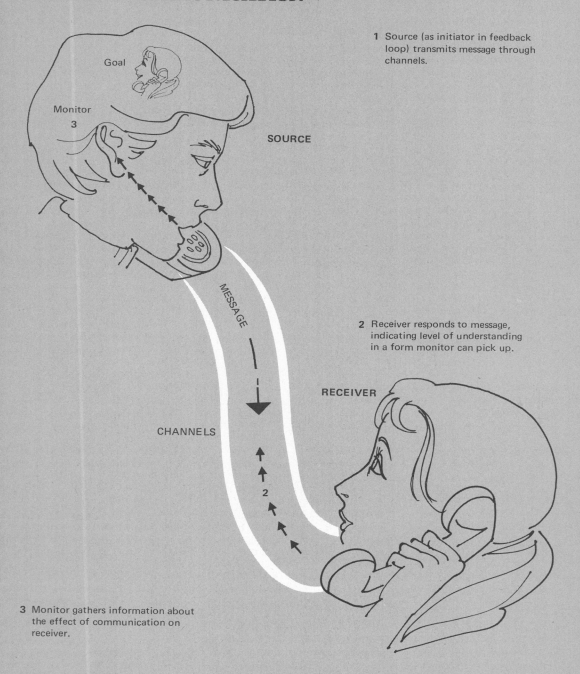

1 Source (as initiator in feedback loop) transmits message through channels.

Goal

Monitor

3

SOURCE

MESSAGE

2 Receiver responds to message, indicating level of understanding in a form monitor can pick up.

RECEIVER

CHANNELS

2

3 Monitor gathers information about the effect of communication on receiver.

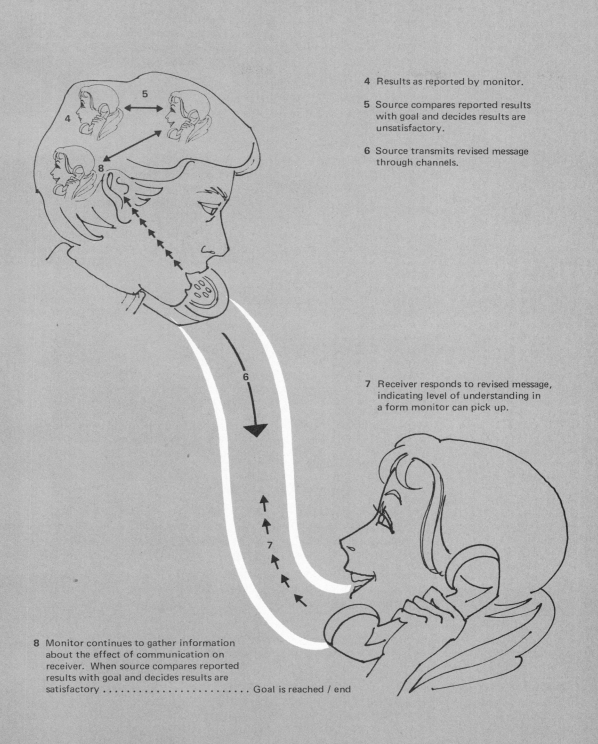

4 Results as reported by monitor.

5 Source compares reported results with goal and decides results are unsatisfactory.

6 Source transmits revised message through channels.

7 Receiver responds to revised message, indicating level of understanding in a form monitor can pick up.

8 Monitor continues to gather information about the effect of communication on receiver. When source compares reported results with goal and decides results are satisfactory . . . . Goal is reached / end

encoding *The process of converting information into a code.*
decoding *The process of translating a message into its original form. Extraction of information from a message.*
code *A system of sympols for representing information, including the rules for their use.*
ESP *The ability to communicate outside of the channels of the senses.*
entropy *The degree of sameness or similarity in a set of messages. An increase in entropy is an increase in disorganization. Information theorists saw information as negative entropy in the sense that information is organization.*

says the teenager as he starts out with the family car.) People often hear what they expect to hear instead of what a speaker is saying. If a teacher assigns a difficult term paper, the student may well not hear the whole assignment. Finally, and most importantly, people tend not to ask questions even when they do not understand because they are afraid a question may make them appear stupid, and they feel that if they keep quiet, at least nobody will know how little they understand.

ENCODING AND DECODING

Figure 4 presents a complete model of the ideal communication event in the message communication style. Remember that the model portrays a dynamic process and that a moving picture would do a better job than any still picture. The parts of the process work dynamically in a give-and-take, step-by-step way. Notice that Figure 4 contains two new terms to indicate some additional important ideas about message communication. Between the source and the message is the process of *encoding*, and between the message and the receiver is the process of *decoding*. Before the source can communicate with a receiver, he or she must invent a message and construct it out of something tangible, something a receiver can sense. People who wish to communicate must fashion some link to establish contact. (Some people believe that contact can be made without going through the senses, and they try to communicate with the spirit world or with others by means of **extrasensory perception** [ESP].) For ordinary purposes, when a person makes a message, he or she encodes ideas into a form that the receiver can perceive. Breaking the **code,** understanding the message, is the decoding process.

COMMUNICATION AS A WEAPON
AGAINST CONFUSION

Influential figures in the early development of the message communication style held a world view which saw the universe as winding down.[11] They saw the winding-down process as a tendency toward disorganization, and they used the word **entropy** to refer to the process. They thought of information as fighting against the natural tendency of things to go toward disorganization. In this view, the creation and transmission of

[11] An excellent presentation of the message theory is to be found in Norbert Wiener, *The Human Use of Human Beings: Cybernetics and Society,* Garden City, N.Y.: Doubleday (Anchor Books), 1954.

Figure 4

COMPLETE MESSAGE COMMUNICATION EVENT

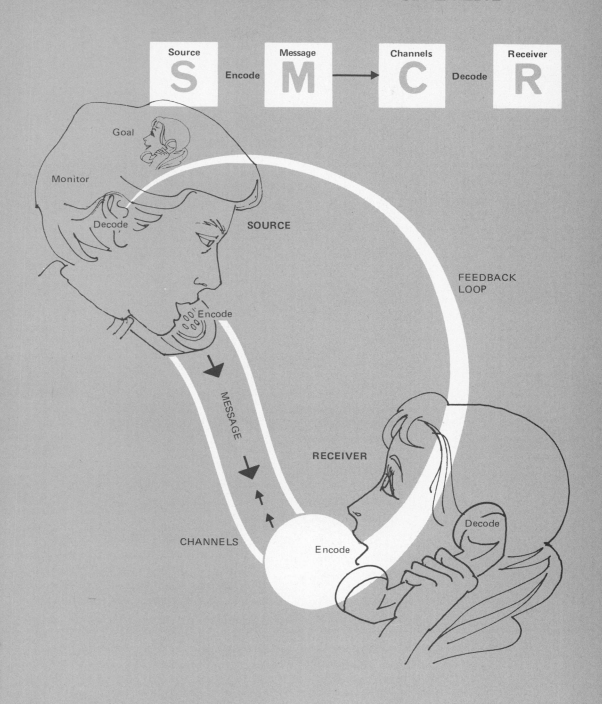

messages required energy and was sustained only by effort and skill. Left alone, organization would decay under the natural entropic forces of the universe. Energy was a value to be protected, and energy for organization and communication was therefore to be expended carefully and sparingly. They valued information; its creation, transmission, storage, and protection became an important feature of the style. Indeed, we call it *the message communication style* because information processing, transmission, storage, and retrieval are the central concerns of the people involved in its practice. The concern with information results, for practical purposes, in an emphasis on the message rather than on relationships or on the speaker.

Norbert Wiener approvingly referred to the aphorism "Speech is a joint game by the talker and listener against the forces of confusion."[12] In the game against confusion, the computer is always cooperative. People talking with one another are not always willing to join the effort to fight entropy. When people enter into competitive communication games, into negotiations where bluff and other devices are used, energy is wasted in terms of protecting information, and indeed, confusion is increased rather than diminished. For the early theorists, the ideal model of communication for humans was that exemplified by efficient machines. Although the programmer might be frustrated and confused on occasion because the machine failed to provide adequate feedback under certain circumstances, he could be assured that the answer was there to be found and that the computer would not systematically change the problem in order to outwit the programmer.

Models of the message communication style are prescriptive and not scientific because of the fact that people often fail to cooperate in the joint game against confusion. They bluff, lie, and try to mislead. They fail to play the role of message receiver. They fail to provide feedback to help the message source achieve a meeting of the minds. If the model were "scientific," all communication events would fall into the pattern described in Figure 4. The model is part of the artistic theory of communication, and as such provides the basis for criticism of events and for instruction on how to be a better communicator. Criticism based on this model is highly useful. If an instructor using the style observes a videotape of a two-person conference and if both he and the people observed share an understanding and appreciation of the style, a

[12] Wiener, p. 42.

comment such as, "The participants are confused because they are not providing one another with adequate feedback," is helpful, and should enable the participants to improve their communication by working on their feedback skills.

The Relationship Communication Style

The American people in the 1950s were, as usual, a diverse and pluralistic lot, but public opinion was generally positive in its evaluation of science and the scientific method. Medical advances and the race to put people on the moon encouraged the generally good opinion many Americans had about science.

COMMUNICATION AS AN END IN ITSELF

The 1960s, however, saw a reaction against science, not throughout the entire society, but on the part of substantial groups of people. The participation of America in the Vietnamese war was divisive; science's contribution to war made science suspect. Young people, particularly, became disenchanted with the Establishment. Anything hinting at the idea of control, of one human being using or exploiting another human being became suspect. The rise of humanistic psychology, the human potential movement, and interpersonal communication all came together to form a new style of communication. Whereas the public-speaking and message communication styles both emphasize communication as a means to an end, as a way to do other things, the *relationship communication style* began to emphasize communication as the most important relationship among people, a positive value in and of itself.

The public speaker communicates to persuade the audience to do something, or to believe something, or to understand something, or to feel greater commitment to the community. A source in the message communication style speaks to achieve understanding and control, to transmit information, to enable groups of people to cooperate to do large-scale tasks, to allow automated factories to produce products, and to allow service industries to work more efficiently. The speaker in the relationship communication style communicates for personal growth or for the reward of making contact with another authentic human being.

Like the public-speaking and message communication styles, the relationship communication style has its theory,

feedback in relationship communication *Any verbal or nonverbal response to another which reveals feelings and the state of the relationship among participants.*

which includes as an important part its description of good communication; it does not, however, use the device of a schematic model to depict the ideal communication. The theorists of the style rebelled against some elements of the other two styles, including the language and the attitude of the engineer and scientists. They disliked mathematically expressed formulas and schema or blueprints of ideal communication systems. Specifically, the followers of the relationship communication style objected to the principle of feedback as it was developed in the message communication style. We have seen that feedback was the key, the crucial principle, of the new field of cybernetics. Feedback, however, implies control, and control implies manipulation, and theorists for the relationship communication style strongly oppose communication designed in such a way that one human being controls another. They reject communication based upon a model of human beings communicating with machines, or like machines, and celebrate instead the uniqueness of the human being and his potential to be different from machines.

"YOU CANNOT NOT COMMUNICATE"

Interestingly enough, they continue to use the term *feedback*, but as they have developed the notion, it has become much more general and abstract than the precise principle of the message communication style. For the proponents of the relationship communication style, *feedback* refers to all the verbal and nonverbal responses that express reaction to another person, or feelings, or response to another's communication and behavior. One of the aphorisms of the style is "You cannot not communicate."[13] The point of the aphorism is that all responses to a participant in a communication setting can be interpreted (and often are) in terms of relationships, feelings, and attitudes. In the message communication style, with its emphasis on high-fidelity transmission of information, the notion that one "cannot not communicate" is simply wrong; observation of the world around us reveals many situations in which the message model of good communication simply cannot be achieved. For example, when noise interferes in a channel, information is lost in transmission. Clearly, communication in which information is lost because of noise is an example of "not communicating," by message communication style standards.

[13] Popularized by the book by P. Watzlawick, J. Beavin, and D. Jackson, *Pragmatics of Human Communication*, New York: Norton, 1967.

For those in the relationship communication style, however, "You cannot not communicate" points up their central rejection of purposive, intentional communication aimed at control of the receiver. Unintentional behaviors communicate feelings, or at least others are stimulated to feel and infer meanings from the entire context of the communication. The relationship style broadens the concern of communication theorists considerably by its assumption that you cannot not communicate. As a result, the theory associated with relationship communication contains much information about nonverbal communication.

The public-speaking communication style devotes considerable theory to the *occasion* and deals with matters of audience position in an auditorium or room, with speaker position, with ceremonial context, and so forth. The message communication style, on the other hand, devotes less time and attention to the immediate context and emphasizes principles such as feedback, noise, and channels to deal with specifics relating to a given communication event. The relationship communication style features context as part of the nonverbal communication: Where do people sit or stand in relationship to one another? What sorts of clothes do they wear? What are their hair styles? How do they walk? How do they gesture? Are they tense? Are they relaxed? How close are they to one another when they they speak? Do they touch? What does touch communicate? What do smells communicate?

One theorist in the relationship communication style illustrated the preoccupation with nonverbal context and cues with the following example of a patient in a doctor's office:

> At the moment he is faintly aware of an antiseptic odor in the room, which reinforces his confidence in the doctor's ability to diagnose his illness. . . . As he glances through a magazine . . . he is conscious of how comfortable his chair feels after a long day on his feet. . . . Looking up, he glances at the Miro reproduction on the wall, but is unable to decipher it. . . . Dr. B., crossing the room, may initiate the conversation. Extending his hand, he says, "Mr. A! So glad to see you. How are you?" At this point, despite the seeming simplicity of the setting and prosaic content of the message, Mr. A. must solve a riddle in meaning of considerable complexity. In a nonclinical environment where the public cues would be different, perhaps on a street corner . . . Mr. A. would regard this message as no more than a social gesture. . . .[14]

[14] Dean C. Barnlund, "A Transactional Model of Communication," in Kenneth K. Sereno and C. David Mortensen, eds., *Foundations of Communication Theory*, New York: Harper & Row, pp. 98–100.

experiential *Experienced directly and personally. Understood through direct personal experience.*
dialogistic *Authentic, truthful communication which accepts others as human beings.*
congruent *Genuine communication without 'front' or facade, openly being the feelings and attitudes which at that moment are flowing in the communicators.*
trusting *A communication quality in which participants rely on each others messages without fear or suspicion.*
open *Willingness to tell others about one's self. Being aware and empathetic to another.*
disclosing *The revelation of information about one's self to another in relationship communication. Going beyond everyday communication interchanges toward a sharing with another person of one's hopes, fears, needs, and so forth.*
authentic *Relationship communication behavior which is real and honest, as opposed to the playing of social games or the assuming of roles or masks which hide the real self.*
transactional *Communication as process of meaning-creating, a circular, complex, irreversible, unrepeatible process involving the totality of each participant.*

THE IDEAL OF THE RELATIONSHIP STYLE

How, then, does the relationship style present its model or exemplar of good communication? The theoreticians of the style describe good communication in a way much more characteristic of the psychiatrist, the philosopher, and the theologian than the engineer. Indeed, certain theologians such as Buber and Kierkegaard, and philosophers such as Sartre, have provided some of the sanctions as well as some of the more complicated words and ideas to support the theory. Ambiguous terms employing high levels of abstraction are used to describe the model communication event. The student of relationship communication discovers the nature of good communication by participating in discussions which deal with ambiguous abstractions drawn from the theory, in which all participants openly share their thoughts and feelings and cooperatively create the insights required to both understand and participate in the style. The students tend to learn the style by participating in special exercises, games, or group sessions and experiencing the joys of communicating in the style. Among the important characterizing terms are **experiential, dialogistic, congruent, trusting, disclosing, open, authentic,** and **transactional.**

To attempt to present a model of the relationship style in clear and simple language with careful and precise definition is to do it an injustice. The relationship style celebrates experience rather than talking about it. Feeling has a higher value than the critical evaluation of ideas. (This does not mean that participants in the style do not critically evaluate communication according to their own standards, however; the style implies strong critical sanctions against beginners who stray from the norms of good communication and become game players or mask wearers; and against people who are tight, controlled, who are unwilling to be open or to accept others, or who treat people like things.)

Having entered our disclaimer, we will try nonetheless to sketch in the main outlines of an ideal model of communication according to the relationship communication style. As there seem to be about as many models of this style as there are teachers of it, you may well find your instructor adding his or her own model.

THE EMPHASIS ON AUTHENTICITY

Like the public-speaking style, the transactional model is dramatistic, but it features not one but several protagonists, who cease to play games with one another and who are real and honest, who take risks and reveal their authentic selves. Their basic attitude is that one should deal with others as authentic human beings and not as things or machines to be manipulated. They are no longer wearing the masks and playing the roles which made (note the past tense) them less human and which shielded them from contact with others. As authentic communicators, they are open and they welcome human contact. They disclose their feelings to one another. Self-disclosure is risky, and they begin communicating about themselves in authentic ways only when a climate of mutual trust is established by active and empathetic listening and by demonstrated honesty on the part of all. People often have trouble talking about themselves honestly, but once risked, the self-disclosing communication tends to open up others, and they in turn disclose. The emotional tone of the communication is warmed by congruent, honest, and open communication, as people take more and more risks and are accepted for themselves.

SELF-DISCLOSURE AND HEIGHTENED AWARENESS

In the warm and trusting climate of a good communication situation, people can reveal their innermost feelings; they can discuss their hopes and fears. The participants can discover their authentic selves, can grow in awareness, can raise their consciousness to higher levels. They can express their feelings, cry, and laugh without worry of acceptance or rejection. As the climate builds to ever more intimate and significant communication, important relationships evolve among the participants. A strong and good self-image is an important ingredient in the ideal relationship communication transaction. One way to build a good self-image includes self-disclosing communication—opening up oneself to others and receiving frank and honest feedback (i.e., response to and evaluation of oneself as exposed: The others describe their reactions to the speaker so an individual can evaluate both self and worth)—and then a frank accepting of the feedback, followed by honest attempts to change. The process of communication, the transactions in which all participate and create meanings, results in the participants' discovering their potential and becoming aware of their authentic selves. In the ideal situation the end result for the individual is a stronger self-image, a greater sensitivity to others as people, and a higher consciousness of the human condition.

A MULTISENSORY APPROACH

The heightened awareness of the relationship communication style also includes more careful and sharper tuning of the senses. The ideal is often multisensory. The evolving theory emphasizes nonverbal communication as more authentic than verbal. Verbal codes tend to deal in content, while the nonverbal codes tend to reveal relationships and feelings. The nonverbal theory deals with such matters as the communication of touching and of making contact through the other senses. Training sessions often stress feeling, touching, smelling, and other nonverbal communication exercises, sometimes causing those who are used to being participants in either the public speaking or message communication styles to be irritated rather than drawn to the relationship style. Those who do not approve of these exercises in heightened awareness in communication situations sometimes refer to the exercises deprecatingly as "touchy-feely" training. Personal experience and testimony by the many who find the relationship communication style worthwhile and satisfactory, however, has drawn many people into its practice—if not all the time, at least on occasions when it is appropriate.

Most speech communication teachers have come to accept the helpful elements in all three styles, and although the bias of your particular instructor will probably be evident in the way your course is structured, you should understand the way these three current communication styles have evolved in our culture. There is no one right way to communicate, and there is no one right communication theory or style. You should learn how to incorporate all of these styles into your communication repertoire, inasmuch as each is useful to you.

Other Communication Styles

Obviously there are more than these three general communication styles operating within the United States. There are a number of other styles related to given subcultures. The three we have discussed, however, all have well-developed communication theories and are, therefore, the predominant styles taught in colleges and universities. In addition, practitioners of the three styles tend to participate in the majority of the public speaking events for live audiences, in television and radio public affairs programming, in small group meetings, in two-person interviews and conferences, and in the general organizational communication which characterizes our corporate society.

The Mixing of Communication Styles

Because some communication theorists have been impressed by the attractive features of each of the three styles described, they have tried to integrate elements from two, or even all three, into an eclectic theory of communication. For example, the writer on communication theory might begin with a discussion of the rhetorical tradition from Aristotle to the present, move to describing the schematic models of the message communication style, and end with a discussion of a transactional model of openness, trust, congruency, and human growth. We have suggested that you learn all three styles and take from each what you feel is useful. What we suggest, however, is based on the assumption that you understand very clearly the distinctiveness of each style. Furthermore, you must not mix the styles without meaning to, for, in practice, the three styles are somewhat incompatible with one another.

THE CONFLICTS GENERATED BY PARTISANSHIP

Partisans of each of the three styles often come into conflict with one another. The issues are drawn around such topics as the charge that those participating in the public-speaking communication style are out of date, since only a few people nowadays give public speeches. (A recent survey, however, indicates that nearly half of those surveyed, particularly those more educated, had spoken to a group (of more than 10 people) in the two years prior to the survey.)[15] Those defending the public-speaking style's usefulness respond that the message communication style has added nothing to the understanding of communication that has not been dealt with adequately in their own theory and that, moreover, those who focus on the communication process itself to the exclusion of speech training are ignoring the basis for which teachers have been considered useful for years, namely the business of improving oral communication skills. In the view of the message communication partisans, the public-speaking practitioners are giving people prescriptive platitudes, whereas they themselves are dealing in scientific, descriptive terms, more useful than mere "how to" conjectures. Those who participate in the relationship communication style charge that the message model is linear, that it emphasizes message source, is

[15] Kathleen Edgerton Kendall, "Do Real People Ever Give Speeches?" *Central States Speech Journal,* 25 (1974), pp. 233–235.

Chapter 2

THE KEY IDEAS

Communication theory is often a mixture of scientific laws and artistic views of good communication.

A communication style is always learned.

Researchers in communication have had trouble distinguishing between the scientific components of theory and the artistic parts.

Three important communication styles in the United States are the public-speaking, the message, and the relationship communication styles.

The model of the public-speaking communication style consists of the speaker, the audience, the occasion, and the speech.

The speech results from the the speaker's dynamic adaptation of topic, ideas, and purpose to the audience and occasion.

The ideal communication event in the public-speaking style is one where the speaker skillfully adapts ideas, delivery, and language to the audience to achieve his or her purpose.

The model of the message communication style consists of a source, encoding, a message, channels, decoding, and a receiver.

The ideal communication events in the message style is modeled after people talking to machines and achieving complete understanding.

The principle of feedback in message communication refers to the output of information which allows a goal-seeking initiator

manipulative, and misses the essential process nature of communication, which the transactional model catches in a much richer and more humane fashion.

THE FLEXIBLE APPROACH TO STYLES
Our approach in the rest of the book will be to provide you with the best of the current theory relating to all three styles.

of a message to continuously monitor performance in order to achieve the goal.

One important feature of the feedback loop in the message communication style is that only the source has the goal.

The ideal of the message communication style is a communication event in which noise is minimized and the redundancy level adjusted to a rate which maximizes fidelity with no unnecessary waste of time or energy.

The message communication process is a step-by-step, give-and-take interaction between source and receiver by which the source reaches the desired goal.

Early theorists of the message communication style held a world view which saw the universe as winding down under the impact of entropy. For this reason, the aphorism "Speech is a joint game by the talker and listener against the forces of confusion" catches the basic theme of the message communication style.

Models of communication in the message style are prescriptive rather than scientific.

The aphorism "You cannot not communicate" catches the essence of the relationship communication style.

The model of the relationship communication style consists of several people who drop their stereotyped roles and social masks and who cease their game playing to become real and authentic human beings interacting with one another honestly.

The ideal communication event in the relationship style is one where the participants can discover their authentic selves, can grow in awareness, and can develop intimate and meaningful relationships.

Feedback in the relationship style refers to the response and evaluation of others to an individual's frank and honest self-disclosure.

The end result of the ideal relationship communication is that participants have a stronger self-image, a greater sensitivity to others, and a higher consciousness of the human potential.

The ideal communication event is multi-sensory in the relationship communication style.

The three communication styles are incompatible in important ways and do not mix easily.

Partisans of each of the three styles often come into conflict with one another.

There is no one right way to communicate, and there is no one right communication theory or style.

The student of contemporary communication should learn to incorporate all major styles into his or her communication repertoire, inasmuch as they can be useful in the student's life.

It seems to us that many current communication problems—and the phrase appears in popular reading material as well as on media programs—arise in part from a confusion among specialists, as well as much of the general public, as to *what style* is being used in a given situation, and that as we learn to differentiate, we will become more flexible as participants, critics, and theorists. You can appreciate good communication in the public-speaking style, you can appreciate good communication in the message communication style, and you can incorporate good communication in the relationship style along with the other two, as you find appropriate. As the public-speaking communication style has a longer tradition, more detailed theoretical development, and more prescriptive advice to offer, we will have more to say about public speaking than the other two. Wherever there is a well-developed and useful theory from message and relationship communication, however, we will provide you with material and suggest where you can look further if you are interested.

SUGGESTED PROJECTS

1 Attend a public speech on campus or in the community. Write a short paper in which you describe the situation in terms of the ideal model of the public-speaking style. Evaluate the speech in terms of the criteria for a good public speech. Were there important things happening that the model could not explain?

2 You may keep the pairs set up in project 2, Chapter 1, for this project, or you may pair up with another member of the class. One of you begins the conversation by playing the role of message source and the other plays the role of message receiver, according to the ideal model of the message communication style. The student playing message source selects one of the terms from the following list and explains what it means. The student playing message receiver actively provides feedback until the source has gotten the idea across clearly. You then reverse roles, and whoever becomes the source selects a different concept.
  entropy
  cybernetics
  fidelity
  redundancy
  code
  After both have been both source and receiver, write a short paper in which you discuss how the model of the message communication style explains what happened. What was the nature of feedback during your talks? Were there important things happening which the model could not explain?

3 Again, you may keep the same pairs set up in project 2 above, or pair up with a different member of the class. Either way, make an appointment to have coffee (or?) with the other person sometime outside of class. Allow an hour or more for the talk. Consciously conduct your conversation in the relationship communication style. Afterwards, separately, write a short paper in which you discuss how well the relationship model explains what happened in your conversation. Were there important things happening that the model could not explain?

4 Keep a diary of your communication for two days. Did you com-

municate in all three styles? Give several examples of the different styles in which you communicated. Did you ever feel you were unconsciously mixing the styles and that perhaps this led to problems? Did you mix the styles consciously? Do you feel you habitually communicate in one style more than any other?

SUGGESTED READINGS

Berlo, David K. *The Process of Communication.* New York: Holt, Rinehart & Winston, 1960.

Stewart, John, ed. *Bridges Not Walls: A Book About Interpersonal Communication.* Reading, Mass.: Addison-Wesley, 1973.

Watzlawick, Paul, Janet H. Beavin, and Don D. Jackson. *Pragmatics of Human Communication: A Study of Interactional Patterns, Pathologies, and Paradoxes.* New York: Norton, 1967.

Wiener, Norbert. *The Human Use of Human Beings: Cybernetics and Society.* Garden City, N.Y.: Doubleday (Anchor Books), 1954.

Winans, James A. *Speech Making.* Englewood Cliffs, N.J.: Prentice-Hall, 1938.

Chapter 3

HOW WORDS COMMUNICATE

In Chapter 2 we discussed the encoding and decoding links in the message communication process. In this chapter we will talk about the verbal code of American English. We will examine such questions as the following: Is there *a* right way to speak English? Should you learn *better* pronunciation? Should you improve your articulation? correct your grammar? Can you move from the lower class to the middle class, or from the upper middle class to the upper class, by changing the way you speak?

If you do not speak black English, can you communicate with black Americans? Are Chinese students, black students from big-city ghettos, American Indians, Chicanos, and Puerto Rican students culturally deprived because their dialects are inferior to white-middle-class speech? Why does the sentence "There ain't no such word as *ain't*" strike some people as funny?

All these questions are important to every person living in the United States today, because they have to do with life style, economic success, feelings of racial and cultural pride, and educational and social opportunity. Before we try to answer the questions, however, we must look at some basic features of language, to lay the groundwork for our response.

Much of the material in this chapter cuts across the styles of communication described in Chapter 2. A public speaker may use a southern dialect, general American, black English, or a Spanish accent. A person may participate in the message communication style in any dialect. A meeting in the relationship style will include participants articulating sounds and pronouncing words in certain ways. The principles of communication we will discuss are common to all three styles.

Much of the information in this chapter about language acquisition and usage and about linguistic structure has been verified by observation and is thus part of the scientific component of communication theory. Much of the information relating to proper usage, to standards of speech, to dialect as the basis for evaluating the social status or worth of the speaker is based upon standards of taste and relates to the stylistic or artistic aspect of communication. At this level of study, however, we are examining materials that cut across all three styles, even though not all of the information can be tested empirically.

The Nature of a Code

To encode and decode messages we must have a *code* which can bridge the gap between source and receiver. You may think first of such things as the Morse code or a secret code such as the one you can make by giving each letter in the alphabet a number and then writing notes in numbers to others who know the code. The important thing about any code is that the people who use it must know all its parts and how they fit together into sentences. If a person has a private code it is useful only to himself. Sometimes people write personal diaries in a secret code known only to themselves. If a code is to carry meaning between a source and a receiver, though, both parties must know the code.

Usually we know the code being used in a communication event, and we can concentrate on trying to use it. Sometimes, however, we think we know the code but find, in the middle of the conversation, that "we don't seem to be talking about the same thing." At that point we have to check to be sure everybody involved is using the same code. Have you ever talked with someone from another country who speaks English as a second language? From time to time he wishes to say something in English but does not know the right English word. Often people who speak in a second language have to ask for the right word by pointing or gesturing, by using words that help their listeners come up with the word they are seeking. The difficulties people encounter talking in codes are easy to see when we talk about a second language and its problems, but there are problems in the use of codes even when all parties involved speak the same native language. They, too, may have to stop from time to time to check and make sure that they are using words that mean the same things to both. Words are highly personal, in that for each word, each of us carries his or her own mental image, or meaning, or several meanings. We will discuss this important concept at greater length in Chapter 14.

THE VARIETIES OF CODES
All natural languages are codes. For most Americans, the common code or language is English. But there are many other kinds of codes besides languages such as English, Spanish, French, German, and so forth. Some, like the Morse code, use dots and dashes to represent letters and are simply a different way of spelling a language such as English. Other

codes are not composed of words at all. For example, the American Indian tribes developed a sign language in which certain hand movements meant certain ideas. Each tribe had its own native language, and a member of one tribe could not talk with someone from a different tribe using that language. All the tribes, however, knew the sign language, and though it was somewhat limited, they could communicate with one another using the sign code.

NATURE'S CODE

We might say that nature communicates with man. A scientist who makes a new discovery breaks nature's code. For example, scientists say that the hereditary genes, which pass on from parents to children things like eye color, nose shape, talent, and ability, do so by means of a code. We can look upon the code as information, and some scientists like Norbert Wiener, a computer specialist and mathematician, argue that some day people may become messages, and when a fast reading device is invented the information contained in a person's body can be sent by radio or telephone across the country where a receiver can build up the body again from suitable materials. Wiener's point is that *we* are primarily information, and not the physical materials—water and other chemicals—that compose us at a given time.

Nature's code enables man to "read" that when we see

lightning, we will soon hear thunder. Nature's codes cannot be changed. We find that we cannot change the code from "lightning means thunder" to "seeing a rainbow means thunder." Lightning is always connected with thunder by the very nature of things.

MAN-MADE CODES, VERBAL AND NONVERBAL

Man-made codes, such as the English language, have no natural connection, and so parts of the code can be made to stand for different things and ideas. For example, if several of us decide to make a code in which the letters of the alphabet are numbered from 1 to 26, starting with A as 1, B as 2, and so on, we can write messages in our code; at a later time we can agree, if an outsider has broken our code, that we will turn the numbers around and have 26 stand for A, 25 for B, and so on. There is nothing in the way the world works to make us assign numbers to the letters in a certain way.

The English language has certain words that stand for certain things. Thus the word *dog* stands for an animal of a certain kind. There is nothing about the animal that makes the word *dog* the one and only word that can stand for it. Other languages use other words: German, *Hundt;* French, *chien.* When we talk in a language, we must learn how the language is used, what the words mean, and how they can be put together in a sentence. For several people to talk to one another, they must all understand the words they use to mean pretty much the same things. When a person has in mind a furry, four-legged, domesticated animal that barks and eats meat, and he encodes a message that has the word *dog* in it, the listener who hears the word *dog* should not decode it to mean a two-legged bird that cackles and is good to eat southern-fried.

Among the important codes used in interpersonal communication are several that use not words but gestures, such as the Indian sign language. For example, when a person looks at another, smiles, and nods his head up and down, this behavior may be part of a code and mean agreement. Shaking the head from side to side, looking the other person in the eye, frowning, moving away, looking at the ground, and other such gestures may also be part of a nonverbal code. Everybody who knows the code understands what these actions mean.

Another important code, which is added onto speech, is like the melody that enhances a poem set to music. The code includes the way the voice changes pitch, the rate of speech, the changes in loudness, and the pauses that separate words

and clumps of words. Thus if two people speak the same body and vocal codes one can say a great deal to another by the way he draws out the sound "ooo" and at the same time smiles, and holds up his right hand in front of his shoulder and forms a circle with his thumb and forefinger.

When we speak to other people we punctuate our comments with pauses and changes in the rate of speech, loudness, and pitch. By proper use of vocal punctuation we can make the same sentence mean several different things. Take the sentence "Youth today is revolting." Can you read the sentence aloud so it means two different things? Try the sentence "Woman without her man is a beast." Can you read it first so woman is the beast and then so man is the beast?

We will call the body codes and the vocal melodies *nonverbal* communication. While we can think of many other languages, and some of these are fun to play with, our concern in the book will be with speech communication that uses some dialect of American English as the verbal code and uses the nonverbal codes common in North America.

The Nature of Verbal Codes

FORM WORDS

There are two basic kinds of verbal symbols used in all verbal communication, no matter what communication style is being used. The first kind of symbol is a form word. When builders want to put in a sidewalk or build some concrete steps, they first prepare the ground and build forms into

form words *Those symbols in a code which provide the structure or shape of sentences or statements according to the rules of the code.*
content words *Those symbols in a code which name things and those symbols which indicate properties of the things named or relationships among them.*
property terms *Those symbols in a code which describe something's qualities or characteristics.*
relational terms *Those symbols in a code which describe two or more things in terms of one another, as when one item is described as larger than another.*

which they will pour the mixture of concrete. The forms hold the concrete in a certain way, shaping it, making sure that where they want the sidewalk, the concrete will harden into a sidewalk, and where they want the steps, the concrete will form steps. Form words in messages are very much like the forms used by builders. The form words structure questions, statements, and commands into their characteristic shape. Some typical form words are *what, when, where, how, is, the, a, if . . . then, or, but.*

Messages require the proper form in order to communicate. Here are some typical form words in place to shape a message: "If the _____ is _____, then the _____ is also _____." "What is the _____ for the _____?" Notice that the first example is in the right form to make an assertion or statement, and the second is shaped to ask a question. We can tell that the form is right simply by looking at the shape of sentences. We do not need to look at the world of objects, things, and events to check the proper form for messages in a verbal code. When a mother tells her child, "Stop that!" even a very young child knows he is not being asked a question.

CONTENT WORDS

The second kind of message symbol is a content word. Content words consist of *names* for things and words that stand for properties and relationships. We commonly think of names as words that stand for important things, such as human beings like *Mary* or *John*, families of humans like *the Smiths* or *the McCoys*, or classes of things like *dogs* or *cats*; but we also name less important things. When we talk of *carrots* or speak of one from a bunch as *a carrot*, we are also using names. When we name some thing, person, or event, we point to it and call the listener's attention to the thing, so we can go on to discuss it in greater detail.

If after we have named something and called the listener's attention to it, we want to say something further about it, we can use either **property** or **relation** words to comment about the thing already named. Property words indicate something that belongs to the object we are talking about. Some typical property words are those that stand for colors, such as *red, blue, orange;* those that stand for shape, such as *square* or *round;* or those that stand for how things feel, such as *rough* or *smooth.* We thus add the properties or qualities that further define the thing we have named. If we name a thing, for instance, *that carrot* and go on to shape a proper sentence that connects several property words to the thing, we can say, "That carrot is orange and hot." Every language has rules about the proper form to use when saying something about a thing that is named. Conventional English would not allow a person who wished to say that the thing named *carrot* was orange and hot to do so with a sentence formed as follows: "That hot is orange and carrot."

Relation terms indicate how two or more things fit together or stand in terms of one another. Some typical relation words that can be used with two name words are *taller* and *above*. Thus, a person could say, "John is taller than Harry." Again the form of the sentence is important in English. If you want to say that the thing named *John* is taller than the thing named *Harry*, you must not say, "Harry is taller than John." Relation words may need more than two names to complete them. For example, the relation term *between* requires three names to properly form a sentence in English: "John sits between Paul and Harry."

THE THREE FACES OF LANGUAGE

To examine language use, we will divide the process into three features. The Romans had a god of the doorways, of beginnings, and of the rising and setting sun called Janus, who was represented by a statue with one head having two faces looking in opposite directions. If we were to represent language similarly, we might create a statue having one head with three faces. One face would symbolize the spirit of work, language as an aid to understanding the world, a giver of information, a servant to solve problems, and a teacher; the second face should be well formed, beautiful, and pleasing, because it follows the formal rules of language; and the third face should be the spirit of enchantment, mystery, magic, confusion, language as a snare and a delusion, language as power.

DENOTATIVE MEANING

The three faces of language are all related, but we can gain a greater understanding of the total process by viewing it from the three sides. We often use the term denotative meaning as a key to the first aspect of language. When we say a word denotes something we mean that the word points to, notes, stands for, or indicates the thing. Thus we can say that the word *chicken* denotes a certain kind of fowl that is a certain general size, is feathered, cackles, and lays our breakfast eggs.

The denotative meanings of a language are the way the

words are plugged into the worlds of the source and the receiver. The words of any language are not related to the objects of our experience by any law of nature or because of any necessary connection. Thunder and lightning, as things that happen, are connected by a law of nature, and we cannot keep the thunder from following the lightning even if we wish to do so. The word *dog*, however, is not connected by any law of nature to the animal that barks, is friendly to his master, and likes bones. Our decision to use a given word to stand for some object, person, or event is up to us. If the language is to work as a code for communication, however, we must decide which words stand for which objects, and we must agree about it and come to share the *common* code or understanding.

We cannot change the denotative meaning of words willy-nilly, because if we did, we would confuse people. Naturally language is continually changing, and we do change the denotative meanings of some words over time. We have inherited a tradition of using certain words for certain objects, however, and we learn its rules when we learn the vocabulary of our language. We all come to have a number of common denotative meanings for words in a language we use to talk with one another. If a waiter gives us fried dog when we order fried chicken, he has violated our rules for the denotative meaning of *chicken*, to say nothing of our sensibilities.

The first aspect of language thus refers to those common meanings, shared by all people who use the language, about what objects, things, people, or events the words of the language denote. A common dictionary is a list of rules connecting words with denotative meanings, and we can read, write, and understand dictionaries because we share the same understanding of how words relate to things. We must point out the difference between the denotative meanings which are common to a number of people and the individual responses we all have to words. Although we may all know what animal is meant by the term *dog*, we may respond to that word in different ways because of our past experience. One of you reading about the notion of *fried dog* may respond differently from another one of you, but both of you will have a clear idea of what the words stand for or denote.

MESSAGE STRUCTURE

The second feature of language has to do with the rules by which the sounds and words can be put together to make sensible statements, ask meaningful questions, or give orders or

surface forms *The arbitrary, grammatical, syntactical choice of words and their order into which we put a thought.*
deeper meaning *The actual thought we wish to convey or express.*
transformational grammar *A system of grammatical analysis that studies structure changes to determine the relationship between surface and deeper meanings.*

suggestions for action. The second aspect of language relates only to the way sounds are arranged to make words and the way words are fitted together to make sentences. If you know the rules for using the language, you can check a chain of sounds and decide whether it is a meaningful sentence without looking at the world to check the denotative meaning of the sentence to see if it is true or false. Thus if you know the rules of forming good English sentences, you know that the string of words "Chicken minus over divided between chicken apple car" is not a good sentence. You would likewise know that "Hetrologue minus over divided between hetrologue aardvark hieroglyph" is not a good sentence even if you did not know the denotative meanings of *hetrologue, aardvark,* and *hieroglyph.* These sentences simply do not make any sense to us.

The first two features of language are closely related, and before a person can say something that is true or false about the world he must encode a message in a form that makes sense to both source and receiver. Both source and receiver must also share a common denotative meaning for the content words. A less obvious connection between form and content of messages is the fact that a source can say the same thing about the world in a denotative sense using a number of different expressions. For example, the same basic proposition about an individual animal and a car in a certain relation can be stated by the following good sentences:

> *Look at that dog running after the car.*
> *Look, that dog is running after the car.*
> *Look at that car with the dog running after it.*

We will call the one common denotative meaning of a group of sentences their **deeper** meaning and the various ways of putting the basic ideas the **surface** forms. Any English-speaking person hearing any one of the three surface-form sentences about the dog-car event knows the deeper meaning of all three sentences, which is what actually happened and what all three sentences report.

An interesting and important area of language study deals with the way the surface forms are related to the deep structures. One result of studying the connection between deep and surface forms of expressions is a set of rules or a grammar to guide a person in moving from one form to another. These rules show how to *transform* a surface form into its deep structure. The technical name for the set of rules is **transformational grammar.** Scholars of transformational grammar have found some important things. For example, their study

denotative meaning *The meaning of a word most usually shared by two or more users of a verbal code.*
connotative meanings *Those meanings over and above the usual denotative meaning which one has for a word.*

of deeper forms of several languages reveals many common features. Finding out how languages are alike helps us understand how languages in general allow man to organize his world. Discovering similarities between two languages also helps with the problem of translating a message from one language to another (from code to code) and reveals what meanings remain and what meanings are lost in the translation process. An expert in transformational grammar can use the same procedure to study differences and similarities among the dialects of a language as well as differences and similarities between languages. Within American English, for example, scholars have studied the similarities and differences between white upper-middle-class dialects and black urban-ghetto dialects. Such studies give us a basis for deciding whether the black English dialects are more or are less able than the white dialects to express denotative meanings about the world and whether the language rules of any particular dialect are simpler or more complex than those of another dialect.

CONNOTATIVE MEANING AND INDIVIDUAL EXPERIENCE
The third feature of language has to do with the total response of the people involved in the verbal communication. We often use the term connotative as a key to this feature of language. Response to language is both individual and cultural. Sometimes we respond to a word or an expression because of our personal experience. According to the first feature of language, the word *chicken* refers to a certain kind of fowl. Both speaker and listener usually understand the denotative meaning for the word to be the same kind of fowl. If the receiver has a violent dislike of fried chicken because of past experience, however, his response to the word will be emotional as well as reasonable. He may not only picture a chicken in his mind but he may feel a shudder of revulsion go through his entire body when he hears the word. Another person using the same dialect and in the same situation might feel a warm, pleasant glow when he pictures the same fowl, because of the favorite pet chicken he had when he was a little boy.

CONNOTATIVE MEANING DERIVING FROM A SITUATION
Sometimes a number of people share a common response to language because they share a common situation. Consider the example of two grade-school boys arguing during recess. A circle of other children is soon ringed around them. The two boys become angry and one yells at the other, "You're

chicken!" The sentence is in the proper form for American English and thus is a good sentence in terms of the second aspect of language. Probably none of the children watching the argument, however, think that the first boy is saying to the second that he is really a fowl capable of laying eggs and cackling. The first feature of language, denotative meaning, is pushed into the background by the situation. The sentence expresses the source's emotional feeling and attitude; he breaks out with a cry of anger and frustration, and he might have expressed his feelings almost as well with a grunt or a shout as with the sentence. The other boy interprets the sentence in a similarly emotional fashion. The context and the culture which suggests that in a conflict the word *chicken* is a taunt and an insult come into play to form the response to the word. Every student of public speaking learns the importance of analyzing the effect of the situation and the occasion on the response of the audience. The speaker finds that an expression which is appropriate and gains him the desired response on one occasion may well be all wrong on another.

CONNOTATIVE MEANINGS LINKED TO CULTURAL DIFFERENCES

Some words and statements are closely tied to the structure of society and tend to arouse a common reaction from entire groups of people. Look at the following examples:

> *Drive slow.*
> *He played it as he should.*
> *Whom did you wish to see?*
> *It is I.*
> *It don't neither.*
> *Dese cigarettes are better'n dose.*
> *Andy, he be with us.*
> *Y'all come back soon, heah?*
> *I hain't seen 'im.*

You probably found some of the examples odd and somehow not right, while others seemed quite right and comfortable. You might decide that some of the expressions were incorrect or bad grammar or show-off ways of talking that only affected people would use, or people speaking with a southern dialect or an urban-ghetto dialect. Your response to the expressions reflects your response to the culture, the way of life, of those who speak the various dialects. Do you like the southern geographic region? Do you feel it is an area of pleasant, cultured, and gracious life? Do you feel the South is a closed society, racist and bigoted? All these feelings come

dialect *The particular pronunciation, articulation, vocabulary, sentence structure, changes in rate and pitch of speaking, general tone, and energy level used by subgroups within any general language group.*

into play when you hear a person speak in a southern dialect. Some critics of political speaking argued that President Lyndon Johnson's Texas drawl damaged the effect of his television talks to the nation, because many opinion leaders, particularly those from the intellectual center of Boston, responded emotionally and negatively to the Texas dialect. Your response to an expression in black English likewise reflects your attitude toward race relations and your feelings about black culture. Whoever you are, wherever you live, you have to accept the fact that *you* speak a dialect. To someone from a different heritage and environment, the way *you* speak is strange.

The third feature of language often reflects geographic regions, social classes, and economic, ethnic, religious, and racial differences. People in different geographic regions have developed different styles of speaking; working-class members use different forms of expression, different vocal inflections, different rules to form sentences, according to the second aspect of language, than do upper-middle-class people. People who live in the black urban ghettos of the North develop some unique patterns of speech, as do bilingual members such as the Mexican-American and Puerto Rican ghetto dwellers.

All the different ways of talking within the United States make up a single complicated system in which people move around from place to place, from one social and economic class to another. We must add to the system the effect of the mass media—film, television, and radio—which transmit a steady flow of messages in a standard dialect. Even within the same geographic regions, such as the southeastern United States, the lower class speaks differently from the upper middle class; the black worker speaks differently from the white worker. In practice, however, since all classes within a region talk with one another and all are exposed to radio, television, and film, the various expressions and ways of speaking rub off on one another. Thus you probably shift back and forth in your style of speaking, depending upon how formal the situation is and on the people with whom you happen to be speaking at the time.

Dialects

We will call the different ways of speaking American English within the United States **dialects.** What is a *dialect?* The differences that make one group's way of speaking a dialect in comparison with another's are part and parcel of the entire language. Dialect differences include the way people say the individual sounds, such as the /r/ sound or the /aw/ sound. Differences include the way people say larger units, such as the word *pin* (denoting a small, slender, sharp thing useful for sticking pieces of cloth together) and the word *pen* (an enclosure useful for keeping babies confined in a small area). Differences also include the way people say clusters of words, such as "Charlie Aunt she be with us" and "Y'all come back soon, heah?"

A dialect differs from other dialects in vocabulary. Some words are commonly used in one dialect and not in another. The same word can denote different things in one dialect than in other dialects. For example, some dialects use the word *man* frequently as a word of emphasis, not merely to refer to a human male. A dialect may use a word to mean something quite different from the usual meaning associated with the same word in another dialect. The words *bread, grass,* and *trip* come to mind in this regard. A given dialect differs from others in the way the various sounds are made and in the way they fit together to form words, as well as in the way the words fit together into sentences.

DIALECT AS A SOURCE OF CONFLICT

Those people who first learned to speak in a given dialect tend to have a common set of emotional responses to it. People who do not know the dialect or who learn it later in life often have a different set of responses to the dialect than do native speakers. Because the third face of language reflects, supports, and influences changes of class structure, race relations, and economic privilege, people respond with deep and profound emotions to dialects and the changing of speech habits. Often a comment intended to correct a dialect is taken as a personal insult or a slur on a class, race, or region. Sometimes it actually is.

Some people we know went to live in Paris for a year. The parents decided to send their two young sons to a private boys' school so that the two Americans could learn a little French that year. What the parents had not counted on was that their boys would be subjected to taunts, teasing, and finally fights and beatings by the French boys, who called them "so stupid . . . they can't even talk!" The American boys did, indeed, learn French that year, first to defend themselves and later to excel in the classroom. We might like to think this is a rather barbaric, isolated instance of language snobbery, and of course it involved two entirely different languages, not merely two different dialects within the same language. But if you have ever tasted the bitterness that can accompany dialect put-downs — being laughed at or misunderstood for speaking as you were taught to as a child — you can understand how belittlement of a dialect can cause conflict and misunderstanding.

Hawaii has a rich, diverse culture composed of many races. For years, speech teachers in Hawaii tried to change the pidgin and other native dialects of students to conform to a standard white-middle-class dialect. Recently the entire program was reevaluated and changed so that the students are allowed to use their native dialects and learn skills using them. In Brooklyn for many years, people who were studying to become teachers and who spoke native Brooklynese were retrained to speak with a standard American dialect. In Washington, D.C., a program to teach black children from the city's ghettos a standard white-middle-class dialect came under heavy fire and was finally discontinued because enough people felt the program was racist and demeaning to black culture and to the students' pride in being black. Nevertheless, even within native dialects, most students need to learn to improve their communication skills. Some people are simply better able to communicate within their native dialect than are others; and most of us could improve our ability to communicate effectively with persons whose native dialect is different from ours.

STUDYING THE FEATURES OF LANGUAGE

If you wish to improve your ability in verbal communication, you must carefully study all three features of language. The first feature requires that you know how the language works to talk about the world and how content words can be defined and sentences can say things that are true and false about facts. Chapter 9, "How To Inform," will deal in detail with these matters of definition and description of facts.

The second feature requires that you know the way words are formed to communicate the deep structure best for a given receiver or audience. Usually you can say the same thing in a number of different ways. The skillful communicator is good at picking a surface expression to convey his denotative meaning in the best way for a given situation and listener.

The third feature requires that you know how language is tied to personal experiences with words, dialects, and expressions. Sometimes words connote something to one person alone, and sometimes connotative meanings are shared by many, but connotative meanings are more likely than denotative meanings to cause problems in communication, because they are more personal, more subtle, more based on people's own life experiences. Because connotative meanings are often not shared by two people, they must be talked about, so that any differences in connotative meanings can be understood by both communicating parties. The student of interpersonal communication needs to be aware that a given individual, because of his uniquely personal experience with words, responds to some terms or expressions in an unusual or surprising way. He needs to know how the situation often affects the way people use and respond to terms and expressions. Finally, he needs to know how dialects affect his own plans to improve his speech and how dialects are related to the responses of various members of social, economic, geographic, and racial groups. In Chapter 11, "How To Persuade: The Persuasive Power of Personality," and Chapter 12, "Persuasion, Propaganda, and Mass Communication," we will examine in detail the third feature of language in use as it relates to individual responses and the influence of context on reactions to language. In the rest of this chapter we will examine the nature of dialects.

ARTICULATION

In order for a person to say a sound, a word, or a cluster of sounds in running speech, he must know the rules for what sounds are to be said and in what order. He must also have the ability to form the sounds asked for by the rules. The rules of *pronunciation* relate to standards of what sounds to say, in what sequence, in order to speak the language. Articulation refers to a speaker's skill in physically forming the sounds of a given language dialect. A person might be unable to say certain sounds required to speak a language and would thus have a problem of articulation. This is particularly true when a person tries to learn some foreign languages, for certain sounds common in one language may never appear in another. Americans learning German as a second language often have trouble saying the guttural sound peculiar to German that is represented by the letters *ch*, as in the word *Ich*. People whose native language is Japanese have trouble saying the American English /l/ sound.

Native speakers may misarticulate sounds in their own language. A person may lisp because he distorts the /s/ sound.

Some speakers of American English cannot form the /r/ sound in certain words, and say *wabbit* for *rabbit*. A speaker can know the standard way of pronouncing a word in his dialect but be unable to form all the sounds in the proper order with the right stress, and thus not say the word properly because of an articulation disorder. Young children often have articulation problems as they begin to speak. On the other hand, a person may be able to make all the sounds of a dialect but mispronounce a word because he does not know the standard way of saying it.

Articulation difficulties can be helped by increasing skill in saying the basic sounds of the language. Just as a basketball player can improve basic skills by practice under guidance, so a speaker can improve his articulation, no matter what dialect he may be speaking. We are all well advised to become skillful at articulation, because to articulate clearly is to be more intelligible. The question of what standards of pronunciation we should follow is more complicated.

PRONUNCIATION

In some countries there is an arbitrary universal standard language. In France, the standards of language usage, including pronunciation, are decided by a group of experts. In Germany, one dialect has come to be considered the dialect for proper speech and is taught in the schools. Educated Germans can speak high German in addition to whatever dialect they may speak at home or with their friends in more relaxed conversation. In the United States, the standards of usage are much less clear-cut. Dictionaries provide some guidance in pronunciation and are particularly useful if you are learning to say a new word. But what does a person do when a word is pronounced differently in different dialects? Perhaps his parents say a word one way, his friends on the block say it another way, and his teacher at school says the same word still a third way. Does he choose one way, or keep various pronunciations for use at different times?

What is the right way to pronounce a word? The dictionary usually suggests a *preferred* pronunciation of a word, and then it may list a second or third choice. Editors of dictionaries are careful not to say that the pronunciation they list as preferred is the right way to say a word. The editors of dictionaries do not make laws about correct pronunciation; rather, they discover the preferred pronunciation by surveying expert opinion and observing usage among those people the editors feel use the language well. In short, the editors take a poll of well-informed people and report the results in the dictionary. The preface of *The Random House Dictionary of the English Language*, for example, characterizes the pronunciation standards in that work as being "acceptable" to "cultivated speakers."[1]

Editors often consult people who are engaged in broadcasting, journalism, lecturing, and writing when they are deciding about the pronunciation of a word. The dictionary's poll is thus weighted in the direction of certain groups of people, and certain dialect patterns tend to be emphasized. The dictionary's pronunciation standards tend to be accepted by the public as prestigious dialect, and those who use the standard speech tend to be stereotyped as educated and cultured.

GENERAL AMERICAN SPEECH

In the United States the standard is often called general American speech. Most radio and television announcers and actors learn and use the general American dialect. No matter what an announcer's native dialect may be, he tries to develop general American speech in order to find employment in any region of the country or to take part in a program or film planned for the entire country. Actors talented in mimicry not only learn to speak in the general American dialect, but also study many American dialects to use in playing as wide a variety of roles as possible. A skillful actor can tell an audience much about a character's geographic origins and social and economic background by a judicious use of dialect as he creates a role.

The influence of the prestigious general American dialect is felt all over the country. For example, at one time the dialects along the East Coast from north to south were divided according to whether people said the sound /r/. In the last few years, the sounding of the /r/ has been standard for broadcasters, and the result is that the prestigious pronunciation of /r/ at the end of words has affected speakers of the old r-less dialects. Most young speakers shift from sounding the final /r/ (hear) to dropping it (heah), depending upon whether they are speaking carefully and formally or just talking casually with friends.

The Best Way to Speak

Should one standard dialect of American English be the prestigious way of speaking? The general opinion of experts in the study of language is that no one dialect should be singled out

[1] New York, Random House, 1967, p. vi.

as better than all others. The test for judging speech ought to be how well the dialect communicates meaning effectively, easily, and appropriately in the situation in which it is used.

SOCIETY'S BIAS AGAINST
NONSTANDARD-DIALECT SPEAKERS

The fact is, however, that despite the efforts of experts in language usage, many people continue to view some ways of speaking as better than others and to take speech as an index of a person's education, sophistication, intelligence, and social position. Labov, an expert in the way various social and cultural groups use language, notes that "for decades, educational leaders have asked teachers to regard the child's nonstandard language as 'another' way of speaking, to recognize it as simply 'different' from school language rather than condemning it as sloppy or illogical."[2] Nonetheless, many people, including many teachers, unfortunately continue to view language as a clue to social and individual worth.

Many citizens of the United States have believed the American dream that the son or daughter of working-class parents could move into the middle or upper middle class, and that the grandson or granddaughter could become a member of the upper classes. Large numbers of Americans have fulfilled the dream and have moved up in wealth and social status. In the happy absence of a hereditary nobility and the influence of family that accompanies inherited social position, one of the few clues to social-class background remaining in the United States is the way a person speaks. After all, wealth can allow a person to get professional advice on hair style, dress, and home decorating, but speech is somewhat more difficult to change. While pronunciations vary among the well-educated, cultivated, and upper classes in the United States, grammar tends to be more uniform. Thus one authority asserts that "grammar is the surest linguistic index of a speaker's education and general culture."[3]

THE EDUCATIONAL CONTROVERSY
SURROUNDING DIALECTS

When people believe that a prestigious standard speech is the only dialect for educated people to speak, some damaging

---

[2] William Labov, *The Study of Nonstandard English*, Champaign, Ill., National Council of Teachers of English, 1970, p. 28. In the discussion of psycholinguistics which follows we are indebted to Labov's work, particularly as it is summarized in this excellent little monograph.

[3] Raven I. McDavid, Jr., "Usage, Dialects, and Functional Varieties," *The New Random House Dictionary of American English*, p. xxii.

things can happen. One of the developments that followed the awareness of the racial problems in the United States during the 1950s and 1960s was an intensive investigation of the teaching of black children. Investigators discovered that black children often did not learn to read and write at the same rate as nonblack children. Some scholars decided that the difficulty was largely a result of the cultural deprivation of the black children. In their view, the black urban-ghetto child was deprived in his early years of the cultural advantages of the white middle-class child, particularly in regard to language development. Proponents of the deprivation view argued that black children spoke a dialect that was impoverished, illogical, and inadequate to meet the demands of schooling.[4] The remedy, they felt, was to improve the child's speech by teaching him standard English.

Another group of scholars emphasized the growing sense of black pride and awareness that developed during the same decades. These scholars argued that black nonstandard English was "a system of rules, different from the standard but not necessarily inferior as a means of communication"[5] and that the black child should be taught that his speech was different from other dialects but not inferior. Typical of the controversies resulting from these two views was the one that arose in Washington, D.C., where a committee of speech therapists in the teachers union argued with the school board that teachers should stop trying to correct the dialect that inner-city blacks spoke at home. The committee called itself Speech Therapists for Human Dignity and argued that the speech-improvement program was another way of robbing black people of their pride. The school board finally directed that the program of dialect change be dropped and told the speech therapists to spend their time correcting speech disorders such as lisps and stuttering. The supervisor of the program, however, opposed ending it and argued against the dialect theory, asserting that the theory was grossly insulting to inner-city children.[6] The argument against using nonstandard black English in the classroom is that it insults black people by suggesting they cannot acquire the language other Americans use and that continued use of the black dialect

----

[4] See Labov, op. cit., pp. 46–50, for a summary and refutation of the deprivation theory. For further discussion of the cultural deprivation notion, see Fred M. Hechinger, ed., *Pre-School Education Today*, Garden City, N.Y., Doubleday, 1966.

[5] Labov, ibid., p. 14.

[6] Discussed in Orlando L. Taylor, "Some Sociolinguistic Concepts of Black Language," *Today's Speech*, 19 (1971), 19–20. This entire issue of *Today's Speech* is devoted to black communication.

will ultimately hold back black children from learning and success. Black as well as white educators are still divided about whether to attempt to change the dialect spoken by children in the big-city ghettos as well as in the Deep South.

The interest in black English soon led to a concern for the speech dialects of bilingual students such as Mexican-Americans (Chicanos) and Puerto Rican Americans. Many of the same issues were raised in regard to Chicano dialects and Puerto Rican dialects as were discussed in regard to black English. In general, the social and cultural implications of the third feature of language came strongly to bear in these discussions. Students who are personally involved in this problem now have strong feelings about it. Countless Americans who now speak standard American English, but whose parents or grandparents or great-grandparents spoke another language before emigrating to the United States, cannot understand why people make such a fuss about it: "We learned it; why don't they?" These people still regard the United States as a melting pot, and they are eager to blend into the general population. Now minority-group members often believe they must build a strong pride and identity as a group so they will be considered equals in American culture. We appear to be on the way toward developing a democracy of differences.

DECIDING HOW TO SPEAK

However you view yourself and where you fit in your own culture, you will make certain decisions about the way you speak, just as you make decisions about other people because of the way they speak. If your native dialect is not general American you may decide you would like to develop that prestigious dialect, at least for more formal speaking situations; in that case you will have to work on modifying your natural dialect. You may, on the other hand, decide that your life is going to be spent among people who speak your dialect and that there is no good reason for you to modify the dialect you speak right now. Except in the case of actors or politicians practicing the "just plain folks" appeal when they speak, most dialect changes are from nonstandard to standard, from working-class to middle-class, from upper middle-class to upper-class. In other words, dialect modification is often part of the upward mobility in American culture the sociologists talk about.

If you speak an inner-city black dialect, a dialect of the Deep South, or Brooklynese, or if English is your second language, the question of what you want to do about the way you speak is of great importance to you. If you speak a dialect of white working-class or lower-middle-class American English, you must face the same problem of whether to work at changing the way you speak. In the final analysis, of course, the decision is an individual one which each reader must make for himself or herself, but your decision should be made on the basis of an understanding of the way dialects are actually used in the United States and of the way in which they reflect social distinctions, class differences, and economic positions.

Language in Use

If English is our first language, all of us have learned a basic dialect before we get to high school. Generally we become native speakers of the given dialect sometime between the ages of 4 and 13. Children do not speak like their parents so much as they speak like the other children in their generation. The neighborhood gang is more influential in setting speaking norms than are parents. A good picture of an individual's dialect comes from his speech in the fourth and fifth grades, when the 10-year-old conforms most strongly to the peer-group pressures.

THE THREE KINDS OF LANGUAGE RULES
When a person learns a native dialect, he learns three kinds of things about the way to speak in the code. He first learns automatic and basic responses that become habitual. These basic rules are never violated except by accident, and without them, we could not speak with one another at all. An example of this first kind of rule concerns when a person can change "she is" to "she's." The rule allows the form "she's here" but does not allow "here she's." People who speak the language know the first kind of deep basic rule, and teachers do not have to teach it. If teachers had to teach the first kind of rule they would have a difficult time improving the student's approach.

The second kind of rule a person learns when speaking a language can be, and generally is, taught in school. Most speakers know that the second kind exists, and they know that it can be violated without destroying the possibility of communication. These are rules about common usage. We are taught not to say "it don't," because it is ungrammatical. The reason is not that people will fail to understand "It don't make no difference to me how I talk," but rather that if you speak in this way, you appear ignorant and uneducated. Violations of this second sort of rule occur in about 1 to 5 percent of the instances covered by the rule in the speech of native speakers of a dialect. Violations are thus unusual enough to become the focus of class and status differences. Recall the notion that grammatical errors are the surest index to a person's lack of education and culture. Whether they ought to be is not the point; they often *are* taken to be important clues to the kind of person you are. People are even sometimes labeled "dumb" if they use poor grammar, which is often an unfair and illogical judgment. Violations of this second sort of rule can be reported and discussed, and teachers can advise students to change their usage when it deviates from what is considered correct. The more common violations of grammatical rules occur during those times when language is in the process of change, especially at the beginning or toward the end of the period of change. Some time back, for example, people did not know whether to pronounce the word *aunt* as "ant" or "awnt." Nowadays most people say "ant," so the question of which to say is no longer very important.

The third type of rule deals with the same language features as the first and second, but native speakers violate it more often than they do the second. Because the usage is so inconsistent, the rule is seldom enforced in school and is much less likely to be used as a clue to education, social status, culture, and background. Even with rules that are often broken, however, consistently extreme violations make a difference in the receiver's response to speech. For example, the sound /th/ can be articulated (especially in isolation) in several ways without drawing much attention to it; however, should a person consistently, or when the the same sound appears several times in rapid sequence, say /d/ for /th/ as in "Dese folks speak better den dose folks do," he might be thought uneducated. People also articulate the sound /s/ in a wide variety of ways without drawing undue attention to their speech, but extreme distortions of the /s/ sound are noticeable as a lisp or a funny way of talking.

In general if a person learns a language rule of the second or third sort after the age of 13 or 14 (the first type of rule is learned by that time), he will never follow the rule as regularly as he follows the first kind of rule. If you practice critical listening to your own speech and find yourself breaking rules of the second sort from time to time, you will have to make a special effort if you want to conform consistently. When a

cultivated usage *A way of speaking a dialect which is generally admired, because of the wealth, education, family connections, and social position of the people who practice it.*

common usage *A way of speaking a dialect which tends to characterize those with some formal education, some sophistication, and middle-class socioeconomic status.*

folk usage *A way of speaking a dialect which characterizes people with little formal education, little experience from travel, and little sophistication.*

person is tired or distracted or highly involved and emotional about something, the newly learned rules give way to the native vernacular speech learned in the earlier years. The more consistent and regular speech of a dialect group is the basic way of talking learned before age 13.

LEVELS OF USAGE WITHIN A DIALECT GROUP

Dialects may contain within them variations reflecting social classes among the people who speak essentially the same dialect. Thus we can talk in general terms of certain people in every dialect group whose speech is effective and prestigious because of their skill in communication and because of their status. Status in a dialect community may be based on a number of things, including wealth, education, skills, or natural leadership. Scholars refer to the speech of the elite within the dialect group as the **cultivated usage** of the dialect.[7] The community also contains members with little formal education, little experience from travel, little status from natural leadership or skills. Scholars refer to the speech of the lower-status members of the community as **folk** usage of the dialect. Between the cultivated and folk usages is a **common** usage, which characterizes much of the speech in the dialect. How different the cultivated usage may be from the folk usage differs from dialect group to dialect group, depending upon the structure of the community. The point is that one person may speak black English with great skill and sophistication, while another person may speak black English with little skill and much less effectiveness. Almost all people could learn to speak their native dialects more effectively than they do, and no student should assume that because his dialect is as good as any other dialect, his speech is necessarily as good as it could be *within the rules that govern that dialect.*

INDIVIDUAL VARIATIONS IN SPEECH STYLE

Just as there are different levels of usage within a dialect group, so there are different styles of speech within the communication of an individual. Every speaker shows variations in speech style depending upon the relations between source and receiver and the power, status, and solidarity ties between them. Speakers also vary styles depending upon the wider social context in which they operate, such as school, job, neighborhood, church or synagogue, and depending upon the

[7] See, for example, Arthur J. Bronstein, "The Pronunciation of English," *The New Random House Dictionary of American English*, pp. xxiii–xxiv.

topic and occasion. Ability to shift styles varies considerably from person to person. Children, for example, may have a narrow range of speech style because they lack experience. Old men may show a narrow range simply because they no longer care about power and status and manners.

Studies of the way people talk in a variety of situations reveal that casual speech can be distinguished from careful speech in terms of the way people use their dialects. A person tends to monitor his speech carefully in formal or important situations such as a job interview, a first meeting with someone he wants to impress, or a formal public speech. Casual speech is the way a person talks when at ease and relaxed with people he can trust and with whom he is willing to be natural and off guard. Studies of casual and careful speech indicate that lower-class speakers tend to model their careful speech upon the standards of the upper classes. The speech of the upper class is not completely different from that of the lower class. Rather, the same differences in usage exist between careful and casual speech in all social classes. The careful speech of the lower class is more like the upper-class speech, and the upper-class casual speech relaxes into the patterns of the lower class. In general, however, the lower social classes have more deviations from careful upper-class speech in both casual and careful speech.

Other style variations come about for rhetorical reasons, as we mentioned before. There is a long tradition in the United States for persuaders to adopt the dialect of the audience, at least in part, to show they are "just like" the people to whom they are speaking. Politicians sprinkle their speech with ungrammatical expressions or use variations in dialect when they are speaking out among the voters informally during election campaigns. The same politicians, however, are careful to confine themselves to correct or even formal grammar on certain state or solemn occasions. The leaders of black nationalist movements rarely use nonstandard black English in their public speeches. Their grammar then is essentially standard. Often, however, they use fragments of black English when talking to all-black audiences.

Considerations About Improving Verbal Communication

Should you change your way of speaking if you use a dialect that is not the same as the standard general American speech of radio, television, and film? Should you change your grammar to that which is commonly used by educated and cultured people of all dialects? You now have an understanding of some basic facts about language and dialects to help you make that decision for yourself.

You should keep the following points in mind as you decide whether you need to change or improve your own language:

1 More middle-class speakers have skills primarily related to school language, but working-class speakers also have a wide range of verbal skills, including many not mastered by middle-class speakers; and in the urban ghetto, speakers communicate in ways that demand ingenuity, originality, and complex language behaviors.

2 Black English and other nonstandard dialects are not deficient uses of standard English. They are logical outgrowths of the linguistic history of the people who speak them.

3 Because of the social, economic, and geographic anchoring of speech, people tend to make stereotyped judgments on the basis of the way you talk. Television announcers, school teachers, office managers, and so forth are stereotyped as having excellent speech with regard to their use of grammar, their articulation, and their pronunciation. A man who uses such nonstandard terms as *dem, dese, dose,* and *dat* and double-negative expressions such as "Don't never do dat to me agin" is stereotyped as a tough guy, one who probably fights a lot. Upper-middle-class and upper-class speakers are stereotyped as using correct grammar, pronunciations, and articulation.

4 The more style changes you have at your command, the better you can communicate in a wide range of situations for a larger number of different receivers.

5 Your instructor can help make you aware of any differences between your dialect and the standard grammar and pronunciation. Simply becoming aware of differences will not teach you to use the standard dialect. Certainly what you learn in the classroom will not become an unconscious verbal habit. Probably the best you can hope for is a control such as when a person learns to use standard grammar at least in more formal speaking situations. Your casual speech will tend to remain much what it has always been.

6 The most important consideration is for you to decide what you plan to do with your life. Do you plan to adopt a life style that requires talking with many different kinds of

Chapter 3

THE KEY IDEAS

Message structure is a necessary part of communication.

After we have named something, we can use either property or relation words to comment about it.

The denotative meanings of language relate to the description of the world.

We make a decision to use a given word to stand for some object, person, or event.

A common dictionary is a list of rules connecting words with their denotative meanings.

We do not need to look at the world of objects, things, and events to check the structure of a message.

The connotative meanings of language relate to the associated, often emotional, responses in addition to the denotative meanings.

Response to language is both individual and cultural.

Every experienced public speaker learns that a word or an expression that gains him the desired response on one occasion may well be wrong on another.

Some words and statements are closely tied to the structure of society and arouse a common reaction, positive or negative, from entire groups of people.

Whoever you are, wherever you live, you speak a dialect.

You will shift back and forth in your style of speaking depending on the formality of the situation and on the people to whom you are talking.

Often a comment intended to correct speech is taken as a personal insult or a slur on a class, a race, an ethnic group, or a region of the country.

Belittling a dialect can cause emotional responses, conflict, and misunderstanding.

Most people can learn to speak their native dialect more effectively than they do.

A person who is unable to say certain sounds used in a language has an articulation problem.

The more clearly we articulate the sounds of a language, the easier it is for a listener to decide what words we are saying.

Editors of American dictionaries do not make laws about the right way to pronounce words; rather, they survey the way educated and cultured people pronounce words and decide what pronunciations are preferred.

Most radio and television announcers and actors learn to use the general American dialect in their work.

The influence of the prestigious general American dialect is felt all over the country.

No dialect should be singled out as better than all others.

When people believe that a certain way of speaking is the only way for educated people to speak, some damaging results may follow.

One of the few clues to social background remaining in the United States is the way a person speaks.

We appear to be on the way toward developing a democracy of differences.

When a person makes a message, he encodes it into a form the listener can take in.

American English is a code.

Codes such as the English language have no natural connection with the objects of the world.

Among important codes for communication are several which use gestures.

Another important code that adds meaning to speech is like the melody that enhances a poem set to music.

By proper use of vocal punctuation we can make the same sentence mean several different things.

Dialect modification is often part of upward mobility in American culture.

All of us have learned a basic dialect before we get to high school.

Children speak more like their friends than like their parents.

Some rules of language use are so basic that they are hardly ever violated, and we are seldom aware of their existence.

Some rules of language are violated often enough so that people become aware of them, and they tend to become markers of social class and status.

Levels of usage within a dialect group vary from cultivated, to common, to folk.

Casual speech is different from formal speech in most individuals.

Persuasive speakers often use the dialect of the audience in an attempt to have their listeners identify with them.

A person is often stereotyped on the basis of his dialect.

If a person wants to be an effective communicator in a mobile society, he is well advised to develop the ability to shift styles within his native dialect and to use other dialects in careful speech.

people? Do you plan to move from one part of the country to another? Do you expect to work with people from different social classes? From different ethnic backgrounds? Do you plan to work at a job in which your native dialect is basic and sufficient? Do you plan a career that would require you to use standard general American dialect and standard school grammar, and do you speak this way now? In general, you should consider that life in the complex, shifting, urban, multiracial culture of the United States will put increasing demands upon college-educated people to be able to shift styles of speech and dialect over a wide range.

SUGGESTED PROJECTS

1 The instructor makes a short tape recording of all of the students' voices. No names are on this tape, only voices. This exercise can be done by the class as a whole, but it is more effective when several machines can be used in smaller groups, members of each group recording only their own voices. The students listen to the voices and try to make a description, oral or written, of the various dialects and ethnic, religious, geographic, and national influences heard in each one's speech. At the end of the hour, the class discusses these dialect variations and further discusses the stereotypes that are sometimes associated with these various dialects.

2 Each student listens to his own voice recording and describes his own dialect and verbal skill. Depending on time, the instructor and/or other class members help make an analysis of individual voices. Each student then writes a short paper analyzing his future career hopes and where and how he desires to live. Then he discusses the adequacies and inadequacies of his verbal communication, at this particular stage in his life, for his chosen career and life style.

3 Find a newspaper article that reports some dramatic news event involving interesting people. Rewrite the news story in two ways. First, emphasize the denotative factual description of the event. Try to keep the names, the relational terms, and the property terms as neutral as possible. Second, slant the message to create an emotional response to the event. Use words likely to arouse positive or negative responses in a reader. If time permits, tape record the two versions for playback to the class, in order to point out the differences in an oral presentation.

SUGGESTED READINGS

"Black Language, Literature, Rhetoric, and Communication," *Today's Speech*, 19 (1971).

Clark, Margaret L., Ella A. Erway, and Lee Beltzer. *The Learning Encounter: The Classroom as a Communications Workshop.* New

York: Random House, 1971. "A Dialect for Meaning," pp. 157–183.

Labov, William. *The Study of Nonstandard English.* Champaign, Ill.: National Council of Teachers of English, 1970.

Lieblich, Malcolm. "Be Proud of Your Brooklyn Accent," *Today's Speech,* 17 (1969), 50–54.

Shuy, Roger W. *Discovering American Dialects.* Champaign, Ill.: National Council of Teachers of English, 1967.

Chapter 4

HOW TO IMPROVE NONVERBAL COMMUNICATION THROUGH VOCAL EMPHASIS

Nonverbal communication consists of the body language and the vocal melodies that accompany a speaker's words. In this chapter we shall concentrate on the way a speaker makes the sounds of a verbal code (language) to communicate meanings beyond those conveyed by the choice of the symbol itself, with its three faces of language, discussed in Chapter 3.

We should never underestimate the importance of the nonverbal elements in the total communication event. One expert, Albert Mehrabian, estimates that the total impact of a message is a result of about 7 percent verbal, 38 percent vocal, and 55 percent facial elements.[1] Of course, we have no way to measure exactly how much effect our use of vocal emphasis has upon our communication; we use such percentages simply to emphasize the importance of nonverbal communication.

All three styles of communication include extensive theoretical treatment of nonverbal communication. The message

[1] Albert Mehrabian, "Communication Without Words," *Psychology Today*, 2 (September 1968), p. 53.

terminal junctions *A distinctive sound feature or modification of a sound feature which marks the end of a word, clause, or sentence.*
degrees of loudness *Four levels of loudness in speaking which add stress and emphasis to American English.*

communication style encourages theoretical discussion of *scientific* studies of vocal emphasis. Usually such studies are based upon observation of human communication which attempts to discover how vocal inflections fit into codes which are meaningful to various communities of language users. For example, many linguists describe American English as having three **terminal junctions**, or ways to punctuate the stream of oral discourse. To illustrate, one terminal junction is indicated by the symbol /#/ and is characterized as a pause in speech combined with an off-glide in pitch plus a stretching out of the last sounds before the pause. The terminal junction /#/ is often used at the end of assertion, or what in writing would be called a declarative sentence. The **degrees of loudness** used to stress elements of a message can also be categorized, as primary, secondary, tertiary, and weak.[2] They have characteristic symbols as follows: primary /´/, secondary /∧/, tertiary /\/, and weak /∪/.

The relationship communication style, because of its emphasis on how people read unintended as well as intended meanings into communication events, stresses the way voice quality and vocal emphasis may convey information about relationships. The public-speaking style has a long tradition of the study and improvement of effective delivery of messages. The theory related to public speaking includes not only models of the ideal way to use vocal emphasis, but also has actual techniques and drills to make the speaker's voice a more effective instrument of communication.

ATTITUDES OF COMMUNICATION THEORISTS TOWARD VOICE TRAINING

Theorists of the message communication style often reject actual training in voice improvement as unnecessary, if not improper. They argue that students are usually well within the normal range of the general public's use of vocal emphasis, that they generally articulate well enough for all the communication they are going to do. These theorists further maintain that those students who fall appreciably out of the normal range should be considered for special help from speech correctionists. They believe that to become a connoisseur and good practitioner of the message communication style, one does not have to learn to articulate sounds more clearly or to use a wider range of pitch, rate, and loudness, or

[2] See, for example, Ray L. Birdwhistell, *Kinesics and Context: Essays on Body Motion Communication*. Philadelphia: University of Pennsylvania Press, 1970, pp. 128–132.

to improve the quality of the voice. The theorists of the relationship communication style also tend to reject formal training in voice improvement, on the grounds that it emphasizes the speaker rather than the dialogue, that an emphasis on how one says something would add even more self-consciousness, when the goal of relationship communication is unself-consciousness or naturalness; they say further than it results in a drastic and undesirable oversimplification of the communication situation. One theorist in the relationship communication style, for example, characterizes the public-speaking style as one which views communication as an act, and asserts that "if you look at communication as an act, and if you want to become a 'good' communicator, you'll obviously have to concentrate on perfecting your communication *performance*." *Performance*, in the relationship style, of course, suggests role playing rather than authentic communication. He goes on to say that the public-speaking style assumes "that skill makes all the difference. If you're smooth, organized, and enthusiastic you'll probably succeed."[3] For the relationship communication theorists, then, vocal emphasis should come from honest emotion openly displayed, and not as a result of skill resulting from training.

The theorists in the public-speaking style have developed the techniques of vocal emphasis to their fullest over a long

[3] John Stewart, ed., *Bridges Not Walls: A Book About Interpersonal Communication.* Reading, Mass.: Addison-Wesley, 1973, p. 8.

paralinguistics *The study of the nonverbal vocal features which accompany sound articulation in speech.*

tradition in voice improvement. The general rationale of the public-speaking style is that while there is a danger of becoming mechanical and unnatural in vocal training, and the students must always guard against affectation, most beginners will need training in the fundamentals of vocal emphasis to become good speakers. The way most of us learn to speak, by imitating those around us, frequently results in slurring, mumbling, monotonous talk which is difficult to listen to and decipher. Further, poor techniques in voice production result in squeaky or nasal or breathy or harsh or weak voices which *do* affect the way others respond to us and to our personalities, which in turn affects how they like us, believe us, or trust us.

Our approach in this chapter is to summarize some of the research discoveries which have become part of the message theory, to summarize the basic attitudes of the relationship communication style, and to concentrate on the well-developed tradition for voice improvement from the public speaking style. We do this because for the student of communication, the question of nonverbal elements is of crucial importance. You not only need to know the attitudes and theories of the major styles, but you also need to be able to compare and contrast them and decide for yourself whether *for your purposes* voice improvement is an important and useful educational goal.

The technical name for the contemporary study of the nonverbal features of spoken communication related to voice production and the articulation of sounds is **paralinguistics.** *Para*, a prefix borrowed from the Greek language, in this instance means "beyond." Linguistics refers to language. The term paralinguistics thus means "beyond language," and refers to that part of talking that goes beyond words.

Many dialects have unique vocal patterns. People whose native language is Spanish, for instance, often speak English with a pattern of pitch inflection and a rate of speech similar to the one used in Spanish. Natives of India, though they often learn English from childhood, often speak English with a very characteristic pattern of vocal emphasis. Ghetto blacks have some characteristic vocal patterns unique to their dialect — for instance, an extreme rise in pitch. People speaking a general American dialect seldom use a high pitch except in times of emergency, when under great emotional stress. Speakers of black English, use a high pitch more often.[4]

[4] Margaret L. Clark, Ella A. Erway, and Lee Beltzer, *The Learning Encounter: The Classroom as a Communications Workshop.* New York: Random House, 1971, p. 176.

HOW TO
IMPROVE NONVERBAL
COMMUNICATION THROUGH
VOCAL EMPHASIS

You should be aware of the nonverbal features of a dialect as you study your own voice and analyze its strengths and weaknesses. Our emphasis in this chapter, however, is on the way you can use your voice to increase your ability to communicate specific meanings on specific occasions. We are primarily interested in how you punctuate and emphasize your messages by the way you say the words of running speech within the rules of a given dialect or communication style.

Nonverbal Communication in the Message Communication Style

As the message communication style evolved over the years, two schools emerged within the general approach. In the early studies at Bell Telephone Laboratories, for instance, investigators often examined the nature of the production of speech, the characteristics of sound waves produced by human speech, and the ways in which speech listeners comprehended speech. Gradually, researchers in experimental phonetics or voice science, discovered a number of things about voice production, about the acoustical nature of vowel

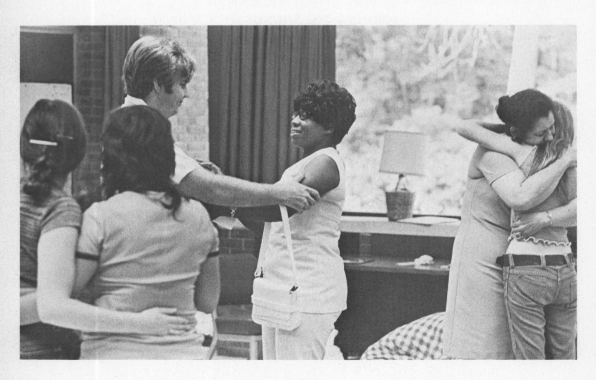

phoneme *The basic units of sound out of which longer units such as parts of words, words, and sentences are formed.*
international phonetic alphabet *An alphabet containing a separate symbol (or character) for each phoneme.*

sounds and consonants, about intelligibility—all of which were essentially scientific; that is, these findings cut across communication styles and are thus the same no matter what language an individual speaks. Meantime, those message theorists who were primarily interested in human, face-to-face communication and the mass media concentrated on other aspects of paralanguage. This second group became more interested in how voice quality influences impressions of the message source; how vocal changes might influence meaning; and the relationships among the verbal components, the vocal components, and the gestures, facial expressions, and postures which comprise human speech.

The material that follows is largely part of the scientific component of communication theory. A channel of considerable importance in the SMCR model of communication is that of hearing. The gap between source and receiver is bridged by sound waves which impinge upon the receiver's ear and, through his sense of hearing, stimulate the listener to decode the message. In order to talk, we must do more than produce a sound wave in the voice box and change its quality by resonating it through the mouth, throat, and nose. Speech requires that we encode messages.

FORMING THE SOUNDS OF A SPOKEN CODE

The physical encoding of American English, for instance, is the result of the *articulation* of individual sounds. The process of articulation is thus of considerable importance to the student of voice science. The technical word for a basic unit of sound in a language is **phoneme**. A small number of phonemes, usually from 20 to 60, is enough to form most of the world's languages. The written symbols which stand for the basic units of sound in a language are part of what is called the **International Phonetic Alphabet.** Devised by the International Phonetic Association, the alphabet is based on articulatory features and provides a consistent and universal system for transcribing the speech sounds of any language. The fact that such an alphabet is possible indicates that the theory upon which such categories are based is scientific rather than artistic and cuts across communication styles.

The English alphabet is also a written code, but is only approximately phonetic: We require more symbols to transcribe the phonemes of spoken English than we require letters to write English. We have many more sounds in our everyday speech than we have letters. Take the sounds in the following English words: *bait, bat, bought, bet, beet, bit, boat, boot,*

soft palate *The muscular part of the back of the roof of the mouth, important in saying sounds like /k/ in Katy, or /g/ in gun.*

proper articulation *Correct formation of the phonemes of a given dialect, in the correct sequence.*

pronunciation *Act or result of producing the sounds of speech (proper articulation) and inflecting and stressing them according to conventional standards of a language or dialect.*

vowels *In American English, a speech sound produced without stopping, diverting, or obstructing the sound wave (/i/, /e/, /ɛ/, /æ/, /a/, /ɔ/, /o/, /u/, /ə/, /ʌ/).*

consonants *In American English, a speech sound produced by stopping (p,b,d,t,k,g), diverting (m,n), or obstructing (f,v,s,z) the sound wave.*

but, *bite*, and *bout*. Each vowel in these eleven words is phonetically different, and yet we encode these sounds when writing with just 5 letters: *a, e, i, o,* and *u*. If we transcribed them in the International Phonetic Alphabet we would use 11 different symbols.

The articulatory mechanism of speech consists of the vocal cords, the **soft palate** at the back of the roof of the mouth, the tongue, the lips, and the teeth. Make the sounds /s/, /t/, or /b/, or any of the vowels and notice how active your tongue is and how many changes you make in the position of your jaw and lips. Exaggerate slightly to emphasize these differences.

Proper articulation is a matter of being intelligible—of being able to make all of the sounds of a dialect so that someone else can understand them. **Pronunciation** is a matter of being able to use well-made sounds in words, with the emphasis in the generally accepted order for a particular dialect. One might articulate the sounds properly and still mispronounce a word.

The phonemes (sounds) can be divided into two main categories: **vowels** and **consonants.** (Phoneticians point to other important distinctions, but for our purposes, this one major difference needs to be stressed.) All vowels require a sound wave of a regular frequency, produced with the oral breath channel open. The tone of the voice and its musical characteristics are therefore a function of the way we say the vowels. Because the vowels are phonated, that is, because the vocal folds are always in vibration to produce them, they contain more sound energy than many of the consonants. The vowels also carry your voice quality. If a person has a pleasant musical voice, it is because of the way he forms his vowel sounds and the way he utilizes his resonators. If a person's voice is breathy, nasal-sounding, weak, harsh, or in any other way distinctive, the vowels are largely responsible. That means that if you want to improve your voice *quality*, you should work on improving the way you make the vowel sounds. You have doubtless all heard the old line "How now brown cow." It is a senseless sentence, the repeated saying of which makes much sense. Now to the other speech sounds, consonants.

THE IMPORTANCE OF ARTICULATING CONSONANTS

Consonants are produced by stopping, blocking, or diverting a sound wave. Consonants tend to come in pairs and to be distinguished by the presence or absence of sound produced by the vocal cords. For example, the difference between /t/ and /d/ is that while the tongue, lips, and teeth are in the same position for both sounds, when one says /d/, he adds a sound produced by the vocal cords. The same is true of /s/ and /z/, /f/ and /v/, and a number of other consonants. Consonants thus may or may not have a regular tone associated with them, but they all have a plosive, noisy, clicking, hissing, or whistling quality. Most consonants are short and cannot be drawn out the way vowels can. Because of the shortness and noisiness of most of them, consonants do not carry the musical or voice-quality features that the vowels do. Their main function is to distinguish among the various parts of an oral code such as the English language. The differences among words such as *bit, hit, sit,* and *bit, bill, big,* is in the consonants that surround a common vowel.

The consonants often contain less sound energy than the vowels. One of the weakest sounds in English, for example, is the unphonated stop plosive /t/. Try saying just the little sound /t/ without adding a vowel such as "eee" to it. Do not say "tee," say only the first sound, /t/. Because the consonants generally have less energy in them, the listener cannot easily hear them. As a result, the receiver cannot always decode the words; if the consonants are not heard the message is lost. Often we can overhear a conversation without understanding it because all we can distinguish are the vowels, and we hear something like "oh, ee, awww, ooo." On the other hand, we can use the same vowel in every word of a sentence, and if the consonants are clear, we can understand the words even though the conversation sounds strange and stilted. For example, say the following sentence using the same vowel every time: "Mu futhur dummunds thut u gu tu culludg."

The lesson to be learned from the nature of consonants is clear. If you want to be understood, in the most basic sense of the receiver's getting the words you are saying, you must articulate consonants clearly. The technical term for the clarity required for decoding the verbal content of a speech message is *intelligibility.* If the message is intelligible, the receiver can reconstruct the words sent out by the source. If someone is talking on a ham radio and says, "John lied out of fright," and the noise and static are such that the receiver of the message decodes it as, "John died last night," the message was unintelligible. Of course even an intelligible message must be interpreted or understood, but intelligibility is a minimum requirement for understanding. The reason the mumbler is often not understood is that the receiver simply cannot hear the consonants well enough to decipher what words the source is saying.

For example, if you are talking over the telephone and find

that because of a bad connection the person on the other end of the line cannot make out the words you are saying, the best procedure is not to yell the vowels more loudly but to articulate the consonants with great care and clarity. The vowels are probably being heard, but the consonants are what counts. Talking more loudly to slightly deaf people often makes them angry; articulating your consonants more slowly and more clearly helps people with hearing impairments understand what you are saying.

To communicate effectively, a person must both articulate clearly and pronounce the words correctly. Of the two skills, clear articulation is the more basic. If a person articulates clearly, others will probably be able to decipher the words even though they may wince at the way a dialect's conventions for saying those words are being broken by mispronunciations; but if a person does not articulate well, the receiver may not be able to decode the word the source intends.

MAJOR ARTICULATION ERRORS

The major articulation errors consist of (1) the omission of a phoneme, (2) the subsitution of one phoneme for another, and (3) the distortion of the phoneme. As a child learns a language, he tends to begin speaking by omitting certain sounds and may first say something like "I wa I tee tone" for "I want an ice-cream cone." As the child becomes more proficient, he tends to add the sounds, but because some consonants are more difficult to form than others, he may substitute easier sounds for the more difficult ones. Notice that the child who is saying "I wa I tee tone" is substituting the easier /t/ sound for the more difficult /k/ sound. Finally, at the later stages, a child may realize the substitution is an error and try to say the right sound, but fail in the effort and, as a result, distort the sound.

Sometimes, because of bad habits, we continue to omit, substitute, or distort sounds on into our adolescent or adult years. No one bothers to point out our error, and we do not listen to ourselves critically as a rule. A common word illustrating two articulation problems is *just*, which ought to have a final /t/ sound, but is often articulated as "jis." When one says "jis" for "just," not only is he omitting the sound at the end; he is also substituting the easier sound /i/ for the /u/ sound. Learn to listen for this in your own speech and that of others. You will hear "jis" frequently. Other common substitutions include "git" for "get," "goin" for "going," "runnin" for "running," and "beaudy" for "beauty." An occasional misarticulation is of little importance, of course, but many people have evolved bad habits of articulation, and their speech is filled with such mistakes.

When a person consistently omits and substitutes sounds in running speech, the result is a mumble that is difficult to understand. Read the following sentence aloud to see how difficult misarticulation is to understand: "Hey, Joe, jeet yet? Lesgo grabbasanwish." Now read the following sentence, carefully forming each phoneme: "Hey, Joe, did you eat yet? Let's go grab a sandwich."

Poor articulation is found in every dialect. You should not confuse a dialect's rules for pronunciation with errors in articulation. Recall that every dialect has a group of speakers who use the dialect well and who set the standards and a large group of speakers who use the dialect in substandard ways. A person who speaks a black inner-city dialect may articulate the sounds of the dialect clearly or may mumble in a fashion that makes it difficult for others *who also speak the same dialect* to understand him. No matter what dialect or dialects you speak, you ought to check your articulation, and where it is inaccurate, you should work to improve it, simply for the sake of being understood—to make your speech intelligible.

PITCH
Pitch is the perception of changes in a sound wave as tones on a musical scale. The pitch of a speaking voice should be neither too high nor too low for general, comfortable use, and every speaker should learn to use variations in pitch to best advantage.

The way a speaker varies the pitch of his voice is an important nonverbal technique to emphasize the meaning in a message or to indicate that the meaning one would normally associate with certain words is to be discounted or interpreted as irony or sarcasm. One can communicate a great deal by the skillful use of changes in pitch in such vowels as "oh" or "eee." You can experiment with the usefulness of pitch variations as a nonverbal technique of communication by saying "oh" so that it expresses different emotions and meanings: "How delightful," "I don't believe you," "That's nothing new," or "How disgusting."[5]

Pitch inflections can be thought of as consisting of three

[5] For a survey of vocal changes associated with emotional states see James C. McCroskey, Carl E. Larson, and Mark L. Knapp, *An Introduction to Interpersonal Communication*, Englewood Cliffs, N.J.: Prentice-Hall, 1971, pp. 116–118.

main types: (1) a downward inflection, (2) an upward inflection, and (3) a circumflex, or upward *and* downward, inflection.

Downward inflections require that the voice start a sound on a relatively high note and then slide down the scale while the sound is prolonged. Downward inflections add the nuance of assertion, certainty, and solidarity to meanings. Try the sentence "I am quite certain about that" and use a strong downward inflection on the words toward the end of the sentence. Notice that the pitch variation supplements the verbal message, making the total message, both verbal and nonverbal, more emphatic.

Upward variations of pitch are useful to add nonverbally a questioning, tentative, light, or sprightly tone to the verbal message. Experiment with saying the sentence, "I am quite certain about that," with an upward inflection. Because the sentence is a statement rather than a question, you may find it difficult to read with a rising inflection or pitch, but with some practice you will be able to do so. Notice that sometimes the rising pitch alone makes the sentence sound like a question, and sometimes the rising pitch makes the remark sound tentative and unsure even though the words themselves assert certainty. Questions are emphasized by an upward inflection of pitch.

The circumflex, or upward and downward, movement of pitch is more complicated in its nonverbal connotations. Usually the verbal context and the situation influence the interpretation of the circumflex. The primary function of the circumflex is to make a portion of the message in which it appears stand out from the context. (Interestingly enough, in English we seldom use a pitch inflection that starts high, glides downward, and then slides up the scale. You might experiment with a U-shaped tonal glide and see if you can interpret its nonverbal meaning.)

Pitch changes are among the most important voice techniques for nonverbal communication. Generally, pitch changes are a result of stepping up or down in pitch, either from syllable to syllable or from word to word, or of gliding from one tone to another while prolonging a vowel sound. (Recall that the vowels carry the musical quality of connected speech, and that pitch changes within syllables are usually associated with vowels.) The pitch variations in Oriental languages often convey different meanings: The same sound pitched at four different tonal levels may be decoded by an Oriental listener as four distinct words.

You should select some sentences, experiment with

shifting pitch in a steplike way from word to word, and then read the same sentences and shift pitch on the vowels in order to get the feel of the two major techniques to suggest mood and meaning with pitch variations.

LOUDNESS

The ear perceives changes in air pressure in the sound wave as changes in loudness. Loudness levels of voice have one basic and vital function in speech communication. The message must contain enough sound energy to travel through the channel to the intended receiver, so it can be picked up and decoded.

Above the minimum required for intelligibility, loudness changes provide another technique of nonverbal communication. Loudness variations add emphasis by making certain ideas within a message stand out. In addition, a generally loud tone communicates excitement, high emotion, boisterous feelings, anger. A soft tone connotes calm, reverence, peace, boredom. We must always be careful not to view the nonverbal codes as though their meanings were as clearly defined and understood as the meanings of words. In a given culture, we tend to interpret nonverbal communication such as loudness or softness of speech in terms of how people talk in given contexts under the stress of certain emotions. Excited spectators at a basketball game may speak loudly, shout, and yell. Mourners at a funeral tend to speak softly.

A speaker can make important elements in a message stand out by saying them either more loudly or more softly than the surrounding verbal padding. We sometimes forget that speaking for a time at one level of loudness and then suddenly dropping the voice and saying the important words softly can emphasize them as much as suddenly raising the voice to a shout.

Try reading the following line in the two ways suggested by the stage directions in parentheses, to get the feel of loudness variations as a nonverbal communication tool:

(*normal level of loudness*) *When you say that, mister,*
    (*drop loudness some*) *you better* (*pause, then very softly*) *smile.*
(*normal level of loudness*) *When you say that, mister,*
    (*louder*) *you better* (*very loud*) *smile.*

RATE

The speed with which one utters syllables and words is the *rate* of speech. Rate is the third major dimension of voice related to nonverbal communication. A rapid rate is usually associated with excitement, danger, the need for sudden action. A slow rate often communicates calm, tiredness, sickness, resignation. Speaking rates tend to vary depending on what section of the country a speaker was brought up in, and much of what we call speech accents are actually variances in rate.

In many respects, variations of rate, like variations in pitch and loudness, function to add emphasis.

PAUSES

Pauses can be thought of as part of the rate of utterance, but they play such an important role in the nonverbal encoding of messages that they deserve separate treatment.

Perhaps the most important feature of the pause is its function as oral punctuation. Comedian-pianist Victor Borge had a comedy routine in which he substituted strange and bizarre sounds, such as whistles, squawks, and clicks, for the various punctuation marks. The result was a hilarious example of the fact that the spoken as well as the written message needs to be properly punctuated to carry meaning successfully.

Generally, short pauses are useful as dividing points, to separate short thought units or modifying ideas, much as commas are used in writing. Long pauses serve to separate complete thought units, much as periods, question marks, and exclamation points do in writing. Notice how pausing punctuates the following sentences so their meanings are changed:

> *The captain (pause) said the mate (pause) was drunk again last night.*
> *The captain said (pause) the mate was drunk again last night.*
> *Woman (pause) without her (pause) man is a beast.*
> *Woman without her man (pause) is a beast.*

Pauses of longer duration may communicate nonverbally in the context of an interview or small group meeting or before an audience. The famous "speaker's pause"—when a public speaker takes the podium and before starting to speak, looks out over the audience and waits for several moments—communicates confidence, a collecting together of important thoughts; it often catches the attention of the listeners, who expect something to happen at once, and when it does not, grow curious about why the speech has not begun.

Within the context of an interview, also, a pause may be interpreted as meaningful. An interviewee who pauses for an appreciable length of time before answering a question may be communicating something such as, "That is a difficult question and I am not sure I know how to answer it," or, "I know how to answer that question, but I am not sure I want to do so right at this point." When a respondent stops talking and the interviewer does not say something in turn, the pause may be interpreted as, "Please go on; I would like to hear you continue talking about this matter."

The first school of message communication theorists, thus, developed considerable scientific knowledge about the nature of the sound wave produced by human speech and the perceptions of that sound wave relating to pitch, rate, loudness, vocal quality, and intelligibility. The second school of message communication theorists, viewing the broader context of communication tended to examine the way voice and articulation communicates impressions of emotion and source personality.

STUDIES OF PARALANGUAGE AND SOURCE IMPRESSIONS

Theorists in the message communication style have assembled the results of empirical studies relating to such questions as what effect changes in vocal quality have upon the listener's impression that the speaker is in an emotional state. A number of studies have documented the conventional wisdom that paralanguage conveys such states as intense anger, contempt, love, and grief.[6] Researchers have investigated also the question of what effect paralanguage has on a listener's impression of the speaker's personality. Again a number of studies indicate that listeners do conclude that a nasal voice goes with a number of undesirable personality features and that a full, round voice in males is evidence of energy, health, sophistication, and other desirable personality features. Still other studies have examined the question of whether vocal characteristics were clues to whether the speaker was male or female, large or small in stature, old or young in age, a high-school or college graduate. In general, the

---

[6] See, for example, J. Davitz, *The Communication of Emotional Meaning,* New York: McGraw-Hill, 1964; E. Kramer, "Judgment of Personal Characteristics and Emotions from Nonverbal Properties of Speech," *Psychological Bulletin,* 60 (1963), pp. 408–420; F. S. Costanzo, N. N. Markel, and P. R. Constanzo, "Voice Quality Profile and Perceived Emotion," *Journal of Counseling Psychology,* 16 (1969), pp. 267–270; J. Starkweather, "The Communication Value of Content-Free Speech," *American Journal of Psychology,* 69 (1956), pp. 121–123.

results of such studies provide evidence for the importance of voice quality and articulation in the communication process.[7]

You might find it inconsistent of the message communication theorists to argue that research indicates that vocal characteristics are extremely important in the communication process, on the one hand, and to assert, on the other, that most students use vocal technique skillfully enough so that they lose little communicative effectiveness. Remember, however, that when those scholars interested in the scientific study of communication divided several decades ago, the group with an interest in voice science and the treatment of voice problems moved in the direction of treating atypical, severe problems. The other group, which formed the core of the analysts of the message communication style, were often in theoretical conflict with those in the public-speaking, oral-interpretation-of-literature, and voice-and-diction traditions. Their solution to the question of whether or not students of communication should be trained to use their voices more effectively was to assert that most people could be divided into either those with speech handicaps, who should be given special attention by speech pathologists, or those essentially normal speakers who did not need further training. It became, for a time, almost impossible for a student to find a class in voice improvement in many colleges and universities. As theorists rather than practitioners, the first advocates of the message communication style felt that prescriptive advice on voice improvement was unscientific, undependable, and unnecessary. As old feuds fade, and as the new concern with paralanguage grows, a swing back to helping people speak better, if they want and need to, seems probable.

Nonverbal Communication in the Relationship Style

Theorists in the relationship communication style tend to view vocal cues as part of a total communication system and

[7] See, for example, D. W. Addington, "The Relationship of Selected Vocal Characteristics to Personality Perception," *Speech Monographs*, 35 (1968), pp. 492–503; and E. Kramer, "Personality Stereotypes in Voice: A Reconsideration of the Data," *Journal of Social Psychology*, 62 (1964), pp. 247–251. For surveys of the research relating to voice quality and articulation see Mark L. Knapp, *Nonverbal Communication in Human Interaction*, New York: Holt, Rinehart and Winston, 1972, pp. 147–174; and C. David Mortensen, *Communication: The Study of Human Interaction*, New York: McGraw-Hill, 1972, pp. 228–229.

elocution movement *A group of communication theorists who devoted their attention to the study of and instruction in oral delivery, including both voice and gesture.*

to stress their importance in terms of relationships. They often discuss the entire context of the communication event — the posture and positions of participants, vocal emphasis, pauses, words, and voice quality — as unique and requiring exhaustive description for complete understanding. Since the communication event is an organic whole, it becomes difficult to isolate features of vocal emphasis and discuss their denotative or connotative meanings. Not only that, but the instruction in the relationship style does not include the practice of techniques of voice improvement or clearer articulation. The relationship style tolerates, and sometimes encourages, mumbling, repetitiveness, vocalized pauses, hesitations, verbal crutches such as "you know" or vocal exclamations such as "hey!" and "wow!" These are seen as valid indications of involvement, feelings, insights, and empathy. As we shall see in Chapter 5, the relationship communication style includes much more attention to gestures, touching, smelling, and physical relationships among participants than it does to paralinguistic features of communication.

The Public-Speaking Style

The public-speaking style has a long tradition of voice and articulation improvement. In the early years of the nineteenth century the **elocution movement** evolved to train speakers, readers, and actors in the skills of vocal emphasis. Much as professional singers learn techniques for producing vocal music, public speakers learned techniques of voice production; proper breathing, voice placement; vocal relaxation; formation of sounds; flexibility in rate, pitch, loudness, and even quality. You could tell if someone had had a course in elocution because he spoke with greater clarity and expressiveness than the untrained speaker. Much as the contemporary actor or television announcer speaks with a more pleasant, clear, and expressive voice than the ordinary speaker, so too did the public speakers of the nineteenth century.

The elocution movement went out of style because of its single-minded attention to the aspect of delivery and was replaced in part by the public-speaking style.[8] The public-

[8] See, for instance, Frank M. Rarig and Halbert S. Greaves, "National Speech Organizations and Speech Education," in Karl Wallace, ed., *History of Speech Education in America,* Englewood Cliffs, N.J.: Prentice-Hall, 1954, pp. 490–517; see also Mary Margaret Robb, "The Elocutionary Movement and Its Chief Figures," in Wallace, pp. 178–201; and Donald K. Smith, "Origin and Developments of Departments of Speech," in Wallace, pp. 447–470.

speaking style was also much preoccupied in its early years with delivery, and judges of speeches assigned a heavy weight to good delivery. Over the years delivery came to be less important, and other matters, such as good reasoning, solid evidence, and important ideas came to weigh more heavily. Delivery remains an important element in public-speaking theory, however, and that theory includes the assumption that nonverbal skills can be taught by practice under the guidance of a professional, much as basic techniques in a sport such as basketball can be developed by practice. The theory also assumes that once a person moves into a communication situation, practice will have made good vocal skills so habitual that the speaker will not have to think about vocal emphasis, will automatically be able to suit melody of voice, pauses, loudness, rate, and quality to his words, much as a basketball player can dribble, pass, or shoot in response to the flow of the game, without thinking about the fundamentals.

The following discussion of voice and articulation improvement comes largely from the public-speaking style, but a similar sort of preoccupation with vocal training and excellence evolved from the public-speaking tradition with the rise of radio and television. A pleasant voice that articulates well is still the goal of many people, particularly those planning to go into the fields of media production, sales, politics, law, administration, education, and religion. Anyone dealing with the public uses his or her voice as a tool of the trade.

Problems of Nonverbal Communication

We happen to teach in an urban area where the general American dialect is spoken. We find that most of our students taking a freshman speech course have never listened critically to their own voices; furthermore, they are rarely enthusiastic about the idea of recording their voices and having their classmates and instructor respond about what they hear. On the other hand, once the exercise has been done, they are as enthusiastic as they had been apathetic, and they say, "Everybody ought to do that." Few of these students are aware of the almost universal montony with which they habitually speak. Comparing the energy level they use in making vocal sounds with the levels produced by trained radio actors, for example, our students find themselves always "in the valley," rarely on the peaks. They find they punctuate their thoughts less effectively than they had thought; they hear sloppy articulation, and they do not like hearing it. When they realize that their voices are not projecting the vocal image they had thought they were, they usually want to work on them to try to make their results more in line with their intentions.

Voice and articulation problems can generally be divided into two categories: those which are the result of some illness or of malformation of the parts of the body that produce speech; and those, far more numerous, which are the result of habits of speaking which do not utilize the vocal mechanism as well as possible. A tone-deaf person will probably never be a fine singer, but even a person endowed with a fine musical ear needs training to reach maximum potential. If you have a severe articulation problem you should consult a trained speech clinician or correctionist. The advice we give here is directed at the vast majority of students who have perfectly normal voices but wish to retrain faulty speech habits to make their voices more expressive and to increase their effectiveness at nonverbal communication.

THE PROCEDURE FOR IMPROVING SPEECH

The same general procedure can be used to retrain most bad speech habits, whether they are associated with poor use of pitch, time, or loudness, with poor articulation or poor voice quality. The first step in any program of improvement is to train the ear to hear the errors. Most of us are so used to speaking that we ignore the way we sound. Few students are aware of the common voice problems. Because speaking is, by nature, imitative, we speak as our friends speak and copy one another's bad habits of articulation and lack of variety.

An excellent way to hear yourself is to record your voice and play the tape back while you listen critically. You ought to take advantage of every opportunity to tape relatively long passages and listen to them. Eventually, however, you must come to the point where you can monitor your own speech—*while* you are speaking. The feedback principle discussed in Chapter 2 is relevant here. You must become the initiator in a feedback loop with the objective of improving your own voice. Your ear becomes the monitor, and the sounds you utter are continually monitored to allow you to bring your practice on target.

The steps in the process go something like this:

1 Train your ear to hear the problem.
2 Gain control of the problem by learning to produce a sample of poor speech whenever you want to.
3 Learn to produce the better sound.

4 Practice the good sound and the poor sound, thus increasing the power of your ear to discriminate, and at the same time teaching your vocal mechanisms how it feels to produce better speech.

5 Once you can control your vocalization so that you can produce poor speech and good speech whenever you wish, begin to introduce the new speech habits into conversation with others—during lunch, for example.

6 Gradually you will find the new speech more comfortable, and as it becomes more habitual, you can introduce it more often into your daily routine.

Eventually, you will use your new speaking voice without having to think about it consciously, and you can concentrate on the ideas you are framing in your message, assured now that you are using the best vocal technique you can to communicate your ideas and feelings nonverbally.

This general pattern can be used to correct slovenly articulation of certain sounds, particularly the tendency to substitute easy sounds for more difficult ones, such as /i/ for /e/ and /d/ for /t/. The general pattern can be used to correct monotony of pitch, time, and loudness. It also works with voice quality problems, as well as with difficulties of rate, which are the easiest to remedy.

If a person speaks too rapidly, for example, careful attention to speaking more slowly, drawing out the vowel sounds in a smooth way during drill sessions, will soon enable him to train his ear. One can speak more rapidly or more slowly without difficulty. A good feedback loop can bring the rate on target quickly. Often a person who speaks rapidly also speaks in a jerky, staccato fashion, so that the articulatory mechanism—the tongue, teeth, and lips, in particular—are asked to form the consonants so rapidly that they are poorly articulated. Slowing the rate and forming the consonants more carefully many times solves an articulation problem as well as a rate problem. Generally, a good rate for reading to audiences is between 140 and 185 words per minute. Daily speaking should not exceed this maximum, and speaking slower than 140 words per minute should be restricted to occasions when one is addressing a large crowd and must overcome problems of general noise, echo, and the like.

A good drill for breaking the monotony of time, pitch, and loudness is to read a passage first in a monotone and then with great expressiveness, much as a Shakespearean actor might read an emotional speech from a play. Overdoing the flexibility of your voice in drill sessions does two good things for your nonverbal communication: (1) It forces your vocal equipment to stretch its range, just as daily exercise stretches muscles and makes them more flexible; and (2) it teaches your ear to discriminate changes in emphasis at the same time it teaches your vocal equipment how these new sounds feel.

FINDING YOUR NATURAL PITCH LEVEL

A whole cluster of voice problems may be improved by finding a suitable pitch level for your voice. Poor pitch flexibility and low levels of loudness may result from speaking at the wrong pitch level for your vocal equipment. Using the wrong pitch habitually may also strain the vocal folds, and one response to such strain is failure of the valve in the larynx to close completely, producing a breathy voice quality. Another typical response to vocal strain is tightening of the throat, which results from forcing the voice to be loud enough to be heard, and produces a harsh or hoarse voice.

We must first note that a person may speak at or around one pitch level habitually, even though that level is not the best one for his vocal equipment. For example, if a girl has a natural alto singing voice but is placed in the soprano section of a choir, she may be forcing her voice to reach the high notes and thus be straining her voice. People learn to speak largely by imitation, and a child may model her speaking voice after her mother's or an older sister's and thus learn to speak at a level that is unnatural for her. Sometimes people adopt a good pitch level as children but fail to adopt the lower pitch level that should come with growth. Sometimes people consciously strive to adopt a low pitch level because they feel it is more attractive. The pleasant voice is not necessarily the low-pitched voice. A man may have a good tenor voice if the vowels are resonant and if he varies the pitch, time, and loudness skillfully.

The *habitual pitch level*, therefore, is the pitch around which a person talks. Somebody with a good musical ear can help you discover your habitual pitch by finding on the piano the tone you tend to use as you speak or read. Contrasted with your habitual pitch is your *natural pitch level—that pitch best suited to your voice.* Just as a certain hair style may make a girl look more attractive because it emphasizes her best features, so will the best (natural) pitch level for you make your voice more attractive.

We have no sure method for discovering a person's natural pitch level. One way to approximate it is to sing the lowest note you can, and the highest, including falsetto, and then find the tone one-fourth of the way up that range, if you are a man, and one-fifth of the way up the range, if you are a woman. Somewhere in the region of the lower fourth or fifth of the range is the place where most people's natural pitch level falls. Another way to approximate your natural pitch is to say a vowel such as "ah" with as low a pitch as you can and then move easily up your pitch range. At some point you will discover you can make a louder sound more easily than you could at the lower pitches; proceed up your range until you again find yourself straining to reach the pitch. Your natural pitch is in the region of the scale where you produce a good, loud tone easily.

A good drill to improve pitch level is to take ordinary prose material and read it in a low tone, then a middle tone, then a high tone. (Sometimes doing this will also reveal whether your present habitual pitch is too high or too low.) If you discover you need to raise or lower your habitual pitch, you should proceed just as you do with other voice problems, by first training the ear to hear the difference, and then, in your drill sessions, reading at the old pitch and then the new pitch.

DEVELOPING GOOD BREATH CONTROL

To have a good resonant and flexible voice, a speaker must provide adequate breath support for the vocal cords. Since pauses are part of our language code and function as punctuation, a person who runs out of breath at the wrong place in a sentence and must pause for another breath will punctuate his thoughts in a confusing way. The technical name for punctuating your ideas improperly is *faulty phrasing.* To phrase properly, people who do not have good breathing habits for speech often tighten the vocal folds and try to conserve breath in that way. The result of tightening the vocal cords and throat muscles, as we have seen, is harshness, or hoarseness. A tight throat also reduces resonances and creates a relatively flat or weak and thin voice. If your voice lacks resonance, the fault may well be bad breathing habits.

Many features of contemporary life contribute to the generally bad breathing habits of Americans. A young lady often consciously sucks in her waistline to improve her posture and figure. A girl who is pulling in on her tummy has no chance to use her diaphragm to draw in a breath or to pull across her stomach to support a tone. She is forced, therefore, to lift her shoulders when she breathes and use only a little bit of the upper lungs to support her speech. She may have a gorgeous figure, but when she opens her mouth she either screeches like a shrew or sounds like a preschool child actress. Athletes who compete in sports that require sudden bursts of energy, such as basketball or track, often develop a habit of breathing in quick, shallow upper-chest pants. The result is often a husky athlete who speaks in a weak, thin, harsh, or husky voice. The common tensions of life also cause people's stomachs to knot up and reduce their use of the diaphragm and stomach muscles in breathing. Indeed, when a person wishes to relax, a good way to start is to take several slow, deep breaths.

Good speech requires an adequate supply of air in the lungs and sufficient skill to control the air pressure during speech. Singers, who face the same problem as speakers, spend much time learning to support a tone properly. The same general approach will work for anyone wishing to improve breathing for speech. You should use the entire breathing mechanism, including the diaphragm, while speaking. To get the feel of diaphragmatic breathing, stretch out on the floor and place a book on your stomach. Now try to get the book to rise when you inhale and sink when you exhale. With a little practice you will discover you can begin to breathe naturally. (You breathe with your total respiratory system when asleep). Notice that as you breathe in slowly from the diaphragm, the tensing muscle inside your body forces the expansion of your waist. The muscle you feel tensing under your lungs is the diaphragm.

Having discovered the feel of diaphragmatic breathing, your next step is to begin to practice support and control of your speech while actually speaking. While breathing exercises by themselves are not harmful and may even be good for your health, alone they do not improve your voice. What is required is training of the habits of breathing during speech. (Interestingly enough, a singer who has excellent breathing habits while singing may have bad breathing habits when speaking.)

A good exercise is to take the old nursery rhyme "This is the house that Jack built" and, taking a good breath before each phrase, try to read the phrases in one breath as they get longer and longer. Thus:

(breathe) *This is the house that Jack built.*
(breathe) *This is the malt that lay in the house that*
  Jack built.
(breathe) *This is the rat that ate the malt that lay in the*
  house that Jack built. (And so on.)

Chapter 4

THE KEY IDEAS

Nonverbal communication consists of the body language and the vocal melodies that accompany a speaker's words.

The technical name for the contemporary study of the nonverbal features of voice production is paralinguistics.

Much of the knowledge about voice production, the acoustics of speech, and the articulation and intelligibility of sounds is scientific and relates to all three styles of communication.

Many dialects have some unique vocal patterns.

Proper articulation is a matter of being intelligible, of being understood.

The vowels carry the quality of the voice.

The main function of the consonants is to distinguish among various words in a language.

If you want to be understood, you must articulate the consonants clearly.

Another good exercise is to count in a whisper in a slow, deliberate manner. See how far you can count on one breath. Practice taking another breath and try to count farther. Several minutes of drill each day will soon increase your ability to support speech with your breath. After you have counted in a whisper, repeat the exercise while phonating. Be careful to count only as long as you can do so with a relaxed throat. The minute you begin to tighten your throat and strain your voice, stop counting.

Quite often, improving the breath support for the voice encourages the speaker to keep the throat open and the vocal cords relaxed. A good athlete is relaxed even when playing a vigorous game of basketball. A good speaker is relaxed even when projecting his voice a long distance. With a relaxed throat and good breath support, a person can speak loudly for long periods without strain. If you find yourself hoarse after shouting at a ball game, you are probably not using your throat properly. When a speaker uses a relaxed and open throat and an adequate breath supply, the quality of his voice tends to be improved. Often simply opening the throat and

If you want to have a pleasant and expressive voice, you must articulate the vowels clearly and vary their pitch, loudness, and duration.

When a person consistently omits and substitutes sounds while speaking, the result is a difficult-to-understand mumble.

Poor articulation is found in every dialect and ought always to be improved in the interest of intelligibility.

Pitch changes are among the most important voice techniques for nonverbal communication.

A speaker can make important elements in a message stand out by saying them either more loudly or more softly than the surrounding verbal padding.

The most important feature of the pause is its function as oral punctuation.

Research indicates that paralanguage conveys emotional states, personality traits, and physical features of message sources.

Theorists in the relationship style view paralanguage as part of the total communication system and stress the natural use of vocal emphasis.

The public speaking communication style has the longest tradition and greatest emphasis on training for voice and articulation improvement.

The same general feedback procedure can be used to retrain most bad speech habits.

A person may have learned to speak habitually at a pitch level that is unnatural.

When a person habitually speaks at a level that is natural for him, his voice quality and flexibility are generally quite good.

Good speech requires an adequate supply of air in the lungs and enough skill to control the air pressure during speaking.

using more of it as a resonator causes less of the sound to go through the nose, and a nasal voice quality is corrected by the change. Another way to improve vocal resonance is to be sure to open the mouth when articulating the vowel sounds. Again, singers are trained to open their mouths wide to improve the quality of their singing voices. The same principle holds for speakers. Too often we develop lazy habits of articulation and speak through clenched teeth, with a rigid jaw. A good drill is to read prose material, opening the mouth in an exaggerated fashion and overarticulating both the vowels and the consonants.

Articulation problems require first a careful analysis. The best procedure is to record your voice reading a passage of prose that contains all the sounds of English, arranged so they fall at the beginning, the middle, and the ends of words. Listen over and over again to the recording. You should be able to pick out the omissions, substitutions, and distortions. If you are fortunate enough to have a voice expert listen to the tape with you and give you a vocal diagnosis, fine. If, for example, you typically substitute /d/ for /t/, you should then practice making the two sounds in isolation. Then drill, saying them one after another. The drill in which you say the correct sound first, then the wrong sound, trains your ear to hear the difference and trains you to associate the correct sound with a certain position of the articulatory mechanism.

If you wish to change your voice into a pleasant and expressive instrument for nonverbal communication and acquire the technique needed to add subtle nuances to the meanings in words you utter, you must drill upon the fundamentals of voice and articulation improvement. You should look at your weekly schedule and select short periods several times a week when you can go off alone somewhere and chant, read, shout, and make weird sounds. Even if you can spare only twenty minutes on Mondays, Wednesdays, Fridays, and Saturdays, and then only in the early evening or just before going to bed, you ought to do so. No one can improve your voice for you. You have to do it yourself. And now you have a good idea of what you need to work on and how to go about improving those things that need improving. So set up a schedule and decide which of your problems require immediate attention. Next develop a list of drills to work on these problems. This is not something you have to do the rest of your life. You can improve your speech noticeably in a matter of months, and you can enjoy the rewards that better speech can bring you the rest of your life, without having to fret about it any more.

You will find that after several months of drilling for short periods, your ear will become much better able to discriminate the sounds you are making; your voice will become a major tool of nonverbal communication. You will become a much more effective communicator in all the communication situations in your life—interviews, group meetings, social conversations, over the telephone, and if the occasion should arise, in public speeches and meetings and over the mass media.

SUGGESTED PROJECTS

1 Each student records his or her voice both talking informally and reading. The reading should be from simple prose exposition, *not* dramatic reading. With the help of the instructor and the other students, each class member analyzes his nonverbal communication in terms of vocal monotony, flexibility, quality, pitch, rate, loudness, and clarity of articulation. Each student writes a brief paper describing his own vocal strengths and inadequacies and in consultation with his instructor, if necessary plans a program of exercises that can be used to improve his nonverbal vocal communication.

2 The class makes a list of popular television newsmen, local or national. After discussion, the list is narrowed to the five the class decides are best. Members of the class then make tape recordings (audio only) of these five and play them back for the whole class, which ranks the five and analyzes their strengths and weaknesses in voice and articulation. To insure that the verbal elements and the meaning of the message do not sway the class, the tapes may be played backwards so that only the nonverbal elements can be judged. How much of the appeal these newsmen had when first chosen seems to come from voice quality and articulation alone?

3 Divide the class into coeducational pairs, if possible. Each pair has two minutes to communicate mutually agreed-upon emotional relationship between two people, using only a variation in the intonations of the words "John" and "Mary." No other words may be used. The male member of the pair will say "Mary," and then the female will say "John," and they alternate these words for two minutes. Gestures and facial expressions should be kept at a minimum. The situation portrayed could be as impersonal as two strangers meeting on a bus and striking up a conversation, as personal as an intimate family incident, a lover's quarrel, or merely two friends gossiping. The class tries to figure out the relationship between the two people from the verbal intonations alone.

SUGGESTED READINGS

Addington, D. W. "The Relationship of Selected Vocal Characteristics to Personality Perception," *Speech Monographs*, 35 (1968), 492–503.

Birdwhistell, Ray L. *Kinesics and Context*, Philadelphia: University of Pennsylvania Press, 1970. "Stress in American English," pp. 128–143.

Bronstein, Arthur, and Beatrice Jacoby. *Your Speech and Voice.* New York: Random House, 1967.

Eisenson, Jon. *The Improvement of Voice and Diction*, 2nd ed. New York: Macmillan, 1965.

Fairbanks, Grant. *Voice and Articulation Drillbook*, 2nd ed. New York: Harper & Row, 1960.

Mehrabian, Albert. "Communication Without Words," *Psychology Today*, 2 (September 1968), 53–55.

Chapter 5

HOW TO IMPROVE NONVERBAL COMMUNICATION THROUGH BODY MOTION

In addition to the paralanguage of voice and articulation discussed in Chapter 4, nonverbal communication can be defined to include a large number of other things. At this point in time, in the theorizing of the message and relationship communication styles, the question of what should be included and what should be left out is a question of concern, debate, and some difference of opinion.

We could restrict the definition of *nonverbal communication* to those body movements and paralanguage accompaniments of the spoken word which are a code. A vigorous nodding of the head up and down several times to mean yes in answer to the question "Would you like to come with us?" illustrates such a nonverbal communication code. Most theorists agree that gestures which convey meanings according to the rules of some code ought to be part of what we mean by nonverbal communication.

Taking the tenet of the relationship style that *you cannot not communicate* as a starting place, however, many investigators define nonverbal communication to include sponta-

context *The setting, surrounding circumstances, and all other background factors which might be considered to have an effect upon a communication event.*

neous and unplanned facial grimaces, smiles, frowns, movements of the head and shoulders, arm and hand gestures, fidgeting of the feet and legs, and overall posture, such as stooping or standing erect.[1] Other theorists have extended the denotations of the term to include an individual's physical features, body type, facial attractiveness, hair style, smell, mode of dress, and use of makeup and perfumes.[2]

THE IMPORTANCE OF CONTEXT

A number of theorists have stressed the **importance of context** in understanding communication, and the need, when interpreting a gesture, to understand the flow of communication prior to and after the given gesture. They have included as nonverbal communication such context features as how close people stand to one another, whether they are facing each other or standing or sitting side by side, and whether they place their hand in front of their face, cross their legs, put their arms akimbo, or turn away from another person while communicating.[3]

Some theorists would define **nonverbal communication** to include still more of the context and would include the notion that objects communicate. They would include traffic signs, a sign of a hand with a finger pointed at a door, a billboard in need of paint. Some would go on to include the arrangement of objects, their framing, disorder, and repetition, such as an arrangement designed for a department store window or food cans in a stack in a supermarket. Others would include the way a person arranges the furniture in an office or the way a person decorates a room or other space as nonverbal communication.[4] Some would include rallies, picketing, rioting, parades, and street marches in the domain of nonverbal communication.[5]

[1] See, for example, Ray L. Birdwhistell, *Kinesics and Context: Essays on Body Motion Communication*, Philadelphia: University of Pennsylvania Press, 1970.

[2] See, for example, Mark L. Knapp, *Nonverbal Communication in Human Interaction*, New York: Holt, Rinehart and Winston, 1972.

[3] See, for example, Albert E. Sheflen and Alice Sheflen, *Body Language and Social Order: Communication as Behavioral Control*, Englewood Cliffs, N.J.: Prentice-Hall, 1972.

[4] See, for example, Jurgen Ruesch and Weldon Kees, *Nonverbal Communication; Notes on the Visual Perception of Human Relations*, Berkeley, Calif.: University of California Press, 1969. Ruesch and Kees maintain that "there is little doubt that the nonverbal and often unconscious exchange of messages codified in material terms fulfills all the criteria of language; for brevity's sake we shall subsequently refer to it as object language." (p. 89).

[5] See, for example, Haig A. Bosmajian, ed., *The Rhetoric of Nonverbal Communication*, Glenview, Ill.: Scott, Foresman, 1971.

Research in Nonverbal Communication

Of course all of the things mentioned above are more or less important in what we think about a communication event. Still, the study of nonverbal communication is confusing, sprawling, and unsatisfactory in many respects, because we have not yet decided exactly what should be included and what should be left out. We will not include in this chapter a detailed discussion of body types or smells, furniture arrangement, use of cosmetics, physical attractiveness, and so forth. Nor will we give you a long list of research studies and point out their inconclusive and sometimes contradictory results. Much of the research has been related to questions of style and culture rather than scientific questions which would tell us something about nonverbal communication in general. The best of the studies give us more a map of nonverbal customs and communication styles in various places and times than a scientific theory of nonverbal communication. Some typical questions have been: What do certain gestures mean? What is the distance that people use for certain kinds of communication? Do these distances vary from culture to culture? Do sequences of gestures indicate sentences something like the sentences we make out of words? What responses are evoked by long hair in males?[6] Usually such research questions yield answers to the effect that we cannot tell for sure, or that the answer depends upon the culture of the region or the country. Some Germans respond differently than some Italians in similar situations and gesture differently; but then, northern Germans are different from southern Germans. Some Americans respond differently than others.[7]

An anthropological approach, which observes and describes gestures in some clearly restricted and defined subculture at some specified time period, may yield relatively sound information about the style of communication used by a culturally homogeneous group. For example, a careful study of the communication of urban blacks in the 1960s may provide an interesting and useful account of a particular group at that time. But the results will not generalize to other places and other times.[8]

Often when you read a research report or even when you

---

[6] For a survey of such studies see Knapp, *Nonverbal Communication*.
[7] See Sheflen and Sheflen, *Body Language and Social Order*, pp. 86–96.
[8] See, for example, Benjamin G. Cooke, "Nonverbal Communication Among Afro-Americans: An Initial Classification," in Thomas Kochman, ed., *Rappin' and Stylin' Out: Communication in Urban Black America*, Urbana, Ill.: University of Illinois Press, 1972, pp. 32–64.

read the results of studies summarized in a textbook you have the feeling that the conclusions are precise and solid. Conclusions are presented in percentages; there are tables and statistical interpretations of findings; technical terms are used and an aura of precision is created for one reading the results of the various studies. For those unaware of the pitfalls of statistics, such presentations of results can be misleading.

AN INCONCLUSIVE RESEARCH PROJECT

Without numbers, then, or technical terms, let us share with you an exploration of some research about nonverbal factors which was undertaken with some of our colleagues and students over the past several years. If you will examine this research with the dubious eyes of the researcher, you will understand why, despite many ways of going at the material, we felt that we never came up with anything scientifically solid enough to justify publication. Others *have* felt their results worth publishing, and many have found these results interesting, as a browse through the psychology or sociology section of any campus bookstore will attest.

Admitting a bias about research results, at the same time we admit a keen interest in the search for "invariables." We tried, over a period of years, to investigate the nonverbal elements of the communication going on in our small group communication laboratory at the University of Minnesota. We used videotapes of group meetings.[9] We looked at all contextual and gestural aspects of the meetings. We looked at where the participants sat in relation to one another. We examined which member sat in the middle or at the head of the table, which members sat side by side, and which sat across from one another. We looked at the positions and movement of the participants' bodies, we looked at whether they were relaxed or tense, leaning forward, or slouching back. We looked at their hand and arm positions and looked to see whether they placed a hand in front of their faces, whether they crossed their legs, whether they protected their personal space using hands, arms, feet, legs, looks, or objects. We particularly looked at facial expressions, at eye contact, looking away, looking down, and head nods and shakes. On one occasion we had an instructor in acting who knew nothing about the groups or their history observe videotapes of some meetings without playing the sound portion.

[9] Although our studies of nonverbal communication have not yielded publishable results, the other studies of small group communication have. The results are published in Ernest G. Bormann, *Discussion and Group Methods: Theory and Practice*, 2nd ed., New York: Harper & Row, 1975.

We discovered that when we had an extensive case history of the group and knew about social tensions, cohesiveness, role struggles, leadership, and the liking or disliking that members had for one another, we could often interpret the complex nonverbal pattern of fidgeting, nods, gestures, postures, and group seating, standing, or pacing arrangements in ways which seemed to make sense *in terms of what we already knew* about the group dynamics. Often when we played the tapes for the participants and asked them to recall what they were thinking or feeling at the time, they agreed with our interpretation. Hoping we had found something of value, we continued, only to find with further study that similar patterns of gestures, positions, facial expressions, postures, and movements could apparently mean different things, both to participants and to nonparticipant observers. We might be watching a tape of group B and decide that a given sequence was just like something we had seen in a tape of group A. When we deciphered the apparent meanings of the two sequences, however, they would turn out to be different. On the other hand, the groups would sometimes be engaged in similar situations such as according someone the status due a task leader; yet each group would be using a distinctive nonverbal pattern to express this behavior.

The acting teacher made some very insightful interpretations of large sequences of movements and interchanges and some interesting personality analyses on the bases of the unique behavior of individuals in the group. But again, other observers did not notice the same things. The acting teacher would say something like, "Notice the way he lights and holds his cigarette. He is 'onstage' all of the time. Everything is a performance with him." The others observing the tape had overlooked the importance of the cigarette. We also had the uneasy feeling that the characterizations were a bit like handwriting analysis or the making of horoscopes. We all tend to be impressed by the aptness of a somewhat ambiguous statement, because we can supply an application; the scientific method, however, requires more precise repeatability.

THE FINDINGS OF OTHER RESEARCHERS
Our researches, to be sure, were preliminary and not conclusive. Some investigators have made much more extensive studies of motion pictures and maintain that for certain cultural groups in North America, in certain situations, they have discovered nonverbal patterns which continually recur, and which always express the same meaning. For example,

the Sheflens have discovered certain courtship patterns which they maintain have been repeated in the North American settings which they have studied. They have found that two people usually face one another to begin the courtship pattern, and the female holds her head high and tilted or cocked. She looks at the male from the corner of her eyes and brings her chest out so that her breasts protrude. She extends her foot and tightens her calf muscles to make her legs look sexy. Her eyes are bright, and her eyelids may be slightly narrowed. She often presents the palm of her hand in gestures such as pushing her hair back, or covering her mouth. The man, meanwhile, is indicating courtship by changing his body position—for example, moving from a slouching posture with his stomach sticking out to one in which he sucks in his stomach, sticks out his chest, squares his shoulders, and stands more erect. If both begin the courtship, they may then go to preening, such as stroking their hair.[10] We were unable, in our brief researches, to discover any patterns so common and detailed that we could describe them as the Sheflens were able to describe the courtship routine.

THE SEARCH FOR A BASIC CODE OF GESTURES

When we discovered that gestures, seating positions, postures, and body motions were so different from one group to another, and from one situation to another, even for the same group, we gave up the attempt to ask scientific questions about these matters. We moved to a simpler question and asked if we could discover a basic code of simple gestures which had similar meanings for both participants and nonparticipant observers. We discovered three kinds of nonverbal cues which seemed promising. They were (1) cues which meant a positive response, (2) cues which meant a negative response, and (3) cues which we could not interpret as either positive or negative. A positive pattern might include a nodding of the head, a smile, looking the other person in the eye, and leaning forward and touching the other's arm; a negative pattern might include a shaking of the head in disagreement, a frown, a leaning back, a look of disgust.

As we continued to use the system we discovered that when the nonverbal was the body motion of the speaker (accompanied the verbal), it could serve different functions than when it was a response by the listener. We divided the category system into the following parts to enable us to study the different functions: Used by someone who was speaking, the

[10] Sheflen and Sheflen, *Body Language and Social Order*, pp. 16–21.

positive nonverbal could be directed (1) to support the words, or (2) to support the relationship the speaker had with the listener; the negative could be directed (3) to undercut the words, or (4) to characterize the relationship. We divided the nonverbal behaviors of the listeners into (1) positive patterns supporting the speaker's verbal comments, or (2) negative patterns rejecting the speaker's words. Even with our simplified category system, however, our observers often disagreed as to how the nonverbal accompaniment of a statement should be classified.

The point of this discussion of our study of the very fascinating puzzle of nonverbal communication is that we had to conclude that we still may not have arrived at questions which are scientific rather than artistic, that we may not have arrived at methods suitable for the study of such a complicated, culture-bound, time-bound set of human behaviors. The further point of our discussion is that while a very global view of nonverbal communication provides us with a chance to tell stories about our personal experiences which are often insightful and useful, the scientific part of our knowledge about nonverbal communication (no matter how it is defined) is small and tenuous. The scientific component being small, the communication theory of all three styles regarding nonverbal communication aspects contains largely stylistic preferences and artificially created norms, no less valid for those who practice them, but artistic in the main, nonetheless.

Theories of Nonverbal Communication in Our Three Styles

Neither the message nor the relationship communication style has developed artistic theories which provide much instruction in how to become a "better" communicator in nonverbal ways. The theory of the message communication style includes definitional discussions of the nature and scope of nonverbal communication, carefully defined categories which subdivide the field, and surveys of research which relate to the categories. One important thing message communication experts do advise is that participants should give more and better feedback to increase the fidelity of information transmission. The relationship communication style includes such advice as that one ought to make the nonverbal express honestly what one is thinking and feeling, and that people ought to expand the role of the senses in communication.

The relationship style grew out of practices which used many nonverbal exercises, games, and group meetings. Such teaching techniques as trust walks, feeling one another's faces, staring into one another's eyes, hugging, and so forth were an important part of the growth of the new style, and certainly the students learned nonverbal techniques by modeling their behavior on that of the facilitators. Albert Sheflen, a psychiatrist whose thinking is often incorporated into the theory of the relationship communication style, points out the way the teaching is carried out without much specific how-to-do-it theory.[11]

> In recent years, since "nonverbal" communication . . . has become a popular subject some people have consciously contrived kinesic behavior. Parlor games are now being held in which contestants are to "express emotions," which others must interpret. Nonverbal parties are held at which guests are to communicate without speaking. . . . Stylized, method-acting versions of emotional expressions, close distance, and touch are also used by many of the new liberal therapies. These contrived kinesic-like acts are used to simulate "real" caring or "real" anger.[12]

Sheflen goes on to argue that theory and practice may be inconsistent, and that the theorists of the new style may not yet have worked out all of the elements in systematic fashion. When a new communication theory arises to support a communication style, such inconsistencies are not unusual. In Sheflen's words:

> The people who use these stylized kinesic behaviors know little about natural kinesic behaviors. They seem honestly to believe that they are expressing "real" emotion as opposed to what they consider the false effects of our culture. However, using and teaching these contrived systems of facial, tactile, and spacing behavior introduces a sad paradox. When we seek to approach communication in this way, we threaten to make kinesic communication as untrustworthy as language.[13]

The public-speaking style, on the other hand, has a well-developed theory relating to the use of gesture, posture, facial expression, and eye contact in the context of a public-speaking situation.

[11] For example, Sheflen's article, "The Significance of Posture in Communication Systems," is included in an anthology which is most consistently about the relationship style; see John Stewart, ed., *Bridges Not Walls: A Book About Interpersonal Communication*, Reading, Mass.: Addison-Wesley, 1973, pp. 224–240.
[12] Sheflen and Sheflen, *Body Language and Social Order*, p. 101.
[13] Ibid.

nonverbal communication *Those body motions and contextual cues which are part of a shared code or are considered clearly meaningful by two or more people.*
kinesics *The study of body movement as related to speech.*

Our approach in the remainder of the chapter will be to define some of the more useful concepts which cut across all three styles and explain the general functions of nonverbal communication. Finally, we will discuss nonverbal communication through body language from the perspective of the public-speaking style.

Our Definition of Nonverbal Communication

We will limit the scope of nonverbal communication to (1) what people do on purpose, intentionally, in order to get something across to others, and (2) what people do out of habit or because of spur-of-the-moment feelings — even if it is without their being aware of it — if other people can generally get the same impression about relationships among the participants from the action.

While we have limited our definition a good deal so we can emphasize some basics, you should remember that an emphasis upon *context* is a good one for the student of contemporary communication. We need to be reminded continually of the importance of the background of our communication in a complex urban culture, in which so much of our environment is artfully and artificially created to make an impression upon us. We must remember that others may read more (or less) meaning into our dress, smell, physical appearance, hair style, fidgeting, facial expressions, home surroundings, and office arrangements than we do. The influence of context or scene is important and cuts across all communication styles. If you would like to know more about the investigations being made of context, the footnotes in this chapter and the suggested readings provide a number of books and articles which you will find of interest.

Categories of Nonverbal Behavior

BODY MOTION
The technical term for the study of nonverbal behavior which involves the motion of the body is **kinesics.** We define *body motion* to include gestures and facial expressions which support, mimic, or pantomime in parallel with verbal communication and which either reinforce *or* reverse the content of what the person is saying; the overall posture, facial expres-

proxemics *The study of body motion in context. Relates to the positioning and movement expressing relationships among the participants in a communication situation.*

sions, eye movements, and so forth which support, modify, or reverse the content of verbal messages.

BODY MOTION IN CONTEXT

The technical term for the category of nonverbal behavior which includes the position of the participants in a communication event in relation to one another and to any other objects around them is **proxemics.** We define *body motion in context* to include what is known in theatrical terms as the stage blocking of a play and what theatre people call *stage business*. A play director will often tell the actors exactly how to stand, move, and gesture in order to communicate the meaning of a scene. On certain lines the director may plan the action so the actors will be face to face, standing very close. On other lines he may direct them to sit side by side, and so forth. When a director stages a scene in which there is conflict among a number of actors, certain characters may be grouped together at some distance from several others to help communicate to the audience the nature of the conflict that is developed in the dialogue of the play at that point. Comedy is often directed in a pattern of circular motion, the effect being that of flowing, intermingling action. High drama with much conflict often has a series of actors "squaring off" with one another, and is angular, abrupt, erratic in motion. The nonverbal elements of body motion in context (proxemics)

concern the same sorts of blocking and business in all communication situations, including the theatrical. The spontaneous and unrehearsed situations are, of course, much more prevalent and are of more interest to us as we look at nonverbal communication in the three styles.

Learning Nonverbal Communication

One question that keeps coming up in the study of nonverbal communication is: To what extent is nonverbal behavior something you are born with because you are a human being, and to what extent is it something you have learned to do?[14] Some studies have tried to see if certain physical actions are always interpreted as "meaning" the same emotion, even when the subjects for the study come from different cultures.

[14] For a survey of thought on this question, see Abne M. Eisenberg and Ralph R. Smith, Jr., *Nonverbal Communication*, Indianapolis: Bobbs-Merrill, 1971, pp. 40–46.

Birdwhistell, a leader in the study of kinesics, came to the conclusion that

> although we have been searching for 15 years, we have found no gesture or body motion which has the same social meaning in all societies. The immediate implications of this are clear. Insofar as we know, there is no body motion or gesture which can be regarded as a universal symbol. That is, we have been unable to discover any single facial expression, stance, or body position which conveys an identical meaning in all societies.[15]

The importance of the nonuniversality of nonverbal aspects of communication in the growing study of intercultural and cross-cultural communication is thus accented. Learning the words of another language is now regarded by communication students as only a first step in learning how to communicate with someone from another culture; the nonverbal aspects of communication assume a position of prime importance as we try to learn more about communicating across cultures and with all nationalities.

Not all researchers agree with Birdwhistell that there is no universality of nonverbal behavior across cultures; other studies have concluded that certain basic facial expressions can be interpreted similarly by subjects from widely different cultures.[16] Whatever the outcome of further research into this important question, the present evidence indicates that almost all of your important nonverbal communication is not inborn but is something that you have learned to do.

THE FACTORS INVOLVED IN BODY LANGUAGE
Four factors are involved in the body language of each of us:

1 We learn a general body language from our particular culture. We learn this general body language as children, just as we learn to speak in the verbal code of our family. The cultural body language includes such things as how closely people stand when they talk to one another, whether people touch one another when talking, whether people look one another in the eye when they are angry or embarrassed, whether a vigorous nodding of the head accompanies agreement or disagreement.

[15] Birdwhistell, *Kinesics and Context*, p. 81.
[16] See, for example, P. Ekman and W. V. Friesen, "Constants Across Cultures in the Face and Emotion," *Journal of Personality and Social Psychology*, 17 (1971), pp. 124–129; and P. Ekman, "Universals and Cultural Differences in Facial Expressions of Emotion," J. Cole, ed., *Nebraska Symposium on Motivation, 1971*, Lincoln, Neb.: University of Nebraska Press, 1972.

2 Every individual, within his culture, develops a nonverbal language to help him communicate. He may use nonverbal gestures while talking to emphasize his verbal messages, or he may use nonverbal gestures alone to convey his meaning. To some extent, nonverbal communication is cultural, but to some extent, it is individual and varies from person to person. Some people are skilled and can use nonverbal communication to emphasize, even to contradict, what they are saying.

3 Every person develops characteristic ways of talking and moving, of standing or sitting while listening, of using the hands while excited. This is highly individual, and often nonverbal communication of this sort is more an interference than a help in conveying meanings to another person. If an individual's gestures call attention to themselves, not to the message intent, these gestures should be modified to allow more meaningful gestures to enhance communication.[17a]

4 Every person develops ways of communicating nonverbally which are modeled after the ideal communication events of various styles of communication, as we saw in Chapter 2. Learning the nonverbal techniques of a given style may take place informally, by individual trial and error, or by practice that is modeled after some ideal (as when a person who wants to be a radio announcer or TV master of ceremonies practices with a tape recorder or videotape recorder, trying to talk and move as a favorite network personality does.) Some nonverbal behavior can be taught more formally, in classes designed for that purpose. In grade and high schools, in community and four-year colleges and universities, instructors provide a variety of courses in the various styles; training programs for facilitators in the relationship style are conducted by churches, mental health organizations, training laboratories, and human development institutes all over the country.

Examples of the contextual cultural basis of much body motion communication are numerous and striking. In the last decade, middle-class white teachers in urban ghetto schools had difficulty communicating with young black children because they did not understand some of the black nonverbal communication which was unique to that place and time. The teachers were from a culture in which eye contact while conversing indicated interest, sincerity, careful listening, and

[17a] For another and similar analysis of the sources of our nonverbal behavior, see P. Ekman and W. V. Friesen, "The Repertoire of Nonverbal Behavior: Categories, Origins, Usage, and Coding," *Semiotica*, 1 (1969), pp. 49–98.

genuine concern. The teachers thought of a person who looked down, even away much of the time, as being uninterested or insincere, perhaps even untruthful. The children were from a culture in which eye contact indicated anger. No wonder the children were disturbed by teachers who always seemed to be angry with them!

The Japanese tend to smile in a certain way when apologetic, embarrassed, and disturbed. When a manager in a Japanese factory calls a mistake to an employee's attention, the latter smiles. Before American managers working in firms in Japan learned of this cultural way of communicating, they often were upset by the smile. One manager broke off, reprimanding the employee with a curse, and forbade the employee to smile like that when discussing an important problem.

When you talk with someone from a different culture, whether that culture is within the United States or outside it, you need to be aware that the culture-based silent language of body position, relationships, and motion can hinder successful communication. We have many different cultures within the United States that affect the nonverbal part of communication. Some authorities maintain that poverty produces its own culture. We are becoming increasingly aware of, and are emphasizing, cultural differences in the minority groups in our national culture. Regional differences affect communication. The dialects of the Deep South are not just matters of forming sounds; they also relate to the vocal inflections and the body motions that accompany them. The same is true of the Yankee dialects of the New Englander or the speech of the Far Western Mountain Region.

When we visit a foreign culture, the strangeness of the nonverbal communication is often quite apparent. Right here in our own diverse society, the nonverbal differences among cultures is quite apparent; however, we are frequently less aware of the differences in nonverbal communication as we move from one style to another. Even if all the participants in a message communication style meeting, or in a sensitivity group, or in a public-speaking situation happen to be white, middle-class North Americans, they may still overlook the fact that different body motion norms are appropriate to each of the three styles. For instance, if a television announcer forgot what he was to do, lost his place in his script, and broke down and cried, it would be out of place and uncomfortable because it would break the conventions of the style. If a participant in an encounter group broke down and began to cry because of the sharing of a deep emotional relationship or some important personal problem, his behavior would be in line with the conventions of the relationship style, and other participants would find his behavior significant and important.

The Functions of Body Language

TO ENHANCE THE WORDS

A speaker may enhance or flesh out the words of a message with the nonverbal. The nonverbal can increase the expressiveness of the speaker and can aid in making information clear in terms of the message communication style. The message source can repeat meanings (add redundancy) by saying the same things nonverbabally as verbally, so that gestures and words reinforce one another. When the receiver sees gestures that support the ideas he is hearing, another communication channel is being used, which adds more information, thus increasing the chance of getting the idea across from source to receiver.

Body motion may also serve to add to the vocal sounds, to frame or package an utterance for a speaker. The speaker may use head nods, arm gestures, or hand and finger motions to show where a comment begins and ends, to underline or emphasize certain parts of the comment, to indicate complete thought units, to separate modifying words, clauses, or phrases, and to point out which of the expressed ideas are more, and which less, important in relation to one another.

Some gestures serve as a tip-off that a person wishes to speak. Maybe that person will lean forward, make mouthing movements, and tense the body as though to move even farther forward, and others will notice that this individual wants the floor.[17b] Once a person starts to speak, he or she may use nonverbal cues such as facial expressions to display emotions and attitudes similar to those encoded in words. The speaker may say, "I don't understand," and accompany the words with a puzzled facial expression. Other gestures may resemble or demonstrate what the speaker is saying. The fisherman says, "You should have seen the one that got away. I swear he was over a foot long," and indicates a size by holding his hands apart. A speaker may say, "I bought that picture in

---

[17b] For a discussion of the way verbal and nonverbal communication can indicate that a person wants the floor, see Robert E. Nofsinger, Jr, "The Demand Ticket: A Conversational Device for Getting the Floor," *Speech Monographs*, 42 (1975), pp. 1–9.

ambiguity *Doubtfulness or uncertainty of meaning; lacking clearness.*

double-edged messages *Messages in which contradictory meanings are communicated at the same time by words and other behaviors.*

Paris," and point to the picture. A speaker may emphasize the intensity of his verbally expressed emotion or resolve. The coach shouts, "We're going to get going next half or I'll know the reason why!" and kicks a locker or pounds his fist on a table.

TO DETRACT FROM OR REVERSE THE WORDS

A speaker may detract from or reverse the verbal message with the nonverbal. The speaker who says one thing verbally and another nonverbally introduces **ambiguity,** or unclearness, and detracts from the redundancy of the message. The speaker implies, "I mean this, but on the other hand, maybe not." In terms of the message communication model of the ideal high-fidelity transmission of information, the conflict of messages transmitted through the two channels becomes a liability. In terms of the relationship communication style, the conflicting messages become an undesirable evidence of game playing or mask wearing. The ideal of the relationship style is to have external behavior and internal feelings and meanings the same, congruent. In terms of the public-speaking style, some ambiguity may be bad, especially if the speaker's purpose is primarily to inform; but it may be good when the speaker wishes to persuade. A speaker can use the nonverbal to reverse the verbal for purposes of irony and sarcasm. A skillful speaker can use irony and sarcasm to make a point which says a great deal with a few words. The rhetorical tradition includes such strategies as learning to simulate emotions nonverbally in order to use sarcasm, irony, bluff, and indirection as part of the available means of persuasion.

Double-edged Messages

Mehrabian uses the term double-edged to refer to communication which says one thing verbally and another thing nonverbally.[18] The double-edged message may have either a positive or negative function, depending upon the context and the communication style of the participants in the transaction. The positive functions include the fact that the double-edged message may at one and the same time make one sort of comment on the content of the words, and another on the relationship between the speaker and listener. If a woman believes that a man who has just traded in his old car for a newer model has wasted $1,000, she may say to him, "You

[18] Albert Mehrabian, *Silent Messages*, Belmont, Calif.: Wadsworth, 1971, pp. 40–55.

dumb nut;" but if she smiles and touches him sympathetically as she says it, she expresses her dissatisfaction with his action but indicates that she still cherishes their relationship. By sending the positive relationship message through the more potent means of body motion she indicates that the relationship is more important to her than her dislike for the thing that he has done. Should she reverse the selection of channels and say, "Aren't you the smart one?" but punctuate the sentence with nonverbal cues which suggest, "You dumb nut! Where are we going to get another thousand bucks?!" she achieves sarcasm and indicates that the negative comment (nonverbal) is more important than the positive (verbal). She may well get an unequivocal message from him, in which the nonverbal supports the verbal, to the effect, "What do you mean by that? It's my money, isn't it? If I want a new car that's my business, isn't it?"

Sarcasm and irony often make points with a sharper cut than long explanations can manage. "How was your date last night?" asks a friend. The woman answers, "He was a nice boy," punctuated with body motion which says that he was nice in the way that a pampered and protected twelve-year-old male can be nice, which makes a point with considerable force for the listener who interprets it correctly. The danger, of course, is that the nonverbal part of the message may fail, if not delivered skillfully, to reverse the verbal, and the listener may end up confused: "She says he was a nice boy, but I don't know for sure what she means." One reason why the public-speaking style includes specific training in voice and gesture is to enable its practitioners to deliver double-edged messages effectively.

By using the double-edged message, a speaker can make a statement with irony or sarcasm and leave an escape route, should the results begin to be punishing. The speaker finds it more difficult to "weasel out" of a clear, unequivocal statement. The woman discussing the purchase of the car in the example above can, if she chooses, answer the challenge, "It's my business, isn't it?" with, "I said you are a smart one, didn't I?" If she changes the nonverbal way she says the latter sentence so that it is now supportive of the words, she has hinted at her displeasure but escaped from the storm.

The double-edged message can, however, have a negative effect no matter what style of communication is being practiced. If people who are in a close personal relationship use many double-edged messages they may well carry on their power struggles largely on the nonverbal level. They may hint at problems and conflicts but not resolve them. The fact that

double bind *The dilemma a person is put in when he or she receives a double-edged message, generally sarcastic, with instructions which are contradictory.*

much of our theory about nonverbal communication has come from psychiatry is an indication of the toll that inconsistent messages can take on the cohesiveness of groups and the emotional and mental health of individuals.[19]

The Double Bind

If a person keeps getting double-edged messages from a friend or relative, the relationship between them is likely to deteriorate; or if the relationship is difficult to break off, the first person is likely to be in a double bind, if the messages are in the form of contradictory instructions: If the person follows the one instruction, the other cannot be followed. One instruction is usually in words and the order is countermanded by the nonverbal. The woman who asks a man, "Aren't you going to kiss me?" verbally, but who nonverbally indicates that she'd just as soon he didn't, puts the man in a double bind.

Birdwhistell tells of a study to investigate differences in the nonverbal communication of a mentally disturbed family compared with a mentally healthy one. Careful observations revealed that the mentally upset mother was sending out contradictory messages. The investigators filmed the way the mother handled a baby girl. They discovered that in changing the baby's diaper, for example, the mother placed her arm around the baby so that her hand was between the baby's arm and body as she was pinning the diaper. As the mother pinned the diaper, she both pushed upward on the baby's arm, sending a message to the infant to raise the arm, and put pressure on the baby's body in such a way that the baby would think the arm should come down. The child was in the unsettling position of being unable to obey either message without disobeying the other.[20]

If this example of Birdwhistell's seems far-fetched, stop and think how a child often learns from his family to do things that are directly counter to the parents' pious pronouncements. "Don't," a father says, "make the mistake I did and drop out of high school. Get a good education. You can't get anywhere these days without it." At the same time the father says this, however, much of what he does suggests to the son

[19] For some typical psychiatric approaches to nonverbal communication and to the double bind which results from two-edged communication and is a possible factor in mental disturbances, see: Mehrabian, ibid., pp. 53–55; Sheflen and Sheflen, *Body Language and Social Order*, pp. 187–198; see also Paul Watzlawick, Janet H. Beavin, and Don D. Jackson, *Pragmatics of Human Communication*, New York: Norton, 1967.

[20] Birdwhistell, *Kinesics and Context*, pp. 20–23.

territoriality *The apparently instinctive stake-out and defense of some area by animals, birds, and humans.*

that he thinks reading books is a waste of time, that he views colleges with suspicion, and that he sees college professors as strange, impractical people. The father communicates in a thousand nonverbal ways that he does not believe his own advice, and then this same father is unable to understand why his son quits school just as he himself did. There is much truth in the old saying that "teachers teach as they were taught, not as they were taught to teach." You must be sophisticated indeed in all aspects of communication to be totally aware of what you are communicating, nonverbally as well as verbally, when you send out messages.

TO INDICATE BOUNDARIES AND TO DEFEND TERRITORY
Nonverbal communication can function in terms of **territoriality** and personal space. Recently, evidence has been assembled to indicate that human beings stake out various territories in which they live, work, and play, just as other animals do. A student may sit in the same chair every time he attends a given class and be disturbed if someone else takes his territory. They exhibit some of the same behaviors in defense of their territory as other species do.[21] In addition, people act as though they had a bubble of personal space surrounding them which they like to keep free of others. The size of the bubble seems to grow larger or smaller depending upon the context and nature of their meetings.

People talking with one another often define territorial limits in a given situation nonverbally. Members of a small discussion group in a classroom will frame or outline the boundaries of their group's territory by the way they arrange the chairs in a circle, by the way they look at one another and away from other people in the room, by the way they hold their arms and legs to protect their turf. When the group finishes its "meeting," the participants often move in ways which say, in effect, "OK, we have finished now, and we give up our hold on this territory." They pull back their chairs, lean back, look around; some may get up, while others stay seated.

One of the important works which popularized the study of nonverbal communication and was evidence that the new styles of communication were preoccupied with the scientific study of such matters is Edward T. Hall's *The Silent Language.*[22] Hall discussed the notion of personal space at consid-

---

[21] For a study of territoriality in animals and fowl, see Konrad Lorenz, *On Aggression,* trans. M. Wilson, New York: Harcourt, 1966; see also R. Ardrey, *The Territorial Imperative,* New York: Atheneum, 1966.
[22] Garden City, N.Y.: Doubleday, 1966.

erable length, and a subsequent flurry of investigations supported the general principle that an individual's personal space may be "invaded" when someone comes "too close for comfort." Hall argued that we are comfortable in some communication situations only if there is a certain amount of space between the other person and ourselves. He described the distances which are common in four different communication situations.

The Four Communication Distances

The first is *intimate distance*, which varies from touching to a space of one or two feet. Intimate distance is appropriate for only the most intimate conversations, usually between a man and a woman who are well acquainted and friendly, or between parents and children, particularly young children. When we are forced into such close contact on a crowded bus or elevator we usually protect ourselves by not conversing. For important and personal communications, however, the intimate distance is often the most rewarding.

The second distance Hall refers to as *personal* and suggests that the space is roughly 2 to 2.5 feet. When two people meet in an office building or on the street and strike up a casual conversation, they usually remain approximately this far apart. Watch the people around you for the next day or so, and see if your own observation bears out this theory, and if you behave this way too.

The third distance, *social* distance, varies from about 4 to 7 feet. The social distance is good for impersonal business. The job interview, for example, is often conducted at this distance.

The final distance is the *public* distance, which starts at about 12 feet and extends as far as is feasible in a large room or auditorium. (You may wonder what happens in the areas between the zones covered, such as the distance from 7 to 12 feet. Other things must be taken into account, and the student of nonverbal communication might be able to determine whether the design of a given room for a speech, a presentation, or a discussion will place the participants in a public or personal zone if they are going to be talking to one another at a distance somewhere between 7 and 12 feet. These distances are simply rough rules of thumb to indicate that distance is an important feature of communication.)

Proxemic Factors

As important as distance is the geographic location of the participants—where people are in relation to one another. If an employer calls an employee into his office to discuss something in a two-person situation, the arrangement of the furniture and the seating of the two people influence the communicative setting. If the boss sits behind his desk and the worker sits in front of the desk, the fact that one is the boss and the other the employee is always part of the situation. With the proxemic nonverbal dimension so strongly a part of the interview, a discussion of personal matters would be difficult. Clearly, the boss who sets up a conference on this basis wishes to keep some distance from the employer as a person and to stress the status difference between them. If the boss comes from behind his desk, pulls up another chair, and sits beside the employee so they can talk at a distance of one or two feet or even touch (a tap on the shoulder to indicate personal concern or emphasis), the situation has been drastically altered by the changed geography of the communicative setting.

The geography of the small group meeting is a fascinating study. In some settings, a place at one end of a rectangular table is viewed as a position of power. Watching the way people sit at a meeting tells a wise observer a good deal about who likes whom and who is competing with whom for position or influence. During the course of the discussion such gross bodily movements as leaning back in a chair, leaning forward and placing the elbows on the table, turning slightly and pulling away from the speaker, or turning toward the speaker respectively indicate interest, boredom, acceptance, or rejection.

In a large group, the position of the listeners in relation to one another and to the speaker is a matter of considerable importance. If the speaker is located on a stage, standing behind a podium some distance from the audience, the speaker's relationship to the audience not only indicates formality but also stresses the separateness between speaker and audience. Should the speaker jump down from the stage and walk up and down the aisles as he speaks, such bodily movement would communicate a desire to break the public distance and move in the direction of more personal space to convey his message.

The distances among the members of the listening audience also affect the suggestibility of the audience. If a few individuals are scattered throughout a relatively large room, with many chairs empty, the effect is much different than if the audience is packed tightly together and some people are sitting on the floor around the edges of the room or standing along the walls. When the audience reacts sharply to a speaker by a sudden tightening of bodily tension on the part of a majority of the listeners, or by a sudden intake of breath, a sigh, a laugh, or a groan, the speaker and the listeners get the message and respond with emotion as well as with interest.

TO FRAME A COMMUNICATION EVENT

Body position and motion can serve to indicate that an informal and spontaneous transaction is to begin, can define the details of the order of speaking and listening and the tempo of the give-and-take, and can mark the end of communication.[23] For example, John sees Mary walking down the hall towards him. He slows up, changes direction so he will walk closer to her apparent path, lifts his eyebrows, widens his eyes, raises his head, holds up his right hand, and says, "Hello, how are you?" The way John emphasizes the words and his body motion invite the forming of a transaction. Mary can answer, "Hi." The way Mary acts as she says the word may reject the invitation, and John may swing back on his former path and go on his way. On the other hand, Mary may respond with a big smile, walking directly toward him until she is within three or four feet and then stopping. John may then continue with, "Classes keeping you awake today?" As Mary answers, he notices an acquaintance, Harry, coming down the hall. Harry smiles and says "Hello," but John nods to him briefly over his shoulder, while turning a bit to close off the turf of the twosome he has formed with Mary. Even though Mary has turned with her head up, looking expectantly at Harry, whom she has not met, Harry gets the nonverbal message from John and walks past them. In the same way, after they have chatted and John has indicated nonverbally a desire to extend and make the transaction more intimate and Mary has replied nonverbally that she is not interested in doing so at this time, she may indicate nonverbally that the transaction is coming to a close.[24] John may accept her cues and nonverbally agree, and they will go their separate ways.

TO INDICATE INTERPERSONAL RELATIONSHIPS

Nonverbal communication may also function in terms of relationships which are beginning or evolving among the par-

[23] Chris L. Kleinke, First Impressions: *The Psychology of Encountering Others*, Englewood Cliffs, N.J.: Prentice-Hall, 1975, pp. 58–59; see also Albert E. Sheflen, "The Significane of Posture in Communicative Systems," *Psychiatry*, 27 (1964), pp. 316–331.

[24] For a study of nonverbal cues to terminating a transaction, see Mark L. Knapp, Roderick P. Hart, Gustav W. Friedrich, and Gary M. Shulman, "The Rhetoric of Goodbye: Verbal and Nonverbal Correlates of Human Leave-Taking," *Speech Monographs*, 40 (1973), pp. 182–198.

ticipants in a communication event. One of the most important ways in which nonverbal messages comment on relationships is in terms of saying "I like you" or "I dislike you." Most people are always on the alert for cues relating to how they are being accepted or rejected by others. Often a verbal response to another person is restricted by custom, norms, or style. The participants in a meeting in the message communication style are restricted by the norms of that style from saying such things as "You arouse me sexually." Innocuous verbal comments can, however, be accompanied by nonverbal messages which suggest the evolving relationship. Frequently, too, expressing dislike or loathing in verbal messages is "not the thing to do" in many social situations, but nonverbal cues may get the message across nonetheless.

Another improtant relationship which nonverbal messages often communicate is that of power. If there is a "pecking order" in the relationships of two or more people and they are meeting together, the nonverbal messages often communicate their pattern of dominance and submissiveness. Nonverbal cues often reveal if one participant is of higher status, or has fate control over others, or is in a "one-up" relationship.

When status is clear and accepted, the participants who communicate with one another tend to have routine nonverbal patterns which indicate that the power relationships are known and accepted by all involved and that the communication can continue based on those relationships. The members do not have to consciously expend effort in building or rebuilding status relationships. In the message communication model, clear and accepted power relationships tend to free the time of the participants to concentrate on information processing and would thus represent a good situation. In other words, with comfortable and acceptable personal relationships established, participants can keep their minds on the content of the messages and use both the verbal and nonverbal channels to support the same information, with a better chance of achieving understanding. When the relationships are disturbed and begin to get in the way of the work, then the recommendation of those in the message communication style would be to tend to those relationships and get them back into harmony, so the participants can once again concentrate on the task at hand.

The relationship communication style, on the other hand, tends to emphasize evolving relationships as people grow—for example, from acquaintance, to liking, to love. For participants in the relationship communication style, the relationship itself often becomes a focus of concern, and both verbal and nonverbal messages deal with relationship matters.

No matter what the style, however, when relationships are evolving, people emit nonverbal messages which are not routine or habitual: They exhibit courtship cues and cues of rejection or acceptance; they exhibit dominance behavior, conflict confrontation, submission, and so forth as they go about evolving relationships.

AS FEEDBACK

Nonverbal communication can serve a powerful function as *feedback* in the message communication model. Indeed, nonverbal gestures, facial expressions, eye movements, postures, are all among the most useful ways in which someone playing the role of receiver can indicate confusion, understanding, agreement, apathy or lack of interest, involvement, acceptance, or rejection as related to the *content* of the verbal message. In the relationship style, on the other hand, nonverbal communication can function to indicate the subtleties of relationships and can display emotions; this is using *feedback* in its larger context, as the relationship theorists do. Since so much of the relationship style is directed to how people relate to one another, nonverbal expression during the beginnings and evolution of interpersonal relationships is extremely important.

TO ESTABLISH AND MAINTAIN COMMUNICATION EVENTS

Finally, nonverbal communication can function to establish the ground rules for a transaction and to maintain the social stability of such an event within a given cultural context. The nonverbal context can set the stage for a communication event in any of the three important styles. Nonverbal communication can indicate the beginning of the transaction, order its tempo, punctuate its agenda, and finally, indicate its termination. In addition, nonverbal gestures can provide a **monitoring behavior** to assure that the people participating will act within the proper rules and norms of the transaction.

If the transaction is in the style of a message communication business meeting in a computer firm, a participant who starts to disclose deeply personal information and to weep and express deep sorrow with his facial expressions will be out of place. Nonverbal gestures can provide monitoring behavior to try to change the out-of-place communication and bring it back into line with what is expected and appreciated in that context, according to that style. The Sheflens call behaviors which are out of context for a given communication event, **transcontextuals.**[25] If the transaction is in the relationship style and a man and a woman are intertwined in each other's arms, and he suddenly pulls back and announces that the agenda for their meeting has three topics which he would like to cover—if possible, in 45 minutes (because he has another important meeting within the hour)—he has exhibited some transcontextuals. The woman is then likely to indulge in some strong nonverbal monitoring. In the public-speaking transaction, should a member of the audience begin to hug and kiss the person sitting next to her, or run up and embrace the speaker, the nonverbal monitoring would likely express embarrassment, amusement, disapproval and rejection, which would suggest to the deviant member that she should cease acting out of context.

Nonverbal Communication in the Public-Speaking Style

We have summarized the major categories of nonverbal communication useful to all three styles first described in the second chapter. We have pointed out some general functions which cut across all these styles with some universality. We can say little more in terms of the message communication and relationship communication styles. The public-speaking theory, however, does contain more information for the person who wishes to become a more effective speaker in that style, and we shall now present the theory of nonverbal communication regarding body language associated with public speaking.

STAGE FRIGHT

Most beginning public speakers find that the thought of talking to a large group of people makes them nervous. Perhaps nothing about a speech-communication course is more on the beginner's mind than this worry about stage fright. It is not an insurmountable problem. There are many things you can do to keep stage fright from showing to the audience, and to make it work for you rather than against you.

If the beginning speaker is anxious, if the audience finds

[25] Sheflen and Sheflen, *Body Language and Social Order*, pp. 76–80.

out about it, it is largely through nonverbal cues. The speaker's hands may shake, his voice may quiver, he may have difficulty looking at the audience, and he may remain poker-faced, wooden-looking. An audience is quick to pick up cues about the way a speaker feels about himself. If the speaker regards his own nonverbal cues as showing that he is worried about his performance, the audience will get the correct impression that the speaker has stage fright. They will begin to worry about him and his feelings and be distracted from the ideas in his speech. Then the speaker not only has trouble getting his ideas across to the audience, but also must combat their view of him as someone with not much to offer them, someone they need to help through the difficult task of giving a speech. Interestingly enough, the same body motions, if perceived by the speaker as symptoms of his intense involvement with, and high regard for, his subject and the occasion, can make a strong positive impression on an audience. We cannot stress too much the importance of how the speaker perceives himself. This perception of yourself is the first thing you communicate to any audience.

If the speaker can control his tension so that his gestures, posture, and facial expression are appropriate to what he is saying, the audience will seldom know he is anxious. Every good speaker gets keyed up before he goes on; even able, professional public speakers get stage fright before they start. Every teacher confesses to some nervousness before meeting a new class for the first time. But like the athlete who is nervous and keyed up in the dressing room but feels fine two minutes after the game starts, the good speaker uses these feelings of nervousness and tension to key him up to do a better job.

The point is that you do not want to stop feeling nervous about giving a speech or standing before a crowd. You want to learn to use this nervous tension to make your mind sharper and less likely to forget, and to give your whole body more focus and concentration on communicating with your audience.

A good way to get the tension under proper control is to feel satisfied about the preparation of your speech. Each of us has a way that works best for him, but if you can feel you have something worthwhile or fun to say to your listeners, something they will enjoy and use, and if you feel you know exactly what you want to say, you will find it easier to get past the few difficult moments as you begin. Throughout the book, particulary in Chapter 7, there is more specific information to help you prepare speaking material.

Another good way to get the tension under control is to pick a spot in the front of the audience, and when you are introduced, get up from your chair, pause, pull yourself erect, and firmly and calmly force yourself to walk to the spot. When you reach the spot you picked, pause again, stand erect, and with the weight balanced comfortably on both feet, look out at the audience and, for just a moment, let your eyes run over the listeners. Be sure and look at the people in the audience *until you can see them.* Some beginners, when they feel particularly nervous at the start of the speech, are unwilling actually to look at the audience. Since they do not know what the people look like or what they are doing, they find themselves growing more and more nervous as they proceed. We are all afraid of the unknown, and if the speaker is not watching the audience, he has no way of knowing what it is doing. In all speaking situations, it is far better for you, the speaker, to look at your audience, to see the friendly faces, the smiles, the frowns, the questioning looks—to realize that an audience is made up of human beings much like yourself, that they usually wish you well (particularly in a speech-communication class), and that they want you to be a good speaker.

And so, having looked directly during this pause at the people to whom you will be talking, take a good deep breath as quietly as you can and begin your speech in a strong voice. By standing erect, by acting confident, by pausing, and by beginning in a good strong voice, you complete the illusion of confidence for your audience.

Furthermore, you will discover that if you can give the audience the impression that you are a poised and confident speaker, their impression will affect you, and you will soon feel more confidence and find that you can keep your tension under control.

Several final hints may help you in controlling nervous tension and using it to make your nonverbal communication more effective. Pick topics that excite you. If you talk on subjects you feel strongly about, you will soon discover that your interest in what you are saying is genuine and is taking your mind off yourself.

Develop an audience-centered approach to speaking. Keep your mind on the listener and his response. Watch individuals. Did the audience like some example you used? Did an analogy work well in getting one of your points across? (Was there nodding of heads in agreement, for example?) Can you think of other such examples or analogies that you might insert to increase audience interest and involvement? Is the audience getting bored? Do any members of the audience look confused? As in the trite but true advice to young people who want to learn how to get over self-consciousness in social situations, get your mind off yourself! By concentrating on the audience, the speaker takes his mind off himself and his performance. Self-centered attitudes are primary causes of stage fright. We devote Chapter 6 to the important matter of audience analysis. Obviously, you must learn how to analyze your audience before you can become audience-centered.

Finally, the fright mechanism is an old one that we have inherited from our prehistoric ancestors, who often had to fight or take flight from personal danger. The person who is frightened generally has an increased heartbeat and increased adrenalin in the system and is charged up either to run fast or to fight hard. When we speak in front of an audience, however, neither flight nor fight is advisable. But if you are by nature a person who gestures in conversations, or if you tend to move about when taking part in a discussion, use this habit of moving when you speak to dissipate some of the nervous energy in strong, purposeful gestures.

POSTURE

The way a speaker stands and holds his shoulders and his head as he speaks communicates a good deal nonverbally to the audience. If the speaker is standing in the region of public distance (12 or more feet from the first row of the audience) and is delivering a speech in a relatively formal setting, the audience expects him to stand erect, with his weight evenly balanced on both feet. The feet should be relatively close together, with one foot slightly in front of the other.

The speaker should not lean on the speaker's stand, slouch first on one foot and then the other, rock back and forth or from side to side, or stand with feet widespread.

If the speaker is in the position of social distance and in a relatively informal setting, and if he wishes to communicate nonverbally that he does not want to give a carefully prepared speech, but plans to ramble on a bit and throw out a few ideas and then ask for questions and comments, he may sit on the edge of a table, sit in a chair, lean on the speaker's stand, take off his coat, and so on.

FACIAL EXPRESSION

One of the most important tools any speaker has for nonverbal communication with an audience is his range of facial expressions. Smiles, grins, smirks, frowns, grimaces, and raised eyebrows can all add emphasis or, conversely, suggest that the descriptive words in the message are to be discounted. Unfortunately, one of the beginner's most common reactions to nervousness is failure to use facial expressions. As a result, the anxious speaker often talks in a monotone, sighs a great deal, and has a blank expression on his face.

The person who is vivacious in conversation, whose face is alive every second in animated talk with one or two others, often tones down his facial expressions when giving a public speech. He should do just the opposite. An expressive smile or grin in the region of intimate space or even personal distance is often lost on an audience 12 feet or more away. Thus, you ought to overdo the smile, the grin, the frown when you are giving a public speech in a good-sized room or auditorium. You have to overdo your platform personality to achieve the effect you ordinarily produce in the more informal and intimate situations.

EYE CONTACT

One of the most expressive regions of the face is the area around the eyes. Again and again the eyewitnesses who reported their impressions of such great American speakers as Daniel Webster, Henry Clay, Stephen Douglas, and William Jennings Bryan noted the arresting and powerful effect of the speakers' eyes.

Generally the speaker ought to give the illusion that he is looking directly at the members of the audience. To be sure, direct eye contact may be a culture-bound nonverbal convention, and you may wish to modify the advice for special situations. However, you are well advised to look a middle-class white North American audience in the eye.

In almost all situations, random eye movements are distracting. Looking over the listeners' heads for no clear purpose, looking out the window, looking at the corner of the room, looking at the floor, or looking always at your speech notes can prove distracting. We have already noted that when the speaker looks away from the audience for the greater part of his speech, he has no way of judging its response, of utilizing the feedback from nonverbal cues.

GESTURE

The beginning speaker often makes an unsettling discovery when he gets in front of an audience. He finds that attached to his shoulders are two arms to which he normally pays little attention, but which now suddenly cannot be ignored. At the ends of his arms are two conspicuous hands. His first thought is to hide his hands, so he puts them both behind his back. When he does this, he feels tied up, and every move he makes with his shoulders seems awkward. He then tries to hide his hands in his pockets, but he still feels restricted, and his hands seem as obvious and as useless as ever. He may fold his arms over his chest or try to hold them rigidly by his sides, in the hope that nobody will notice them, but there is no hiding either the arms or the hands. The only solution is for the speaker to learn to use his arms and hands to make gestures in support of the material in his speech.

Once the beginner realizes he must move his hands and arms, he may make a second mistake by keeping his elbows close to his sides, using the forearms for short, jerky gestures. His nonverbal communication at this point is that he wants to use some gestures but feels inhibited in front of his listeners.

You can get the feel of good ways to gesture by practicing at home in front of a mirror. When you practice gestures suitable for a speech, you should make them broader than you first feel necessary. Experiment with gesturing with both arms. Remember to use the space above your shoulders, particularly if you are speaking from a stage and are some distance from your audience. Move your hands to express ideas. Make sure the movement flows through the entire arm to the tips of your fingers. Do not let your hands and fingers flop about loosely; do not use gestures that distract from, rather than add to, the meaning of what you are saying.

The entire body can gesture to suggest nonverbal meanings. The speaker may hunch his shoulders and crouch to suggest a certain mood or feeling. He may step toward the audience, pull back, turn to one side or another, or stand on tiptoe. A good speaker may use the techniques of pantomime, the art of getting across emotions, actions, and feelings by mute gestures. He may turn slightly, crouch, and make an imaginary pistol out of his extended index finger to suggest to the audience the character of a holdup man in a story. He might next turn, stand rigidly erect, and hold both hands high, this time suggesting his own response to the feeling of having the gun in his back.

THE USE OF NOTES

The question of whether to have notes for a public speech may seem a minor matter. Yet in the hands of a speaker who does not know how best to use them, notes can inhibit eye contact, facial expression, posture, and gesturing, and thereby affect the speaker's total skill at nonverbal communication. Many speech instructors prefer that students not use notes in class, simply because notes hinder development of good habits of nonverbal communication through body language. Some instructors also feel that beginning speakers should learn to keep the outline of their ideas in mind, without notes, as they speak. We do not use notes in most informal communication situations. We may use notes for formal speaking situations, however, and the Teleprompter and other devices provide ready notes, even whole speeches, for television performers. It seems to us that the situations calling for speeches without any notes are rare. However, listeners are impressed when a speaker uses no notes, and you should keep this in mind for your most polished and important speeches. If you can develop a way to prepare speeches that allows you to keep the main points of your outline in mind, you can usually easily remember the examples and other supporting material that fit under the main point. If you can speak extemporaneously without notes, you can keep your eyes on the audience and gesture more freely.

Many students find it difficult to speak without notes, and plan to use notes in the speaking they will do after they finish the class, so they prefer learning to speak well using them. The most important point about using notes in a speech is not to pretend that you have no notes. Few things a speaker can do distract an audience as much as the pretense that he has no notes. Sometimes a speaker writes his notes on small cards and stacks them on the speaker's stand or holds them hidden in the palm of his hand. He cannot fool anyone. The first time he sneaks a look at his notes the audience picks up the cue and watches for him to steal another look; he may create more suspense with this nonverbal behavior than with what he is trying to say! So if you need notes, bring them out into the open, then use them naturally, trying not to cut down on eye contact and facial expressiveness any more than necessary. Perhaps in the instance of quoting a statistic or a special sentence from some authority, the speaker can even hold up the notes and point to the place where he has his information; this communicates nonverbally that what he is saying is absolutely correct and he has it written down to make sure he says it correctly.

Avoid the common pitfalls of using notes. Do not look at them whenever you feel embarrassed; look at the audience, keep your poise, and pause to collect yourself. To the audience, your poised look at them as you pause communicates that you are about to say something important and are thinking about exactly the right way to say it best. Do not play with your notes; a nervous speaker with something in his hand is often tempted to fold it, roll it, tap it, or bend it. The audience may, again, become more interested in what you may do next with your note cards than in what you are saying.

Do not clutch your notes tightly in front of you with both hands; you cannot gesture with your hands if they are in this rigid position. Hold the notes in one hand and use the other arm and hand for gesturing, although you may certainly gesture with both arms if it seems appropriate—the notes, held up in one hand, will not distract from the gesture; if anything, a vigorous arm gesture that includes the display of notes may communicate that you are prepared, you have in your hand what you are going to say, and you are very much in charge of the situation.

The more imagination you can develop to enable you to see yourself as the audience does, the better your nonverbal communication will become.

Nonverbal communication is sometimes called the silent language. We are all vaguely aware of the implications of gesture, facial expression, and body attitudes when we talk with people from day to day. When we are involved in public communication events, we need to become more sophisticated about the implications of nonverbal body-motion codes so that if we are speaking, we know what to do to make our nonverbal communication support our intention. If we are viewing and hearing someone else speak, we need to be aware of the many signals given by the speaker's body, eyes, and vocal intonations. All these are elements of nonverbal communication, and they are important components of messages; there is much truth in the saying, "What you *do* speaks so loud, I can't hear what you *say*."

SUGGESTED PROJECTS

1 The class divides into groups of two or three, and each group selects a brief emotional scene one of the members has witnessed. (An example would be the reactions of downtown shoppers witnessing a serious automobile accident, or of ardent basketball fans watching a local hero take a final shot at the basket, with the score tied and 2 seconds remaining. Or the scene might be much more intimate, involving a tense and critical interview between a doctor and a patient, a parent and child, or a lawyer and a witness.) For 1 minute the group tries to communicate the emo-

Chapter 5

THE KEY IDEAS

The best of the studies of nonverbal communication give us a map of nonverbal customs and communication styles in various places and times rather than a scientific theory of nonverbal communication.

We need to be reminded continually of the importance of the background and context of our communication in a complex urban culture.

Present evidence indicates that almost all of our important nonverbal communication behavior is learned rather than innate.

We learn a general body language from our particular culture, an individual body language within the restraints of the cultural norms, and a characteristic way of nonverbal communication which is highly individual and not common to the culture.

tions involved to the rest of the class, using only hand and body gestures. No facial expression should be used at this stage of the exercise. For a second minute, the group continues to use hand and body movement to convey the emotions but also adds facial expression. The third minute, they add movement in relation to one another (proxemics.) The class then discusses the importance of various elements of body language in communicating emotion.

2 Five members of the class are given a current, preferably controversial topic to discuss. They go to the front of the classroom and conduct a brief unrehearsed discussion. Half of the remaining members watch and make notes about the proxemics of the discussion group, their nonverbal gestures, postures, and facial expressions. The other half of the class watches the nonverbal proxemics and gestures of the entire classroom, including the instructor. After the discussion, a general class meeting analyzes the nonverbal dimension of the discussion group and the entire classroom setting.

3 Prepare a stage fright analysis of yourself. Show this initial analysis to your instructor, then keep it throughout the course. It is to be a personal record, so be frank and honest. Begin with a brief discussion of the types of communication experiences in which you feel most anxious. Write a brief description of physical symptoms that you notice at such times, such as shaky knees, a

Every individual learns the nonverbal components of a communication style as part of the study of the style.

Body language may function to enhance words, to detract from the words, to indicate boundaries and defend territory, and to frame a communication event.

One of the most important functions of nonverbal communication is to indicate relationships such as liking or disliking, and power and status differences.

Nonverbal communication is an important means of providing feedback in terms of the model of the message communication style.

Nonverbal communication helps establish and maintain the ground rules of communication events.

Monitoring behavior serves to keep communication within the bounds set by a given context and communication style.

The public-speaking communication theory contains much knowledge about the art of using body motion to communicate within the style.

Audience members often pick up that the speaker is nervous because of nonverbal indications.

A speaker should watch the listeners and see how they are responding to the speech nonverbally.

One of the most important ways a speaker can communicate nonverbally with listeners is by means of facial expressions.

Whether or not the speaker looks directly at the audience affects how the listeners interpret the speech.

Random body motion unrelated to cultural norms, communication styles, or meaning, tends to distract the listener. .

dry mouth, sweaty palms, or trembling hands. Keep a record of your communication experiences throughout the quarter or semester, and describe in some detail your feelings during each class exercise. Prepare one of your final communication assignments with the express purpose of achieving maximum control of your tensions. Select a topic about which you have strong feelings, prepare your message carefully; use strong, convincing language. Concentrate on the audience response. Write a final progress report of your tension during this final assignment. Compare your response to communication tension toward the end of the class to your initial analysis, and particularly note your progress in controlling and using stage fright.

SUGGESTED READINGS

Birdwhistell, Ray L. *Kinesics and Context: Essays on Body Motion Communication*, Philadelphia: University of Pennsylvania Press, 1970.

Bosmajian, Haig A. *The Rhetoric of Nonverbal Communication: Readings.* Glenview, Ill.: Scott, Foresman, 1971.

Clark, Margaret L., Ella A. Erway, and Lee Beltzer. *The Learning Encounter: The Classroom as a Communications Workshop.* New York: Random House, 1971. "Nonverbal Behavior," pp. 52–65.

Eisenberg, Abne M. and Ralph R. Smith, Jr. *Nonverbal Communication.* Indianapolis: Bobbs-Merrill, 1971.

Hall, Edward T. *The Silent Language.* Garden City, N.Y.: Doubleday, 1959.

Jensen, J. Vernon. *Perspectives on Oral Communication.* Boston: Holbrook Press, 1970. "Perspectives on Nonverbal Intercultural Communication," pp. 133–160.

Kleinke, Chris. *First Impressions: The Psychology of Encountering Others.* Englewood Cliffs, N.J.: Prentice-Hall, 1975.

Knapp, Mark L. *Nonverbal Communication in Human Interaction.* New York: Holt, Rinehart and Winston, 1972.

Leathers, Dale. *Nonverbal Communication Systems.* Boston: Allyn and Bacon, 1976.

Mehrabian, Albert. "Communication Without Words," *Psychology Today,* 2 (September 1968), 53–55.

_____. *Silent Messages.* Belmont, Calif.: Wadsworth, 1971.

Ruesch, Jurgen and Weldon Kees. *Nonverbal Communication: Notes on the Visual Perception of Human Relations.* Berkeley, Calif.: University of California Press, 1969.

Sheflen, Albert E. and Alice Sheflen. *Body Language and Social Order: Communication as Behavioral Control.* Englewood Cliffs, N.J.: Prentice-Hall, 1972.

Chapter 6

HOW TO COMMUNICATE IN THE PUBLIC-SPEAKING STYLE

Some courses in speech communication stress the public-speaking communication style to such an extent that much of the material on the message communication and relationship communication styles which form an important part of this book is neglected. The communication theories from other styles are very valuable, and we include the two-person conference, small group discussions, interviews, and mass media persuasion in the book because we want to stress the relevance of improved daily communication in all areas of our lives. We do not want, however, to go to the extreme of some of the partisans of the other styles and argue that public speaking is out of date and that nobody gives public speeches anymore. We personally spend too much time teaching these specific skills to postgraduates, men and women who, some years after assuming supervisory positions in businesses and organizations, need public-speaking skills because they have information they need to share with others. A recent survey by Kendall indicates that for people with a college education, public speaking remains a significant, useful communication style, and that furthermore, communication transactions in the public-speaking style are important to blue-collar workers and their families.[1]

Every culture needs to have the right spokesman say something formally at important periods in the life of the family, institution, community or nation. (Today in our culture the right spokesman may be male or female, but this is not true of all cultures, nor was it always true in the United States. When women first took to the platform and began giving speeches in public, they were greeted with outcries of public displeasure.)[2] At times of beginning or ending—at the start of a new public building or civic enterprise, at the end of a project or large program, at birth, at marriage, at death—we often feel the need for words to recall the past, to celebrate the present, and to dream of the future. We need to add perspective to the everyday hustle and bustle that occupies most of our time. The speech to celebrate community, family, or individual is firmly embedded in most cultures, and ours is one which has historically prized such public statements.

THE PUBLIC—SPEAKING TRADITION IN THE U.S.

In the United States, the value of public discussion and debate is widely accepted. Every state, as well as the national government and most local and county governments, has a policy-making group of elected officials who debate important issues before settling matters by vote.

Few countries in history have been as involved in adult education and social uplift on as large a scale as has the United States. An early and important expression of the adult-education movement was the lyceum, a group of people who formed an educational club and hired a series of lecturers to talk on various educational topics. As these clubs grew in popularity, they were tied together by state and national associations and were able to establish routes or circuits so that nationally prominent speakers could tour the country, assuring that even lyceums in remote towns could hear famous speakers. You should recall that this was happening in the days before the development of the mass media. The arrival of a visiting speaker was a big occasion in towns and cities all

[1] Kathleen Edgerton Kendall, "Do Real People Ever Give Speeches?" *Central States Speech Journal*, 25 (1974), 233–235.

[2] See Ernest G. Bormann, ed. *Forerunners of Black Power: The Rhetoric of Abolition*, Englewood Cliffs, N.J.: Prentice-Hall, 1971; see also Kathleen Edgerton Kendall and Jeanne Y. Fisher, "Frances Wright on Women's Rights: Eloquence Versus Ethos," *The Quarterly Journal of Speech*, 60 (1974), 58–68.

across the land. Supplementing the lyceum was the chau-
tauqua movement, which provided the public with lecturers
in an outdoor setting, much like the religious camp meeting.[3]

Today we continue the traditions of the lyceum and chau-
tauqua. Most every high school has a series of assembly lectures; every college campus has a number of similar speeches
on varied topics by different speakers. At larger schools a

[3] Waldo W. Braden, "The Beginnings of the Lyceum, 1826–1840,"
Southern Speech Journal, 20 (1954), 125–135; Henry L. Ewbank, Jr., "Current
Interest Topics Discussed in the Lyceums, 1832–1837," *Speech Monographs*,
23 (1956), 284–287.

student can usually attend one or two special lectures a week if he wishes.

Every business and educational, governmental, or religious organization uses a form of communication called the *presentation*. The presentation is a carefully prepared message officially ordered and sanctioned by the organization. To be sure, the members of the modern organization do use many written messages, but in the United States, the preference for oral communication is strong, and many important topics are discussed in meetings that begin with a well-prepared, carefully rehearsed multimedia presentation.[4]

General Features of Communication Context

In Chapters 4 and 5 on nonverbal communication we described the well-developed theory of the public-speaking communication style relating to use of voice, articulation of gestures, posture, facial expression, and eye contact. We also discussed the larger nonverbal context, which can indicate the nature of a communication event, when it is to begin, and how it is to proceed, which can monitor behavior that is not appropriate (transcontextual behavior), and can end the interchange. The Sheflens indicate that there are culturally sanctioned transactional forms which persist for a number of years, and that people who have learned the expected patterns of nonverbal communication can participate in specific transactions with understanding and with satisfaction. They note:

> With so many possible variations in behavior, the degree to which transactional forms remain relatively standard in a tradition is extraordinary. We can go almost anywhere in the United States and see the same kinds of games, work scenes, meeting formats, and forms of discourse. Many of these forms have not changed greatly from one generation to the next.[5]

The public-speaking style consists of a family of transactional forms, and part of its theory consists of their description. The forms of public speaking are among the important transactional forms that have not changed greatly from one

[4] For a comprehensive treatment of the business presentation as a special transaction in the public-speaking communication style, see William S. Howell and Ernest G. Bormann, *Presentational Speaking for Business and the Professions*, New York: Harper & Row, 1971.

[5] Albert E. Sheflen and Alice Sheflen, *Body Language and Social Order: Communication as Behavioral Control*, Englewood Cliffs, N.J.: Prentice-Hall, 1972, p. 104.

generation to the next. If you could climb into a time machine and return to the Connecticut Valley in 1741 you could tell by the way the people in the audience were sitting and listening, by the way Jonathan Edwards was standing, gesturing, and speaking, and from the content of what he was saying that you were part of a transactional form in the public-speaking style called a sermon. If you had the time machine drop you off to watch a big crowd collect in Charleston, Illinois in the late summer of 1858 and you could listen to Stephen A. Douglas and Abraham Lincoln take turns speaking in the open air from a temporary platform, you would soon be able to tell that you were listening to a political debate.[6]

The public speech is thus a cultural event with rather clearly understood rules and customs in most societies. Beyond the general set of conventions that govern the public-speaking style, there are specific conventions governing a number of common situations, which tend to arouse in the people participating a similar set of expectations. People who attend a political rally have not only the general expectation of all who come to a public-speaking occasion, but have in addition some more restricted notions about what will happen and what will be an appropriate response. People who go to a revival meeting, to a funeral, to an after-dinner speech, to a lecture, or to a keynote address at a political convention, all have a common general mental and emotional set toward a public speech, but also have some more specific expectations aroused by their understanding of, say, what a funeral eulogy should be, or how a good lecture ought to be given.

AUDIENCE EXPECTATIONS REGARDING FORMAT
For many public speeches the participants anticipate that one individual will deliver an extended message. The audience comes to hear a certain person speak on an advertised subject or title. The public-speaking transaction has a definite format that usually includes a time at which the audience is to gather and the speech is supposed to begin, and quite often, a time when the speech is to close. Americans are time conscious and pay a great deal of attention to the length of a speech. If the speech draws out longer than they have anticipated, audience members often grow restless.

For many public speeches the audience expects and appreciates activities that set the stage for the speaker. A simple format for a speech is to have a local dignitary call the meet-

[6] Paul M. Angle, ed., *Created Equal? The Complete Lincoln-Douglas Debates of 1858*, Chicago: University of Chicago Press, 1958.

ing to order and introduce the speaker by identifying his background and experience. The speaker then delivers his message, and the dignitary who introduced him thanks the speaker and closes the meeting. The basic format is often elaborated so that the speaker is preceded by music, group singing, or performances by lesser personalities, to increase the audience's susceptibility to the main speaker. Big revival meetings, for instance, often have prayers, announcements, songs, and introductions before the evangelist delivers the main message of the evening. Political rallies generally have music, introductions, and some enthusiastic partisan comments before the main speaker comes to the podium.

After the speech, the audience may participate in questioning the speaker or in making comments. The occasion may call for more music or some additional comments by other people.

Generally, the people planning the public speech arrange things so the audience has some place to sit or stand, so distractions are minimized, and so the speaker is provided with a public-address system in good working order in order that everyone present can hear him.

EXPECTATIONS ABOUT AUDIENCE AND SPEAKER BEHAVIOR

The variety of specific expectations aroused by such situations as the after-dinner speech, the revival speech, the agitator's speech at a political demonstration, and the funeral eulogy praising someone who has died can be identified by questions such as: Does the audience expect and enjoy humor? Does the audience listen quietly to the speaker? Does the audience interrupt and heckle? Does the audience interrupt to reinforce the speaker with shouts such as "Hallelujah! Praise the Lord!" or "Right on!" or "You tell 'em, George!" Does the audience expect the speaker to read a carefully prepared message? Does the audience expect the speaker to deliver an extemporaneous speech with high feeling and vigorous nonverbal communication? To some extent, of course, expectations of audiences are culturebound; more than likely a black rural southern congregation will expect a different funeral eulogy than will a small-town Scandinavian Lutheran congregation in Minnesota.

An adept speaker may sometimes break one or two of the expected conventions that relate to a certain speech occasion and even benefit from the novelty of the violation—people usually enjoy a mild surprise—but if he violates a number of the conventions surrounding a public speech, the audience will often be confused, indignant, bored, or even angry. If a minister, for example, introduces some humor into an ordinarily serious religious meeting, most of the audience will respond as the speaker hopes. If the minister violates other expectations in addition — for example, in the way he is dressed, his style of language, his dialect, his use of profanity, his use of bald humor, or in his appearance of drunkeness while delivering the sermon, the audience's responsiveness will be seriously disturbed. In the Sheflens' terms, such action would be transcontextual and would result in much nonverbal monitoring behavior.

All the general and specific expectations of an audience attending a public speech put some pressure on the speaker to adapt his ideas to the form of the occasion.

People gathered in a large group to hear a public speech respond differently than they would in two-person conversations or even small discussion groups. Because one person is the center of attention and the primary source of messages, and because a large group of people plays the role of receiver, the dynamics of the situation are changed in several important ways. The social pressure of four or five people is strong, but the power of 50 or 100 is much greater, and when thousands of assembled people stand up or shout, the influence of the crowd upon any individual is immense. Have you ever been part of a large audience — at a football game, a student demonstration, a religious revival — when the crowd began to groan or shout or chant, and felt personally the emotional impact of thousands of voices moved by a common feeling or emotion?

If the audience comes to a public-speaking situation expecting to hear a fire-breathing politician, a hellfire-and-damnation revival preacher, or a violent revolutionary, the members are often predisposed to respond with high feeling. The planners of the meeting, trying to fulfill these expectations, may precede the main speaker with music and warm-up speeches, as we mentioned earlier. By the time the speaker begins, the audience may be quite excited, and if he is skillful, the orator will soon have focused the attention of the listeners upon his speech.

AUDIENCE-SPEAKER INTERACTION

If the audience is warmed up and the speaker delivers a particularly good line, some audience members may begin to clap, yell, and shout encouragement. The response of the audience stimulates the speaker. He loses his preoccupation with self. Encouraged by a positive audience response, he is stimulated to proceed along the lines that strike a reaction. He is now more effective, and the audience responds more strongly. Not only does the audience stimulate the speaker, and the speaker in turn stimulate the audience, but the audience members stimulate each other. Excitement and emotions are contagious in a large crowd, and a person is hard put to keep quiet or remain calm in the midst of an audience caught up in the emotional response of the moment.

We have, admittedly, taken the above examples from that group of public-speaking situations which conventionally arouse expectations of emotional excitement. The same principles of audience behavior, however, apply to other situations. The audience attending a lecture by a Nobel prize winner, for instance, places equally strong pressures to conform on individual members. If the speaker is wearing a tuxedo, if the ushers whisper as though loud and boisterous talk were out of order, if the audience sits upright and with great dignity, the pressure is strong on all audience members to do likewise. If members of the audience begin to cough, grow restless, look at their watches, all these behaviors put pressure on the speaker and other audience members alike.

The larger the audience, the more likely it is to expect an elevated style of language from the speaker. The keynote speaker at a political convention generally uses a more careful and formal speech style (and is expected to do so by the audience) than the same politician uses when he is talking over a strategy move with five of his staff members in his hotel room.

THE EFFECT OF AUDIENCE SIZE ON EXPECTATIONS

The larger the audience, the more it expects and demands that the speaker appeal to the so-called "higher" motives of mankind. The new president of the United States giving an inaugural address is expected to appeal to the better nature and the more unselfish motives of the American people. The late President John F. Kennedy said in his inaugural address, "Ask not what your country can do for you—ask what you can do for your country."[7] His statement was in line with the expectations for the occasion and with the vast size of the television audience. If the president were to express similar sentiments in the same lofty style in a meeting with an assis-

[7] Delivered at the presidential inauguration ceremony, January 20, 1961 and widely reprinted.

tant and three leaders of the antipoverty movement lobbying for legislation to guarantee everyone an annual income, he might well get, and deserve, a scornful laugh. On the other hand, the speaker at a high-school commencement would receive an outraged reaction from much of his audience if he said he knew the seniors were not interested in a lot of pious baloney from him, that all they wanted was to get out of the auditorium, out of their robes, and into their cars to head for the nearest pot party or beer bust to get stoned out of their heads in celebration of the end of their four miserable years in high school, and that he, for one, thought they had the right idea.

The larger audience enjoys a message which paints a rosy picture of the world and mankind, whereas the same message in a group of one or two people in a casual setting causes embarrassment or laughter. By the same token, the tough-minded recognition of basic desires which is appropriate to small groups of people sounds crude and disgusting in large assemblies.

One of the reasons we predict the continued importance of public speeches to large groups is that such speeches provide one of the few places in our culture where people expect and get fantasy themes peopled by heroes with high motives and where they are appealed to on the basis of their better nature. No matter how shoddy the community or how crude the general mode of conduct, people require some sense of worth and significance. The appeal to the better nature of the audience is a high form of flattery and is a source of pride and significance. Aside from the speech to a large audience, the only other major source of mass communication is television, and it does not provide many rosy depictions of life and of the community. The predominant style of the newscast and the television documentary, with few exceptions, is the style of the inside dopester (a person who has all the inside information).[8] Television newsmen tend to cut all public figures down to size and point out that important people are not larger than life, but ordinary people just like the rest of us, maybe even a little worse in some regards. The general tone of the story presented on television is factual and is tinged with skepticism about high motivations; the reporters appear to be continually searching for shoddy or unethical behavior. Saints are not dramatic; sinners, on the other hand, make good news copy.

[8] For an analysis of the "inside dopester" vision of the television news reporters see Ernest G. Bormann, "The Eagleton Affair: A Fantasy Theme Analysis," *The Quarterly Journal of Speech*, 59 (1973), 143–159.

The Persuasive Speech

The participants in one common communication transaction in the public-speaking communication style come with the general expectation that the speaker will deliver a persuasive message: The audience expects a persuasive message when a speaker known to take a definite stand is scheduled to talk on a controversial subject. Our discussion of the persuasive speech will concentrate on the stylistic features of the message.

The persuasive speech tends to influence the listener's choices and to narrow audience response to the one the speaker prefers. Notice that the speaker designs the persuasive speech to arouse a specific response or change of attitude from the listener. The good communicator must be audience-centered; when you are preparing a persuasive speech, the importance of studying the specific audience for your speech and of learning its hopes, dreams, hobbies, interests, loves, and hates cannot be overemphasized.

PERSUASION AND MOTIVATION

The concept of motive, properly defined, can be used not only as a tool to criticize persuasive speaking but also to help the person preparing a speech. Our concern here is with motive as what, in fact, drives members of the audience to act the way they do. Many people talk of motivating other people. When a salesman says he must motivate the customer to buy the product and a teacher says he must motivate the student to study for a test, they seem to be saying that they can install within the customer or the student a motor which will impel the customer to buy and the student to study. We must realize that whatever basic motives the listeners possess are in them already, and as persuasive speakers, we have to adapt to the motives present in the audience. We cannot install motives in people, because motives develop in a complex way, usually over a period of time. A person's motives are influenced by his heredity, his upbringing, and the people after whom he has decided to model himself.

A person may develop further wants, motives, and goals while caught up in a chaining fantasy in a meeting or in a series of deep conversations with another person; but when a person goes to hear a persuasive speech, his motive structure is largely formed. The speaker has little hope of changing that structure. When we manage to persuade a member of an audience, we do so largely by attaching our suggestions to the motives he already has. Only by hooking into previously held motives can we make individuals in an audience want to do or believe what we are trying to persuade them to do or believe.

People tend to do what they want, even though, upon careful study of the facts, what they want at the moment may not always be the best thing in the long run. A good automobile salesman tries to make the customer *want* his car first; then he suggests logical reasons why the person should buy it. The salesman often suggests, "Why don't you get in and drive it around awhile?" He hopes that when the customer gets behind the wheel and drives the car, he will come to want to have the car for his own. The persuasive speaker should carefully evaluate the wants of his audience and then present his ideas in such a way that he makes the audience *want* to do what he suggests.

DEALING WITH AUDIENCE HABITS

We all perform much of our daily routine out of habit, those learned behavior patterns that are repeated so often they become almost involuntary. When you first started senior high school, or later, college, your old habits and patterns were torn up; you had to develop new ones. Usually such periods of our lives are troublesome for us. We do not know where to go next, what to do. We often feel homesick for the good old days, or really for the good old ways. When you analyze the audience for your persuasive speech, remember that if you can show that by following your advice the members of the audience can continue in the same comfortable ways, they will often choose your suggestion. On the other hand, if you want to change things, you will have to shake up your listeners and make them believe that their present habits cause serious trouble and that they must change their ways. If a person is in the habit of smoking cigarettes, then before you can persuade him to change his habit, you have to prove to him that he may be in for serious trouble if he does not stop smoking. You must remember that your persuasive message may "cost" the listener a comfortable habit; you have to be ready to meet the challenge of his resistance to change.

THE TWO TYPES OF PERSUASIVE SPEECHES

Persuasive speeches arise in two main situations. First, a number of people have grown increasingly restless with the way something is being done. They are unsatisfied with some basic part of their lives. These people begin to think up new and, to them, better ways to do something about it. They are now ready to attempt to persuade other people to support their drive for a change. Once a substantial number of people begin to argue and persuade the community to change things, the second situation arises: Another group becomes disturbed because it feels the present situation is satisfactory, and fears the proponents of change will succeed. This group begins to take steps to persuade the community to reject the proposals for new programs. Persuasive speeches are given either (1) to get the audience to work for, vote for, or in some way help adopt a new law, program, or way of doing things, or (2) to get the audience to work against, vote against, or in some way prevent the adoption of a new law, program, or way of doing things.

The Speech for Change

If you are disturbed or upset by the way things are going and wish to advocate change, you should develop a speech outline that has three main parts. The first point in a persuasive speech for change is "Things are a mess." Take the topic of the rate of inflation. Someone who wishes to change it should begin with the point, "The present rate of inflation is a mess," and then use the basic building blocks of communication (a point to be proved and the evidence, examples, statistics, and testimony of experts that support the point) to build his case against the draft. The second point in a persuasive speech for change is "Here is my program to solve the problem." In developing this point, the speaker for change explains his recommendations. He describes his recommended changes and urges the audience to take some positive action to help get the changes made. He may say, "My program for solving this mess is to lower interest rates and balance the federal budget. You can help in this regard by signing the petition I have here in my hand." The third point in a persuasive speech for change is "If you do as I say, here is what is in it for you." The speaker then describes in graphic detail the benefits that will accrue if the listeners follow his advice and support his proposal.

Persuasive Speech to Change Things
I. Things are a mess.
    A. Point to be proved
       (statistics, testimony, examples)
    B. Point to be proved
       (statistics, testimony, examples)

II. Here is my program to solve the problem.
   A. Point to be made clear
      (examples, analogies, narrations)
   B. Point to be made clear
      (examples, analogies, narrations)
III. Here is what is in it *for you* if you adopt my program.

Of course, you will not find many occasions when the exact phrases "Things are a mess" and "Here is my program to solve the problem" can be used in your speech. You will need to phrase the points differently for each specific occasion.

The proof of the case tends to come in the first point, where the speaker describes the present conditions and explains the nature of the problem. The persuasive impact tends to come in the third point, where the speaker describes how the wants of the audience will be satisfied by the new program. Here, in shorthand form, is a quick, persuasive speech:

> *Your present car is a mess. The paint is scratched, the tires are shot, the motor needs overhauling. The repairs will soon cost more than new-car payments, and in the meantime you can't count on your transportation. Here's my program for you. Let me put you into this neat little Rattlesnake four-cylinder convertible. You not only get dependable transportation, but you get a whole new outlook on life. The girls who won't date you now will begin to flock around you. You'll get a new sense of zest for life as you tool down the freeway in this sweet little sports car.*

The Speech Against Change

The speaker who wishes to persuade an audience *not* to adopt a new proposal has several different options in planning his speech. Essentially, the basic outline consists of three points that take issue with the three main points of the speech advocating the change. Thus the first point is "Things are going along just fine"; the second point is "The proposal would not work"; and the third point is "The proposal would make things a lot rougher on you." The speaker need not use all three points, however. For some arguments, he may select only one and argue simply that things are just fine and submit two or three major reasons for believing change is unnecessary. He may pick several points and argue, for example, that there is no need for a proposal as drastic as the one under consideration, and even if there were a need, this plan would not help matters any.

Let us see how the entire outline works:

Persuasive Speech Against Changing Things

I. Things are going along just fine.
   A. Point to be proved (evidence)
   B. Point to be proved (evidence)
II. The proposal would not work.
   A. Point to be proved (evidence)
   B. Point to be proved (evidence)
III. The proposal would make things a lot rougher on you.
   A. Point to be proved (evidence)
   B. Point to be proved (evidence)

The persuasive part of the speech against a proposal can come in the first point, if the speaker describes the desirable aspects of the way things are and makes the audience appreciate and want to keep the good things they have. Of course, the speaker can also be persuasive in the third point, by presenting the dangers in vivid and graphic terms, so that the audience is repelled by the results of the new plan as the opponent presents them.

The Lecture

Another common transaction in the public-speaking style of the United States is one in which a speaker has important information or know-how to give to an audience. The audience comes to learn from the expert. The speech form expected under the above circumstances is the *lecture* (sometimes referred to as a *speech to inform.*)

In our culture, we expect a lecture to be an objective and many-sided view of the material. The lecturer does not intend to narrow the choices of the listener, but rather aims to open up new horizons and give the listeners new perspectives for viewing the topic. Of course, few of the real-life lectures we attend are just what we expect them to be. Every lecturer has some biases, and often is not as objective as the model suggests. Still, though we tolerate some departure from the ideal cultural norm, if a speaker advertised as a lecturer gives, instead, a powerful persuasive pitch for a pet legal project, we are disturbed by this violation of a cultural norm.

The material in Chapter 9 on how to inform illustrates the

general tone and expectations about content that people in the United States have for a lecture. The lecturer is supposed to encourage feedback and strive to achieve understanding by answering questions in a complete and open way. We expect the lecturer's language to be a clear and careful reporting of denotative meanings and descriptions of factual information. While we anticipate that the persuasive speaker will select language to slant the speech in favor of his bias, we expect the lecturer to use language in a way that represents various positions and arguments fairly; his tone is "These are the facts, and these are the various ways people look at the subject, and you can draw your own conclusions after I have given you all the information."

The Presentation

The presentation is a speech form that has emerged within the public-speaking communication style in the last few decades to meet the needs of our highly developed urban culture. Most of us now work in organizations, institutions, or corporations. Representatives from various groups within the company, the church, the governmental agency, or the school

multimedia communication *A communication event which employs a number of media channels simultaneously or in sequence.*

need to give and get information in formal communication settings officially approved by the organization involved. Because these official speeches are so important, the people preparing them have called upon the latest communication technology to aid in their preparation. Recent developments in film, audiotape recording, television or videotape, photography, and graphic arts, stimulated by the use of commercial advertising on television, are used in preparing a presentation. Music and sound effects may be employed. The result is that the presentation is essentially a multimedia communication. The speaker uses every trick in the book and even tries to invent new gimmicks to make his message effective and persuasive.

Supervisors or employees with the power to do so usually authorize a given presentation, assign the people to work on it, and decide who will actually give it. The person who gives the presentation is often not a professional speaker, because the organizational position and status of the message source are important parts of the presentation. Thus, even though the vice-president in charge of personnel is not a particularly able speaker, he may have to give a presentation because the content of the message is such that someone in a position of authority in personnel has to deliver the speech. All of us who come to work in business and industry, in governmental, educational, or religious institutions, may well expect to deliver presentations at certain key times in our careers.

How you give a presentation on the job can be crucial; when you present yourself and your ideas about your particular specialty to your peers and your superiors, they will make judgments about your skill, understanding, and competence on the job. Also, many of the highest-level decisions are influenced by presentations. Lower-management people often work up proposals and make a presentation of their recommendations to the higher level people within the organization, who make a final decision.

Sometimes presentations are given repeatedly, especially for purposes of public relations. A company representative might give a presentation to visitors touring a plant. Another representative might go out to groups and schools in the community and give a presentation about the organization. The most common situation, however, and the more critical or important occasion, is the instance in which a presentation is prepared with a definite persuasive purpose, with a specific audience in mind. The audience for a presentation may be one or two people only, as is the case when a salesman for combination doors and windows gives an elaborate presentation in a customer's living room, complete with models of various windows, a series of brochures, slides of installations, and a demonstration of the way the various models of the windows work. More usually, of course, presentations are given to groups of people ranging in size from five to twenty, or even, occasionally, hundreds.

Presentations are the most carefully prepared, rehearsed, and tested messages given by members of organizations. Quite often, the organization's top management and best specialists review a presentation before it is given. The dry-run rehearsal is the rule rather than the exception in presentational speaking.

AIDS IN MAKING PRESENTATIONS: AUDIENCE PARTICIPATION

One effective way to make a presentation is to have the audience directly experience the material in the message. In order to do this, the speaker could take the audience on a field trip, or he or she could bring an illustrative event to the audience. Suppose a person is making a presentation about the teaching of reading to children in an inner-city school. He might take the audience to the school and have them observe the teaching as it is going on. He could, on the other hand, have a teacher and some pupils from the school come before the audience to demonstrate the teaching there.

Another way to make the audience participate in the presentation is to allow it to take part in a simulation or model of a process being discussed. For example, members of the audience might go to a planetarium and see, projected overhead, a simulation of the heavens, or they might operate an automobile simulator while the speaker adds verbal information about highway safety.

THE DEMONSTRATION

A number of multimedia aids are useful even though they do not furnish the audience with the active participation that often yields the highest interest and understanding; there is the *demonstration*, which allows the audience to be present while the speaker participates, as when a speaker mixes and bakes a cake while talking about the merits of a new cake mix and rapid-baking oven.

THE EXHIBIT

Exhibits are displays which resemble a demonstration without as much direct intervention from the speaker. The presentation associated with an exhibit usually involves the speaker's taking the audience on a guided tour of the exhibit. The speaker may pause at certain stations along the tour and demonstrate, for example, a process or recreate a historical event. Exhibits may consist of an almost unlimited variety of materials, including posters, models, mock-ups, objects, chalkboards, recorded sounds, videotape playbacks, and still or motion pictures.

VIDEO AND AUDIOTAPE

Closed-circuit television and audiotape-recording equipment are extremely useful aids to the presentation. The speaker can produce one reel of videotape, for instance, which has on it photographs, diagrams, graphs, charts, filmstrips, slides, clips from motion pictures, models, mock-ups, scenes recorded on location, posters, cartoons, interviews, excerpts from speeches, and his own narration or comments. The speaker may also give his presentation and incorporate segments of videotape as he proceeds. A speaker may use audiotape in much the same way, to supplement a demonstration or exhibit or to illustrate a point in a presentation.

FILM

Motion pictures provide excellent aids for a presentational speaker, but at a considerably greater expense than videotape. A person making a presentation may be able to find segments of commercially prepared film which are suitable for incorporation in his speech. The expense of shooting and editing film for a given presentation is so high that only extremely important presentations use specially prepared film segments.

OTHER VISUAL AIDS

Still pictures, graphs, charts, line drawings, and cartoons are dependable and useful techniques for communicating messages. Carefully developed and integrated into a well-prepared presentation, these aids are often used in our modern organizations.

Speakers continue to use the old reliable aids to presentation, such as the chalkboard (blackboard), which anyone studying presentational speaking should learn to use well. Large cards with information on them can be placed on an easel beside a speaker so that all members of the audience can read whatever diagrams, charts, illustrations, or photographs the speaker wishes to use. A flip chart is a good aid in giving presentations; this consists of a pad of newsprint-sized paper, mounted on an easel and designed to be flipped back and forth to show various charts or diagrams as needed. The speaker can have blank flip cards on which he writes visual aids with a heavy marking pen as he gives his verbal message.

The flannel board is a large board covered with fabric; the speaker can prepare display items backed with the same material so they will stick to the cloth on the board. The speaker can place illustrations, figures, and so forth, on the board as he speaks.

Speakers often supplement their presentations by using slides or film strips projected on a screen. Still pictures may show people, events, fossils, geologic features of the earth—whatever would be useful. Graphs, charts, diagrams, maps, and other graphics are easy to see when projected on a screen with a slide projector, and slides are easy to store and carry. One of the most useful devices is the overhead projector which throws an image of whatever is drawn on a transparent surface upon a screen in front of the audience. The speaker can prepare drawings and diagrams on the transparencies in advance, or he can write upon a transparent sheet while he speaks, much as he would use a pad of paper, and the writing will be projected onto a screen in front of the audience.

THE PRESENTATION IN THE FUTURE

More and more evidence is accumulating that the presentation is the public speech of the future in our culture. The brief persuasive commercial messages on television have become a popular art form and the style-setting edge of communication in our society. Children who start watching television at an early age are often so intrigued by the commercials that some of their first words and songs are those they learn from television advertising. As a spin-off from the large investment of money and talent in television commercials, we now have a well-developed multimedia technology of persuasive and effective communication. More and more organizations are drawing upon the multimedia knowledge for aid in the development of important presentations. The implications of the presentational techniques developed in business for the whole field of education are enormous. The truly gifted lecturer is probably as rare and difficult to find as a gifted golfer or chef, but with the wealth of presentational aids available many more people can give highly effective messages which will both instruct and impress listeners.

Speeches About People

Persuasion is often concerned with the human personality. People are interested in personalities. We come under the spell of striking and dramatic people, and we grow to love or hate individuals until they dominate our thoughts and dreams. Our chapters on persuasion will give detailed descriptions of the techniques of suggestion speakers can use to project an image of a person to an audience. On some occasions in our culture the audience expects that almost the entire speech will be devoted to biographic information, praising or blaming that individual's life and character.

THE EULOGY

The technical name for a speech devoted entirely to praise of a person is a *eulogy*. When someone dies, often a speaker gives a funeral eulogy describing the deceased's life and interpreting its meaning in a favorable way. Usually speeches about people present them in a favorable light. Sometimes, however, a speaker devotes an entire speech to damning a person, and the name for a speech that cuts down a person in this manner is a *dyslogy*. Few dyslogies are given in the United States, although in many political campaigns there is a large element of personal attack against the opposition by the partisans.

On some occasions people gather to hear a speech celebrating their history, heritage, culture, or community. Often the speech to build group cohesion consists largely of praising heroes and attacking villains. Certain key persons, such as the founders of an organization, club, fraternity, company, state, or nation, become the focus of attention, and the speaker praises these people for values the community wishes to celebrate and recall. The typical nineteenth-century Fourth of July address in the United States was such a speech form. The speaker would praise the "Founders of the Constitution," and the "Signers of the Declaration of Independence." Many Fourth of July orations included eulogies of George Washington.

Although relatively few people find themselves called on to give eulogies, many of us are called on to give short speeches in praise of a person; we refer to the duty that often falls to an officer of a club or organization, the job of introducing a featured speaker at a meeting. The speech of introduction is another culturally developed message form.

THE SPEECH OF INTRODUCTION

The audience expects a *speech of introduction* to be brief, but it also expects certain things to be taken care of in this speech. The listeners expect the introduction to tell them enough about the main speaker to enable them to evaluate his expertness and to make them more eager to hear his speech. Usually the audience expects the person giving the introductory remarks to say only favorable or complimentary things about the speaker. A good speech of introduction, however, should be more than a simple listing of accomplishments ("He has written fourteen articles and three books, holds eight degrees, and has won twelve honors and seven national awards"); it should recognize the uniqueness of the audience and occasion and humanize the speaker by revealing some part of his personality that warms the audience to the individual.

The good speech of introduction, in our culture, avoids too much praise of the speaker. Whereas in general an audience does not object to overstatement or flattery from the speaker himself, most audiences tend to become embarrassed when one person overdoes the praise of another person who is also on the speaker's platform. (The exception to this cultural norm is the political convention or rally. We expect and tolerate outrageous flattery in partisan political meetings. There are also ethnic groups in our culture that practice more public personal praise. In considering this matter if you are to make an introduction, you must rely on an analysis of your particular audience.) Experienced speakers live in fear of the inexperienced person who gives them a glowing introduction no one could live up to! More than one speaker has had to use some stock retort to acknowledge an overblown introduction without publicly embarrassing the person who gave it. One such retort we heard was, "Thank you for that great introduction. I was wondering where you heard all those things, and then I remembered my mother knew I was speaking here tonight."

If possible, the best procedure if you are making an introduction is to check with the speaker ahead of time to find out what material the speaker himself would particularly like to have included in the introduction. In this way the introduction can tie in with what the speaker plans to say and help set the tone the speaker plans to use. Moreover, once you meet the speaker, even briefly, you have a better idea of what remarks he will prefer and what remarks he might find embarrassing. If you have an introduction written out in advance, he can check it out for himself.

THE SPEECH OF WELCOME

At times in our culture a meeting or a conference has an opening session which features a speech of welcome to all the delegates. A *speech of welcome* is expected to deal with the person or organization sponsoring the meeting and giving the welcome (for example, "On behalf of the college . . ."), with the people receiving the welcome ("I am particularly pleased to talk with students dedicated to ending pollution"); or with the occasion ("We are most pleased to be the site for this vitally important workshop in changing attitudes toward the human environment"). Generally we expect the speech of welcome to praise the hosts, guests, and occasion. The speaker aims to make the guests feel that they are important and the event is significant. Like a speech of introduction, the welcoming speech should be brief.

Both the introduction and the welcoming speech serve a primarily ritualistic function. A ritual is a set way of doing something which has long been the habit of a group, an organization, or a culture. Both speaker and audience will be satisfied with a brief, routine comment. All of us, however, appreciate a touch of originality and artistry in our ritual speeches, and we appreciate a speech of welcome that both fulfills the needs of the occasion and goes on to do more. An assistant to the mayor of New Orleans managed this some years ago when he gave a welcoming speech on behalf of the city to the members of the national Speech Communication Association convention. The speaker was a black man who began in the expected way by praising New Orleans much in the style of a tourist advertisement. He praised the tourist attractions, the charm and history of the city. Then, with a quick transition, he caught the audience by surprise and began describing the seamy side of New Orleans. He talked about the poverty, racial injustice, and crime. Many audience members found themselves sitting forward in their chairs at this unexpected turn in his remarks. The speaker then concluded with an optimistic note that the citizens of New Orleans were working on all these problems, and that a new day would dawn. His skillful blend of the expected plus the unexpected aroused the admiration of the teachers of public speaking who heard him; he had definitely made a routine speech of welcome into a much more memorable, though brief, message.

THE SPEECH IN HONOR OF ACHIEVEMENT

A final sort of speech about persons is one of praise which is given when an individual wins an award or is honored for past achievements. Again, the speaker making the award or noting the occasion is primarily praising good motives, honorable actions, good character, and effective work.

Analyzing the Specific Audience

While the audiences of public speeches share many similarities, each audience is also unique in many important respects. A substantial portion of your planning time for any public speech should be given to an analysis of the specific audience and occasion. A good public speaker is not self-centered (not worried about personal looks, about how his voice sounds, about gestures, about how well he or she is impressing the listeners) or message-centered (not worried solely about polishing the message as an end in itself), but is *audience-centered*. The audience-centered speaker makes all his final planning decisions in terms of his analysis of the listeners. Indeed, the art of public speaking is largely the adaptation of ideas, world view, information, and arguments to a listener, to several listeners (a small group), or to many listeners (an audience.) The first question a skilled public speaker asks about a given audience is "How much alike are the audience members in terms of background, experience, interests, and attitudes?" If all the audience members resemble each other on important features related to the speaker, the topic of the speech, and the occasion, the problem for the speaker is clear and can be handled directly. If the audience members are greatly diverse, the problem becomes much more difficult, and the speaker may have to seek some broad and abstract common ground or some overriding goal that can in some way unite such a varied group.

A speaker may start by finding out the composition of the audience in terms of such obvious but often important qualities as age, sex, socioeconomic class, race, ethnic background, religion, and occupation.[9] Not all factors are always important. For many speeches, the audience's age may be irrelevant, but for other situations it may be crucial. We noted in Chapter 3 that dialects reflect social structure, and so a speaker planning to adapt language and grammar to his audi-

[9] For a detailed survey of research into audience characteristics and their relationship to credibility and persuasibility see Gary Cronkhite, *Persuasion and Behavioral Change*, Indianapolis: Bobbs-Merrill, 1969.

ence would need to know if the members were primarily from the working class in an inner city or from an upper-middle-class suburb, if they were predominately Mexican-American, or black, or Indian, or white. A speaker often adapts to an audience by selecting an appropriate example or analogy to clarify a point, and if the audience is composed of farmers and their families, he selects different examples than he would if the listeners are members of the American Medical Association.

More important, often, than the general information about age, sex, and social economic background, are the audience's attitudes and interests. A person planning a persuasive speech in behalf of more state-supported community colleges would like to know if the audience is generally in agreement that community colleges ought to be supported, or hostile to paying more taxes for community colleges, or interested but undecided, or apathetic to the whole question. He would benefit even further from knowing *how many* of the audience members hold attitudes toward his position that are friendly, hostile, undecided, or apathetic.

A speaker making a thorough analysis of his audience finds that specific details are vital; the general features of the audience provide only hints that help when making a more complete study. The speaker with the time and opportunity to study the audience and the occasion would do well to raise some more detailed questions, such as the following: What sort of person will these people more likely trust and believe? What can I say to get their confidence? What are the public dramas that excite and move these people? Who are the heroes of their group fantasies and public dreams? Who are their villains? What dramatic actions do they use to build a sense of community and purpose? What attitude do they take toward these lines of action? For example, if all the audience members participate in a public drama which casts the president of the United States in a heroic role, then the speaker who says that the president, whoever he is at the time, is a man of low morals, insincerity, and bad motives will find himself in trouble with that audience. On the other hand, if all the audience members participate in a common drama in which the president is cast as villain, a negative statement about him may draw a strong positive response from the listeners. If the audience members are strongly divided in terms of their political fantasies, so that some see the president as a sympathetic figure fighting villainous forces, and others see him as a dark and evil personality, the speaker may well decide not to mention the president at all!

Gathering Information About the Audience

Often the experienced speaker knows what sort of information about the audience would be useful to him, but does not have the resources to collect it. In those long-range and important campaigns of persuasion where the success or failure of a new product, the election of a candidate to major office, or the organization, recruitment, and administration of a social or political movement is at stake, the campaign planners generally have sufficient resources for elaborate formal surveys of their potential audiences.

THE MORE SOPHISTICATED TECHNIQUES

Experts in persuasion have brought scientific marketing and polling techniques to a high state of perfection and proved usefulness. Most public-relations firms, advertising agencies, professional fund-raising companies, and experts in political campaigning and revolutionary organization know how to sample the audience, administer attitude tests or questionnaires relating to opinion, and discover what a target audience thinks about a product or an issue or a particular personality. Some of the public-opinion polls publish their results in newspapers, and even speakers with little time or money can find out how various age groups with various educational backgrounds are currently responding to such general questions as How well do you think the president has been doing? When money is available, pressure groups often take their own polls to discover audience attitudes.

Sometimes the main themes of a persuasion campaign are pretested by showing samples of the persuasive material to people who indicate their reactions by pressing buttons on special monitoring machines or by answering questionnaires.

LESS COSTLY TECHNIQUES

We mention these elaborate and expensive techniques of audience analysis mostly to show how far the art has been developed beyond the mere collection of information about age, sex, and geographic origin. Most of us do not have the resources to use these sophisticated audience-survey techniques; yet we can often acquire useful information quickly and cheaply. While the following example is hypothetical and exaggerated, it contains elements that resemble the speech situations in which you might find yourself.

Professor Gilbert Johnson, our example, teaches at State University. He has been a lifelong student of the process of eutrophication (too much plant food in a lake causing a lush growth of water plants, which, in turn, decay in the late summer, sucking the oxygen out of the water). When ecology became an important issue in the 1960s and 1970s, Johnson suddenly found his specialty popular with the general public. He won several awards and then attracted national notice on a television program. Soon he found himself in great demand as a speaker around the country.

Unfortunately, Professor Johnson's previous speaking experience had been in lecturing to classes of students who were already to some degree interested in the subject and willing to listen to a detailed, solid presentation. He found his public audiences growing restless, coughing, even dozing off. Gradually, over a period of months, and with the help of a fellow faculty member knowledgeable in speech communication, Johnson discovered that his problem was one of audience adaptation. He began to change his approach and in a while was getting standing ovations and receiving more invitations to speak than he could comfortably accept. (And here the authors indulge in some fantasizing about the value of their field, their careers, and this book!)

Back to Professor Johnson. He has just accepted an invitation to give a speech entitled "Eutrophication and What We Can Do About It" for the Sandy Hill City Commercial Club's bimonthly luncheon. He immediately sends his secretary to the campus library. She brings back a pad of notes about Sandy Hill City and its surrounding county, Goodwin. The secretary has found that the main industry derives from the gravel pits and stone quarries south of town; a cement factory has the second most important town payroll. Sandy Hill City is one of the oldest settlements in the state and is the site of the Goodwin County Historical Society Museum, which contains, among other things, the personal effects of the town's most famous son, Brigadier General Allan Snyder, World War I ace of aces and leading proponent of the development of air power prior to World War II. Armed with this information and various devices he has learned about audience adaptation, Johnson begins his speech to the Commercial Club as follows:

"Eutrophication and What We Can Do About It." (He smiles.) I guess the first thing we can do about it is define it. (Audience chuckles.) I will define it in a minute, but first I'd like to share some of my thoughts with you as I was flying here over the lush farmlands of the central part of the state. I think far too often those of us living in cities forget the contribution the farmers

of counties like Goodwin and the thriving towns like Sandy Hill City make to our economy and our quality of life. The countryside was beautiful, fertile, tilled—productive. I could see this as we landed. And as we taxied up to the Goodwin County airport terminal (which is, I was surprised to discover, a remarkably handsome facility, the newest in the five-county area I'm told), I was impressed by the thriving bustle at the airport. The growth and power of this nation is made up of the dozens of cities such as Sandy Hill City.

When my taxi drove north toward the downtown area from the airport, I was struck by the immense size of the Terrara gravel pits. I asked the driver to pull in so I could get out and look at them. Producing, as they do, 35 percent of the gravel and crushed rock used in this state, the Terrara gravel pits make a real contribution to the entire state's economy and progress and really put Sandy Hill City on the map.

When we started driving toward town again, we had no sooner gotten under way than we came upon the imposing buildings of the Snyder Cement Works, and I suddenly recalled the name of Allan Snyder, World War I flying ace and far-seeing statesman in the air force—a native son. I had a little time left before I was due at the hotel, so I asked the driver to take me by the Goodwin County Museum. . . .

In the real world, most audiences would consider this much overdone; still, it demonstrates that our professor could find out a great deal about his Commercial Club audience in a short period of time; he combed the public sources of information (libraries, newspapers, and the like), and he allowed some time in the area to talk to the natives themselves before he was to speak.

Often when we are asked to give a speech we can learn about the audience we will address simply by interviewing the person who contacts us to make the talk. This person will probably be able to tell us about the room or auditorium where we will speak, about who will attend, and what they will expect. As a person gains experience speaking to various sorts of audiences, he develops an awareness of what is expected from him in various speaking situations. A PTA meeting in a large urban school presents one kind of audience; a PTA meeting in a suburb presents another kind of audience—similar in many ways, different in others. The luncheon meeting of a businessmen's service club is a different audience than a social-business dinner of the same group.

Chapter 6

THE KEY IDEAS

Every culture needs to have the right spokesman say some formal words at important periods in the life of the family, institution, community, or nation.

In the United States all forms of public speaking are prized, cultivated, and practiced.

The public speech is a cultural event with clearly understood rules and customs in most societies.

If a speaker gets an audience response, he is stimulated to greater effort; this in turn further affects the audience, who also affect each other.

The larger the audience, the more it appreciates an elevated style of speaking and appeals to its higher motives.

Our best advice, therefore, is that you should remember that there are many sources of information about audiences and that you should collect as much information as you can. Further, you should give public speeches whenever and wherever you can if you want to develop skill in audience analysis and adaptation; by so doing you will gain a personal knowledge about varied audiences, how they respond to you, and how you adjust to control their response. If you have the chance to give a speech to your class, set aside enough time to study your classmates as members of an audience. If you focus on them as potential members of an audience, you will find that you know a lot about them simply from interaction with them as you go to and from the classroom, from class participation, and from discussions. Think of them as individuals in a real audience rather than as "just our speech communication class." Try to think through their response to you quite objectively, and plan and rehearse your speech keeping your specific audience in mind. Adapt your examples, analogies, evidence, and positive and negative suggestions to these people—these individuals collected at a particular time to hear you.

When giving a public speech you will often have to work

Public speeches fill our need for fantasy themes depicting heroes with high motives.

Television, with its emphasis on exposing shoddy and unethical behavior, is a poor medium for building community-sustaining myths.

The speaker should remember that people tend to do what they want at a given moment, even if the evidence indicates it will be bad for them in the long run.

The speaker who wishes to change an audience's habitual routine has the burden of proving that change is necessary.

In our culture we expect a lecturer to give us an objective, many-sided view of his topic.

A new speech form that has evolved to meet the needs of an urban culture is the multimedia presentation.

The speech of introduction is a special speech form in our culture.

Many speeches in praise of individuals serve a primarily ritualistic function.

An important question for a speaker is "How diverse is the audience in its attitudes toward my position?"

When preparing a public speech we often have and need less complete and less accurate information about our listeners than we do when we plan an interview or a committee meeting.

A public speaker can use broad strokes and get the desired response from a large audience.

with less complete and precise information about the listeners than you can have when you are speaking in an interview or small group situation. As a public speaker, you seldom get as much information from the audience about how well your messages are comprehended and how they are evaluated as you can get in less formal communication situations. At the same time, however, you do not need as much specific information from larger audiences, because the public speaker can use broader strokes and get the desired response with less carefully adjusted messages. A member of a large audience adjusts his listening to react to someone talking to *us* rather than just to *me*. He thus does not expect the same person-to-person adjustment he would demand if you were engaged in a conversation.

While we live in an age of electronic communication and a time in which intimate and informal conversation is prized and common, we also live in a culture which uses the formal public speech for many important occasions and purposes. Although the present age stresses the need for high-quality informal daily communication, the complete communicator also needs to know about audiences for public speeches and about how to adapt his ideas to them.

SUGGESTED PROJECTS

1 Assume that a visiting speaker asks you to brief him about his probable audience. Analyze students at your school. Identify their heroes, villains, and dreams, as well as their general interests and attitudes.

2 Pick some city or town within 100 miles of your school and analyze its chamber of commerce as an audience for a speech to be made by a student, concerning student attitudes today towards business as a career. What sources would you use in informing yourself about this audience?

3 Select a topic for a persuasive message. Using the same topic, pick two different audiences and prepare two short messages adapted to each of the audiences. Explain your audience analysis in each instance, and explain your objectives in tailoring each of the messages as you do.

4 Select a topic of some complexity that will require careful explanation for the audience to understand. Develop a multimedia presentation, using a range of visual and audio aids to help you clarify your ideas for your audience.

5 During one of the rounds of speeches or presentations suggested above, your instructor will assign you the task of giving a brief introduction to a classmate's speech.

6 Select a person, living or dead, whom you admire or dislike and prepare a five-minute speech either praising or attacking that person.

SUGGESTED READINGS

Clevenger, Theodore, Jr. *Audience Analysis*. Indianapolis: Bobbs-Merrill, 1966.

Cronkhite, Gary. *Persuasion and Behavioral Change*. Indianapolis: Bobbs-Merrill, 1969.

Dickens, Milton. *Speech: Dynamic Communication*, 2nd ed. New York: Harcourt Brace Jovanovich, 1963.

Eisenson, Jon, J. Jeffery Auer, and John V. Irwin. *The Psychology of Communication*. Englewood Cliffs, N.J.: Prentice-Hall, 1963.

Jeffrey, Robert C., and Owen Peterson. *Speech: A Text with Adapted Readings*, 2nd ed. New York: Harper & Row, 1975.

Chapter 7

HOW TO ORGANIZE A PUBLIC SPEECH

When one must organize a message, the artistic nature of communication becomes very apparent. A message must be organized according to the theory that underlies a particular style, and it must meet the criteria of the best practitioners of that style. Whereas a person may be beautifully articulate when talking to another person in a one-to-one relationship style of communicating, this same person will have to learn how to organize a public speech according to a different set of standards. Similarly, a person well schooled in message communication theory will have to use the standards of the public-speaking style when he wants to make a public speech. None of us is born knowing how to highlight main points, how to relate these main points to a central idea, how to lead the audience along from point to point by verbal and non-verbal transitions; all such organizational skills must be learned when any of us move into the public-speaking style of communication.

For persons listening to a message such as a lecture or public speech, the speaker must create a message within the norms and rules of one of the various transactional forms of public speaking that will fit the needs of the listeners involved. Over the years, experts have learned how audiences respond to oral messages and have evolved ways of organization that meet the various requirements of the context. Organization of an oral statement is not like the organization of a written statement on the same subject matter. An audience that has to listen to material cannot flick its eyes back over the material as it could if reading the same message. A reader may even take a pair of scissors and cut up an article or letter and paste it together in different order if it makes more sense to him another way. Listeners, on the other hand, must participate in a public speech as it unfolds, and if they try to recall something the speaker has said to see if it relates to something the speaker has just said earlier, they may miss something important that the speaker is saying right at that moment. As speakers have practiced communicating in such clearly defined circumstances, the public-speaking style has developed detailed rules about proper organization to guide speakers and critics.

Qualities of a Well-Organized Spoken Message

People who have not studied public speaking are likely to have only a vague notion of what constitutes "organized material" according to the ideal model of that communication style. If they can outline a message when they listen to it, or if a speaker presents a message in the form of an outline, they often assume that it is organized. Indeed,

many students keep their notebooks in outline format, and many business and professional people present their material in outline form; it *looks* organized. Unless a speaker is trained, however, his material usually is actually disorganized. All you have to do to outline is to list and number some points. You can list points with numbers and letters even though the ideas do not fit logically together. Sound organization in the public-*speaking* communication style requires more than listing, and using numbers and letters to label items on the list. A well-organized spoken message must have the qualities of unity, coherence, relevance, conciseness, and comprehensiveness.

UNITY

A good public speech has unity. A critic can tell if the speech is unified by looking for a central idea to which each part of the speech relates. Often a speaker helps unify the speech by stating and highlighting the central theme in a way which makes it stand out clearly for the listener. When this is done well, almost all of the listeners can later recall the speaker's main point. If the speaker does not state the central theme in so many words, the speech may still be unified if the subpoints are arranged and presented in such a way that the listener is led to figure out the main conclusion by inference.

A speaker further achieves unity by clearly and logically relating all major subpoints to the central theme and to one another. You can explain the relationship among ideas to your audience by telling them how you will arrange the main subpoints. "I will begin by . . . Next, I will . . . And, finally, I will . . ." "First I will discuss . . . Second, I will deal with . . . Third, I will . . ." "I want to examine two main questions with you this evening. The first question is . . . The second question is . . ." You can also indicate when you have completed your comments on one point and are moving on to a new part of your speech. "So in summary, my answer to the first question is . . . , but remember that I said the answer to the first question is not enough. We must also answer the question . . ." Finally, you can indicate relationships among points by summarizing what you have said and pointing out to your listeners what you have so far accomplished in terms of your overall plan. "We have now seen that, first, . . . and second, . . . With this evidence I have proved what the lawyers call a prima facie case, that is, a case that, unless answered, gives you enough evidence to render a verdict of 'yes.' But I promised you more than a prima facie case. Let's look now at the most important evidence. . . ."

The speaker who makes comments such as the above helps the listeners see the overall structure of the speech and understand how the details fit together into a meaningful "big picture." The next time you watch a television drama, notice how the director arranges the shots. He will often begin with an establishing shot, that is, a picture of the larger scene, so you can understand how the actors are arranged and how they fit into the larger context. He may then cut to a closer shot of several actors, and cut again to a close-up picture of one actor's face as the scene builds to a dramatic climax. At a transition point, he will often use another longer shot to once again establish context before moving the camera to more detailed close-ups. Such "big picture" establishing shots are useful for the speaker as well as the television director. You must verbally and nonverbally unify your speech for your listeners throughout.

COHERENCE

A well-organized public speech is coherent. Coherence refers to the way the parts of the speech cluster or hang together. Each part of a good speech relates to every other part in a way which reveals some clear design. A coherent speech is like a jigsaw puzzle of a picture of, say, a horse; when it is properly put together, the resulting picture is unmistakably a horse. A speech which lacks coherence is like the puzzle when it is only partially put together, with a portion of the head completed but much still missing, and with other parts spread over the table in jumbled fashion.

When sections of a speech are brief, just the fact that one comment comes on the heels of another may be enough to indicate that it is closely related to the first idea. When the parts of the speech are longer, the speaker may use pauses or vocal inflections (paralanguage cues) and gestures and facial expressions (kinesic markers) to show the connection among divisions of the speech. With very large sections, the speaker ought to provide verbal as well as nonverbal transitions, to indicate such things as how the last third of the speech relates to the first third. Remember that the audience receives only those pieces of the puzzle that you give them, and that you must supply all the pieces and relate each to the whole if you want the audience to get the total idea in all its richness.

RELEVANCE

A well-organized public speech contains main points with supporting information and evidence that clearly and directly relate to the central theme. The speaker who feels that something which is not obviously related to the central idea is nonetheless important and relevant, should explain his reasoning to the audience. Speakers who organize a public speech poorly often include much material that is not related to the topic under discussion. When you are first preparing a message you may "free associate" ideas and list them just as they come to mind. You may daydream along so that one idea follows another, one image triggers another, one story causes you to think of another, one experience reminds you of another. You may be tempted to include these materials in your speech plan because they interest you at the moment. If you were part of a group in the relationship communication style, others in the group might evaluate your comments as "great," even though their organization is in a stream-of-consciousness style, if they judge them all to be honest expressions of your feelings. In the public-speaking style, however, rambling and disjointed speeches are undesirable. Everything you say should have clearly understood relevance to your central theme.

CONCISENESS

A well-organized speech is concise in the sense that it does not contain a high proportion of repetitiveness. The speaker deals with each point in a good speech in enough detail for the purposes of the situation and occasion and then does not deal with it again except for emphasis in summaries, transitions, and conclusions. A common fault in the organization of a public speech is for a speaker to deal with a topic, drop it, take up another topic, perhaps a third, and then return to the first point again. The beginner in the public-speaking communication style is learning good technique when he or she can cut a poorly organized message into parts and paste it together again so that all statements about a point are put together and unnecessary repetitions are eliminated. Keeping your speech concise for the listener helps the listener come away with your ideas intact, as you hoped to present them.

COMPREHENSIVENESS

A well-organized public speech is comprehensive in the sense that it deals with the leading topics relating to its central theme. Of course the speech's comprehensiveness must be evaluated in relation to the audience, the occasion, and the amount of time that the speaker has to discuss the central idea. A skillful speaker will restrict the scope of the speech so that the topic can be dealt with in sufficient detail in the time available. A less skilled person often works out a central theme that is vague or too broad; he must then deal with the topics in abstract fashion or leave out so many important ideas that the speech, as heard, is sketchy and lacking in completeness. The public speaker who covers the stated topic as thoroughly as the context warrants, has produced a speech with sufficient comprehensiveness.

Preparing the Speech

A speech that is unified, coherent, relevant, concise, and comprehensive tends to result from a three-step process of preparation. The first step of speech preparation is the creative analysis of the topic; the second is the audience-adaptation step; the third is the step of crafting the individual parts and fitting them and shaping them to create the speech. If someone wanted to develop a new car for a particular category of auto racing, the designer might go through a similar three-part process by first creatively solving the basic design

problems; then adapting the design to the specific rules and requirements as to weight, engine power, and so forth for a given category of racing car; and finally, actually building of the car.

ANALYZING THE TOPIC

A creative analysis is important to understand a topic. Once a speaker has decided upon a general topic for a speech (or once the people arranging the occasion have given the speaker a general topic) the next step is to assemble all of the information possible within the time available. At this point your ability to use the library, to interview for information, to assemble and remember all of the information that you know from personal experience becomes important. We will not give a detailed set of directions on how to use the library in this book. Excellent books devoted to library use and research are readily available in your own library. If you want to learn to use your library more effectively see if a reference librarian will give you a short tour and explain the main reference tools available to you. You will find the skill of using a library effectively important not only for your career as a student but for the rest of your life. A course in speech communication, particularly one which includes the study of the public-speaking style, provides a good stimulus and context for you to learn the very important skills of collecting and recording information for further use in writing and speaking. One expert in the use of the library boasted that, given a first-class library and two weeks' time, he could become the second-best authority on any topic in the world. Such claims are probably, like the expert, legendary, but there is a good point to the story. An important part of anyone's education involves learning how to gather information quickly and efficiently.

Once you have an assignment to deliver a speech and have selected (or have been given) a general topic, you should assemble all the information you can and begin to analyze it. *Analysis* is the process of dividing the information into parts, examining the parts, and discovering the important questions that relate to understanding the subject. Some of your thinking ought to be systematic and disciplined, and some ought to be freewheeling and creative. You start by being systematic. Collecting and reading the basic information sets the stage for the more creative analysis later.[1]

[1] Our analysis of creativity is indebted to that of Graham Wallas. See his *The Art of Thought,* New York: Harcourt Brace Jovanovich, 1926; see also Ernest G. Bormann, *Theory and Research in the Communicative Arts,* New York: Holt, Rinehart & Winston, 1965, Chapter 7, "Creativity," pp. 123–144.

Preparation

As you begin the creative "mulling over" of the information you will undoubtedly make false starts and run into dead ends. You may find the topic confusing and be unable to see a pattern in all the information you have collected. You are in the first stage of the creative process, the *preparation phase*, which is a warm-up period in which you systematically try to make sense out of the material you have available for the speech. Often you seem to be wasting time, getting nowhere. Do not be discouraged by your seeming lack of progress. You must immerse yourself in the material before you can make a sound analysis of it. Often a person becomes frustrated in the preparation stage and stops working on the analysis. If the person has really worked for a sufficient period of time, however, putting the topic aside may be exactly what he should do for a while. The key to the successful ongoing creative process is doing each step sufficiently so that the next step can take place. You must prepare thoroughly, gather everything you can find; try to organize it systematically in as many ways as you can. Then, if you have really filled your mind with the material, you are ready for the second stage to happen.

Incubation

As you can consciously put the topic of the speech out of your mind for a while and work at other tasks (preferably manual work!), the second phase of the creative process, the *incubation period*, should begin. In the incubation period, although you are not apparently working on your speech, your subconscious is mulling it over. Many people are aware of this process when they suddenly see the solution to a personal problem, such as a difficult decision, right in the middle of doing something completely unrelated to the problem itself. But not everyone is aware that this is a natural, creative sequence and that *we can make it happen;* and that the more often we work at it, the more easily it becomes a source of problem solving. In terms of organizing a speech, while you are doing some routine job such as washing dishes, mowing the lawn, or driving the car, you may suddenly find yourself thinking about the speech in a stream-of-consciousness way. Maybe you hear yourself giving parts of the speech. The words sound "right" in your mind. You are not purposely trying to work on the speech, but it just seems to happen as your ideas associate freely, and you combine ideas, seeing yourself give the speech maybe, image following image. At first these ideas and images bubble up to your consciousness in bits and pieces.

Illumination

This bubbling up of ideas signals the beginning of the third part of the creative process, which usually comes after a period of incubation and is a most exciting part of any creative job. When you are thinking of something else, suddenly and unexpectedly you may clearly see the important ideas relating to the topic of your speech and how they fit together. Inspiration seems to strike and you suddenly know what your central theme for the speech will be, and you see how you can best approach it. The answers seem so right and good that you become excited and enthusiastic about the project. The third part of the creative process is this moment of *illumination*.

Verification

The final part of the creative analysis comes after the illumination phase and consists of the careful and conscious checking out of the details of the solution. Sometimes, upon reflection, the moment of illumination will turn out to have been a "flash in the pan"—when you check out the answer for consistency and plausibility, you discover it is not such a good idea after all. Often, however, the moment of illumination turns out to present a good solution to the problem, and your final task then is to verify, check, shape, and fill in minor details. This final part of the creative process of analysis is called the *verification phase*.

Disciplining Creativity

The creative process often seems groping and unstructured. Yet there is a method to the creative madness; it is not completely random, nor is it the same as arriving at an answer by trial and error. Creativity requires disciplined work habits. The person who waits for inspiration to strike before beginning to prepare a speech is seldom lucky enough to be struck by the divine lightning. Professional writers who must continually stimulate their creativity to meet deadlines often suggest that the best way to learn to write is *to write*. Successful creative people repeat the slogan endlessly that creativity is 10 percent inspiration and 90 percent perspiration. This advice and the slogan about creativity may seem to be simpleminded, if not question-begging, but they contain the important idea that disciplined work habits are essential to the use of creative talent. Good public speakers also advise that the best way to learn the art is by disciplined practice. One popular slogan that catches the spirit is "If anybody is foolish enough to ask you to give a public speech, be foolish enough to accept."

The more creative you are, of course, the more difficulty you will have getting started on a creative task. Talent acts as though it were lazy, and your creativity will think up all sorts of good excuses for not getting to work. You sit down with a blank piece of paper to begin organizing a speech, and suddenly you remember that you need a glass of water. Having gotten the water, you sit down once more and realize that your typewriter needs a new ribbon. Once the new ribbon is in, you realize it is twelve o'clock and time for lunch. Finally you do get down to work, but as you strike the first key and start the first sentence, you remember that you really ought to go to the library and look up some more information before you proceed. All too often, the beginning public speaker puts off the analysis of the topic until the very last minute and in the rush to meet the deadline the creative process never really has time to get under way. Undoubtedly most of you found some of the above "creative" excuses very familiar. On the other hand, if someone asks you how "creative" you are, you may not rate yourself too highly. Most people are more creative than they realize; they have simply never learned to use their creative energy in any controlled and accountable way.

You can discipline your creativity by developing systematic work habits. Set aside certain times during the week to do creative work such as writing papers and preparing speeches. Make it an iron rule to spend that time doing your projects. If possible, pick the same desk, work table, or corner of the library for your preparation and writing. Gradually you will discover that the familiar surroundings and the habit of regular work sessions will make the warm-up period less painful, often shorter. You must be faithful to your schedule, however; you must push ahead even when you feel little inspiration and the work is not going well.

Often, with a little planning you can allow enough time for your analysis to go through all four stages of the creative process. You cannot make a creative analysis all at once in a period of several hours or by cramming it into an all-night session as you might prepare for a final examination. Begin your preparation early and allow time for the incubation period. Set aside some time each day for contemplation. If you can do some routine activity such as walking, running, jogging, sweeping the floor, mowing a lawn, or gardening, the incubation process will be encouraged. Be careful about reading, though; reading occupies your mind too much and keeps it from moving into the free association of ideas and images that is useful for incubation.

When you are in the creative phase of analysis you need the proper mental set. Welcome farfetched ideas and elaborate on them. Imagine as many solutions as you can for a given problem. Modify, change, combine the ones you read about. Play with the ideas, and do not worry too much about how stupid or crazy they may seem at first glance.

Once the creative process discovers the basic issues in a body of discourse, you can find a suitable central idea for your speech by answering one or more of the basic questions to your satisfaction. Next, you need to find the most important subpoints that fit under your central theme and the logical relationships that hold among them. When the process of analysis reaches its conclusion you should have a logical arrangement of reasons in support of your idea, something like a lawyer's brief, which lays out the basic points in a case in a tightly ordered and reasoned fashion.

THE AUDIENCE-ADAPTATION STEP

After you have made a creative analysis of your topic you should have a thorough understanding of the material. You will have done your "homework" and will have a firm grasp of the ins and outs of the question. You will not yet be ready to speak to a specific audience, however.

Too often, people untrained in the public-speaking style but very knowledgeable and authoritative in a given profession or field, will be called on to give lectures; they do a poor job, because they present their logical analysis of the topic, period—no matter what the audience and the occasion. They act as though there is an ideal lecture on their topic which has universal appeal to all audiences and they need only find that lecture.

Another problem is that untrained public speakers often want to present everything that led to their own understanding of the question, and since they do not know where to begin in cutting down the information, they find time limits frustrating. "You just can't do justice to this topic in one hour," they may say.

The public-speaking style requires that the speaker take the results of an analysis of a topic and skillfully adapt it to a specific audience and occasion. For the study of public speaking, therefore, the second phase of analysis is of utmost importance. In the second stage, you turn your attention to analyzing the audience according to the recommendations in Chapter 6, and you plan how best to arrange the material for the needs of your particular audience.

THE SPEECH CONSTRUCTION STEP

The speaker constructing a message for an audience has to do three main things in order to organize his speech for maximum effect: He must *select* the material to include, he must *arrange* the items in some order, and he must *proportion* the items by deciding how much time to give to each point.

Although the speech construction step involves many concrete problems relating to the details of the nuts-and-bolts aspects of fitting a speech together, a speaker still profits from applying our advice about creativity to these matters. Even though you have a general theme for a speech and have analyzed it you will need to develop a clearly worded central idea for each specific occasion. The central idea for a persuasive speech should be worded as a positive suggestion: "Buy this Bearcat now!" "Picket City Hall tomorrow!" The central idea for a lecture or an informational presentation should be a simple declarative sentence. A central idea for a lecture might be: "I will explain a good basic model of message communication."

Vaguely worded central ideas such as, "I will tell you something about message communication," are poor guides to use in organizing a speech. Complex sentences which contain several ideas, such as "I will explain a basic model of the message communication style and discuss the nature of communication theory," are likewise troublesome, because they require a speaker to keep *two* main ideas before the audience.

Once the speaker has picked a specific and clear central idea for his speech, he can select material which is appropriate for his audience and which fits logically under his central idea.

The next task in organizing a speech is to arrange the material in some order. In the case of the persuasive message, we have already provided the basic outlines for speeches in favor of and against a new program. If a speaker is preparing a lecture, he might arrange his ideas around a logical progression of main ideas growing out of the information. For instance, a person lecturing on the process of communication might use three points: (1) the nature of the process, (2) the parts of the communication process, and (3) how the parts function together.

Speakers often arrange the points in a lecture in a time

sequence, according to spatial relationships (that is, where things are located in relation to one another), or according to complexity (starting with simple concepts and ending with the more complex ideas). The time order is a good one for explaining a process in terms of what happens first in time, what second, and so on. Lecturers talking about history often use a time sequence. The space order is useful for subjects such as architecture or geography. Lectures in mathematics or the natural sciences often move from the simple concepts to the more complex applications. A speaker needs to think through his material and decide which kind of arrangement would best suit it, as well as his audience. As a rule, he should stick to the one kind of arrangement only. Later in the chapter we will discuss three important patterns of arrangement in greater detail.

Deciding how much time to give to each point is a matter of judgment, depending on the total amount of time allotted to the speech and on the audience's attitude and knowledge. The speaker has to think carefully about his arguments, deciding which is the most important, what material is familiar to the audience, and what is unfamiliar and must be more fully developed.

A good speech has a beginning, a middle, and an end. The beginning is called an *introduction*, the middle is called the *body* of the speech, and the end is called the *conclusion*.

A good introduction catches the audience's attention, arouses and holds its interest, and lets it know what the speech is to be about. Because a speech is different from a theme or essay in that the speaker is talking directly to people sitting in front of him, he must spend some time at the beginning of his remarks just getting everybody's attention. The listeners need a chance to size up the speaker as a person, to get acquainted with him.

The body of the speech contains the main points that make up the message proper. If, instead of speaking, you were writing an article about the same material, the bulk of the article would be similar to the information contained in the body of a speech.

The conclusion of a speech is a brief comment that rounds off the message and gives the audience a feeling that you have finished. A conclusion tends to be a summary of the main ideas in a speech, an appeal for action or reaction, or a summary plus an appeal.

When a speaker constructs a good unified speech from the basic building blocks of communication (a point to be proved plus its supporting material), he not only needs to arrange the blocks into a satisfying structure, but he must provide some connecting links among them. Thus the final important skill in organizing a speech is the ability to provide transitions. *Transitions* are brief comments composed of statements or questions or both that lead the hearer from the point just finished to the next point in the speech. Transitions tie the various points of a speech together.

Inexperienced speakers feel the need for transitions but have a tendency to use one or two words over and over again. Novice speakers say "and another thing" and "another point," or overuse the word *next* or *also*. The good speaker has to learn to use varied transitions that summarize the points just made, forecast the point coming next, or better yet, both summarize and forecast. A speaker might say, for example, moving from his first to his second point, "Now that we have seen how present marijuana laws encourage drug abuse among the young, what can we do about it? The answer is to pass a law legalizing but restricting the use of marijuana similar to the laws we now have for the use of tobacco." The speaker then goes on to develop the point about passing a new law.

Patterns for Organizing Public Speeches

The three-part division of a speech into an introduction, body, and conclusion is a good standard way to frame your remarks, but it does not help you much in selecting and arranging the main points, supporting ideas, and transitions in the body of the speech. Over the years the theorists in the public-speaking style have discovered a number of recurring patterns that have proved useful in organizing speeches.

If you learn some of the "tried and true" ways of arranging the points in a speech you may be able to use them in planning a speech of your own. At least you will have a place to start. You might buy a coat from the rack in a clothing store and wear it immediately. The coat is cut to a standard pattern, and it will fit you more or less well. You might buy a coat cut to a standard pattern but have a tailor alter it, modifying it to fit you better. And finally, you might have a tailor measure you and design a one-of-a-kind coat to your taste, made out of your chosen material. As a speaker, you are in somewhat the same situation as when you buy a coat in that you can use a good standard outline and often end up with a well-organized speech which fits the audience and occasion more or less well; or you can alter a standard outline and make it fit better; or you can design a unique organizational pattern tailored especially for your specific audience and occasion.

We will not provide a long and detailed list of various patterns of organization that the theorists in the public-speaking style of communication have compiled over many years of practice and criticism. As we said, the public-speaking style has been taught for over a half-century now. Many of the variations are relatively minor, similar to changing the lapels of that coat we talked about above. We recommend that for important speeches, you try to alter one of the three very basic patterns that follow or that you design a unique outline tailored for your audience alone. An understanding of these three most important and widespread patterns will certainly help you get started in the practice of organizing public speeches.[2]

STATE YOUR CASE AND PROVE IT

The state-your-case-and-prove-it pattern of organization is the basic, straightforward development where you "tell them what you are going to tell them, tell them, and then tell them what you told them." You begin with an introduction, state your central thesis and the points that you will develop in support of it, take up each point in turn, and end with a summary.

State-Your-Case-and-Prove-It Pattern
I. Introduction.
II. Overview consisting of central idea and listing of points.
III. Development of each point.
IV. Conclusion consisting of a summary.

The pattern of stating a case and proving it is a good one for a speaker dealing with a familiar and much-discussed controversial topic. When a person talks on a well-worn issue, the audience members probably know a good deal about the pros and cons of the subject. The speaker dealing with a much-discussed issue does not need to explore the topic comprehensively and go over as much background information as is often necessary with a fresh topic. If you are dealing with such a topic, you might well just state your position and support it in line with the basic pattern.

[2] Our analysis of the three patterns follows closely that of William S. Howell and Ernest G. Bormann, *Presentational Speaking for Business and the Professions*, New York: Harper & Row, 1971, pp. 122–132.

THE IMPROMPTU VERSION

Because of the elementary nature of the pattern, you can use it in situations where you have little or no time to prepare your remarks. Have you ever received an honor and been in a situation where, to celebrate the occasion, people began to yell at you to give a speech? "Speech, speech" is a familiar call. Often you can shrug off such a request, and people are good-natured about it and let you off the hook, but sometimes you really must respond. Sometime you may be told before you sit down at a banquet, for instance, that after the meal the sponsors of the banquet would like to have you "say a few words." The technical name for the speech you give when you are asked to say a few words on very short notice is an *impromptu speech.* You can remember a variation of the basic pattern, which is ideal for impromptu situations, and by carefully following the directions for each step of the speech, you can end up with a well-organized speech on the spur of the moment.

The impromptu speaking pattern we recommend consists of the following four steps; you will notice they parallel fairly closely the basic state-your-case-and-prove-it pattern:

Impromptu Pattern
    I. Begin with an illustration.
    II. Give an overview consisting of the central idea and listing of points.
    III. Follow through (cover each point in turn).
    IV. Recap, with a twist (conclusion consisting of summary).

By memorizing the key words *illustrate, overview, follow through,* and *recap,* you can recall the directions for quickly organizing your remarks.

You begin the impromptu pattern with an example, preferably a narrative with human interest which illustrates the central idea you want to make. You do not set the stage for the story or example in any way; you simply begin to tell it:

"In the Old West, when they got civilized and stopped hanging the socially undesirable citizens from the nearest tree, they turned to finding a long, thin fence rail, and they'd tie them to it, and then they'd form a long procession and run 'em out of town on a rail. One such individual gained notoriety by asserting, 'If it wasn't for the honor of the occasion, I'd just as soon walk.'"

If you have some ability to dramatize the story, audience

members will become interested. Furthermore, they will become curious as to why you are telling the story and what you are driving at. You catch their attention, arouse their interest, and make them want to continue listening.

The second step of the impromptu pattern consists of a statement which leads easily to the central idea of your speech. You then give an overview (state what you will talk about) by listing the two or three points which you will talk about:

> "You really surprised me just now by making me team captain. But I know what it takes to be captain of this team, and I feel a little like the old westerner. Let me tell you why. We can win the title this year, but to do so, we must do two things; first, it's our tradition that the team captain is the leader of the team, not a figurehead, the leader; and second, all of us will have to level with one another about any problems we have as a team."

In the third step of the impromptu pattern you take up each point in turn and comment on it, supplying the examples and evidence that come readily to mind.

The fourth step is to conclude the speech with a recap and a twist. The recap is a short reminder of each of the points, phrased in different words than you used when you first made them, and the twist is a surprise ending which makes the speech sound unified and rounded off. A good twist is to refer back to the opening example or story with a tie-in that again shows the relevance of the introduction, thus unifying the speech:

> "If we do those two things, we can win the championship this year. If you are willing to do these two things, I will be willing to ride the narrowest, sharpest rail you can find. If you aren't willing to do these things, despite the honor, I would just as soon get off now."

The state-your-case-and-prove-it basic pattern of organizing a speech is simple but effective. It is an adaptable form, including the impromptu speech outline we used, and it is a straightforward, useful pattern for you to consider.

THE PROBLEM-SOLVING PATTERN

The problem-solving pattern is one where the speaker describes a problem, discusses its causes, suggests possible solutions, and recommends a course of action most likely to solve the problem. In its simplest form the pattern consists of (1) a description of the problem, (2) an analysis of its causes, and (3) an explanation of the best solution. A useful variation is a pattern similar to the one that the philosopher-educator John Dewey introduced at the beginning of the twentieth century. Dewey presented an analysis of what he called *reflective thinking* and discussed the way the trained mind studies problems in the scientific laboratory.[3] According to Dewey, reflective thinking is not random stream-of-consciousness thought, nor is it trial-and-error problem solving. When you daydream, your mind moves from image to image and does not focus on any specific problem. When you solve a problem through trial and error you simply try everything that pops into your head, until finally you reach a solution. Reflective thinking, on the other hand, begins when someone has what Dewey called a *felt difficulty*—a disturbance of the environment or pattern of life that becomes so strong that the individual begins to work to try to do something about it. The person begins to search out the problem and find out what is causing the difficulty. As the individual's vague feeling of puzzlement and difficulty comes under rational analysis, the problem comes into focus and the pattern of reflective thinking begins. As the person gets a clearer picture of the problem, possible solutions come to mind. The individual postpones trying out the solutions, as would be the case in trial and error, and instead *reflects* upon each, weighing the solutions against one another in terms of the causes of the problem. After methodical and reasonable analysis, the individual tries what seems like the best solution, in an effort to relieve the felt difficulty.

Dewey's analysis provides a step-by-step, logical progression which a speaker can use in organizing the materials for a speech. The pattern is as follows:

Problem-Solving Pattern
  I. Introduction.
 II. The nature of the problem.
     A. Definition of problem.
     B. Exploration of causes.
III. Listing of representative solutions.
 IV. Examination of representative solutions.
  V. Selection of the best solution.

The problem-solving pattern is a particularly good one when the problem is complicated and the audience is hostile

[3] *How We Think*, New York: Heath, 1910.

to the speaker's proposed solution, or when the problem is complicated and the audience is relatively unfamiliar with the facts of the situation. The pattern gives the listener an easy-to-follow and logical path through what might otherwise be a baffling and chaotic topic.

The problem-solving pattern encourages the listeners to adopt an objective, thoughtful attitude toward the speech, and this can help to disarm them of some of their emotionalism and prejudices. The speaker should adopt an appropriate tone in giving a speech in the problem-solving pattern. When the speaker says, "Let us explore the problem and see if we can decide what is causing it, and let us list all of the good solutions we can think of and compare them to see which is best," the openness of his approach should lead the audience members to follow along thoughtfully. One must be careful, however, when using the pattern, to adopt a scientific, objective manner and not use emotional or "loaded" language or any of the typical persuasive devices. Use matter-of-fact, direct language which conveys objectivity to the listener.

If you make a speech examining a number of possible solutions to a problem, and then eliminate all but the one you recommend, you will be following the natural tendency of much human decision making and problem solving. Research into the problem-solving dynamics of small task-oriented groups indicates that groups use this method in making decisions and solving problems.[4] People tend to eliminate undesirable solutions first and let the decision emerge as the only remaining option. Often they find it easier to decide which solutions they do *not* want to follow than to decide what they would prefer to do. The pattern of organization which eliminates the undesirable answers until the one best solution is left, is the *method of residues.*

THE PSYCHOLOGICAL-PROGRESSION PATTERN

The third and final pattern which we will consider in detail is another common and useful way to organize public speeches. The psychological-progression pattern was an important part of the communication style of evangelical preachers in the early part of the nineteenth century. The evangelical communication theory supported a speech practice of revival sermons and prayer meetings aimed at the "new birth," or conversion of the hearer to a religious vision. The steps to conversion included (1) awakening the interest in salvation,

[4] See Ernest G. Bormann, *Discussion and Group Methods: Theory and Practice,* 2nd ed., New York: Harper & Row, 1975, pp. 289–296.

(2) self-examination and the discovery of guilt (the breaking up of the old foundations), (3) conviction of sin, (4) the searching for the way to salvation, and (5) yielding and peace.[5]

In developing the public-speaking communication style, such theorists as Woolbert and Weaver combined early twentieth-century psychological theory with a modification of the steps to conversion. They classified the five responses which speaking tries to arouse as follows: (1) attentiveness, (2) understanding, (3) deciding, (4) acting publicly, and (5) yielding fully.[6] Monroe adapted these ideas to include the arousal of all five responses as steps within one public speech; he arrived at a pattern of organization in the 1930s which he called a *motivated sequence*, and the pattern has served as a useful and popular one in the public-speaking style of communication.[7]

Howell and Bormann developed a modification of this historically effective speech organization to the needs of contemporary communication and called it the psychological-progression pattern. In it are the following steps: (1) arouse, (2) dissatisfy, (3) gratify, (4) picture, and (5) move. We make only a slight change in the pattern. We prefer the term *dramatize* for *picture*, in step 4.[8] As we shall see in the following chapters, recent research into small groups indicates the great importance of dramatizing to persuasion, in all styles of communication.[9]

An attractive feature of the psychological-progression pattern is that you can easily remember it by committing the five key words (arouse, dissatisfy, gratify, dramatize, move) to memory. When you need to develop a persuasive speech you can think of each key word in turn and begin to draft a section of a speech aimed at that purpose. The end result is a speech arranged in a psychological sequence proven effective for North American cultures, one in which Protestant and evangelical speech forms have influenced secular communication. The fact that you cannot easily reverse the parts of a speech that is organized around the psychological-progression pattern indicates its organic unity. Many professional speakers use this pattern to adapt material that they

---

[5] For a description of the psychology of conversion see Joseph Tracy, *The Great Awakening: A History of the Revival of Religion in the Time of Edwards and Whitefield*, Boston: Tappan and Dennet, 1842, pp. x–xi.

[6] Charles W. Woolbert and Andrew T. Weaver, *Better Speech*, New York: Harcourt Brace Jovanovich, 1922, pp. 250–266.

[7] Alan H. Monroe, *Principles and Types of Speech*, 4th ed., Glenview, Ill.: Scott, Foresman, 1955.

[8] Howell and Bormann, *Presentational Speaking*, pp. 130–131.

[9] See, for example, Ernest G. Bormann, "Fantasy and Rhetorical Vision: The Rhetorical Criticism of Social Reality," *The Quarterly Journal of Speech*, 58 (1972), pp. 396–407.

know very well to specific audiences. You might well want to memorize the five steps, and when you next have to give a persuasive speech you can draft your outline by asking the following questions about your audience: How can I arouse their interest? How can I make them dissatisfied by showing them the things that are wrong with their present situation? How can I show them that my solution will meet the problems and be gratifying to them? How can I dramatize an attractive future for them once they accept my solution? How can I move them to implement the plan?

Another good thing about the psychological-progression pattern is that you can often eliminate some of the early steps if the audience is already highly interested in the topic and very dissatisfied. You can then simply remind them of your common problem and concern and move quickly to the gratification step. Sometimes, of course, one speech is part of a whole campaign of persuasion. Much contemporary advertising is planned as a campaign. Revivalists often talk of a crusade, a campaign which is designed to create a total persuasive climate through the use of a large number of integrated messages, prayer meetings, public speeches, revival meetings, and sermons. If a speech is part of such an ongoing and elaborate campaign, a given speech might concentrate on arousing interest, and subsequent messages and speeches could take up the other steps in the psychological-progression sequence.

The psychological-progression pattern can be used to bring about change. The pattern is basically a persuasive one and usually includes both logical support and nonlogical support such as dramatizing, which generally arouses audience emotions.

How to Outline a Speech

We are going to conclude this chapter with a general sample speech outline which indicates one good way to plan a speech or presentation. Any speech you give is bound to have individual requirements that you will have to work out for yourself. This outline includes a wide column (to the left) in which you can comment about the communication techniques you plan to use to achieve your purposes. This method has proved useful to our public-speaking students over the years. It helps develop some objectivity about why you put a speech together in a particular way, and it helps develop a

Chapter 7

THE KEY IDEAS

A message must be organized according to the theory that underlies a particular style.

Over the years, experts have learned how audiences respond to public speeches and have evolved ways of organization which meet the requirements of the public-speaking context.

People who have not studied public speaking are likely to have only a vague notion about how to organize material for a speech.

If a public speech is unified, the listeners can usually recall the central idea and the main subpoints.

In addition to being unified, a good public speech contains only relevant materials, concisely presented in a coherent and comprehensive pattern.

A creative analysis is important to understanding a topic and is the result of the

sense of control over material. Many beginning public speakers can dig out much material on a subject for a speech and can make a fair prediction about the probable response of their audience (the other members of the class), but when it comes to deciding what material to use, what to leave out, and how to order the material once they have decided to include it, they are lost without a model outline to follow.

The outline on the following pages is for a persuasive speech, but the same sort of outline can be used for all other forms of public speaking if you modify the content according to the kind of speech.

No one way to organize a speech guarantees its effectiveness. Everything that you learn in this course—about language usage and structure, audience-centered messages, and the many factors involved in persuasion—are vital factors in public speaking. Outlines can aid structure, but the individual art, the creativity, the fun of speechmaking comes when you make the *choices* of what will go into the outline.

four-phase creative process of preparation, incubation, illumination, *and* verification.

You can discipline your creativity by developing systematic work habits, such as working on a regular schedule at a specific time and place.

The public-speaking style requires that the speaker skillfully adapt the creative analysis of a topic to a specific audience and occasion.

The final step in preparing a public speech is the construction of the speech itself.

A good speech has a beginning, a middle, and an end, usually called an introduction, body, *and* conclusion.

The body of a speech consists of points supporting a clear central idea, all tied together by good transitions.

The state-your-case-and-prove-it pattern is the one in which you "Tell them what you are going to tell them, tell them, and then tell them what you told them."

The problem-solving pattern is the one in which the speaker describes a problem, discusses its causes, examines possible solutions, and suggests a course of action.

The method of residues is the pattern of organization in which the speaker lists a number of solutions and eliminates the undesirable ones, thus leaving the recommended one as the only remaining alternative.

The psychological-progression pattern evolved from revival preaching and is well adapted to persuasive speeches.

The psychological-progression pattern consists of the steps of arousing, dissatisfying, gratifying, dramatizing, and moving to action.

To use the outline, start with the left-hand column. Write out what you plan to do. Put in some detail. Then in the right-hand column write a comprehensive outline of the content of your speech.

Introduction

I am starting with a science fiction dramatization of the future, to catch the attention of the audience and also to reveal that my speech will be about the energy crisis.

I will begin by taking the audience into the future where they set their alarms at 6:00 A.M., in time to rush out when the gas stations open, so they can join the mile-long line to fill their tanks with $3.00-a-gallon gas—if there is any gas left.

This is my central idea.

Urge your representative and senator to support gas rationing.

Body

Point 1

I. Our current energy crisis, particularly as it relates to petroleum products, poses a major problem for all of us, for

Supporting material

    A. Our current laws allow short-sighted waste of gasoline.

    B. Our current laws will result in a crisis for our economy in the near future.

This is my transition from point 1 to point 2

Clearly our present laws relating to the sale of gasoline are intolerable. What is the answer? The best solution is gas-rationing legislation with teeth in it.

Point 2

II. Gas rationing is a good solution.

    A. Gas rationing can work, because [example of the way the new law would work].

    B. Gas rationing is fair, because [literal analogy of current situation with the plan for gas rationing].

This is my transition from point 2 to point 3

Gas rationing is a workable solution to our present petroleum energy crisis. What difference does a change in the law make to you? How do you stand to gain from change?

Point 3

III. Gas rationing will be beneficial to you, for

    A. It will assure you of a fair share of the available gasoline in the future.

    B. It will enable us to adjust our economy to a future of limited petroleum resources without a depression.

Conclusion

I will summarize the main points of my speech and make an appeal referring back to my example in the introduction of the miserable future without rationing, and I will dramatize a future where, if they accept my plan, they can drive into a station at any time and purchase their just ration of 50-cent-a-gallon gasoline.

SUGGESTED PROJECTS

1 Select a topic of concern to you and, taking a controversial stand on the matter, develop a five to eight minute persuasive speech on the topic. Prepare a carefully planned speech outline to turn in to the instructor prior to giving your speech, as directed in this chapter or as modified by your instructor.

2 Your instructor will have prepared a number of topics suitable for impromptu speeches. Draw three of the topics, pick any one, and return the other two. You will be allowed to step out of the classroom for five minutes to prepare your speech. Follow the directions for an impromptu speech outline in this chapter in preparing your talk.

3 Prepare a five-minute commentary suitable for reading on radio or television. Your commentary should relate to some important public issue or some recent news event. Outline your speech carefully and write it out and revise it. Your commentary will be judged in terms of its unity, coherence, relevance, conciseness, and comprehensiveness.

SUGGESTED READINGS

Jeffrey, Robert C. and Owen Peterson. *Speech: A Text with Adapted Readings*, 2nd ed. New York: Harper & Row, 1975.

Howell, William S. and Ernest G. Bormann. *Presentational Speaking for Business and the Professions*. New York: Harper & Row, 1971.

Monroe, Alan H. *Principles and Types of Speech*, 6th ed. Glenview, Ill.: Scott, Foresman, 1964.

Chapter 8

HOW TO LISTEN

When we explain the importance of listening, most people say, "You know, you're right! I never thought about it much, but listening *is* important. From now on I'm going to pay better attention. I'm going to listen better." Like most communication skills, unfortunately, listening is not much improved merely by trying to "listen better."

Speaking and listening are learned skills, learned in much the same manner as reading and writing. The major difference is that we all learn to speak and listen at such an early age, long before starting formal schooling, that we tend to feel that everything we need to know about speaking and listening is already learned before we start school; many come to the mistaken conclusion that we do not need to study speaking and listening. We learn to walk and to run long before we enter school, too, but any person with a talent for running dashes can profit from expert coaching and diligent practice, and it is the same with speaking and listening skills. Anyone can learn to listen more efficiently and effectively, given increased awareness of the factors involved plus practice guided by an expert in listening.

In addition to some general principles of listening which apply to most styles of communication, there are some attitudes and techniques which are unique to each of the three main styles we are studying, just as some general principles apply to running all track events, while specific skills are more appropriate for individual events such as dashes, cross country races, or running hurdles. When you are a student you listen to many lectures; when you work or are involved with any task-oriented group, you are involved in many transactions in the message communication style; much of your most important listening involves relationship-style communication interactions.

How to Listen in the Public-Speaking Communication Style

Often members of an audience listening to a public speech do not listen carefully, and as a result they do not comprehend all of the ideas in the speech, nor do they critically evaluate those ideas they do comprehend. Some members of the audience may be poor listeners because they are taking flight from the situation, doing anything *but* listen. There are a dozen places they would rather be, and a dozen things they would rather be doing. Playing the role of listener is a time-consuming, tension-producing job. A person must often exert effort to keep his attention from wandering.

If we are at all creative, our attention can find materials more interesting than the speaker's comments. We have a colleague who claims that for years he has organized his next week's lectures every Sunday morning during the church sermon. Mental energy which could be used for listening is often spent in less constructive ways than organizing our week's work, however; perhaps the speaker has interesting mannerisms of speech or gesture, and we can count the number of times he says "y'know" or the number of times he twitches his eyelids, looks at the floor, or tries to put one hand in a nonexistent pocket in the back of his coat jacket. Perhaps a young man has spotted a great-looking girl sitting three rows in front of him in the audience and spends his time thinking how he will approach her after the lecture is over.

DECIDING TO LISTEN

All too often, our minds drift away from, then back to, a speaker; we thus unthinkingly listen for a while, then fail to do so, then find ourselves back in the role. It often happens that if we work at listening carefully to the people we least want to hear, we are amply rewarded by what we learn. In any case, we would be wise to make a conscious choice about whether to listen; we should think about whether we will concentrate in a listening situation and not leave the matter to chance.

Think through your own experiences and list some situations in which you were unwilling to listen. From time to time the decision not to listen is probably justified (as our colleague insists is the case for him when he sits in church), but the question of when you should be willing to listen and when not, deserves more study than it usually receives.

For the remainder of this chapter we will concentrate our analysis on those situations in which you have decided that you *will* try to listen. Even when you willingly take the part of a listener you will discover that the role requires some specific skills which need to be understood and practiced in order to increase listening competence.

CONTROLLING YOUR ATTENTION

A runner may tire at the midway point in a race but force him- or herself to continue, despite pain and fatigue. A person listening to a public speech can do much the same thing by forcing his or her attention to stay on what is being said. Concentrated effort to focus on the message and understand it can overcome listening fatigue and the natural tendency of our attention to wander.

A little practice can help you become aware of those moments when your attention begins to waver. As you listen, you need to keep part of your mind on how well you are listening; you can learn to pull yourself back to the message when you catch yourself losing interest. If the speaker is developing an idea that seems dull, trite, or uninteresting, or if he or she is going so slowly that we find ourselves thinking ahead, we may be tempted to relax and indulge in daydreaming.

One way to keep from drifting away from a dull speaker's slow-moving train of ideas is to anticipate what point he will make next. By guessing where he will go, we can arouse our interest in checking to see if, indeed, we were correct. And if we have guessed correctly, we have then thought about the idea twice and are more likely to remember it than if we had not made the prediction. If we guess incorrectly, we still may wonder why the speaker took the turn he did instead of the one we thought he would take, and in either case, we have tricked ourselves into attending to what he is saying.

Another tactic that can help combat the boredom of listening to a slow speaker is to take 10 to 20 seconds from time to time to review quickly what the speaker has just said. You will find that summarizing from time to time helps you recall the important ideas later.

We have to focus our attention on any message before we can begin to interpret it. You will no doubt recall the old story about the farmer who told his neighbor he was going to teach his mule how to drag a log by a chain. After announcing his intention, the first thing the farmer did was pick up a big board and hit the mule over the head with it. "What'd you do that for?" the startled neighbor asked. "I thought you were going to teach him how to drag logs!" "Yup," the farmer nodded in agreement, "but first I have to get his attention."

FOCUSING ON MESSAGE STRUCTURE

Assuming that we now know how to force our attention to the speech, we can learn further techniques of effective listening. We should focus on the structure of the message. People who listen for factual details tend to have trouble recalling the main ideas, and seldom remember many of the facts, either. They thus end up with a vague idea about a mass of undigested material. All of us tend to remember patterns more easily than isolated details. Whole systems of memory improvement depend upon connecting the things to be remembered with something we know well. For example, when we meet a number of people at a party and wish to remember their names, if we can connect each person and each name with a house on a street that we know well, we can often recall the names of the persons later. Simply trying to remember a series of names without associations is difficult.

If you practice listening for the main outline or structure of a message, you will find your understanding increasing. You will know that you are a professional listener when you can hear a badly organized message and refit its parts into your own organizational pattern. You may, indeed, be able to recall more of what a rambling speaker said during an impromptu speech than the speaker himself can if you organize the material more effectively than he did.

CONTROLLING EMOTIONAL REACTIONS TO LANGUAGE

Finally, an important key to misunderstanding, even when a person is seeking actively to listen, is related to the third aspect of language discussed in Chapter 3. Certain words arouse

our emotions. Moreover, a speaker's dialect may cause us to respond with anger, suspicion, or fear. The power of words to cause emotional responses is a factor in poor listening. A person in an emotional state is generally upset and acts to some extent as though he were in shock. He loses his ability to think clearly, just as he loses his ability to make small, isolated, subtle physical movements. Even when we want to listen, we may respond emotionally to a word or phrase and lose some of our listening abilities. Just as we lose our ability to make fine adjustments with our fingers when we are nervous and upset, we begin to mishear.

Of course a certain amount of excitement can improve our ability to listen, just as stage fright can be used to help us give a better public performance. Excitement, under control, makes us function better. People can experience a considerable level of excitement and high feeling and be keyed up to more efficient use of skills and talents. Students giving speeches before a class often exhibit both the crippling effects and the positive use of excitement. Occasionally a student may become so emotional that he goes into a sort of shock reaction, is unable to think clearly, and makes many random physical gestures. (We are glad to report that in this day of family picture-taking, making reports to classes at the elementary-school level, and excellent high-school courses in speech, we rarely encounter this degree of nervousness in a college student of public speaking.) Most often, students find that the excitement of giving a speech can be used to make their minds work more efficiently. Coaches of athletic teams are well aware of the fine line between working the team up for the game and getting the players wound so tightly they do far less than their best.

In listening as in speaking before an audience or participating in athletic events, the trick is to be genuinely involved, interested, and efficient. Remember that when you find yourself getting boiling mad, you are also losing your ability to listen well.

After we have learned the techniques of keeping our attention on a message, or structuring the message as we hear it, and controlling our emotional responses to language, we can listen with *understanding*. When we listen to a speech with the aim of understanding, we *comprehend* the message.

Much of the difficulty we experience in working with one another we attribute to communication problems. Marriages are often said to fail because of a breakdown in communication. A colleague of ours argues, in an ironic way, that if it were not for misunderstandings, we would have a world with much more conflict and violence than we do have. He argues that most people filter their incoming communications in such a way that they protect their self-image. Thus they often rearrange what others say so that it fits in with their own comfortable preconceptions, biases, and prejudices. If we always had a clear understanding of what other people were trying to say, he argues, we would come in conflict with them much more often! His point is worth making, if only as an antidote to the popular assumption that communication problems are the basic causes of all conflicts.

Nonetheless, interpreting a speech to mean something other than what the speaker intends can cause difficulty, and most occasions require that we at least comprehend what the other person is saying before the conversation can proceed to either agreement or disagreement.

LISTENING CRITICALLY

Many times we need to do more than just understand what denotative meanings a speaker wishes to convey to us. We must also critically evaluate the speech. We need to examine the speaker's assertions to see if they accurately describe the purported facts. If we can personally check what is said by observation, we can discover whether the message is true or false. Once we discover a message is false, we may go on to infer a motive or intent on the speaker's part to account for the falsehood. We may decide that the speaker has deliberately misled us, in which case we may say he has lied about the matter. We may decide that the speaker intended to tell us the truth, but made an error. In either case, of course, although we understand what the speaker is saying, we do not accept the statement as an accurate depiction of events.

We may also listen critically to the form of the message and decide that it is an unsatisfactory message on formal grounds. In Chapter 10 we will discuss the nature of reasoning and how the form of a message can often reveal whether it is logical. When a message says both that something is the case and that the same thing is not the case, the message contains a contradiction. We discount the contradictory message as illogical and cannot tell anything about the facts from it. The contradiction is a matter of the form of the message, the second aspect of language. Often a speaker asserts that several assumptions about the world are true, and if we conclude that they are true, then we can conclude that some other statements he makes are also true. But unless the message is in a logical form, the concluding statement may not follow even from true premises. For instance, if we know it is true that John has three apples and it is also true that Mary has five apples, we may still reason to a false conclusion if we decide that together they have nine apples. In this case, the assumptions are true, but the form or logic of the message is wrong. The proper form for the sentence is $3 + 5 = 8$. When we use an improper form, such as $3 + 5 = 9$, we have made an error in the form of the argument. We do not need to check the world to see if there are 3 and 5 apples that will combine to total 9 apples; we can tell that $3 + 5 = 9$ is wrong simply by looking at the form of the statement.

Finally, we must listen carefully and criticize speeches reflecting rumor, propaganda, and persuasion. People encounter rumors frequently and usually listen to them with interest. Rumors are messages in general circulation which cannot be factually confirmed, such as gossip, unofficial messages based upon guesses, or incomplete hints. Many times the rumor relates to official organizational secrets that are of considerable importance to the people in the organization. Rumors in the form of gossip often relate to matters that are socially unacceptable, and thus the concerned parties will keep them secret if possible. Gossip may relate to such things as the boss's wife becoming an alcoholic, the know-it-all neighbor's daughter's illegitimate baby, the professor who passed out drunk at the president's party—the list is endless. Most people enjoy listening to gossip.

If a rumor is the best source of information about something of importance to us, we should try to figure out what the facts are as best we can, remembering how things get distorted as they are passed on by word of mouth.

Even after a person is sure he understands a message, he should critically evaluate the propaganda elements within it. In Chapter 12 we will examine in detail the techniques of suggestion. A critical listener should evaluate the words a speaker picks to name things and people and to refer to properties and relations. Does the speaker always choose a word with a bad connotation to name certain people? Does he use words to slant his message in favor of some people and some programs and against other people and other courses of action? (The authors often catch their children sending out such loaded messages; two school acquaintances are always spoken of, for instance, as Dumb-Bill and Icky-Elizabeth.)

You should also consider the dramas in the message. Who are the heroes and who are the villains? What values are suggested by the dramatic actions? A critical listener should look at the motives attributed to various actors in the dramas.

(Also remember that social scientists who try to study human behavior are often disillusioned about research that attributes motives to people. Attempts to study motives scientifically tend to break down in disturbing ways.)

How to Listen in the Message Communication Style

One of the important distinctions between the role of message source and that of message receiver in the S M C R model is that the evaluation of good or bad communication is dependent upon the ability of the participants to jointly achieve the source's intent. The receiver may legitimately later become the source in another, consecutive exchange of information; but for purposes of judging how good or bad a single event is in the message communication style, we must judge the feedback of the listener in terms of how well it helps the source know that its message has been understood. The critic using the model will judge the fidelity of the transmission in terms of the information the source intended to transmit. Or if the source intended control, the critic will evaluate success in terms of whether or not the message achieved the source's intended control. When one person talks with another in the message communication style, therefore, the problem of whose goal will control the communication must be faced early in the interchange.

When the apparent listener in a communication transaction that is getting under way comments in a manner designed to assume the role of a message source, then what the person says and does is not feedback according to the model of the message communication style. Recall that feedback refers to those verbal and nonverbal cues which the receiver provides about how the message is being decoded. The respondent who tries to assume the role of source encodes a message to achieve a different goal; the comment of the respondent is thus not feedback at all.

Recall, also, our discussion in Chapters 3 and 4 of how nonverbal communication functions. Nonverbal communication can help establish that a communication transaction is to begin, can set the ground rules for the transaction, and can monitor the behavior of the participants to keep deviant communication from disturbing the event. When you begin a communication transaction in the message communication style assuming that you will be allowed to be the message source, you must be very alert to the verbal and non-verbal response of the others involved. In this regard you must "listen" with your eyes as well. You must make sure that your listener or listeners are playing the role of receiver, and providing feedback rather than trying to assert a different role.

THE CASE OF THE UNWILLING RECEIVER

Often people refer to a situation where nobody wants to be a receiver and everybody wants to be a message source as an instance of poor listening. "We were all talking at once. Nobody was listening. We all had something we wanted to say, and we didn't even hear what anybody else said. We've got to start all over again and *listen* to one another." The problem in such cases probably is not lack of listening skills so much as the unwillingness of the participants to take on the role of receiver at that time. When two people both try to play the role of message source and encode messages aimed at achieving different personal goals, the results do not fit the message communication model; instead we have two incomplete communication events that happen to take place at the same time. We have the not unfamiliar spectacle of two people talking past each other, or of two people talking in one another's presence without talking with one another. In terms of the ideal model, two message sources speaking in one another's presence are certainly not communicating. The critic of message communication calls such events a failure or a breakdown in communication.

Unwillingness to be the receiver of messages often stems from poor interpersonal relationships, particularly when people are forced by organizational structures to talk over a common task. Above we referred to those informal communication transactions which are signaled and marked by nonverbal communication, and which tend to be maintained or broken off by mutual agreement. The meetings required by formal structures often cannot be terminated in the same way. The doctor and patient may be required to talk about the case history of the patient's illness; the applicant and the personal director may be required to conduct a job interview; the supervisor and the subordinate may have to discuss details of a job. Sometimes, two people trying to work on a common task and needing to talk effectively in the message communication style should switch for a time into a transaction in the relationship style; after having created a suitable relationship, they can then switch styles and move into the task-oriented interview or conference more comfortably. The person who does not know the one who is the source of a message may be ill at ease, tense, and unsure, and may not be willing to play the role of receiver until the source is better known. The person who is suspicious, hostile, or antagonistic to the message source often refuses to assume the role of receiver, because to do so would be to help the source achieve an objective, and the last thing the respondent wants is to be helpful. For all these reasons it is vital to remember that listening is not a passive state that just happens; listening is an activity, and a person has to agree to listen, be able to listen, and work at doing it well.

PLAYING THE ROLE OF RECEIVER EFFECTIVELY
When participating in a conversation in the style of message communication, you should willingly accept the role and duties of message receiver at appropriate points in your interaction. If you anticipate conflict, you should allow the source to develop a complete message first, and then you should provide feedback and work to understand the message until both of you are satisfied that you understand one another. Then if you decide that you are not going to cooperate to achieve the source's intent, you ought to assert yourself clearly in the role of source for another round of communication. Conversely, the other person should willingly assume the role of receiver until your message is understood. Understanding does not assure harmony and cooperation. The participants in a communication event in the message communication style may still disagree or grow to dislike one another, but they will do so on a more realistic basis and not because of misunderstandings stemming from lack of communication skills—particularly from either's lack of willingness to play the role of receiver.

Once you have agreed to play the role of message receiver, the communication skills of good listening come into play. Some of the same psychological powers of focusing attention, searching for structure in the message, predicting and summarizing ideas which were important in listening to a public speech or lecture are equally necessary to the listener in the message communication event. A most important difference in the two types of communication, though, is that the skills of providing feedback which are central to the message communication style are less stressed in public speaking. In message communication, the receiver tries to attend carefully to what is said, to decipher denotative meanings, and to provide continuous feedback. The speaker, in turn, willingly plays the role of message source, searches constantly for feedback, and keeps encoding new messages to achieve a satisfactory level of understanding. If both source and receiver play their roles willingly and with skill, the whole process becomes a classic expression of the basic model of ideal message communication.

Nonverbal Feedback

The communication skills required of an effective receiver of messages include skill in providing nonverbal feedback. Facial expressions are extremely important. As we saw in Chapter 5, research indicates that facial expressions are among the most important nonverbal cues to response and reaction.

The poker game, which is a situation which puts a premium on bluffing, lying, and systematically misleading other players, also encourages the "poker face," the careful suppression of any facial expression which might give away what cards a player is holding. The poker game is thus a communication situation which goes counter to all the values of the message (as well as the relationship) communication style. (If you want to study how to be a better bluffer—in a poker game or when you are negotiating to buy a used car, for instance—you might simply take the advice provided by the theory of message communication and turn it inside out: Do not accept the other person's intention, but push ahead to achieve your own. Do not provide feedback to achieve high-fidelity transmission, but use a poker face or nonverbal cues which go counter to your actual inner thoughts.)

The poker face is a liability rather than an asset for the receiver in the message communication style, however. A skilled receiver makes clear facial expressions and gestures to indicate understanding or acceptance or misunderstanding or rejection. When participating actively and willingly as receiver, you should smile, frown, look puzzled, allow a look of illumination to spread over your face when you see what the source is trying to say, and so forth. Head nods and shakes are another good technique to provide feedback. One of the authors of this book once took a driving examination for a license and was graded down because he drove across a set of railroad tracks without clearly turning his head first in one direction and then the other, although he stoutly maintained that he had looked carefully in both directions. The tester wanted to see an unmistakable swing of the head, first to the left and then to the right. (Said author then clued in your other author, and when she took the examination later the same afternoon, she looked so long and hard in both directions the tester chuckled and asked, checking the names on his list, "Say, was that your husband earlier . . . ?")

When playing the role of receiver, a person is as active as the individual playing the role of message source. Although the receiver may not say as many words as the source, the receiver will be providing nonverbal feedback continuously; his cues are intentional and done consciously.

Verbal Feedback

Verbal feedback, too, is a communication skill necessary for an effective receiver of messages. The receiver can feed back error statements to the source indicating the nature of the problem: "You seem to think I know all about what the group decided last night, but I haven't any idea, really." "I'm confused." "Well, I thought I understood, but now I think it just doesn't make sense. Maybe you'd better . . . " "I don't think I heard that right." Questioning is an important technique for feedback: "What was that last word? Did you say 'would' or 'wouldn't'?" "What do you mean by *entropy*?" "I'm sorry but that whole business about negative entropy confuses me. Would you go over that again, please?" The receiver can also give feedback by repeating, echoing, or rephrasing the message: "OK, now let me repeat what I think you just said." "Just a minute; here's what I got out of that." "Let's see now if I've got that straight." "Do you mean . . . ?"

The individuals involved in a conversation in the message communication style alternate the roles of source and receiver, but those playing the receiver roles must be willing to bide their time and listen, provide feedback, and come to an understanding with the source before they launch into their own turn at playing the role of source. They must be willing to provide feedback, even if it seems to put them in a one-down position, make them lose status, or appear ignorant at the time. Finally, they must take the initiative when necessary and stop the communication flow (just as a computer does, automatically) and indicate to the source, either verbally or nonverbally, (1) that there is a problem (misunderstanding), (2) what kind of a problem it is, and (3) where the receiver is in terms of what is understood and what is not.

How to Listen in the Relationship Style

According to the model of the relationship style the participants in an ideal communication event are involved in a significant and important transaction. Someone speaks and the listeners not only comprehend and evaluate the comment, but they also sometimes discover meanings in the message that had not occurred to the speaker. They search for nonverbal context and cues and try to understand the feelings implied by the comment as well as the denotative meanings encoded in the words. Much as a creative reader can discover more in a book than the author intended, a creative listener can make a comment that adds new meaning to the original statement. When the listener feeds back ideas into the event, the speaker may be stimulated to see a still deeper meaning in the messages that begin flowing rapidly between or among the participants, generating much increased excitement.

In discussions and conferences, people sometimes find themselves caught up in a chain of fantasies similar to the creative moments individuals experience when they daydream about a creative project or an important problem. Someone makes a suggestion, and the idea is picked up by another participant, then by another, and soon a number of people are deeply involved in the discussion, excitedly adding their reactions and ideas to it. Under the suggestive power of the group fantasy the constraints that normally hold people back are released, and people feel free to experiment with ideas, to play with concepts and wild suggestions and imaginative notions. This sort of idea interplay can also happen between two people who have reached a high level of supportive interpersonal communication.

The total involvement of the listener in a communication transaction creates a situation where the flow of meaning is no longer from source to receiver, as is the case when a programmer works with a computer, but where all participants are adding to a common reservoir of meaning until the result is greater than any one person could have managed by himself. The final growth and insight and learning in such a communication event take place in both the person who originally discussed the topic and the individual who began the transaction as listener. The creative involvement of all participants requires all the communication skills, including the highest levels of listening ability. Interpersonal trust, a positive social climate, skill in expressing ideas, sensitivity to dialect and suggestion, ability at nonverbal communication — all these components are important to the deep and important communication event.

An athlete does not spend all his time running important races at top speed; so, too, we should not hold up the pattern of deep significant communication as the formula for all communication. But when the time is right, and the people are in tune with one another, the deep and significant communication transactions in which we participate are among our most exciting and rewarding experiences.

Creative listening skills are as important in all communication styles as are the skills of speech. Good listening requires effort within the frameworks of the various dynamic exchanges of personalities and ideas. You have to stay tuned in to someone when you listen to him.

Listening as a Supportive Technique

Putting it too simply of course, the analyst listens. The analytically oriented psychiatrist listens. You pay a great deal of money to have such a professional *listen* to you. Why? Because the kind of listening they can do is a very special kind; they are trained to try to hear what you are *really* saying. There are times when all of us are aware that we are not saying what we really want to say because we are having difficulty getting the words our right, but professional helper-listeners are not listening for the right words. They are listening for the feelings that are being expressed, or, in the case of many disturbed people, not being expressed—because the person himself or herself is sometimes not aware of the feelings, or does not know why he has these feelings or what they mean to him and why they are bothering him. In any case, professional listening designed to help disturbed people and all the research that has resulted from the study of this special kind of therapeutic listening has provided much interesting material for the normal person interested in becoming a more effective listener.

DEFENSIVENESS AND COMMUNICATION BREAKDOWNS
Much of the material regarding communication breakdowns relates to *defensiveness* and its destructive effect on a person's ability to listen. The first step any good analyst makes is to try to break down his client's defensiveness so that a climate of trust can be built. Because disturbed people are more obviously upset or paranoid than normal people, their defensiveness is usually very apparent; they express their defensiveness verbally or nonverbally, either in an outgoing, obvious manner, or by retreating into silence.

When a person becomes defensive, his listening ability is

lessened. All of us have to maintain sufficient defensiveness to protect our inner images. When we are insecure in a situation, always waiting for evaluation and criticism, we often hear only the "what you did wasn't up to your usual standards," and not the "but then, even second-best from you is better than what most people turn out!" that follows. All of us know people who seem to take nearly everything that is said to them the wrong way, or as we say, "personally." On a bad day even the healthiest of us can feel unduly attacked and begin to respond defensively when it is not necessary.

Because defensive communication plays a part in everyone's natural communication behavior, but is so often an obvious source of trouble, it has been studied carefully. Jack Gibb discovered certain types of behaviors in messages which appeared to convey attitudes which set up defensive responses in listeners; he also recorded those messages and attitudes which seemed to set up a climate of support and acceptance in listeners. As you might expect, the supportive climates, as he calls them, are mirror images, exact opposites, of the defensive climates.[1]

The defensive climates are generally manipulative in intent and include messages which are (1) evaluative (I'll tell you whether you're good or bad); (2) controlling (me over you); (3) strategic (I've figured out how to get you to do it my way); (4) neutral (I really don't give a damn); (5) superior (you're a nothing; I'm "it"!); and (6) certain (It's going to go this way, and that's that). Our normal response to anyone communicating these attitudes is to be defensive. The problem, of course, lies in the fact that so often we are unaware of how much of this sort of defense-producing material creeps into our messages. And as listeners, we are often not fully aware why we are not listening well, when, in fact, we have become defensive, riled up, angry, and probably hurt.

We all find it much easier to listen to someone whose messages create a supportive climate. Gibb includes among these (1) description (Tell me more about it); (2) problem orientation (What's the problem as you see it?); (3) spontaneity (Hey, let's see what we can do about this!); (4) empathy (You sure feel bad about it, don't you); (5) equality (Two heads are better than one; let's see what we might work out together); and (6) provisionalism (Looks like you feel you could go about it this way, or that way.) These are very brief statements derived from the Gibb article, and you may well want to look into his account of defensive communication more thoroughly. De-

[1] Jack R. Gibb, "Defensive Communication," *The Journal of Communication*, 11 (1961), 141–148.

THE KEY IDEAS

Deciding to listen is not enough; guided practice in listening techniques is also necessary.

Listening is as difficult as reading.

A listener often must exert effort to keep his attention from wandering.

We should make a conscious choice about whether or not we will listen to a speaker; we should not leave the matter to chance.

People who listen for factual details have more trouble remembering what a speaker has said than people who listen for the main ideas.

If we respond emotionally to a speaker's language, we lose some of our ability to listen.

We need to understand what the other person is saying before we can intelligently agree or disagree.

When we listen critically, we need to ask if the denotative meanings are true to the facts.

fensive climates are characterized by put-downs of the listener by the source, whereas supportive climates stress equality and a constant reassurance, verbally and nonverbally, that the listener is as valuable a human being as the source and has capabilities and feelings that matter. There is no evaluation of anyone by anyone going on in supportive-climate communication.

In terms of the message communication style, when defensiveness interferes in the channel between the source and the receiver, it is that kind of psychological "noise" that makes good listening and accurate, feedback almost impossible. In terms of the relationship communication style, defensive communication builds barriers between people that make trust and openness and authentic interaction difficult, if not impossible. In terms of the public-speaking style, to the extent that any speaker creates defensiveness in his audience when making a public speech, his effectiveness is lessened.

Even after you understand a message you should critically evaluate the propaganda elements within it.

Feedback in the message communication model only takes place when some participants in the communication willingly try to understand the source's message and systematically provide cues as to how they are decoding it.

Often what we think of as poor listening in the message communication style is due not so much to a lack of skill as to the unwillingness of the participants to play the role of receiver.

The unwillingness of the participants in a message communication event to be receivers of messages often stems from poor interpersonal relationships.

Once you have agreed to play the role of message receiver, then the communication skills of good listening come into play.

A student of the message communication style should learn skills of nonverbal and verbal feedback.

The relationship style of communication often requires creative listening that discovers meanings in a message that go beyond a speaker's intentions.

When a person becomes defensive, his listening ability is lessened.

Defensive communication climates often result from manipulative messages which imply evaluation, control, strategy, neutrality, superiority, and certainty on the part of the speaker.

Supportive communication climates often result from messages which imply description, problem orientation, spontaneity, empathy, equality, and provisionalism.

Active listening involves an empathetic involvement with the other person to the extent that you cannot sit in judgment, because, for the time involved, you share the other person's feelings and point of view.

ACTIVE LISTENING

Another form of listening that interests those involved in the study and practice of the relationship communication style is that advanced by psychologist Carl R. Rogers. Originally conceived as a therapeutic technique for counselors, *active listening* contains principles well worth our consideration as we explore the facets of listening in contemporary communication.[2]

Working with upper-level college students studying small group theory and techniques, we have become increasingly aware how well the American educational system prepares its students for competition, and how poorly it prepares anyone for the cooperative skills necessary in our increasingly urban

[2] Carl R. Rogers and Richard E. Farson, "Active Listening," in Richard C. Huseman, Cal M. Logue, and Dwight L. Freshley, *Readings in Interpersonal and Organizational Communication*, Boston: Holbrook Press, 1969, pp. 480–496.

society and complex business and industrial organizations. We preach equality and reward excellence; we evaluate one another from babyhood on. Parents criticize so children "can learn." Teachers pit students against one another "to get a little healthy competition going." Competition exists in most modern societies, in and out of school; but it seems unfortunate to us that the students we encourage to work together in order to learn first-hand how group dynamics develop and how cooperation must be worked on throughout the class, report that this class is the first in which they *had* to cooperate to make the class work out. Most students have had to live with being ranked since kindergarten. Despite every device educators have come up with (no grades, no "smart" or "slow" groupings, no "failures"), students are constantly told, verbally and nonverbally, where they stand. No wonder our antennae are always out for cues about our personal worth.

We are so used to being evaluated, so used to having our statements accepted or rejected, that when someone actually listens to what we say *without evaluating it in any way*, we want to talk forever. There is an old Spanish proverb, "He who keeps silent consents." When someone listens so nonjudgmentally, we dare to assume he agrees with us, accepts us as we are, is "on our wave length." This is the core of active listening, and yet there is much more to it. If as a listener you never respond, the person talking cannot be sure how you are responding; your mind could be a thousand miles away, or you could just be bored. The person talking needs some indication that you are empathetic to what he says.

If you are listening actively, as Rogers describes the concept, your mind is right with the person who is talking. You are trying to walk that mile in his shoes for the time involved, and you atune yourself to the person to such an extent that you cannot sit in judgment of him because you share his feelings from his point of view. Does it sound a little impossible? Perhaps it would take years of practice to become a totally supportive, nonevaluative active listener, but the basic premises and some of the techniques themselves have proved very interesting and useful to some of our students. They point out the slightly "manipulative" character of the technique: After all, you *do* have a purpose when you practice active listening; you are witholding yourself and your opinions for the express purpose of helping someone else discuss and sort out his own feelings, and work out his own solutions. Even when you are asked, "What do you think? What's your opinion?" Rogers says you must turn the question back to the speaker and give neither negative nor positive evaluation.

Certainly in terms of relationship communication skills, to be able to actively listen is extremely valuable, but such listening must be totally honest, verbally and nonverbally. You cannot "con" people by pretending to listen actively; if you try to use active listening as a manipulative tool, as we define *manipulate*—doing things for your own ends, not anybody else's—you will be found out sooner or later.

SUGGESTED PROJECTS

1 Make a list of words that tend to make you respond in such a way that you can hardly listen to what comes next.
2 Think back to the experiences in communication you have had in the past week. Select which of the three styles of listening would have been the most appropriate for three situations you choose. Write a short paper analyzing your experience as a listener in each of the three situations. Was your listening style the most appropriate one, as you think back over each instance? If not, can you figure out why not?
3 Select a group that is important to you—your family, your fellow workers, or your close friends. Analyze the listening skill of several other people in the group, and then analyze your own listening in that group. Can you suggest ways to improve the others' listening ability, as well as your own?
4 Do you think that any one of the three listening styles is more "natural" to you than the other two? If so, why do you think it is, and if not, why not? What style of listening is the most difficult for you, and why?

SUGGESTED READINGS

Barker, Larry L. *Listening Behavior.* Englewood Cliffs, N.J.: Prentice-Hall, 1971.

Bormann, Ernest G., William S. Howell, Ralph G. Nichols, and George L. Shapiro. *Interpersonal Communication in the Modern Organization.* Englewood Cliffs, N.J.: Prentice-Hall, 1969. "Listening to the Spoken Word," pp. 167–177; "Getting the Message," pp. 183–199; "Evaluating the Message," pp. 203–212.

Huseman, Richard C., Cal M. Logue, and Dwight L. Freshley. *Readings in Interpersonal and Organizational Communication.* Boston: Holbrook Press, 1969. "Communication through Listening," pp. 457–496.

Lewis, Thomas, and Ralph G. Nichols. *Speaking and Listening: A Guide to Effective Oral-Aural Communication.* Dubuque, Iowa: Brown, 1965.

Nichols, Ralph G., and Leonard Stevens. *Are You Listening?* New York: McGraw-Hill, 1957.

Chapter 9

HOW TO INFORM

The Emphasis on Information in Our Three Basic Styles

As we saw in Chapter 2, information is a basic concept in the message communication theory. Programmers often think of computers as data processors or information-processing systems. Organization, an inherent property of information, is basic to the fight against entropy. High-fidelity information transmission is a value of the style. Because of the importance of information, the question of how to inform is particularly important to people communicating in the message communication style. Much of what we discuss in this chapter is pertinent to learning to communicate effectively in that style.

The public-speaking style places less emphasis upon information than it does upon persuasion, yet the question of how to inform is important to public speakers as well. One common cultural communication transaction within the style is the speech to inform, or the lecture. The public-speaking theory also emphasizes the importance of clarifying ideas and informing the audience as a means to proving a case and to persuasion in general. Much of what we discuss in this chapter is pertinent to learning to be a good public lecturer.

The relationship communication style places the least emphasis of all three styles upon the question of how to inform. One collection of essays on interpersonal communication, for example, contains only one brief article on clear interpersonal communication and that turns out to be largely a discussion drawn from the message communication style.[1] Another essay in the same collection discredits the theory that "the aim of communication is to transmit ideas from one person to another." Such theories, according to the essay, "minimize or overlook completely, the interactive and dynamic nature of the communicative process."[2]

As we have seen, the relationship style is a relatively new one and is still evolving, so we can expect such inconsistencies and ambiguities relating to aspects of the theory. In our survey of the writings on relationship communication we have not been able to find a coherent and consistent treatment of material relating to communicating information. Some writers take the first approach above and borrow from the message communication style, using the term *feedback* in a way which is inconsistent with its usual use. Some writers take the second approach and suggest that theories based upon information transmission are unsatisfactory; they then go on to stress the importance of context, the process nature of communication, and the active involvement of all participants in a good communication event. They further note that the communication process creates meanings which are personal, unique, and only brought into communion with the greatest difficulty.

AN EXERCISE IN INFORMATIONAL MESSAGE COMMUNICATION

Theorists in the message communication style often advise that as a message source, you may increase the fidelity of information transmission by analyzing the available channels for your message and selecting as many channels as possible to assure high-fidelity communication. You should analyze the noise in the system and find ways to reduce it if possible. You should seek ways to maximize feedback. You should use the proper amount of redundancy to overcome unavoidable noise and to adapt to the attitudes, communication skills, and

[1] John Stewart, ed., *Bridges Not Walls: A Book About Interpersonal Communication*, Reading, Mass.: Addison-Wesley, 1973, pp. 116–130.
[2] Dean C. Barnlund, "Toward a Meaning-Centered Philosophy of Communication," in Stewart, ibid. pp. 44–45.

understanding of the receiver. You should also seek the ideal rate of transmission, given the capacity of the system.[3]

One common instructional technique in the message communication style is to have a student play the role of message source and inform the rest of the class (playing the role of receivers) about how to make a geometric pattern with paper and pencil, or how to fold a piece of paper into the shape of a bird, or a drinking cup. In one variation, for instance, the instructor gives the message source some patterns made by tracing around the edges of a domino. The instructor also gives each receiver a domino, and they supply several sheets of paper. The source's intent is to get each receiver to duplicate a given pattern. The instructor will often repeat the exercise with different patterns, increasing feedback and the number of channels each time. For example, in the first try, the instructor might restrict the source to one channel—hearing—by placing the student behind a screen so the receivers cannot see the source. Screening the message source also eliminates nonverbal feedback, and the instructor may approximate the condition of zero feedback by not allowing the receivers to speak or make any paralinguistic sounds that could be interpreted as nonverbal feedback. In the second version, the instructor might increase the channels by allowing the receivers to see the source and might introduce some feedback by allowing the source to monitor the nonverbal feedback of the receivers. In a third try, the instructor might keep the multiple channels for the source's messages and add verbal feedback to the nonverbal to achieve a condition approximating unlimited feedback. The instructor thus creates an ever closer approximation of the model communication event in the message communication style as the controls on feedback are relaxed. The exercise requires some clear check on the comparative fidelity of information transmission as levels of feedback and number of channels change, such as the comparison of two geometric patterns.[4]

[3] For typical advice from message communication theorists see James C. McCroskey, Carl E. Larson, and Mark L. Knapp, *An Introduction to Interpersonal Communication*, Englewood Cliffs, N.J.: Prentice-Hall, 1971, "Suggestions for Achieving Greater Accuracy," pp. 32–34.

[4] A study by Leavitt and Mueller used a research design similar to the exercise above but they conducted the data gathering with greater care. They discovered that the condition of free feedback resulted in the highest-fidelity communication; partial feedback resulted in higher fidelity than no feedback, but under conditions of no feedback, sources took less time trying to achieve understanding. Put another way, feedback in the message communication style increases fidelity but takes a greater expenditure of time. See H. J. Leavitt and Ronald A. H. Mueller, "Some Effects of Feedback on Communication," *Human Relations*, 4 (1951), 401–410; see also William V.

AN EXERCISE IN INFORMATIVE PUBLIC SPEAKING

The theory of the public-speaking communication style contains considerable material on how to inform a listener in terms of briefing sessions, lectures, and so forth. One common instructional technique in the public-speaking communication style is to have the student speaker prepare a five- or six-minute speech to inform. After several minutes of the speech, the instructor tells the audience members that they may interrupt the speaker and ask for clarification. They are told, however, that they must confine their interruptions to one of three questions: "What do you mean?" "How do you know?" and "So what?" The instructor directs the student to proceed with the speech only when the audience members indicate they have received a satisfactory answer to their questions.

SIMILARITIES IN INFORMATIONAL SKILLS IN THE TWO STYLES

The instructional techniques used in the two styles of communication indicate that many of the basic skills for making ideas clear cut across these styles. The theory and practice of the public-speaking style and the message communication style in regard to information transmission and the speech to inform are comparable in many ways, even though the terminology of the two approaches may differ. We do not as yet see anything analogous to the theory of information transmission emerging clearly in the theory of the relationship communication style. For the remainder of the chapter we will discuss the most important theoretical formulations regarding techniques for communicating information. We will indicate when a skill is particularly pertinent to the message communication model by referring to elements of that model, such as the *source* and the *receiver*. When a skill is especially useful in public speaking, we will indicate that by referring to *speaker* and *listeners* or *audiences*.

The Message to Inform

Often when we are the source in the message communication style, we have as our basic purpose telling the receiver something about the world. We are emphasizing the first face of

Haney, "A Comparative Study of Unilateral and Bilateral Communication," *Academy of Management Journal*, 7 (1964), 128–136.

language usage — the denotative. For example, when we tell someone how to get from one place to another, we are informing him about the geographic location of various places. The basic content of a message discussing facts is *information*. A common dictionary definition of *information* is "a message about facts."

What are facts? *Facts* are those things which two or more people can see and agree on. We encode factual messages about such things as chairs, tables, cars, people, buildings, and their relationships to one another. Someone may come to a meeting, look about the room, and ask, "Where is John?" If you have the information, you may encode a message in reply as follows: "John just called. His car is stuck in the ice in his driveway, and he will be late." The information in the message relates to things such as the human being called John, his automobile, his driveway, and the relationships among these things, for example, the relationship contained in the words "he is stuck in his driveway." Further, the message provides information about John's relationship to the building in which the meeting is being held: that he is in his driveway, that the driveway is some distance from the place of the meeting, and that he is there now and will be here somewhat later than expected.

A message to inform consists of information about facts. We need to understand and have skills in the denotative use of language in order to make ideas about facts clear. We begin our study of how to inform by examining techniques for describing and explaining facts.

Definitions

One of the most important tools a speaker has to help make ideas clear is the ability to define a word. Before a person can tell someone about facts, he must decide whether his listener understands the words he hopes to use. If the listener does not know what is named by a word in the speaker's message, he is likely to misunderstand or be confused by the message.

When a speaker defines a word, he tries to make clear to his listener the thing, property, or relationship he means to indicate when he uses the word in their conversation. If the source and receiver have the same meaning for the content words in messages—that is, they both use the same words for naming things and the same words to stand for properties and relationships—they can talk about the facts of their common experience. They can then talk about the things in a room. For example, one person might say, "Please sit in that red chair." Or, "Be careful of sitting on that red chair, because it is weak and may break." People can also speak about chairs that are not present at the time of their conversation. For instance, the source may describe the color, size, and shape of a chair which he is selling. Should the receiver decide to buy the chair, he will expect it to have certain properties because of the information he decoded from the message. If the chair is not what he expected, either the source misled him by claiming that the chair had certain properties it did not possess (his information was false) or the source and he did not have the same definitions for the words in the message (the receiver misunderstood).

When you are trying to make an idea clear you must look carefully at the words you use in your messages. You must ask yourself, "Will all the people taking part in the communication decode a name as standing for the same thing?" If not, can you use another word for the same thing that everybody will understand? If not, you must select the best word, in your opinion, for the thing to be discussed and carefully define it for your listeners.

One way to define a term is to find other words that say the same or nearly the same thing, and by using these other words, clarify how you plan to use the term in the communications to follow. Many of the terms that we have used earlier in the book have been defined in other words. The dictionary definition of a term usually supplies other words that mean the same thing. For example, one meaning of *communicate* in a good dictionary is "to give thoughts, feelings, or information by writing, speaking, and so forth."

IMAGINARY DEFINITIONS

If one can describe the thing or events named by a term clearly in other words, the result is a definition. An interesting by-product of the process of definition is that we can describe an imaginary thing, person, or event, and give it a name. For example, we can describe a person who is "the present king of the United States" and refer to such a person in our messages. Of course, the United States has no king, so no real person is named by the definition. Yet we can go on talking about "Samuel Rex, the present king of the United States," as though such a person existed. We can also pick a name such as *unicorn* and supply such a precise description of the beast that an artist can draw a picture of one, even though the animal does not exist.

Take the case of the *rockslide cornberet*, a strange, gray bird the size of a crow with a crown of feathers resembling a beret. The rockslide cornberet gets its name from its love of corn, its beretlike headdress, and the female's peculiar practice of laying a single egg in some stones at the top of a mountain and then kicking egg and stones over the edge, thus starting a rockslide. When the rockslide comes to rest in the valley, the pile of stones serves to protect and incubate the egg so the female does not have to sit on it. Since neither source nor receiver can observe the non-existent rockslide cornberet, if they argue about it they are talking about individual impressions and not about anything in the world which they can observe to correct their impressions.

We do not get into serious trouble talking about mythical animals or the present king of the United States, but we do get into difficulties when we talk about *the Establishment, a racist society, duty,* or *Women's Liberation* and cannot find any observations to correct our impressions. Much misunderstanding and many arguments come from discussions of terms that, like the rockslide cornberet, stand for nothing but the meanings we put into them. Equally important is the problem posed by defining terms such as *democracy, capitalism,* or *communism* without reference to actual events. The process of definition allows us to name a nonexistent economic system called *pure capitalism* or a governmental arrangement called *pure communism.* Having named these fictitious things, we can go on to discuss them as though they were real events with real implications. If we define something called *world communism* in terms of a powerful force of millions of people dedicated to the violent overthrow of capitalism and the destruction of the United States, we may act as though the thing we have defined actually exists in the world. If the thing defined is as unreal as the rockslide cornberet, we might act foolishly because we are responding to definitions and not to things. (What of the man who spends years in the Rockies with his camera, trying to get a photograph of the rockslide cornberet?) The same thing can happen with definitions such as the *conspiracy* to kill Black Panthers or the *conspiracy* to overthrow the government by violent means.

If you wish to inform people, therefore, you should be sure that both you and your listeners understand whether the terms defined refer to the things of the world that can be observed and whose definitions can be checked, or are names for mythical people or events or for abstract concepts.

FALSE INFORMATION

One final problem relating to clarifying ideas and conveying information concerns confusion resulting not from lack of skill in definition, but from the intent to mislead. On occasion a source uses words that all his hearers understand and says something about the things under discussion which is not true. In short, the source asserts something about the world which he knows is not true, and he does so with intent. The information contained in his message is *false*, and the result of the intent to mislead is a lie. A communicator who exploits the situation where the receiver expects clarification and information by purposely telling a falsehood has been unethical, not lacking in communication skill.

Explanations

DESCRIPTION

One of the most important ways in which a person can make something clear to another is to explain it. Perhaps the most basic and important way to explain something is to describe it. When we describe something, we find a suitable name for it—one that all involved in the communication understand—and then proceed to use descriptive words that denote properties or relations to explain the thing. When either the source or the receivers of the message (or both) have fewer words for the properties or relations of the thing under consideration than they need, they use comparisons (figures of speech) to indicate that the thing is like something else in certain respects; they may also point out how the thing differs from other commonly understood things and thus, by pointing out what it is not, begin to explain what it is.

When we describe a situation, a thing, a happening, or an event, we can use language to appeal to the listener's imagination. One of the most important ways in which people acquire information about their world is through their senses. By skillful descriptions of how a thing appears, sounds, smells, tastes, or feels, a message source can make a receiver understand the thing almost as though the listener were experiencing it himself. When trying to explain a complex experience or situation, we ought to use descriptions that appeal to as many of the senses as possible.

We can also describe something by *listing its parts.* We explained the model of message communication by using the *S M C R* key to the parts of the process. We might explain the government of the United States by listing the three main branches: the legislative, the executive, and the judicial. We could then go on to list the parts of the legislative branch, such as the House of Representatives and the Senate.

Another good way to explain certain things is to *describe the way they work.* We could explain an internal-combustion engine by showing how the gasoline is changed into a mist as it moves through the carburetor and is drawn into the cylinder by the vacuum created by the stroke of the piston moving out of the cylinder. We could go on to describe how the stroke of the piston pushing back into the cylinder compresses the mixture of air and gasoline until the spark from the spark plug ignites it and the resulting explosion drives the piston forward.

CAUSAL EXPLANATIONS

We can explain some things by pointing out the *causes or scientific laws* that account for them. Why do some people who shoot heroin get hepatitis, or inflammation of the liver? We could explain that hepatitis is caused by small organisms that can be transmitted from one person to another through the bloodstream and that such small organisms can live for a time on a dirty injection needle.

We can explain some human behavior on the basis of the *goals and desires* of the people involved. Why does a student become nervous before giving a speech in front of a class? We might explain stage fright in terms of the student's desire to get a good grade and to make a good impression on the others in the class. Since the student knows that the opportunity to get up alone in front of everybody and have the spotlight on him for a short period of time offers a great chance to impress the others (and the instructor), he realizes that much is at stake. What if he forgets his speech and makes a fool of himself in front of everybody? Since he is risking a great deal, he approaches the speech with mingled hopes and fears. He might win a great deal, but he might lose as much. He feels something like a gambler who is risking a lot of money in a crap game or at poker. He is tense, excited, and fearful.

THE PLAUSIBLE STORY

We can explain some things by telling a *plausible story* that includes all the facts to be explained and makes them hang together so they sound possible. Children who like to do things they are not supposed to do sometimes get caught. A child might become adept at telling stories to keep from being punished. Bill comes to school late after playing hooky, and he has not done his homework. He tells a story about how he overslept because he had to stay up late taking care of his sick mother and how, because of all the extra work taking care of things at home, he could not do the homework. The ancient Greeks explained many important events in their lives through stories about the gods on Mount Olympus. Lawyers often explain the events surrounding a crime by placing them into a plausible story. Thus the prosecuting attorney might account for certain events by accusing the person on trial of having stolen property in his apartment because he was the boss of a ring of burglars, with whom he was meeting at his place to lay plans for future crimes. The defense attorney might say that the accused knew some of the burglars but was an innocent victim, because one of his friends had asked him to keep the stolen stuff. The accused did not know where the goods came from and had no idea they were stolen. The meetings in the apartment were to play cards, and while the accused may have been unwise in his choice of card-playing friends, he was not guilty of any crime.

CLASSIFICATION

We may also explain something by *fitting it into a class.* If we create several classes on the basis of some common feature of the things in each class, we can explain some characteristics of an individual thing by fitting it into the proper class. For example, if we take a number of children and divide them into classes on the basis of their ages, as is often done in an elementary school, we can further divide the fourth graders on the basis of reading ability, so that we have bluebirds (fast readers) and redbirds (slow readers). We can explain some things about Johnnie by saying he is a fourth-grade bluebird. We use classification systems to help explain things in a number of different areas. In botany we divide plants into classes and subclasses. In biology we divide animals into genus and species. In sociology we divide people into socioeconomic classes.

Definition and explanation are basic ways of clarifying a point and informing others. We have discussed some important ways to define and explain. Several additional tools are available to the person who is trying to make ideas clear. These additional tools can be used to define terms and explain things, but they are so important for other purposes as well that we will deal with them separately and in some detail. The most important tools for clarifying ideas are the example, the analogy, and the narrative.

Examples

One of the most important skills you should develop to improve your communication is the ability to recognize and use examples. What we call *examples* are sometimes also called *illustrations*.

An example is one (of a number of things) taken to show (the nature or character of) all. The example illustrates some important points about all the things like it. An example may also be an instance that illustrates the operation of a law or a general principle.

Earlier in the chapter we used several examples to clarify an abstract idea. In discussing the notion that the process of definition allows a person to describe a fictitious event or person and supply a name for it, we used the examples of the present king of the United States and the rockslide cornberet.

REAL AND HYPOTHETICAL EXAMPLES
When a person submits an example to make a point clear, he may select an instance that actually happened, or he may invent an example, much as an author makes up a story. When a speaker uses nonfictional accounts of actual events or people, he is using a *real* example. When he dreams up a fictitious incident that might have happened, but in fact did not, he is using a *hypothetical* example.

Real examples are useful in making a point clear, but they may also be evidence to prove a point in an argument. If a person wants to prove that the smoking of marijuana does not necessarily lead to the use of heroin, he may submit as proof the real examples of a number of people who have smoked marijuana but have not used heroin. Hypothetical examples, on the other hand, are not proof, because if you were in an argument and made up a number of examples to support your side, another person could make up an equal number of examples to support his side. Suppose one person argues that juvenile delinquency is caused by poverty and miserable living conditions in the inner city. "Take the case of Johnnie," he says, "growing up in the ghetto. Johnnie is much more likely to become delinquent than a child in the suburbs." "Not at all," answers the other person. "Take the case of rich Billy, whose parents have no time for him and who give him every material thing he wants instead of giving him enough love, time, guidance, and discipline." Both parties in such an argument can dream up make-believe characters such as Johnnie and Billy as long as they like and match hypothetical example with hypothetical example. When using real examples, however, the debaters can submit only actual happenings as evidence.

Real examples carry more weight, because they are factual and because the person in a conference, interview, group discussion, or public speech who explains ideas by using real examples gives his listeners the feeling that he is speaking from a firm basis of facts and that he is an expert.

We may have trouble using real examples, however, when we take part in informal talks and do not have notes with us. If a point comes up in a conversation or an interview and we need an example to make the idea clear, we may not remember the details of a real example and may not have time to look them up. Even if we have time to prepare for a discussion or business meeting or public speech, we may search the library in vain for exactly the right example to make a point. We can tailor the hypothetical example to the needs of the audience, the point to be clarified, and the time available. Thus, although hypothetical examples are not evidence, they are a good way to make a point clear.

THE ARTFUL USE OF EXAMPLES

Why are examples so important to basic communication skills, no matter what the setting or the occasion? Examples are concrete and make broad principles and laws easy to hear, smell, see, taste, and feel; when we stop talking about the law of gravity and start using the example of the falling basketball, the listener can visualize the event and see how the law works in actual practice. Examples add interest to a message. A good example makes a difficult idea easier to understand. We enjoy the understanding that comes from seeing how or why something works. We like to be able to understand things, and so an example which brings understanding also brings interest.

People appreciate the skillful use of example. Most of us enjoy watching an expert perform. Even though we may not be good musicians, we probably enjoy watching and hearing a skillful pianist. Although we may not care much for baseball, we may enjoy watching a talented shortstop field ground balls. When a talented and skillful speaker uses a good example—one well suited to the listener, the occasion, and the point under discussion—we get a similar sense of interest and appreciation.

The use of examples is an art that can be acquired through practice. Some aspects of communication discussed in this book are difficult if not impossible to change; the most you can hope to do is understand them, take them into account, and develop the right attitude about them. We cannot change time limitations; we cannot change the way dialects reflect social and geographic differences; we cannot control the complicating effects of status on communication situations; and we cannot change the basic rules of the dynamics of small groups. We just have to allow for these things in our conduct within the particular situations. But some aspects of communication can be controlled, and a good communicator is one who has learned to encode messages more skillfully than a poor one for a given receiver (or receivers), for a given purpose, in a given situation. One of the arts of communication is the invention and use of examples to make a point clear. Any speaker can pick an example to clarify a given idea. A good speaker is able to pick an example that interests the listener and is within the listener's experience and level of understanding. By skillful use of examples he can connect even abstract, difficult ideas to the experience of the other person.

When you pick examples to clarify a point you ought to be listener-oriented. A good speaker has a number of different examples available for illustrating the same point. He invents examples from different situations. The speaker who picks an example that interests the listener helps ensure the success of his attempts to inform. By selecting examples of different lengths, the speaker can make his comments shorter or longer. The speaker who has a good supply of examples can be guided by feedback and supply the listener with additional examples until he is sure he has been understood.

Suppose we wish to clarify the point we made in Chapter 3 that each person should carefully decide whether to learn the standard general American dialect if he does not already speak it. Suppose, too, that we know quite a bit about the people who will hear our speech. We know how old they are, whether they are male or female, what jobs they have, their hobbies, their social and economic class, whether they are from the South or the North, from the city, the suburbs, or a rural area. We have available the following examples to clarify the point about the decision to learn a new dialect:

> *An actual person who is a network television announcer and grew up in Tidewater Virginia*
> *A hypothetical person who is an education major from Brooklyn and plans to teach in Brooklyn*
> *An actual person who is a business major at Louisiana State University and speaks with a Cajun accent*
> *An actual person who is a community-college student with no major as yet and who comes from a suburb in Los Angeles*
> *An actual person who is a black star in the National Basketball Association, attended a Big Ten university, and was originally from a ghetto of New York City*
> *A hypothetical person who is a Chicano from New Mexico and attends a junior college there*
> *An actual person who is from an aristocratic old family in North Carolina, is proud of her background, and is studying art*
> *An actual person who is a militant black from an inner-city ghetto in Detroit, studying to be a social worker*

Each of the above examples contains a great deal of information in addition to what we have described. Some are quite detailed and take longer to explain than others. Some are humorous, some serious, and some full of conflict. When we prepare to talk to a given group of people, we have to pick the example which seems best for this audience in this setting, at this time. Decide which of the above examples would be best for each of the following occasions:

> *A meeting of the Parent-Teachers Association in a wealthy suburb of Detroit*

*A meeting of the Parent-Teachers Association in an
inner-city school in New York City*

A speech communication class in a Los Angeles College

*A group of students at a high-school careers-day con-
vocation in Atlanta, Georgia*

*A meeting of the Black Student Union at a Big Ten uni-
versity*

Since examples can add interest and emotional tone to a
message, the source must consider the occasion as well as the
audience when selecting which examples to use. If a person
plans to discuss a topic in an informal two-person conversation over coffee in a cafeteria, he might use a light, humorous
example. If he plans to clarify the point in an important
presentation before a large group in a formal setting, he
should pick an example which has a different tone and treatment. One should not use humorous or sexy examples on solemn occasions, nor should he use serious, weighty, or complicated examples in an after-dinner speech.

Analogies

The analogy is another important way to clarify ideas. If you
become good at using examples and analogies, you will be
able to meet 80 to 90 percent of your needs in making a point
clear. An *analogy* is an extended comparison. When a speaker
takes two things or two events and points out that they are
the same in important respects, he is making a comparison. If
he continues to point out several similarities, he makes an
analogy. The short comparison is a figure of speech. "She has
a neck like a swan's" is a figure of speech, a simile. If we take
the figure of speech about the girl's neck and extend the comparison of girl to swan, we may invent an analogy as follows:
"She has a neck like a swan's. She swims with the grace of a
swan, but when she walks she waddles like a swan. Her voice
is a swanlike screech, and her nose looks like a swan's beak."

Analogies are like examples in many respects. Like examples, analogies come in two major types—the literal and
the figurative. A *literal* analogy resembles a real example. The
literal analogy is a comparison between two things, people, or
incidents drawn from the same class or genus. The speaker
who compares Metropolitan Community College to North
Oaks Community College in regard to size of student body,
quality of instruction, courses offered, and extracurricular
activities available is using a literal analogy. He can find and

verify this information. A *figurative* analogy, on the other hand, resembles a hypothetical example. It is a comparison between two things that, at first glance, do not seem comparable. A girl's neck is not really like a swan's neck. A girl does not have feathers on her neck, nor is a girl's neck as thin and long as a swan's. And yet the listener understands when we say that the girl's neck is like a swan's. Life is not really like a football game, although many a coach has used that figurative analogy in his annual speech for the team.

The literal analogy, like the real example, is an important tool to prove a point as well as to inform or clarify. If you know a great deal about one event you can often reason about what will happen in a similar situation. Let us say that a student did well in science courses at a small liberal-arts college in the East. In his sophomore year he transfers to a small liberal-arts school nearer his home in the Midwest. We might argue that since he did well in science courses at the first school he will do well in science courses at the second; this argument is based on a literal analogy.

We often think in terms of analogies and try to reason from past experience to the present and future on the basis of literal comparisons. The literal analogy is an important way to make ideas clear to a listener. The ability to identify literal analogies is basic to better thinking. If we practice inventing analogies and expressing them, we can improve both our thinking and our communication.

The literal analogy can build on the past experience of a listener. A good way to make a new idea or a new situation clear to another person is to compare the new idea to the old. Moving the listener from the familiar to the unfamiliar creates interest and understanding. The listener often finds familiar material dull. If the content of a message is unfamiliar, on the other hand, the listener is often so confused that he rejects the material and makes no attempt to understand it. In a good message the content is familiar enough so the listener can keep his bearings, yet is novel enough to create interest. If a recent graduate returns to his high school after his first semester at college, a young friend still in high school might ask, "What is college like?" The college freshman might answer with a literal analogy comparing the high school they both know to the college only the speaker knows.

Literal analogies, like real examples, usually depend upon factual material for their development. You cannot always find a good literal analogy to use in an informal conversation or discussion. When you do find an apt literal analogy, however, you have a powerful tool for making ideas clear.

Figurative analogies resemble hypothetical examples in that they are largely fictitious. Often the message source can express an emotion or an attitude toward some person or event more by comparing two things that might not, on the surface, seem comparable. For example, the president of a large steel company might argue:

> *My company is criticized because we have a large share of the market for steel. I can't understand the criticism. The steel industry is like the National Football League. If a team wins a large share of its games in the league everybody thinks it is a great team, because that is what football is all about — winning games. But when we win a large share of the steel market we are criticized for being a monopoly. Yet that is what the steel industry is all about — winning a share of the market.*

The comparison of the steel industry to the football league expresses a strong positive attitude toward the industry on the part of the speaker. Try to invent an analogy that would express a different attitude toward the steel industry on the basis of this following hint: "Big steel is like an octopus that has its tentacles into every aspect of our lives including the government!"

Figurative analogies add interest to a comment designed to clarify an idea. They reveal the speaker's basic communicative skill, and we enjoy the artistry of a good comparison, whether it is a short figure of speech or an extended figurative analogy.

Figurative analogies can help make complex notions and principles easier to understand. One common figurative analogy is the comparison of the functioning of the human nervous system to a telephone exchange. Another is the comparison of the structure of an atom to the structure of the solar system.

Narratives

The final important device for making a point clear is the narrative. *Narratives* are stories, either true or fictitious, long or short, that contain characters, situations, and action. Stories are about one central character who draws the audience's interest. Usually the main character has a clear object in view and attempts to achieve his goal; in the process he runs into trouble, and the story tells about his good and bad times as he works for his objective. The old formula for a love story, for example, is boy meets girls, boy falls in love with girl, boy loses girl, boy gets girl. The fun of the story is in the many different ways in which the boy may lose the girl and the unusual ways in which he may win her back. In a good story, the forces that keep the boy from getting the girl ought to be evenly balanced with the chance the hero will get the girl. Conflict and suspense result from the hurdles the character must overcome to win his objectives and the even odds on his success or failure.

Narratives may be factual; among real-life stories, some of the most effective are the speaker's personal experiences. Perhaps it would be appropriate to tell about the time he was trying to get to school for a big examination, but stayed up late studying and slept through his alarm. When he did wake up he had only a short time to get to school. Racing to make it in time, he was stopped by a policemen, and so forth. The personal-experience story is one of the most common and effective ways to make a point clear. A well-told personal-experience story can amuse, illustrate, clarify, and present the speaker in an attractive light as a person of insight and humor.

The *anecdote* is a short narrative concerning one particular happening of an interesting or amusing nature. When the anecdote is amusing, it also may be called a *joke.* Both serious anecdotes and jokes tend to have a sudden twist at the end which is called the *punch line.*

Narratives may be used as explanations by fitting facts into a plausible story, as we noted earlier. Narrative material is often worked into analogies and examples to add human interest, conflict, and suspense. Narratives also play an extremely important role in the process of persuasion, as we shall see in Chapter 12, where we discuss the way dramatic stories present heroes and villains acting out dreams which people often strive to achieve.

The Basic Message Unit

In discussing communicating to inform we must consider any technique, such as an example or an analogy, in terms of the point the speaker wishes to make. The basic building block for messages consists of two parts: the point to be made and the material to support it. Sources may encode messages composed of single blocks placed in some order or structure. The

Chapter 9

THE KEY IDEAS

One of the most important skills in making ideas clear is the ability to define words so that your listener fully understands you.

A description of a thing or event named by a term results in a definition of the term.

Definition can also be the process that creates imaginary things and assigns them names, as in the case of unicorns and other mythical beasts.

Abstract names such as democracy, capitalism, communism, youth, *and the* Establishment *cause communication problems when used without reference to actual events and things.*

People get false information because of inept communication or because the speaker intentionally lies to them.

The most important tools for making ideas clear are the example, the analogy, and the narrative.

The example illustrates some important points about all things like it or provides

basic building block is used in talking with another person informally, in casual conversation, in a conference or an interview, in a small group discussion or a business meeting, and in a presentation or a public speech. No matter what the reason or setting for your message, you need to know how to construct the basic message units.

When a communication source presents only his main points, without supporting or amplifying them, his messages sound and read like a telegram or an outline of the major headings for a theme in an English class. Brief comments on points to be made are hard to understand. Telegraphic talking has the advantage of brevity but usually produces confusion.

STATING A POINT
A point to be made clear should be expressed in a complete, simple, declarative sentence. We use the terms *complete*, *simple*, and *declarative* in their technical meanings for English grammar. Complete sentences include both subject

an instance of the operation of a law or general principle.

When a person uses an example he may select one that actually happened or one he made up.

Real examples not only clarify points but can be used as evidence in an argument.

We can tailor hypothetical examples to the needs of the listener, the point we are making, and the time available, but since they are fictitious, we cannot use them as proof, only as clarification.

A good example makes a difficult idea easier to understand and arouses the interest of the listener.

The choice and use of examples is an art that can be learned.

A short comparison is a figure of speech; an extended comparison is an analogy.

Literal analogies are comparisons between things from the same class or genus.

The literal analogy can build on the listener's past experience by comparing the thing to be explained to something the listener already knows.

If we know a good deal about one event, we often use a literal analogy to reason about what will happen in a similar situation.

Figurative analogies are based upon comparisons that are unusual; they add interest to a message because of their novelty.

In a narrative, conflict and suspense result from the hurdles the main character must overcome to win his goal.

Stories may be factual or fictitious.

Among the most effective factual narratives for a speaker are those dealing with his or her personal experiences.

The basic building blocks for messages consist of a point to be proved and the material that supports, explains, or illustrates it.

A message can be too brief, because points that are not explained or illustrated are hard to understand.

and predicate, as follows: "You must know black English to teach black students," "The operators of the numbers games pick the winning numbers from common experiences," "The moon's gravity affects the way a person can walk on the moon's surface."

Remember that a simple sentence has but one subject and one predicate. Put another way, the point to be made in a message unit ought to contain only one idea. The following sentence would make a poor point for a message unit: "The operators of the numbers games pick the winning numbers from common experiences and generally pay off the police to keep in business."

A declarative sentence states something, in contrast to a question, which asks for information, or a command, which tells somebody to do something. "How do they pick the winning numbers for the numbers game?" is not a good point for a basic message unit. Neither is the command "Stop playing the numbers."

Never underestimate the importance of finding a good,

clear way to state the point you wish to make. If you can express what you want to say in a good, clear, simple sentence, you have gone a long way toward getting your point across.

SUPPORTING MATERIAL

After you have found a good statement of the point to clarify, provide supporting material to make the idea clear. Give an example (real or hypothetical), an analogy (literal or figurative), or a narrative that applies directly to the point. (Of course, if the idea is difficult for the receiver to understand, you may give several examples or analogies or stories to clarify one point.) An important mistake of beginning speakers is to use an example that does not have much to do with the point they are trying to make. Here is a hypothetical example of the does-not-apply mistake:

> *The operators of the numbers game in my neighborhood pick the winning numbers from most anything. For example, I know this one bookie who pays protection money all the time, and he's been working this one place for a long time and nobody has bothered him or given him any trouble.*

In the above instance, the so-called "example" has nothing to do with the point made before it.

PATTERNS OF FORMING MESSAGE UNITS

Basic message units can be formed in several ways. The following four patterns are often used:

Type 1
Point to be made clear
Supporting material (examples, analogies, stories)

Type 2
Supporting material (examples, analogies, stories)
Point to be made clear

Type 3
Supporting material (examples, analogies, stories)
Point to be made clear
Further supporting material

Type 4
Supporting material (several examples, analogies, stories): The point is never stated in so many words, but the audience is supposed to be able to figure it out

from the mass of supporting material; the point is made *by innuendo.*

As a general rule, the patterns that state the point to be made clear first or last are the best; certainly you seldom will be wrong using message-building blocks of these first two types. Burying the point in the middle of a message block often hinders the receiver's efforts to dig it out and follow your comment. Leaving out the point entirely is quite risky. However, if you are reasonably sure of your listener's ability to identify the point on the basis of your clear examples and analogies, the fourth pattern can be effective, partly because it provides variety and partly because it creates the illusion that the point is the listener's own notion and facilitates his willingness to accept it. We recommend, therefore, that you use the basic message unit without a clear statement of the point primarily for persuasive situations and that you stick to types 1 and 2 for most efforts to inform.

SUGGESTED PROJECTS

1 Write 10 statements illustrating good points to be made clear. Make sure that each statement is phrased as a simple declarative sentence.
2 This is an oral exercise in making ideas clear. Select a complex concept from one of your other courses, such as the concept of comparative cost advantage in economics, or the concept of valence in chemistry, or the concept of mitosis in biology. State the point to be made clear, and using only one extended real example or one extended hypothetical example, make the point clear to the class. Your example should be 2 minutes in length. You should announce to the class *before you begin* which form of example you will use.
3 This is another oral exercise in making ideas clear. Select a concept similar to the one used in project 2 above. State the point to be made clear, and using only one extended figurative analogy or one extended literal analogy, make the point clear to the class. Again your analogy should be 2 minutes in length, and you should announce which analogy you will use before you begin.

SUGGESTED READINGS

Braden, Waldo, and Mary Louise Gehring. *Speech Practices.* New York: Harper & Row, 1958.
Jeffrey, Robert C., and Owen Peterson. *Speech: A Text with Adapted Readings.* New York: Harper & Row, 1971. "The Use of Supporting Material: Exposition," pp. 266–285.
Olbricht, Thomas. *Informative Speaking.* Glenview, Ill.: Scott, Foresman, 1968.

Chapter 10

HOW TO PERSUADE: THE PERSUASIVE POWER OF EVIDENCE AND REASONING

No aspect of communication is more important to our daily lives than persuasion. We are urged to vote for political candidates, to support reforms, to buy products, and to establish relationships with other people. The message with persuasive intent comes at us in two-person conversations and interviews; in face-to-face small group conferences; in public speeches and business presentations; in newspapers, magazines, letters; in films, radio shows, and television programs. Billboards proclaim suggestions about how we should act or believe; neon signs entice us to drink, eat, or buy. The lyrics of popular songs sell a point of view or a life style. We go to a job interview and try to persuade the interviewer to hire us. We take a job as a salesman and try to get a customer to make a purchase. We see an attractive person and try to persuade her or him to go to a movie.

Persuasion Defined

Persuasion is sometimes called changing another's behavior. It can also be defined as changing attitudes or belief, as win-

persuasion *Purposive communication aimed at a target audience and designed to influence
choice.*
coercion *The use of force or threats
of force to get people to do what the
coercer wants them to do, no
matter what their choice would be
in the matter.*

ning friends, influencing people, gaining cooperation, or selling a product or an idea. When we talk somebody into doing something, we have persuaded him. When we suggest ideas or beliefs or argue for a position with evidence and logic in such a way that the listeners change their behavior, attitudes, or beliefs, we have persuaded them.

We will define persuasion as communication to influence choice. When we speak to inform (make a point clear), we often provide the listener with information that opens up new horizons and increases choices, but when we speak to persuade we try to influence the listener's choices and narrow them to the one we prefer.

Notice that persuasion is communication intended to get a response from the receiver, to change the receiver's attitude or beliefs. The source of the message, the person giving a persuasive comment or making a persuasive point, has a specific purpose in mind and drafts the persuasive message to achieve that goal.

Persuasion is not the same as force. We can control human beings to some extent with the use of force or the threat of force. **Coercion** restricts choice. If you are forced to do something, your options are closed. Coercion eliminates choice, while persuasion influences it. Coercion does not require artistry. "Do this or I will bash in your head" may get results, but requires little skill—only the brute strength and the desire to deliver the blow. A good salesman, on the other hand, is skillful and has developed the art of persuasion to a high level. If selling were as easy as bashing in heads, more people would be making $50,000 a year in commissions.

Persuading someone is not the same as inducing him to do something by offering a powerful reward. A father might get his son to cut his hair by promising him a new car. Offering a large reward is similar to offering a threat of force. The boss who says, "Come to work on Saturday or I will fire you," is operating on the same level as the one who says, "Come to work on Saturday and I will give you a bonus." Neither offering a large reward nor threatening punishment involves much communication skill or selling ability.

The Importance of Persuasion

Persuasion cuts across all three of the major communication styles. As we have seen, persuasion is the core of the rhetorical tradition. The public-speaking style values the skillful persuasive speech above all other speech forms, and its theory relating to persuasion is extensive and detailed. Some of the theory of persuasion in the public-speaking style is artistic, and to be influenced, a person must be trained to appreciate public speeches in the appropriate style. Some theory of persuasion in the public-speaking style, however, is validated by practice and transfers to other settings, such as the television commercial, the political message on radio and television, and the therapy session of the psychiatrist.

While some elements of persuasion which are featured in the public-speaking style are ruled out of the message communication style, the latter nonetheless gives control equal emphasis with information transmission in terms of the intent of communication. Usually the rationale for control is scientific. According to one theoretician in the message communication style, for example, the theoretical goal of the scientific investigation of communication is to arrive at laws such that communicators "would be assured of maximum predictability, as well as the opportunity to manipulate their environments through communication in a way calculated to bring about desired behavioral responses on the part of their receivers."[1] A good deal of research effort has gone into discovering the variables which affect attitudes and behaviors of receivers. Such research and the resultant discoveries become part of the theory of the message communication style, and, in effect, that style is much concerned with persuasion.[2]

As we noted in Chapter 2, in the recent past, critics of the public-speaking and message communication styles have found these styles, with their emphasis on persuasion (control), manipulative and ethically bankrupt. This criticism of the older styles contributed to the rise of the relationship style, and as a result, the theory of the relationship style contains less specific treatment of persuasion than the other two. Nevertheless, persuasion is pertinent to the practice of the relationship style. Facilitators of training and sensitivity

[1] Gerald R. Miller, *Speech Communication: A Behavioral Approach*, Indianapolis: Bobbs-Merrill, 1966, p. 42.

[2] The study of variables which change attitudes has been voluminous but largely disappointing, because many of the questions asked have related to stylistic matters such as fear arousal, the order of arguments, presenting one-sided or two-sided arguments, language intensity, source credibility, and so forth. For typical summaries of research results see Erwin P. Bettinghaus, "Structure and Argument," in Gerald R. Miller and Thomas R. Nilsen, eds., *Perspectives on Argumentation*, Glenview, Ill.: Scott, Foresman, 1966, pp. 130–155; James C. McCroskey, "A Summary of Experimental Research on the Effects of Evidence in Persuasive Communication," *The Quarterly Journal of Speech*, 55, 1969, 169–176; C. David Mortensen, *Communication: The Study of Human Interaction*, New York: McGraw-Hill, 1972.

machiavellianism *Intentionally deceptive and manipulative behavior designed to get others to advance one's own goals.*

groups, of encounter groups, and of interpersonal communication exercises, as well as therapists and counselors—all use persuasive devices such as indirect suggestion to create the norms they desire in communication events. They apply techniques of indirect suggestion, group pressure for conformity, and the power of fantasy to achieve communication that approximates their model of the ideal. Mehrabian, for example, notes that, "Despite such therapists' firm intention not to maneuver their patients, researchers who have viewed therapy sessions through one-way mirrors have found that these therapists do influence patients, albeit in subtle ways."[3] Many of the subtle suggestions in the therapy sessions are nonverbal indications of approval and interest, or monitors of disapproval. The therapist may lean back, turn away, lean forward, change eye contact, and so forth.

PRIMARILY MANIPULATIVE STYLES

In addition to the major communication styles operating in contemporary society that we discuss in this book there are a number of other styles with a strong interest in persuasion, styles which are less important, less widespread, but which nonetheless fill the air and the electronic waves with persuasive messages. Some of these styles are manipulative and have as their main criterion for excellence the success of the communicator in manipulating the response of listeners. They include systematic deception as to facts, bluffing, spying to gain an advantage in bargaining or selling situations, secrecy to guard one's own position, the use of threats, the staging of charades to give a misrepresentation of the situation, and other, similar subterfuges.

Some communication scholars refer to manipulative styles as machiavellian. A famous Italian statesman and political philosopher of the fifteenth century named Machiavelli wrote a book on politics which placed political success above morality. He therefore came to symbolize a style of politics called **Machiavellian,** a term which refers to unscrupulous cunning, deception, and dishonesty. Investigators in social psychology and communication have studied the character of manipulative communication and have developed a test of Machiavellianism. They have tried to discover what sorts of communication are used by people who score high on a test of Machiavellianism when compared to people who score low

[3] Albert Mehrabian, *Silent Messages*, Belmont, Calif.: Wadsworth, 1971, p. 133.

zero-sum game *A game in which the same amount of value comes out as goes in, although the value may be distributed differently at the end of the game; thus, for some to win, others must lose.*

on the same test.[4] To this point attempts to test for machiavellianism have resulted in inconclusive research findings.

Many of the manipulative communication styles evolve from communication situations in which participants are in conflict.[5] When people choose sides and pursue contradictory goals, so that if one side wins the other loses and vice versa, the result is often a bargaining or negotiation style which is but a step away from violence and physical combat. Parties to a dispute may see the situation as a **zero-sum game.** Poker is a classic example of a zero-sum game: The same value (money) goes into the game as comes out; however, some of the players leave with more money than they put into the game, while others suffer a loss. During the cold war period of the 1950s and 1960s, the intelligence agencies of the leading powers saw themselves as involved in a zero-sum-game, a situation which generated a communication style filled with secrecy, spying, bluff, and threat.

BARGAINING AS A ZERO-SUM GAME

Even the simply daily transactions of buying and selling can approximate a zero-sum game. In North America we tend to have fixed prices for most of the less expensive items that we buy, and we do not haggle about the price, as is standard practice in some foreign cultures. We do, however, tend to bargain

[4] See for example, Arthur P. Bochner and Brenda Bochner, "A Multivariate Investigation of Machiavellianism and Task Structure in Four-Man Groups," *Speech Monographs*, 39 (1972), 277–285; Michael Burgoon, "The Relationship Between Willingness to Manipulate Others and Success in Two Different Types of Basic Speech Communication Courses," *Speech Teacher*, 20 (1971), 178–183; Michael Burgoon, Gerald R. Miller, and Stewart L. Tubbs, "Machiavellianism, Justification, and Attitude Change Following Counter-Attitudinal Advocacy," *Journal of Personality and Social Psychology*, 22 (1972), 366–271; M. Lee Williams, Vincent Hazleton, and Steve Renshaw, "The Measurement of Machiavellianism: A Factor Analytic and Correlational Study of Mach IV and Mach V," *Speech Monographs*, 42 (1975), 151–159.

[5] Recently there has been a growing interest in gamesmanship (how to get the best of the other person) and communication relating to bargaining, negotiation, and confrontation. In a sense the theory of communication associated with gamesmanship (sometimes called game theory) is a turning inside out of the relationship style of communication. For some typical discussions of the manipulative style, see *Speech Monographs*, 41 (1974), no. 1. The entire volume is devoted to conflict and conflict resolution. See also Paul Diesing, "Bargaining Strategy and Union-Management Relationships," *Journal of Conflict Resolution*, 5 (1961), 369–378; Harold H. Kelly, "Experimental Studies of Threats in Interpersonal Negotiations," *Journal of Conflict Resolution*, 9 (1965), 79–105; David H. Smith, "Communication and Negotiation Outcome," *The Journal of Communication*, 19 (1969), 248–256; Thomas C. Schelling, *The Strategy of Conflict*, New York: Oxford University Press, 1968; Kenneth E. Boulding, *Conflict and Defense*, New York: Harper & Row, 1962; Fred E. Jandt, *Conflict Resolution Through Communication*, New York: Harper & Row, 1973.

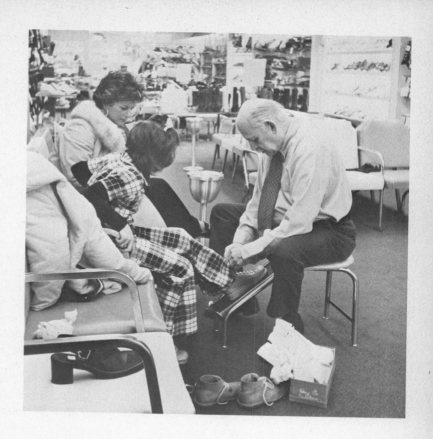

over large and important purchases such as homes and automobiles. When we go to buy a car, for example, we may adopt a Machiavellian style. We try to discover the so-called minimum disposition of the salesman (that is, the lowest possible price that he can sell the car for). In order to discover this, we may threaten not to buy at all, may bluff that we are disinterested, or may misrepresent the cost of other cars that we say we are considering. The salesman, in turn, may have a number of similar strategies to try to discover the most that we will pay to get the car. He may, for example, quote a price, and when we seem interested, qualify the offer with the reservation that the sales manager will have to approve. "But," he will add, "let me write this up, and I'll see what I can do to persuade the manager." After conferring with the manager, the "disgruntled" salesman will return with the bad news that the manager absolutely will not accept the offer but has made a counteroffer; and so the negotiation proceeds. The salesman's elaborate charade of joining forces with the nice customer against the hard-nosed manager appears to make the

forensic speaking *Speaking related to the practice of law; also contest speaking including debate.*

salesman and customer a team negotiating with a tough third party, and this puts the salesman in a much better position. It also puts the onus of negotiation on the third party, the manager. Even as we are venting our disgust about the counteroffer of the manager, the salesman, the one with whom we are really negotiating, is sizing up the limits of our best offer, and he may well leave and come back with a compromise that suits us both.

Persuasion concerns us all in many situations in addition to those in which we use the predominant communication styles. We are all producers and consumers of persuasion, but with the rise of radio and television, most of us tend more often to be consumers. In the chapters on persuasion which follow, we will emphasize persuasion for you as a consumer, although we will also point out how persuasion relates to you as a practitioner in all three communication styles. Because of the overriding importance of persuasion in all our lives, we will present a general treatment of the subject and point out its stylistic applications along the way. This chapter deals with the general theory of argument. Some of the material in this chapter is drawn from the public-speaking style, particularly **forensic speech,** which relates to legal arguments before judges and juries. Much of it is drawn from the disciplines which are concerned with formal argument, such as mathematics and logic. Some of it is drawn from research into the scientific aspects of persuasion. But the principles of straight thinking, or the uncommon use of common sense, apply in a very general way to all the different contexts of persuasion in our society.

ELEMENTS OF PERSUASIVE MESSAGES

For many years a basic assumption of public-speaking communication theory was that argument was different from persuasion, because man is a creature of reason and of will. Argument appealed to the mind, and successful argument resulted in convincing the listener. Persuasion appealed to the nonrational faculties, and successful persuasion resulted in the movement of the will. Subsequent research has indicated that the separation of head from heart, of reason from emotion, is artificial. Human beings tend to react as total organisms. We have divided the material on persuasion into three parts for the purpose of emphasizing various aspects of the process, but all are closely related. To be a successful persuader you must use all three components, and to be a good critic of communication you must be aware of all three.

dramas in persuasive messages Persuasive appeals carried by stories in which there is conflict, and in which most likely there is a sympathetic hero or heroine who battles for control. In Chapter 12 we use the term fantasy theme to refer to the dramas in persuasive messages.

As consumers of persuasion, we must learn to separate personality from drama and drama from evidence and reasoning; we must demand a direct and realistic link between the dramas presented to us in a persuasive campaign and actual events. In other words, although we can expect that reasonable people will disagree about what an event means, we still must demand that all speakers provide a complete and accurate description of the event. We call this connection between public dramas and the facts, *reality links*.

The reality links in a persuasive message consist of those words that describe things along the lines discussed in Chapter 3. Naming objects and ascribing properties and relations accurately provides a persuasive message with its reality links. We can think of the correspondence between the suggestion in a message and the reality of a given situation as the reasonable or logical portion of a communication. The reasoned elements of the persuasive effort consist of proving the points that make up a case and fitting the individual points into a logical pattern.

The **dramas in persuasive messages** can be attractive and interesting, but if they are false or unrelated to the facts, they should not move us to action simply because we like them. Monitor your TV set and count the number of dramas that relate to the simple matter of washing clothes. The actors are attractive, or funny, or folksy. The dramatic action is simple: The unhappy heroine with a laundry problem washes her clothes with a given laundry product, waits eagerly for the result, discovers the clothes are brighter-and-whiter-and-cleaner-than-ever, and is happy once more. For the consumer of these dramas, the problem is that five different manufacturers use essentially the same drama to suggest that the viewer buy their respective products. If in fact there is no difference in the way a given washer will perform with any of the five laundry products, the decision to buy one or another is made, not on the basis of facts, but on the basis of name identification or the attractiveness of the commercial. In this case, the advertisers have no facts that can be used in the persuasive message; we, as consumers of the persuasion, should be aware that no facts are presented to us in the message. This is persuasion with a key element missing.

A powerful factor for persuasion is evidence in support of an idea or product or course of action. For many years the public dramas suggesting that we buy a given brand of toothpaste were similar to those selling laundry products. The situations in the dramas varied, but the plot was generally that an attractive person could not get his or her teeth clean and thus had dingy teeth and bad breath, making him or her unpopular. Every toothpaste advertised could, of course, give the hero or heroine sweet breath, shining teeth, and popularity. Then the American Dental Association tested a new product ingredient and found that it reduced tooth decay. Controlled experimental conditions provided evidence that one product was better than the others, and immediately the advertising campaign for that toothpaste switched to extensive reports of these tests, long quotes about the results, personal testimonies from participants in the experiments, and heavy emphasis on the endorsement by the American Dental Association. When facts are added to the persuasive impact of personality and drama, the strength of the message is greatly increased.

Proving a Point

When we discuss proving a point for an audience, we must remember that we cannot tell whether a given piece of information is proof until we look at it in relation to the point to be proved. The best way to prepare or evaluate the reasoned part of a persuasive message, therefore, is to look at message units. Each unit, to be complete, must contain a point to be proved, worded in a clear way, and the material that supports the point. Information that may be excellent proof for one point may not be logically related to another. We will not always mention the point being proved in our explanations of evidence, but you should keep in mind the idea of a message unit as you study the art of proving a position. Refer back to the section "The Basic Message Unit," in Chapter 9, if you want to refresh your understanding.

Evidence is material that furnishes grounds for belief or makes evident the truth or falsity, rightness or wrongness, wisdom or folly of a proposition. It is a technical legal term that refers to material supplied by lawyers in support of their arguments in court. Legal evidence may include testimony of witnesses, written documents, or actual items, such as pistols, knives, or clothing.

Proof is the process of gathering together, ordering, and presenting enough evidence to convince the judge or jury (or us, the listener-consumers) to accept a given proposition.

Although we can look at evidence and make some decision about how good or bad it might be in terms of general rules about evidence, we must look at proof in terms of the audi-

ence. We can evaluate evidence against some absolute and general standards of excellence, but proof has to convince somebody. A given message unit, consisting of a proposition and supporting evidence, may convince one individual but not another. An old folk saying claims that "the proof of the pudding is in the eating." Even though the cook thinks the ingredients are good and his recipe interesting, if the people eating the pudding do not like it, for them anyway, the pudding is no good. No matter how good the speaker thinks his evidence is, no matter how sound his reasoning, if the listener is not persuaded, his proof is no good.

In Chapter 9 we described the way to phrase a point to be made clear. We also discussed the ways the point and the supporting material can be arranged in relation to each other. The message unit containing a point to be proved is developed in the same way as a unit containing a point to be made clear.

The three major forms of evidence used as proof for persuasive messages are statistical descriptions of facts, real examples, and testimony. A speaker uses evidence for two main functions: to describe and to evaluate the facts. The first and most important use of evidence is to describe what is the case. Factual information consists of statistics, real examples, and eyewitness accounts of what happened. The second use of evidence is to present expert opinion about what the facts mean. The testimony of authorities provides expert interpretation.

Statistics

Statistics are numerical comments about facts. A person may comment that Bill is tall. This is a simple descriptive statement. A similar statement may say that Bill is 6 feet 6 inches tall. This last statement includes numbers and is thus a statistical comment. When the statistics are true, they give us more precise information about facts than can most other forms of description. When a person wants to talk about many things and has only a short interview or conference in which to make his statement, his use of statistical description enables him to pack a lot of information into a few sentences.

Suppose a student asks the dean, "What are my chances of going on to the university if I enroll at Pleasant Hills Community College?" If the dean answers, "Of every 1000 freshmen who start at Pleasant Hills, 300 go on to the university," he covers a large number of facts (implicit in his answer is the information that while 300 go on, 700 do not), and he has given this information in a short sentence.

However, because the answer provides only a little information about a lot of students, we may get an incomplete picture. How many of the 700 who do not go on for further education wanted to or planned to? Many community and junior college programs are designed as two-year programs and are complete in themselves. How many of the 300 who go on for more education finish with university or four-year college degrees? In other words, many things are left unsaid by the dean's initial statistical statement. Many persuaders and pressure groups use figures to fool the public as well as to inform people. Even when used carefully and honestly, as in the dean's statement, statistics are abstract and present only a part of a larger picture. In our discussion of statistics, we will particularly look at both the sound use of statistics and the dangers of presenting factual information in the form of figures without explaining exactly what these figures mean or, almost more important, without explaining what the figures do *not* mean.

Numbers suggest precision and accuracy. Most of us think of figures as being factual and scientific. We do not know how to answer a statement such as "Twenty percent of inner-city teenagers use heroin" unless we have some statistical information of our own. We may say, "I find that hard to believe," or, "That figure seems awfully high," but if the other person repeats the statement, the suggestive power of the number itself, "20 percent," is persuasive, making it difficult for us to answer.

NUMBERS AS MEASURES

We all use numbers to talk about such things as our age, height, and weight. We count things like apples, pennies, and oranges, and we know how useful counting and measuring can be. One important way to reason is to count things and then, applying addition, subtraction, multiplication, and division to the numbers we have, compute further answers for ourselves. If I make $50 a week, and $11 is deducted in taxes and insurance, I figure that I will have $39 in my weekly pay check. As long as my basic premises are right (I make $50 and $11 is deducted), then when I make my mathematical computations, my experience will agree with my predicted outcome. I calculate that I will have a $39 pay check, and when payday arrives, I *do* have a check for $39.

All this seems somewhat obvious to us at this stage in our lives. We have no difficulty counting apples or people, because we can tell one apple from another and we can differentiate people. But the use of numbers becomes much more complicated as soon as we leave individual, single items. Counting the length of a table, for example, is more difficult than counting the number of tables in a room. A table is one long uninterrupted length. We have, then, to make arbitrary divisions or units along the length of the table, so that we can count each division just as we counted the apples. The units we set up for counting the length of the table are inches or centimeters. Each inch is the same size as every other inch. We mark off the inches along the length of the table and add them up. Our hypothetical table, however, does not consist of an exactly even number of inches; when we mark off the last full inch, we find that the table extends a little further, but less than 1 inch. Then we have to deal in fractions, or parts, of an inch. In spite of the complications of measuring and

IQ *A score arrived at by dividing a number said to represent a person's mental age by a person's chronological age.*

counting, however, we can achieve fairly accurate results when we measure a table or count apples. We can compare lengths of various tables, and we can compare the total number of apples in one box with the total number of apples in another.

NUMBERS AS EVALUATIONS

Because numbers are such useful labels, we tend to use numbers for many things that cannot be counted in the simple way apples and inches can. When we do this, the accuracy with which the numbers represent the real world is decreased. You have all taken essay-type tests in which the instructor assigns points for each answer. Question 1, you are told, is worth 25 points. The instructor has the job of deciding whether the answer given by a particular student is worth all 25 points, or only 20 points, or 10, and so on. What can the instructor count to arrive at a conclusion that the answer is worth 20 points? Nothing, really. The number 20 is a number evaluation which corresponds to a word evaluation of the answer, such as *good* or *fair,* and the instructor is simply using the convenience of a number to make his general evaluation of the answer.

If you say that Mary is 5 feet tall and weighs 100 pounds, you have made a measurable, accurate statistical statement. Suppose you are told that Mary has an IQ **(intelligence quotient)** of 140. Is this an accurate, dependable statistical statement? Not so much so. We are impressed that Mary's IQ is 140, because we know that this value borders on the genius range of human intelligence, but what have the testers counted to arrive at the number 140? They have certainly not been able to count anything like apples or inches or pounds. Mary has done certain tasks, and the tester has assigned number values to them. He has added up the number values of the tasks Mary completed correctly (her score) and has compared her score with those of others her age who have taken similar tests, in order to determine her mental age. On that basis he has assigned the number 140 as a measure of Mary's intelligence. To say Mary has an IQ of 140 is a less valid statistic than to say Mary is 5 feet tall and weighs 100 pounds.

When we use or listen to statistics, we must make sure we know how the people who observed the facts picked the numbers they assigned to the facts as statistics about them. Did the person gathering the statistics count something that could easily be counted by you or by anyone else, so that several people would come up with the same numbers, or did he use the number as an evaluation or a name? Numbers that come from counting tend to be more useful and accurate than numbers used as names or evaluations.

Many people and organizations are engaged in counting and evaluating things and publishing statistics. Today's student acquires facts and figures from many different sources. In organizing communication messages, we seldom have any trouble finding statistics; the newsstands are full of magazines that are, in turn, full of statistics we can repeat in a communication class. Our trouble comes when we begin to puzzle out what the numbers we find actually mean.

The basic information we need to understand something or to make a wise decision is often a comparison of how two things are similar or how they are different or how they are changing in relation to one another. The things we want to know can often be described by such terms as *enough, too much, on time, gaining, out of reach, leveling off, losing ground, the weakest regions, the strongest area, ahead of schedule, above average,* and *less than we expected.*

USING FIGURES IN COMPARISON

One of the most important ways people use figures is to make comparisons. Basically, we compare figures to get a clear indication of *more* or *less.* We can use figures to find out about more or less by looking at two things at about the same point in time (we measure Joe's height and Harry's height and say that Joe is at this moment 2 inches taller than Harry) and by looking at the same thing at different times (Metropolitan Community College had an enrollment of 1500 in 1965, 2200 in 1970, and currently has 3100).

When we compare figures we must be sure not only that the numbers are a result of counting and not of naming or evaluating, but also that the units counted are comparable in terms of the point we wish to prove. The most common thing people try to count which is not comparable from time to time, is the dollar. Usually the dollar buys less this year than last, although in some periods of American history the reverse was true. Suppose an older person says to a high-school student, "When I started my first job I made only $1 an hour and here you are beginning at $2. Are you lucky! You're making twice what I made then." The idea that a student making $2 an hour today is earning twice as much as a man making $1 an hour in 1945 is wrong, because the value of a dollar depends on its buying power—how many hours a person has to work to buy a good dinner in a restaurant, or a car, or a bag of groceries. Someone making $2 an hour today can buy little, if anything, more than a person making $1 an hour in 1945.

Even on the same day in different parts of the country, the dollar is not comparable in terms of buying power. If someone says welfare payments are much higher in New York City than in Jackson, Mississippi, what is he saying? Maybe the dollars paid in New York City buy less than the dollars in Jackson. What you buy for a dollar in one part of the country often costs more, or less, in another part of the country. This is even more true in various cities around the world.

Even when the things compared are the same size, or are corrected to make them comparable, the people who compare figures for today with statistics from the past often ignore the effect of the increasing or decreasing numbers of people in a given city or region. For example, the latest figures regarding deaths in automobile accidents, arrests for using illegal drugs, or the occurrence of venereal disease are usually larger than the same statistics from 10 or 20 years ago simply because the population of the United States has increased in the last 20 years. Comparisons of absolute numbers are poor evidence to prove a trend toward better or worse. Comparing the total number of deaths on the highways 10 years ago with the total number this year is not as valid a statistic for proving the increased rate of automobile-related deaths as is the number of deaths per 1000 cars in those years or, better yet, the number of deaths per 100,000 automobile-miles driven in those years. Because some cars are driven so much more every year than others, a comparison of car-miles driven is more meaningful than a comparison of deaths per so many automobiles. Airlines usually present safety statistics in terms of passenger-miles rather than in terms of number of flights or length of flights.

THE RANDOM SAMPLE

To this point we have assumed that the figures under discussion are the result of observing everything we want to know about. That is, if we want to know how many students are enrolled at our college, we find out the number by tabulating every student. Many important statistics are the result of such complete counts. If the counting is complete and no item is overlooked, the numbers that result are most useful. Much statistical information, however, comes from observing only part of the total and then trying to figure out what the whole picture looks like by making educated guesses about the whole from the part actually counted. The argument is that you do not have to drink the whole glassful to know the milk is sour.

Statisticians often take a sample from the population they are studying and then count the occurrence of some important feature in the sample. If they are careful and follow the formulas of statistics, they can usually figure out, with a rather small margin of error, the occurrence of that feature in the entire population. Taking a sample saves counting, and thus time and money. A good sample must be large enough and selected in such a way as to be representative of the total population. A good way to acquire a sample that is representative of the total population is to select it so that every member of the total population has an equal chance of being picked for the sample. Suppose you want to know how the students at your school feel about the library hours. You can ask 20 people in your English course, but since people in an English class might use the library differently from people in another class, you will know about the students in your English class but not about all the students in your school. You can obtain a list of all the students in the school, assign a number to each name on the list, and then pick 20 names by using a table of random numbers which you can find in most elementary statistics textbooks. The result is a random sample, and you will have a more representative sample for determining what the whole student body thinks about the library hours.

Many of the figures we hear and use come from samples and are thus less accurate than those resulting from counting every item under study. Still, if we are careful how we study and evaluate statistics, we can learn a great deal about factual matters by the sampling procedure.

Most polls of public opinion are based on the answers of several hundred or perhaps several thousand people to various questions. Surveys of television viewers also record the responses of a sample of the total viewing audience. Often surveyors report their results in specific figures. One may read that the most recent poll shows that 53 percent of the American people approve the way the president is doing his job. These same polls seldom also indicate that, given the number of people polled and the error that creeps into such sampling, the results are accurate only within 2 or 3 percentage points.

AVERAGES

In addition to describing numerically the whole of a group, statistics can be used to describe the average of a group. For instance, the average student at a state college is 21 years old. We often want to know what is typical, and averages help us find out. But an average can be misleading as well as useful. For example, if all 20 members of a class have part-time or full-time jobs, we may not discover the typical salary if we add all the salaries and divide by 20 because, for one thing, those with full-time jobs probably earn more than those with part-time work. Even if we limit our group to 10 students with full-time jobs, averaging may be misleading. For example, if one student is a highly successful door-to-door salesman who makes $20,000 per year, including this high salary in the averaging gives us a misleading figure. Say the 9 remaining students have salaries between $6000 and $8000 a year, averaging for the 9 people about $7000 per year. Including the single $20,000 salary produces an average of $8300 per year, which is higher than the earnings of 9 members of the sample and lower than the earnings of one.

All numerical statistical evidence must be carefully examined when you use it or hear it as part of a persuasive campaign to prove a point.

Real Examples

In Chapter 9 we discussed real examples as ways to make a point clear. Examples that are factual can also support a point as evidence of its truth or wisdom. A person trying to find out the truth about a particular problem must weigh the real examples carefully to be sure they are factually accurate and typical of the things they are supposed to illustrate or represent. We can take one or two examples as being representative of a class of people or events. We imply that the examples are able to stand for a great many more just like them that we could use if we had the time to discuss them all. The danger, therefore, is that we may, in the interest of proving a point, use an extreme example. In the early 1970s, two dramatic and compelling events caught the imagination of the American public. The first was a series of bloody murders of Hollywood personalities, for which a long-haired commune leader named Charles Manson and several of the women in his "family" were convicted. The second was a war atrocity in which a number of Vietnamese women and children were killed at a village called My Lai, for which an infantry lieutenant named Calley was convicted. Some people argued that the hippy culture was morally bankrupt and vicious and submitted the Manson murders as an example to prove their point. Other people argued that the military-industrial complex was morally bankrupt and vicious and submitted the My Lai massacre as an example to prove their point. Both groups were guilty of using extreme, rather than typical, examples.

The use of extreme examples as proof is characteristic of popular magazine articles. A writer in search of an attention-catching device for his opening paragraph often describes a dramatic but unusual case and implies that it is typical.

Students of straight thinking have found so many instances of the use of a few extreme examples to prove points that they call such errors of thinking the fallacy of *hasty generalization.* If one of your friends did something your parents thought was out of line, they may have made a hasty generalization about your whole group of acquaintances. When someone submits an extreme example to another person in a conversation or discussion, and then jumps to the conclusion that the example is typical, both speaker and listener may be misled about the facts of the case. When we make mistakes about the way the world really is, we can usually expect a rude awakening sooner or later.

DETERMINING WHAT IS TYPICAL

The notion of typicality ties together the use of statistics and examples. An important part of statistical analysis is the discovery of the fact or facts that are the most usual or that are in the middle of a range. We have mentioned the average—the sum of all the numbers divided by the frequency of their occurrence—which is often an appropriate device for indicating what is typical. When it does so, it is called the **mean.** If we take the weight of each of the 11 players on a football team, add them to find the total weight of all players, and divide by 11, we have the average weight of a player on the team. If the average turns out to be 220 pounds, that statistic gives us a better impression of how heavy the players are than would the extreme example of Harry Potter, a 180-pound quarterback, or William Jones, a 167-pound scatback. As the two lightest-weight players on the team, Harry and William would be poor examples of the weight of the team as a whole. There may not even be a player who weighs the exact average, 220 pounds, but if we use Fred Smith, a 223-pound end, or Elbert Reed, a 217-pound running back, for our example, we have selected an example close to the actual average weight.

Another way statisticians discover the typical is by arrang-

median *A measure of the central tendency in a statistical distribution which is arrived at by ordering the statistics by size and locating the midpoint of the distribution.*

ing all of a group of statistics in order from larger to smaller, and then picking the statistic at the middle point and using this to show what is usual. If we made a list of the incomes of all the families on the Red Lake Indian Reservation and arranged the incomes in order from the highest to the lowest, we could count halfway down (or up) and consider the income in the middle of the list to be the typical example of the income of these families. In the discussion of salaries used earlier to illustrate the pitfalls of averaging, a midpoint or **median** example would give a more accurate indication of what was typical than would a numerical average. The median example is often a good statistic to use when the figures you are discussing range from unusually high to unusually low. These extremes are accounted for when you pick the point in the middle.

Real examples add interest to statistics because they relate the dry figures to the human world. Statistics can express many facts in a short statement, but without examples, they often seem dull and boring. Facts presented in terms of people who are heroes or villains, who suffer and have moments of joy and happiness, are more interesting and more understandable. Real examples are vital also because they serve as reality links to the highly persuasive dramas we will discuss in Chapter 12. Because examples can contain characters in action, they can be persuasive as evidence and as *indirect suggestion*. As a student of persuasion, you should watch how skillful speakers use examples for maximum effect. Try this exercise: Present the same real example in several different ways to achieve different impressions. On one occasion, have the main character be the good guy. In another version, let the main character be the bad guy. Make us sympathetic with your example; then make us detest him. Learn to think of examples as highly effective tools in persuasive communication, and practice using them.

Eyewitness Testimony

"When in doubt, go see for yourself" is generally good advice. In other words, if you don't believe someone, go find out with your own two eyes and ears. We depend upon the evidence of our senses in deciding many factual questions. If you want to know if it is raining, you go to the window and look outside. Say that a fight breaks out in the hallway. You run to see what is going on. Someone else runs up after the fight is over

hearsay evidence *The testimony of witnesses who have not been involved in given events but have been told about them by someone else.*

and asks, "What happened?" You describe the fight. This other person says, "I don't believe you." You shrug your shoulders and say, "Suit yourself. But that is what happened." We believe the evidence of our own senses.

However, many times in our communications with others we want to prove a point about some facts, but have not had the time or the chance to see the particular facts for ourselves. Maybe the facts, such as what happened in the fight in the hallway, occurred at only one place in time, so that unless we happened to be there, we have to depend for information on the story of a person who did see the event. Some facts are complicated and occur over a period of time or at a considerable distance, so that we would need much time to observe them all. During the years the United States did not have diplomatic relations with Communist China, the facts about what was going on in China existed, but could not be observed by Americans. If we wanted to know how things were going in China during those years, we had to rely on the testimony of people who were there — foreign correspondents from countries that did have diplomatic exchanges with China: we often read reports about China that were written, for example, by Canadians who went there to observe at first hand.

Thus an important source of evidence is the testimony or word of an eyewitness. In a court of law, the only testimony about facts allowed is that of an eyewitness. Sometimes in everyday living, we are willing to depend upon what the law terms **hearsay** (second-hand information, gossip, or rumor; the word of somebody who got a story from someone else), but when we are trying to prove something, rumor is a shaky substitute for eyewitness accounts. Think of several rumors you have heard recently. How many turned out to be entirely accurate?[6]

Many times we quote testimony from a witness who has written up an account of what he saw in a newspaper or magazine. Sometimes we refer to a statement made on radio or television by an alleged eyewitness. When using the testimony of a witness to prove a point, we ought not to assume that just because the person saw the event he is necessarily telling the truth about it or giving a good picture of what happened.

[6] A number of psychological studies have demonstrated the fallibility of eyewitness accounts of events, but eyewitnesses still provide a more accurate account for the most part than rumors or hearsay. For a summary of studies in the psychology of recall as well as a study of rumors, see Gordon W. Allport and Leo Postman, *The Psychology of Rumor,* New York: Holt, Rinehart and Winston, 1947; see also, Tamotsu Shibutani, *Improvised News: A Sociological Study of Rumor,* Indianapolis: Bobbs-Merrill, 1966.

Suppose we ask a friend of Bill's what happened in the hallway fight between Bill and Harry. Bill's friend may well say that Harry did not knock Bill down, that Bill slipped. Another eyewitness who has no stake in the matter, such as friendship with one of the participants, may say that Bill provoked Harry, and Harry hit Bill a solid blow to the jaw and knocked him down. Which eyewitness do you believe? How do you decide which reporter is the more reliable witness to what actually happened?

When trying to decide what happened in any given instance, we have to examine the testimony of eyewitnesses carefully. You should ask yourself such questions as:

What exactly did the witness intend to say?
Was the story a put-on? Was it supposed to be funny?
Was the person able to make a good report? Was he in a position to see? Did he have the training that would make him better able to keep track of what was going on? Is he a reliable person?
Was the person willing and able to tell the truth?
Was there any reason for the witness to lie or distort the truth?
Did the witness have a bias? What did the witness expect to see? (We all have a tendency to see what we expect to see. Each of us has a personal bias built in when we view or hear an event.)

Expert Testimony

Speakers frequently use direct quotations from well-known authorities in interpreting facts. Usually we use *expert* witnesses to testify about what the facts mean. If we go to a doctor and he shows us our X rays, we may still ask, "What does it mean?" He could then tell us that the X rays indicate there is a fracture of a small bone in the right foot. Many facts are difficult to interpret, and people who specialize in a given area can often help us decide what the facts mean. An expert in foods may testify that the diet of the poor people in an area is not good enough to keep them healthy; he may testify, further, that studies have shown a direct relationship between diet and intelligence in young children. Another expert on drug usage may testify that the facts indicate that the use of marijuana does not affect a person's physical ability to drive a car as much as does the use of alcohol in comparable amounts. Speakers often quote the interpretation of facts by widely-known experts to support their case.

Another way in which we may use testimony is to decide what we ought to do in a given case. We might ask the doctor who told us we have a fractured bone in the foot, "What shall I do?" He might advise us to have the foot put into a cast to keep it immobilized for six weeks while it heals. We often depend upon an expert's advice; in the case of the doctor, his advice is testimony you should consider as you decide what to do about the facts. Obviously, when you want advice, you must ask the right expert. Suppose an unmarried pregnant girl asks her mother, "What should I do?" Suppose she asks her boy friend, a girl friend, or her doctor the same question. Her mother might say, "Get married." The boy might say, "Have an abortion." The girl friend might say, "Keep the baby." The doctor might say, "Take these pills, they're vitamins; don't gain too much weight, and come back to see me in a month." The girl has received testimony from four sources. Whose testimony is more persuasive? Whose testimony ought to be more persuasive? Has the girl perhaps not asked the right expert or the right questions yet? Consider the involved interests of her sources. Speakers may quote or allude to advice from leading authorities who recommend the same proposals as does to speaker.

One widely used propaganda technique features the testimony of glamorous and famous people telling us we ought to buy or do something. The form of the argument is similar to the legitimate use of the testimony of experts to support a case discussed above. However, the persuasive power of the testimony comes from the old propaganda device of nonrational transfer of glamor and prestige of a popular or famous name to a product or proposal. We often see baseball or basketball or football players advising us to buy a certain kind of shaving cream, cologne, or breakfast food. Movie stars advise us what political candidates to vote for. Supposedly, if we admire and value the opinions of a sports or television star, we will transfer our liking to the product he tells us to use and will buy it.

When an expert tells us what to do about a health problem, or getting an education, or voting for or against a tax increase or school bond, or to support an antiwar position or candidate, or to support a disarmament conference or an antipollution effort, we should be sure that the person is an expert *in the field* he is talking about. We should not follow a person's advice just because he is likable or glamorous. If the person talking about facts has a vested interest in how he interprets the facts to us, we must keep that in mind when we consider his testimony.

Making a Persuasive Logical Case

Most people find good evidence and sound reasoning persuasive.[7] One of the most effective ways to persuade others about what they should believe or do is to give them good reasons, well supported with evidence.

We have seen that the clear statement of a point to be proved and the evidence that supports that point are the basic building blocks for a logical argument. We now turn to how basic building blocks can be fitted together to form a strong case for a particular position.

For our purposes we will define *logic* as the process of drawing a conclusion from one or more points that need to be proved with evidence. When we present the results of straight thinking to a listener or an audience, we can begin with the conclusion and then give the reasons for believing the conclusion, or we can begin with the reasons and draw the conclusion at the end of our message. An audience generally requires proof composed of both evidence and a logical conclusion.

In an interview or conference between two people, the give-and-take of question and answer, statement and answering statement, tends to break up the connections between evidence and point and general conclusion. Even so, many interviews contain chains of hard, logical thought. In an interview, a person may present a conclusion and have it accepted without further proof. He may present another conclusion and have it challenged, then submit a reason to support the conclusion and have it challenged, then present more evidence until the other person accepts the argument. In a two-person conversation, the possibility for source and receiver to interact and to thus indicate when evidence is understood or misunderstood, or when a person is convinced or is skeptical about a point, allows them to think together in a productive fashion.

Much the same opportunity for give and take and for discovering when members are convinced of a point exists in the

---

[7] Again the communication style will modify the extent to which good evidence and sound reasoning are stressed. For quantitative research results see James C. McCroskey, "A Summary of Experimental Research on the Effects of Evidence in Persuasive Communication," *The Quarterly Journal of Speech*, 55 (1969), 169–176.

small group discussion; in this regard the interaction is much the same as in a two-person situation. For larger groups, however, the speaker often plans the logic of the case ahead of time, structures the message with the audience in mind, and presents larger chunks of proof and logic without interruption. The pressure of arguing in persuasive fashion before large audiences often makes a speaker examine the reasons behind his conclusions and analyze the way the parts of his arguments hang together. We should also plan for the interview, conference, or meeting by thinking through the logic of our argument beforehand. We have more difficulty keeping arguments in mind when they can be questioned or challenged as we go along. All of us have a tendency to underestimate the need for ordering our evidence when we hope to be persuasive in informal communication.

Lawyers call the paper they write that contains the logic of an argument a *brief*. Someone working on an important persuasive project might well outline the main conclusion and the points that support it, much as a lawyer briefs a case. By following an outline, a person can see the connections from reasons to conclusions clearly and decide whether they fit together logically.

CHECKING LOGIC

When someone questions our logic, he often asks the short but troublesome question "Why? When we answer a *why* question, we usually provide a *because* response. One good way to check the logic of a conclusion following from reasons is to write the conclusion clearly at the top of a sheet of paper and list the reasons supporting the conclusion under it, beginning each reason with *because*. If — keeping in mind our common-sense meaning of *because* — the outline makes good sense, the logic is probably all right.

For instance, here is a conclusion with its supporting reasons, using *because* to indicate logical connections:

> *Black English is a good legitimate language dialect*
>   because *Black English is not a substandard dialect*
>   because *black English is not a deprived language.*

One can also test the logic of conclusions drawn from a set of reasons by listing first the reasons, and then the conclusions introduced by the word *therefore*, as in the following example:

> *Many teachers believe that blacks fail to use standard English because of a cultural deficiency; and, many*

teachers refer thousands of black students to speech correctionists to bring their speech up to standard; therefore, many black students are being destroyed psychologically in our schools.

When checking your own logic, keep in mind that the evidence must relate to the point you want to prove and that the reasons you present must support your conclusion. One of the most difficult things to do when trying to think clearly and logically is to make sure that every step of an argument is to the point. Here is an example of an argument that makes a mistake by trying to fit two related reasons together, as reason and conclusion:

> *Many black students are being destroyed psychologically in our schools* because *many blacks get a psychologically damaging image of blacks from motion pictures and television.*

The point to be proved relates to the effect of schools and the reason supplied to prove the point says something about motion pictures and television. Although both ideas are related to the general topic of the psychological effect of certain experiences on black students, they do not fit together as main point and supporting reason.

When we prove to someone the wisdom of acting, believing, or thinking in a certain way by means of evidence and logic, we have used one of the most powerful means of persuasion. Often the decision based upon facts and careful inferences from evidence is better than the decision made solely on the basis of the advice of a person we like and trust or on the basis of suggestion. We all need to know the methods of straight thinking, not only for our formal communications but also for group discussions, interviews, and other two-person conversations. Most importantly, as consumers of persuasion, we need to be skillful in testing messages for their factual content and the soundness of their logic.

Fallacies of Argument

The public-speaking tradition contains more theoretical material both on sound argument and on fallacies of reasoning than either of the other two communication styles.

Over the years, rhetorical theorists with an interest in argumentation have classified typical mistakes in reasoning. (A minor communication style which is an offshoot of the public-speaking style is high-school and college debating. Intercollegiate debating is almost a pure communication style in miniature. Practitioners have a highly developed theory and a practice so stylized that only trained critics can evaluate good and bad efforts. Nonetheless, the debate style has influenced public speaking particularly in the area at logical proof for an argument. Many of the standards of a good argument are the same in both styles.) Artistic theories often are organized around a system of classification. The classifications of fallacies are useful because they enable a person to criticize an argument, for example, by asserting that it contains a certain class of mistakes in reasoning. The system thus provides a convenient shorthand for evaluating arguments and discussing technical problems. The system is also useful for the instruction of beginning speakers. A debate coach, for example, can point out that a given argument contains a fallacy of a certain kind, and the student can then try to remedy the problem.

Sometimes argumentation and debate theorists use Latin names for the fallacies, such as *post hoc ergo propter hoc, ad populum, ad hominum, circulus in probando.* Scholars have a long tradition of using Latin names for classes in a classification theory. Botanists, for example, use Latin labels for their classification system. Generally Greek or Latin terms are attractive only to the most professional of professionals in a given art of science. Latin labels can be easily translated into basic English. The Latin term *post hoc ergo propter hoc* refers to the common error of assuming that because one event followed another, the first caused the second. The term *ad populum* refers to the mistake of arguing along the lines that "everybody knows" or "everybody is doing it," or asserting, "The voice of the people is the voice of God." The phrase *ad hominum* indicates the mistake of arguing against the individual who supports an argument rather than the argument itself. The term *circulus in probando* refers to the common practice of arguing in a circle. These four fallacies are illustrative and by no means exhaust all of the mistakes in argument that have been discovered, classified, and studied. One additional logical error which is extremely important in the public-speaking style is inconsistency or contradictoriness. We will examine the fallacies of after–therefore-caused-by reasoning, of circular reasoning, and of contradictory argument in more detail.

FAULTY ANALYSIS OF CAUSATION

The error of assuming that because one event followed another the first caused the second is a very common one. In general, the entire question of causation is a difficult one for the public speaker. Usually events are interrelated in very complex ways, and when a person assumes that event A caused event B, many factors which contributed to event B are probably ignored. Generally you should be suspicious of any argument which asserts that a single cause brought about a complicated event. Consider the following faulty argument:

> *Herbert Hoover was elected as a Republican president before the depression of the 1930s; Dwight Eisenhower was elected as a Republican president before the recession of the 1950s; Richard Nixon was elected as a Republican president before the recession of the 1970s; therefore, Hoover, Eisenhower, and Nixon caused the economic problems.*

If we were to indulge in another common fallacy, which is to make a hasty generalization on the basis of too few examples, we could assert that Republicans cause economic depressions and recessions. Both fallacies are present in the next argument:

> *Woodrow Wilson was elected as a Democratic president before the United States entered World War I; Franklin Roosevelt was a Democratic president when we entered World War II; Harry Truman was a Democratic president when we entered the Korean War; and John F. Kennedy was a Democratic president when we escalated the Vietnamese War; therefore, the Democrats always get us into war.*

The error of assuming that because one thing preceded another it caused the event which followed is an easy one to make. You ought to be careful in evaluating the arguments you hear as well as those you use yourself to be sure they do not contain the fallacy.

CIRCULAR REASONING

The fallacy of arguing in a circle is illustrated by the following assertions:

> *"The Bormanns are authorities in speech communication because they have written several books."*

"Why have they written several books?"
*"Because they are authorities in speech com-
munication."*
*"Liz is in the movies not because she is a good actress
but because she is a personality."*
"Why is she a personality?"
"Because she is so widely known."
"Why is she so widely known?"
"Because she is in the movies."

The above examples may seem rather trivial, even though
they illustrate the fallacy clearly, but the circular argument
can crop up in important political and economic discussions
as well:

"Detente with the Russians will not work."
"Why?"
"Because you cannot trust the Communists."
"Why?"
*"Because the Communists will never keep their treaty
obligations."*
"Why?"
"Because Communists are untrustworthy."

THE CONTRADICTORY ARGUMENT

The inconsistent or contradictory argument is probably the
most basic logical fallacy. In the study of formal logic, an
argument which contradicts itself is always invalid, and on
that basis, the public-speaking style puts a premium on logical consistency. The debater who can convincingly point out
that the opponent's argument is contradictory carries the
issue. In the debates at the Virginia Convention, called to
consider approval of the new Constitution of the United
States, Patrick Henry argued against Virginia joining the new
government, and James Madison argued for the Constitution.
During the course of the long debate, Henry presented a great
many different arguments against the proposal, and Madison
was able to challenge Henry's reasoning on the grounds that
he contradicted himself. For example, Madison first pointed
out that Henry had argued that the provision that three-
fourths of the states would be sufficient to start the new government was a bad one, because this would allow too few
states to form the new government. Next, Madison pointed
out that Henry had later argued that the stipulation that two-

Persuasion is communication designed to influence choice. Coercion, like persuasion, restricts choice but, unlike persuasion, requires little artistry.

Little persuasive skill is involved in offering a reward or threatening punishment.

Persuasion cuts across all three major communication styles although the public speaking and message communication styles give it greatest emphasis.

In addition to the three styles discussed in this book there are a number of manipulative communication styles which encourage any means which achieves success.

Many of the manipulative styles evolve from communication situations in which participants are in conflict or can profit to some extent at one anothers' expense.

Reasonable people may properly disagree about what events mean, but before differing, they should agree about the facts.

The dramas in persuasive messages can be attractive and interesting and still be false.

Evidence is material that furnishes grounds for belief in the truth or falsity, rightness or wrongness, wisdom or folly of a proposition.

An important use of evidence is to describe what is the case.

Expert interpretation of facts if a form of evidence.

Statistical descriptions of factual material often contain much information in a few words.

thirds of the states be required to ratify amendments would make it too difficult to change the government. Madison pointed out that Henry's argument was inconsistent, in that Henry said three-fourths of the states were too few to start the government, but two-thirds were too many to amend it.

Skillful charlatans can juggle statistics to fool the listener by distorting or misrepresenting the facts.

Even when carefully and honestly presented, statistics often give the listener an incomplete picture.

Numbers that come from counting tend to be more useful in informing about the world than figures used as names or as evaluations.

Some units, such as the American dollar, are not comparable from time to time.

The latest figures regarding any vital statistic are usually larger than the same figures for several years ago simply because the population has increased.

Much statistical information comes from observing a sample of the total population and making an educated guess about the whole on that basis.

A random sample allows a more precise guess about the total population than most other kinds of samples.

Extreme examples are poor evidence.

The fallacy of hasty generalization results from jumping to a conclusion on the basis of a few extreme examples.

An important part of statistical analysis is the discovery of facts that are usual or typical of a wide range of things.

Real examples are a good way to add interest to statistics, and statistics provide a good guide to typical examples.

Real examples serve as reality links to the persuasive dramas that are part of many messages.

We depend upon the evidence of our senses in deciding many factual questions.

The testimony of reliable eyewitnesses is an important source of evidence about factual matters.

In an age of specialization, expert testimony interpreting complicated factual matters is often an important part of persuasion.

A widely used propaganda technique is to cite the testimonial of a famous and glamorous person in behalf of a product or service.

If someone testifies that we ought to do or believe something, we should examine that person's authority carefully.

Logic is the process of drawing conclusions from one or more points.

Decisions based upon careful inferences from evidence are often better than those made solely on the basis of the persuasive power of personality and suggestion.

One common logical fallacy is to assume that because one event followed another the first caused the second.

Other common logical fallacies include arguing in a circle, and being inconsistent or contradictory.

In the message communication style the major emphasis on logical consistency comes from balance "theories" or the principles of "cognitive dissonance" or "congruity."

Consistency and the Message Communication Style

The matter of reasoning is treated in the message communication style largely in terms of the usefulness of the assumption that people try to keep their thinking and behavior consistent. The public-speaking communication style uses the analogy of rhetoric with logic to explain why arguments ought to be consistent. The message communication style, on the other hand, assumes an innate drive for logical consistency in human beings. Several people have put forward the hypothesis of consistency in one form or another to explain communication events and to guide research. Osgood and Tannenbaum have formulated the principle of congruity; Heider has suggested a balance hypothesis; and Festinger has used the term *cognitive dissonance* to indicate an uneasy feeling on the part of people who discover logical inconsistencies in their thinking and behavior.[8] On occasion, writers refer to these hypotheses as "theories," so you may read of Heider's "balance theory," or Festinger's "cognitive dissonance theory," but as we saw in Chapter 2, scientific theories are systematic and consistent sets of invariable relations or laws. Assumptions such as "A contradictory argument is always invalid," or "People try to make their ideas consistent," or "When someone you like takes a position you do not like, you try to balance your likes and dislikes so you feel more comfortable" all may be parts of communication theories, but they are not a scientific part of them.

The congruity notion, the balance hypothesis, and the cognitive dissonance assumption all relate to the idea that human beings try to be consistent in their reasoning and behavior. That is, people try to work out logical contradictions and provide plausible reasons, good or bad, to bring their attitudes, beliefs, values and behaviors into more comfortable consistency. The various consistency hypotheses have encouraged a number of studies to investigate whether or not people do behave reasonably, as the assumption predicts.[9] These studies tend to be less than clear-cut in their outcomes, although most people who survey the research conclude that the studies tend to support the human drive for logical consistency.[10] The practical advice which flows from the consistency research is that to change attitudes, values, and beliefs, the

[8] Charles E. Osgood and Percy H. Tannenbaum, "The Principle of Congruity in the Prediction of Attitude Change," *Psychological Review*, 17 (1955), 42–55; Fritz Heider, *The Psychology of Interpersonal Relations*, New York: Wiley, 1958; Leon Festinger, *A Theory of Cognitive Dissonance*, Stanford, Calif,: Stanford University Press, 1957.

[9] For a survey and summary of the research results see Elliot Aronson, *The Social Animal*, San Francisco: Freeman, 1972, pp. 90–139.

[10] For a critical review of studies relating to consistency notions see Robert N. Bostrom, "Motivation and Argument," in Miller and Nilsen, eds., pp. 110–128.

communicator (the source) should create a feeling of imbalance or dissonance within the receiver, and this feeling will provide the listener (the receiver) with the motive to change, in order once again to achieve logical consistency.

SUGGESTED PROJECTS

1 This is a project in proving a point. Select a controversial point, phrase it in suitable form, and then, using only statistical information, support the point for two minutes.
2 Select an argument presented in a newspaper, magazine, or on television. Note the point to be proved and then analyze the supporting material critically. How could the argument have been better supported, in your estimation?
3 Although it is seldom possible to ignore your emotional reactions to the personalities and suggestions, direct and indirect, involved in decision-making, it is always good practice to work toward making decisions as much as possible on the basis of evidence and reasoning. Consider a recent decision of some importance to you that you had to make. It could have been a decision about what course of study to take at school, what career to prepare for, a decision to participate more fully in your religious group or to cease your participation completely, to move into an apartment with friends—something you had to think about quite a while. Now, looking back, list in the order of their importance in influencing your final decision, the evidence and reasoning you considered.

SUGGESTED READINGS

Bettinghaus, Erwin P. *Message Preparation: The Nature of Proof.* Indianapolis: Bobbs-Merrill, 1966.
Huff, Darrell. *How To Lie with Statistics.* New York: Norton, 1954.
Miller, Gerald R., and Thomas R. Nilsen (eds.). *Perspectives on Argument.* Glenview, Ill.: Scott, Foresman, 1966.
Mills, Glen E. *Message Preparation.* Indianapolis: Bobbs-Merrill, 1966.
Newman, Robert P., and Dale R. Newman. *Evidence.* Boston: Houghton Mifflin, 1969.
Walter, Otis M., and Robert L. Scott. *Thinking and Speaking,* 2nd ed. New York: Macmillan, 1969.

Chapter 11

HOW TO PERSUADE: THE PERSUASIVE POWER OF PERSONALITY

Since the times of ancient Greece we have records that scholars have known and understood the persuasive power of the human personality and the kernel of truth in the saying "What you *are* speaks more loudly than what you say." Aristotle wrote several thousand years ago:

> The character [*ethos*] of the speaker is a cause of persuasion when the speech is so uttered as to make him worthy of belief; for as a rule we trust men of probity more, and more quickly, about things in general, while on points outside the realm of exact knowledge, where opinion is divided, we trust them absolutely. . . . We might almost affirm that his character [*ethos*] is the most potent of all means of persuasion.[1]

RESEARCH ON PERSONALITY AND PERSUASION

In 1949, as the message communication style was evolving, a scholar in the public-speaking tradition put the hypothesis to empirical tests. An empirical test is an experiment to test a

[1] Lane Cooper, trans., *The Rhetoric of Aristotle*, Englewood Cliffs, N.J.: Prentice-Hall, 1932, pp. 8–9.

hunch or hypothesis by means of systematic observation of data under controlled conditions. Haiman at Northwestern University played a tape-recorded speech for three audiences and told one group the speech was by the surgeon general of the United States, told another the speech was by the secretary of the Communist party in America, and told a third that the speech was by a sophomore at Northwestern. Haiman discovered that when he said the speech was given by the surgeon general, the audience members changed their opinion more than when it was attributed to either of the other sources.[2]

In 1951, two psychologists at Yale, Hovland and Weiss, did a similar study with a written argument and discovered similar results.[3] The psychologists used the term *source credibility* to describe the subject of their study, whereas Haiman had used *ethos*, which was the term that had come down through the rhetorical tradition from Aristotle.

The research techniques of Haiman, Hovland, and Weiss became models for a host of other investigators who did studies of essentially the same form, with minor variations, and the new message communication style encouraged and incorporated the experimental discoveries related to source credibility.[4] The studies tend to support the discovery of Aristotle, and we can consider the persuasive power of personality as an empirically supported, or scientific, part of our communication theory which cuts across all communication styles. Indeed, the fact that Aristotle could discover the principle in a culture as remote in time and space from ours as classical Greece, and that Roman theorists of rhetoric made

[2] Franklyn Haiman, "An Experimental Study of the Effects of Ethos in Public Speaking," *Speech Monographs*, 16 (1949), 190–202.

[3] Carl Hovland and Walter Weiss, "The Influence of Source Credibility on Communication Effectiveness," *Public Opinion Quarterly*, 15 (1951), 635–650.

[4] For summaries of important studies and conclusions, see Kenneth Andersen and Theodore Clevenger, Jr., "A Summary of Experimental Research in Ethos," *Speech Monographs*, 30 (1963), 59–78; Kim Giffin, "The Contribution of Studies in Source Credibility to a Theory of Interpersonal Trust in the Communication Process," *Psychological Bulletin*, 68 (1967), 104–120; Herbert W. Simons, N. Berkowitz, and J. R. Moyer, "Similarity, Credibility, and Attitude Change: A Review and a Theory," *Psychological Bulletin*, 73 (1970), 1–16. For some recent studies in the continuing research tradition see, Ronald F. Applebaum and Karl W. Anatol, "The Factor Structure of Source Credibility as a Function of the Speaking Situation," *Speech Monographs*, 39 (1972), 216–222; E. Scott Baudhuin and Margaret Kis Davis, "Scales for the Measurement of *Ethos:* Another Attempt," *Speech Monographs*, 39 (1972), 296–301; Raymond G. Smith, "Source Credibility: Context Effects," *Speech Monographs*, 40 (1973), 303–309; Christopher J. S. Tuppen, "Dimensions of Communicator Credibility: An Oblique Solution," *Speech Monographs*, 41 (1974), 253–260.

the same observations, is further evidence that the relationship may be applicable across cultures as well as across communication styles.

We know that some people are more believable than others, for certain people, in certain contexts. We know, in general, that the personality of the individual who utters the message is an important part of the persuasive context. What we do not yet know much about are specific ways in which source credibility functions. Some investigators have searched for specific factors (character traits) which account for a person's credibility or ethos. They have found factors such as qualification, dynamism, authoritativeness, objectivity, expertness, and so forth.[5] However, attempts to replicate the studies and agree on some small set of general factors have failed. Indeed these studies may have asked an unanswerable question, because the factors that go into source credibility may well be specific to communication styles or even to specific contexts within communication styles.[6]

Quite possibly, the sorts of people who are credible within a culture or community practicing a certain communication style will be different from those in cultures participating in other communication styles. For example, a John Wayne-type western he-man might be a credible source for some communities, but he might be a source of very low credibility for other communities whose members value a sensitive, low machismo-type male.[7]

A recent line of investigation has been the study of how people evaluate others in contexts even more restricted than those of culture or communication style. For instance, one study examined how people evaluate others as work partners or as social companions.[8] If such studies develop reliable conclusions, they will seriously undercut the notion that we can find general factors relating to source credibility.

[5] For some typical studies of this sort see David K. Berlo, James B. Lemert, and Robert J. Mertz, "Dimensions for Evaluating the Acceptability of Message Sources," *Public Opinion Quarterly*, 33 (1969–1970), 563–576; James C. McCroskey, "Scales for Measurement of Ethos," *Speech Monographs*, 33 (1966), 65–72; Jack L. Whitehead, Jr., "Factors of Source Credibility," *The Quarterly Journal of Speech*, 54 (1968), 59–63.

[6] See, for example, Applebaum and Anatol, "The Factor Structure of Source Credibility."

[7] See, for example, Charles U. Larson, *Persuasion: Reception and Responsibility*, Belmont, Calif.: Wadsworth, 1973. Larson discusses an attempt to analyze the electorate in the state of Oklahoma by using marketing research techniques to try to discover what sort of television personality would present an attractive image as governor. See footnote pp. 184–185.

[8] Jesse G. Delia, Walter H. Crockett, Allan N. Press, and Daniel J. O'Keefe, "The Dependency of Interpersonal Evaluations on Context-Relevant Beliefs About the Other," *Speech Monographs*, 42 (1975), 10–19.

charismatic role *A position of power over others which stems from personal spiritual qualities of the individual.*

In this chapter we will present information about the general nature of ethos or source credibility as it pertains to communication, with special emphasis on each of the three styles where appropriate. In our discussion of such things as likability, competence, and conviction as elements of credibility, we are probably reflecting a predominant North American culture rather than providing features that are universal. In addition, we will point out contextual effects upon source credibility.

Persuasion and Personal Relationships

One of the most important factors in persuasion in a communication situation is the quality of personal relationships that are established.[9] If people who are discussing a topic like and trust one another, attempts by either one to influence the other are more likely to succeed than if they are suspicious and dislike one another. The dimension of persuasion that has to do with the influence of human relationships enters the relationship style of communication in important ways. The fact that successful facilitators and instructors in the relationship style often develop a group of committed disciples and emerge in a **charismatic role** in which they can be very influential, is partially accounted for by the power of strong, positive personal relationships.

Persuasion often consists of advice. When we receive important advice we usually face some risky choices. Many of the big decisions of life pose some risks. Should I enlist in the army? Should I take that job with Pulver Motors? Should I get married? Should I go to college? Should I take a shot of heroin? When the choices are risky and I need advice, I tend to turn to someone I can trust.[10] Trust assumes that the other person will give me advice that seems to him or her to be the best for me. When I trust a person, I can count on his strength, integrity, sincerity, and expertness, and his concern for me.

[9] For a summary of a study by Franklin B. Evans of the things which go on in successful life insurance interviews which discovered that one of the most important things is the quality of the personal relationship between salesman and client, see William S. Howell and Ernest G. Bormann, *Presentational Speaking for Business and the Professions,* New York: Harper & Row, 1971, p. 283.

[10] For a summary of research on trust and source credibility see Giffin, "The Contribution of Studies in Source Credibility." See also, W. Barnett Pearce, "Trust in Interpersonal Communication," *Speech Monographs,* 41 (1974) 236–244.

Persuasion and Likability

Often, liking and trusting go together, but they are not necessarily always connected. We might find some people likable but not trustworthy in important matters, because we know they are forgetful, unreliable, or easily swayed by emotions. On the other hand, some people whose advice we take and whom we trust are not likable. We might trust a certain medical doctor because we know he is well trained, sober, and a talented physician, even though we do not like him much as a person.

Nonetheless, if we like a person, we are tempted to believe and accept his ideas and his advice. We often *feel* better about taking the advice of someone we like than about accepting the recommendation of someone we dislike. An important part of the study of persuasion, therefore, concerns how people who talk with one another come to *like* one another.

Picture in your mind a person you like. Recall your conversations with that person. What do you talk about? How do you talk? What is your attitude toward the person before you start a given conversation? Does the likable person have certain characteristics, such as physical appearance and habits of dress, that carry over from conversation to conversation? What does the likable person do and say that is attractive?

FACTORS IN LIKABILITY

Physical beauty is a factor in being likable.[11] Peoples' ideas about what is beautiful are as individual as people. Just the same, Americans spend billions of dollars each year in the search for beauty, because, for many, physical attractiveness is the key to popularity and friendship. Physical beauty is not enough by itself to assure likability, but other things being equal, the beautiful people have an advantage. Slogans such as "slim is beautiful" and "black is beautiful" clearly tie physical beauty to persuasive messages. Advertisers often use the persuasive power of handsome men and beautiful women shown using a product or simply being present in the same picture with an advertising slogan. The persuasive message is

[11] A large number of studies have demonstrated the importance of physical beauty in terms of likability. For a survey of the research see Chris L. Kleinke, *First Impressions: The Psychology of Encountering Others*, Englewood Cliffs, N.J.: Prentice-Hall, 1975, pp. 1–15; Elliot Aronson, *The Social Animal*, San Francisco: Freeman, 1972, pp. 215–219; Mark L. Knapp, *Nonverbal Communication in Human Interaction*, New York: Holt, Rinehart and Winston, 1972, pp. 64–68.

clear enough: "Beautiful people use this product; buy this product and you too will be beautiful."

Speaking ability is a factor in being likable.[12] A pleasant, flexible, resonant voice quality communicates a dynamic personality, an alive and vibrant person. The person who can find the right word at the right time and who can express an idea clearly and with interesting examples or analogies draws attention and interest. The person with a lively and vivid imagination, who can make small talk, spin out dreams or fantasies, dramatize characters, tell interesting stories, and ask unusual questions, is interesting and can be likable.

Listening ability is a factor in being likable. Listening is a real talent and is often underestimated. The person who is willing to listen to others and find out who they are, what they are interested in, and what they are worried about is often liked. Genuinely good listeners are always welcome.

People who come to like and trust one another often do so by means of serious, deep conversations that take place over a long time.[13] To be sure, some try to achieve such liking and trust in a week or two, or even a few days, by means of intensive sensitivity or encounter groups, but such forced feeding of significant communication is usually less successful than the growth of a relationship over more time. Instant trust is much like instant coffee; it just does not have the same flavor as a well-brewed cup. One of the charms of alcohol, drugs, and other mind changers is a "let's pretend" state of instant trust, but the feeling is the result of the altered mental state; it is not real. Trust cannot come without testing over time.

The Importance of Our Attitude Toward Others

All the basic personality characteristics mentioned above, such as physical appearance and speaking and listening ability, enter into our significant communications, but equally

[12] See, for example, Ronald J. Hart and Bruce L. Brown, "Interpersonal Information Conveyed by the Content and Vocal Aspects of Speech," *Speech Monographs*, 41 (1974), 371–381; W. Barnett Pearce and Forrest Conklin, "Nonverbal Vocalic Communication and Perceptions of a Speaker," *Speech Monographs*, 38 (1971), 235–241; W. Barnett Pearce and Bernard J. Brommel, "Vocalic Communication in Persuasion," *The Quarterly Journal of Speech*, 58 (1972), 298–306.

[13] For a summary of studies see Sidney J. Jourard, *Self-Disclosure: An Experimental Analysis of the Transparent Self*, New York: Wiley, 1971; see also P. C. Cozby, "Self-Disclosure, Reciprocity and Liking," *Sociometry*, 35 (1972), 151–160; B. C. Certner, "Exchange of Self-Disclosures in Same-Sexed Groups of Strangers," *Journal of Consulting and Clinical Psychology*, 40 (1973), 292–297.

important is the attitude people bring to their interpersonal communications. When we engage in significant communication, we let others know what we think, where we stand, and how we feel. We disclose our hopes, our dreams, and our fears. People are more likely to disclose themselves to those whom they think have a real interest in them. The salesman who seems interested in us only as long as he thinks we will buy something so he can make a commission, irritates us. People who use the others in a working group for their own ends or who treat others like things rather than like authentic persons seldom create trust and liking.

An attitude of willingness to help creates a feeling of trust and liking in others. A genuine offer of help is a powerful force of persuasion.[14] A good salesman often has a sincere and dedicated desire to help the customer. Well-managed stores instruct the salespeople to ask, "May I help you?" The opposite attitude works to build trust also: "I *need* your help" is another persuasive message. A person who asks for help, accepts it without bitterness, and then thanks us, makes us feel good. When people have helped one another, they feel freer to ask for help when they need it. When we create a climate of trust, we often accept the people we are talking with for themselves *as they are.* Acceptance does not mean approval of everything said or done by the participants in a communication; it means that the worth and importance of each person are unquestioned.

People who wish to persuade others in order to exploit them often try to cover up their real intentions. In face-to-face situations like the interview or small group meeting, such persuasive tricks usually fail. No matter how hard the manipulator tries to make the others believe he is sincere, unselfish, and dedicated to the welfare of all, his facial expression, vocal intonations, and bodily posture and gestures give him away.[15] Others come to think of the manipulator as slick, oily, phony, insincere. If a person is only pretending to be interested in another, his nonverbal messages communicate his real feelings. A common example of pretended interest is

[14] See, for example, Aronson, *The Social Animal,* pp. 207–212.
[15] For a report of research in small group communication relating to the inability of the manipulator to con others, see Ernest G. Bormann, *Discussion and Group Methods,* 2nd ed., New York: Harper & Row, 1975, pp. 265–266; see also, P. Ekman and W. V. Friesen, "Nonverbal Leakage and Clues to Deception," *Psychiatry,* 32 (1969), 88–106; Albert Mehrabian and M. Williams, "Nonverbal Concomitants of Perceived and Intended Persuasiveness," *Journal of Personality and Social Psychology,* 13 (1969), 37–58; Albert Mehrabian, "Nonverbal Betrayal of Feeling," *Journal of Experimental Research in Personality,* 5 (1971), 64–73. For a survey of research see Kleinke, *First Impressions,* pp. 54–55.

the child who courts another child only to ride his new bicycle. The result is that the receiver dislikes the person more than if the speaker had been honest in the first place.

Sometimes, a speaker's nonverbal cues create a wrong impression, so that he fails to establish friendship and trust without knowing why. Often if several people are having trouble talking with one another because of unintended nonverbal mannerisms, they can discuss the things that bother them and come to an understanding.

Persuasion and Source Competence

In addition to being likable and working to engender trust, the speaker should suggest competence, expertness, and credibility if his advice is to be persuasive. We expect a competent person's talk to contain a wealth of good and relevant information about the topic under discussion. The speaker who is

clear, whose comments are easy to follow because they are well organized, whose language is precise, and who has a fluent and expressive way of speaking, further suggests to us that he is competent. This is as true of the person talking to us face to face as of the person speaking in a more formal setting to a group of people in an audience.

Persuasion and Source Conviction

Finally, a powerful force for persuasion is the speaker's deep personal conviction that he is right. The first person a good salesman persuades is himself. The father who discusses the dangers of the use of tobacco and advises his son not to start smoking as he himself drags on a cigarette is not persuasive. The persuasive power of dedicated reformers is in large part a result of their willingness to make great personal sacrifices for a cause. William Lloyd Garrison, a leading figure in the fight to free the slaves in the nineteenth century, once wrote of his own part in the battle to abolish slavery:

> It is my shame that I have done so little for the people of color; yea, before God, I feel humbled that my feelings are so cold, and my language so weak. A few white victims must be sacrificed to open the eyes of this nation, and to show the tyranny of our laws. I expect and am willing to be persecuted, imprisoned, and bound for advocating African rights; and I should deserve to be a slave myself if I shrunk from that duty or danger.[16]

Since Garrison was writing from a jail cell in Baltimore, his sincerity was obvious, and his credibility was increased. One of Martin Luther King's most persuasive messages was his "Letter from Birmingham City Jail."[17]

Persuasion and the Speaker's Reputation

Up to now we have been talking about persuasion as it applies to the man in the street, to you and me. When an important public figure takes his platform to the people, persuasion

[16] Quoted in Archibald H. Grimke, *Williams Lloyd Garrison, The Abolitionist*, London: Funk and Wagnalls, 1891, pp. 82–83.

[17] In Haig A. Bosmajian and Hamida Bosamajian, eds., *The Rhetoric of the Civil Rights Movement*, New York: Random House, 1969.

moves from informal communication, where people talk directly to one another in what we called intimate and personal space in Chapter 5, to communication from the region of public space.

Two factors influence the public speaker's ability to persuade his listeners: his reputation and the particular speech he is making. When we study the persuasiveness of well-known public figures, therefore, we must examine both the effect of the speaker's reputation and the impact of the message itself. If we hear from others of a basketball player's skill and high scoring ability, his reputation affects the way we watch the start of the game but our final opinion is also influenced by how well he lives up to his reputation during the game. The reputation of a speaker influences our acceptance of his ideas, but our final decision usually depends upon what he says to us.

A number of different terms are used to stand for the concept of the source's reputation. A popular term is *image*. Advertisers talk of image to designate what communication researchers refer to as source credibility and what students of rhetoric term *ethos*. Most politicians have professional help in building an image (reputation) that will gain votes. Business firms, motion picture stars, rock musicians, government agencies, and other institutions often try to create a favorable image of themselves.

THE DYNAMIC NATURE OF IMAGE
A communicator's ethos or image is not static. Rather, when people talk with one another, they develop images related to that talk. For example, in a two-person conversation between John and Mary, their images of one another grow out of what they say to each other and how they say it. The images involved in conversations are thus more like motion pictures than like still snapshots; a given message source does not project one image now and forever, nor is the persuasive impact of an image independent of the receiver of the messages.[18]

The personality of the listener influences the effect of a persuasive message, as well. Research reveals that the listener's scores on dogmatism tests (which show how bullheaded or inflexible a person is) or personality inventories cor-

[18] For a study which illustrates the dynamic nature of ethos or source credibility, see Robert D. Brooks and Thomas M. Scheidel, "Speech as Process: A Case Study," *Speech Monographs*, 35 (1968), 1–7.

relate with how much the listener changes his attitudes after hearing a message.[19]

A listener's prior opinion of a speaker comes from many sources: previous in-person communications between them; what others have said to the listener about the speaker, what the listener has read about the speaker, and biographic information the listener may know about the speaker. Sources of information need not be individuals, of course. We receive communication from organizations, as well, and they too have prior reputations. The Defense Department has a reputation that affects all messages sent out by that particular unit of government, just as the John Birch Society, the Black Panthers, the United States Steel Corporation, the Communist party, the Republican party, and the Symbionese Liberation Army all have images or reputations that affect the persuasive impact of messages they send.

Consider the images of two mythical candidates as they have been created on television and in the national publications. One is a senatorial candidate named Wayland, who is said to be young, slim, handsome, educated at Harvard College, dynamic, polished, a man who inherited wealth but who has been giving his life to public service. Photographs of Mr. and Mrs. Wayland attending cultural and social events often appear in the slick magazines. They have several attractive young children. Wayland has appeared more and more frequently in recent months on television news shows, in brief scenes that show him stepping off airplanes, talking informally to reporters at airports, or speaking before audiences. His voice is pleasant, his manner serious but with some lightness and humor. He has a good smile and looks like someone you would enjoy knowing. Wayland's enemies say he is a lightweight and has gotten as far as he has largely through the power of his inherited wealth and social connections. There are ugly rumors about an impending divorce and about his extramarital sex life. Wayland is a liberal, and he is strongly committed to international disarmament.

Wayland's opponent, also mythical, is the incumbent Senator Homer Beardsley. Beardsley is approaching 60 but is said by his friends to be amazingly vigorous and young at heart. He is frequently shown jogging, playing tennis, and chopping wood for the fireplace of his cabin in the western mountains. Beardsley is a self-made man, the son of a poor tenant farmer;

[19] For a thorough survey of the research findings relating to audience characteristics and their relationship to credibility, see Gary Cronkhite, *Persuasion and Behavioral Change*, Indianapolis: Bobbs-Merrill, 1969.

he worked his way through college and law school, won a scholarship, and went abroad to study. Beardsley is said to be a brilliant man, but he has some difficulty expressing himself in speeches. He is a man of few words and has something of a poker face. He is by no means a charmer. He has the reputation of being a powerful member of Senate committees, although he does not get many headlines. Mrs. Beardsley is a plain but pleasant woman who likes to recall her farm background. They both enjoy country music and camping trips in wilderness areas. Their children are grown; they have grandchildren. Beardsley has been a strong defender of what he calls "preparedness" and is suspicious of all plans to disarm the country.

Say that some students in your speech class (with our myth in mind) are presenting a debate on disarmament, and the student speaking *for* disarmament quotes candidate Wayland. The student speaking *against* disarmament quotes Senator Beardsley. The reputation of each man influences response of you the listener to the statements. However, should Wayland appear on campus to give a speech, his reputation would be a factor as you *begin* to listen to him, but his platform personality and his demonstration of the personality traits others have attributed to him would be important factors in your final image of the man.

THE BUILDING OF IMAGES

Building a good image of candidates and institutions is the object of much organized persuasive campaigning. As an individual, you are projecting a public image every day. You can learn much about how your own image appears to others and how you can improve your projection of it by studying the professional image-makers' techniques. What are they primarily interested in doing? Professional persuaders often go to great lengths to discover attractive images for clients. Obviously, you are also trying to project your own image in the most favorable way.

Interestingly enough, persuasive images vary from audience to audience and from culture to culture. You will certainly try to project your most responsible image to your father when you ask for the family car for the evening, but 10 minutes later, on the telephone, you may try to project your most exciting, devil-may-care image to the date you expect to pick up in an hour. Consider our mythical political candidates once more. Did you find Wayland's image more attractive than Beardsley's? If so, you might well be from the suburbs of a metropolitan area. If you found Beardsley more attractive, you are probably from a small-town, rural, or midwestern area. Psychologists tell us that we identify with people with whom we feel we have much in common.[20] In this instance, the word *identification* refers to the feeling that you and another person could walk awhile in one another's shoes. Consider a candidate who is black, was raised in an urban ghetto, went to college on a basketball scholarship, became a star in the National Basketball Association, and subsequently worked with ghetto youths and became a militant advocate of Black Power. Would you find his image attractive? Anyone wise in the arts of persuasion takes a close look at the image he projects and then works hard to find out what images will be attractive to the audience he hopes to persuade.

You are all familiar with the national public-opinion polls—Gallup, Harris, and others. These polls are national trend-takers. Many campaign experts hire private survey firms to make depth studies of public reaction to images. In these studies, the experts collect responses from a group of people and, using those responses as a guide, estimate the responses of the large group that will be involved in the actual voting. The use of computers has, according to the pollsters, increased their accuracy and effectiveness in predicting actual voter performance. The methods they use to discover why people choose this man over that man are often unique. One poll-taker showed his respondents a list of some of the more popular television characters and asked them which of these personalities they would most like to represent them in Congress. On the basis of their findings about what a candidate's public considers attractive, the image-builders select the elements in the candidate that they feel will be most attractive to the voters and stress these elements in news releases, in television commercials, and in the candidate's speeches.[21]

THE LIMITS OF IMAGE BUILDING

From all this, however, you must not conclude that image-makers are always or even usually successful in creating false impressions of candidates or institutions. Persuasion must work within the limits of the facts. The basic personality of the candidate or the nature of the institution being "sold"

[20] For a less research-oriented and more philosophical analysis of the concept of *identification* see Kenneth Burke, *The Rhetoric of Motives*, Englewood Cliffs, N.J.: Prentice-Hall, 1950.
[21] See Larson, *Persuasion*, pp. 184–185.

forms a framework within which the persuaders must operate. The best public-relations firm in the world cannot make Homer Beardsley appear to be a member of the jet-set or socialite Wayland appear as a soul brother. If a public realizes it has been fooled, the reaction is usually swift, and disastrous for the unwise candidate. All the persuaders can do—but this is of considerable value to candidates and to you as an individual—is to learn what is attractive in a personality being "sold" and to help a person stress the attractive portions of his image and minimize the less attractive elements.

Our society has been undergoing a refreshing scourging of phonies. If you consider it hypocritical to sell yourself when you wish to persuade, you should remember that there are times when a man believes in a cause so strongly that if he finds his persona is alienating people, he will work hard to change his image in order to build more favorable response for the cause he is promoting. Thousands of college students hoping to stop the Vietnam War "went clean for Gene," cutting their hair, dressing conservatively, talking at length, quietly and without profanity, to potential voters as they campaigned for Senator Eugene McCarthy for president in 1968. By emphasizing the positive features of their cause and themselves, the students improved their ethos in an ethical way. They were able to level with the voters and still be honest with themselves. Accenting the positive is no sin; accenting what does not exist, on the other hand, is unethical. If a potential candidate sells himself to the voters as a churchgoing, sober man, when in fact he never goes to church and drinks heavily in secret, he will usually be found out and his ethos will be damaged.

We all form first impressions of people we meet. On getting to know these people better, we often change our opinions of them as the friendship grows or does not grow. In the case of national political figures, we are given much information from news media and magazines, and we are given information by the political figures themselves. We form opinions about all sorts of well-known people because we see and hear them or read about them; but about many people we have little information prior to our initial communication. What happens when we know little or nothing about the source of the communication?

ROLE-RELATED IMAGES

We often decide how much to accept from such a source on the basis of the stereotypes we have all built in our minds since childhood. We accept or reject messages because they come from people whose roles in society we accept or reject.[22] We know that many professional people have spent years acquiring the knowledge needed to label themselves landscape architects, medical doctors, lawyers, certified public accountants, or college instructors, and when they speak to us as professionals we tend to accept what they say as being useful (truthful or persuasive) whether or not we find them personally attractive. We are accepting the image of the expert rather than the personality image, and we accept messages from such experts more readily when they are speaking about their particular area of competence. When a professor of economics argues that the Federal Reserve Board is following the wrong policy to get the country out of a recession, we listen to him and tend to think he knows what he is talking about. We expect his judgment to be professional and based on careful research. When this same professor argues that the salaries of economics professors ought to be increased, we may not accept his message as being as persuasive, since in this second instance, he is speaking as a man with vested self-interest, and not as a scholar making an objective study of a subject. (On the other hand, should he testify against his own self-interest, the source's credibility would be enhanced.)[23]

The authors watched with interest one evening as a well-known surgeon nearly tore up his hat in anger and frustration after an elementary-school building committee wisely declined his carefully worked out plans for a new school. Although his judgments were accepted immediately in his day-to-day hospital world, his expertise dropped dramatically when he spoke as just another parent in the school meeting. The parents preferred the opinions of the teachers, administrators, architects, and city planners present, and wisely so. An expert, to be persuasive, has to stay within his area of competence.

[22] For a study which discovered that students asked to rank 10 religious, political, and social groups in terms of general credibility, ranked doctors, physicists, and civic leaders at the top, and labor-union members, high-school dropouts, and sexual deviates at the bottom, see Alvin Goldberg, Lloyd Crisp, Evelyn Sieburg, and Michele Tolela, "Subordinate Ethos and Leadership Attitudes," *The Quarterly Journal of Speech*, 53 (1967), 354–360. Of course, these opinions are subject to change through time and would probably differ with different populations of subjects.

[23] Elaine Walster, Elliot Aronson, and Darcy Abrahams, "On Increasing the Persuasiveness of a Low Prestige Communicator," *Journal of Experimental Social Psychology*, 2 (1966), 325–342.

Direct Knowledge of the Source

WHAT THE SPEAKER COMMUNICATES NONVERBALLY

In the final analysis, of course, a great deal of any speaker's ethos is generated by how he talks and what he says. Any speaker can do much to make his image more attractive right at the moment he is communicating.

He can use nonverbal suggestion to make himself more influential with his listeners, more persuasive. The speaker in the public-speaking style should work hard to appear to be in charge of the situation and his material, though in a relaxed and friendly way, not in a dictatorial or wise-guy manner. Remember that we are more likely to be persuaded by someone we accept as a person—a person we feel we could like. If the speaker's manner conveys the impression that he is calm, confident, sincere, and honest, we are more likely to trust and believe him. In a question-and-answer period after a formal speech, or in any face-to-face communication event, if the speaker's manner of fielding questions, dealing with disagreements, and handling challenges is confident, his credibility with the listeners is increased. If, under such stress, he loses his temper, his credibility often correspondingly plunges. If further, the speaker can communicate to the listener that he genuinely appreciates questions and respects the questioner, and if he responds fairly and candidly to the best of his ability, admitting honestly when he is stumped, he tends to build good will. If the speaker's manner suggests that he has something to hide, or if he hedges in such a way that he appears insecure and afraid of making a mistake, then his ethos is damaged. All these instances refer mostly to the manner in which the speaker conducts himself, to his nonverbal signals.

WHAT THE SPEAKER SAYS

What the speaker says, his verbal message, certainly has a considerable effect on whether we like and trust him, on whether we accept what he is saying and are persuaded by him. If the speaker is to be trusted he must say things that reveal him to be unselfish, interested in us, guided by a suitable code of ethics. (A suitable code of ethics would vary somewhat from situation to situation, depending on the speaker and the audience.)

If a person communicates verbally and nonverbally that he is trying to control us, that he is trying to outwit us and make us do something *he* wants but that we do not know about, that he is not really interested in us but in what he can get out of us, that he thinks he is a lot better and smarter than we are, or, that he is so set in his ways he will not be changed, no matter how wrong others may feel him to be, then we are likely to reject him as a person and to reject his message as well. He will not persuade us, because we do not think much of him or his ideas.[24]

On the other hand, if the speaker communicates verbally and nonverbally that he is absolutely fair, candid, and honest; that he is not defensive about his status or his expertness; that he is deeply involved with and dedicated to our common objectives; that he is willing to make personal sacrifices for our common good; that he is competent; that his advice is good and is given in our best interest; then his ethos is likely to be persuasive for us. He just may persuade us as he speaks, because he inspires confidence that he knows what he is talking about and wants to share his know-how with us for our own good.

The speaker may well create an advantage by reminding the audience of factors in his background, experience, and training that make him particularly competent to discuss the topic. This should not be done in a boastful way, of course. Often the speaker's expertise is known beforehand, either from advance publicity or from an introduction before he speaks.

The speaker may also imply his status. For example, he can add as he talks about what kind of tires we should use on our cars, "I've been racing stock cars for some years, and I've found that . . . " A speaker can dramatize his or her expertise as in the following example. A woman, a special counselor in the welfare department, was being introduced as a speaker to a group of young mothers, all newly receiving aid-to-dependent-children benefits. These mothers were more than a little wary of listening to another expert tell them how to manage their lives, particularly their finances, now that they were on relief. The program chairman introduced the speaker as a woman who had earned a degree in social work from the university and whose experience in the field was extensive. The listeners were only mildly impressed. The speaker won their attention and hearts at once when she began. "Fifteen years ago I was sitting in your seat. I'll tell you how I got up here, and I'll tell you how you can get yourself back on your own two feet, and I know that's where you want to be. I *know* each of you wants to do the absolute best

[24] For a survey of the effect of such communications see Jack R. Gibb, "Defensive Communication," *Journal of Communication*, 11 (1961), 141–148.

you can for your children, and for yourself, and that's why you are here." Wiping away the feelings of guilt that had washed over the young mothers as they had filled out the myriad papers necessary to obtain public assistance, the speaker had immediately told them: "You are great women with problems; I had the same problem a while back, and I learned a lot of answers which I am going to pass on to you."

If a speaker can rise above the self-absorption that comes when one is the focus of attention and can work to raise the status of his listeners with genuine compliments about the organization they represent, warm comments about individuals in the audience, or requests for help and advice (giving every indication that he plans to take such suggestions seriously), then he will certainly build good will.

THE PERSUASIVE USE OF HUMOR

One final element always useful in developing a persuasive ethos as a speaker comes from the fact that we all like to laugh. If a speaker can amuse us, if he can share his sense of humor with us, we are going to find him more likable. If he can communicate to us that he takes the subject, but not himself, seriously, we will be drawn toward him. If his humor is gentle rather than cutting or sarcastic, if he turns his humor back on himself rather than using it against others, we will trust him more. A person who can amuse his audience seems secure and in command of the situation. You must be careful not to overdo the use of humor, of course, particularly if you have a serious point to make. People love comics and clowns and try to place in that role any person who has some talent for comedy. The rewards for amusing speakers are

Chapter 11

THE KEY IDEAS

Much persuasion is dependent upon the quality of the personal relationships established among the people involved in a communication.

When the choices are risky and a person needs advice, he turns to someone he can trust.

People who come to like and trust one another, often do so by means of a series of deep conversations.

Trust seldom comes without a period of testing.

People are more likely to disclose themselves to those they feel are really interested in them.

A genuine offer to help is a powerful force for persuasion.

great—laughter, congeniality, and the knowledge that they are well liked. But just as the expert must stay in his area of expertness, so the comic is expected to stay the comic. If the clown tries to make a serious point, to give advice about important matters, we feel uncomfortable and tend to ignore his advice. Funny guys are not listened to on serious matters. Use humor in your persuasive speeches, then, but keep in mind your overall purpose.

There is much persuasive power in the personality of the source of the message. We have now seen how the use of evidence, reasoning, and personality contribute to persuasion. In the next chapter we will consider the power of suggestion.

SUGGESTED PROJECTS

1 Select some important personal decision, such as which college to attend, whether to get married, whether to buy a car, or which career to pursue. Think of the one person whose advice you would be most likely to accept in regard to the decision. Make a list of reasons why this person is a credible authority for you in regard to this particular decision.

2 This is actually a project within a project. Using the personal experience oral narrative, tell the class in two minutes about some exciting or emotional thing that has happened to you. Your aim will be to portray your participation in, or response to the

We tend to believe people whom we think are competent, expert, and interested in our welfare.

A powerful force for persuasion is a person's deep personal conviction that he is right: Sincerity is persuasive.

The image of a public figure is closely related to his credibility as a source of messages.

Organizations and business corporations also have images that affect their believability when they issue corporate messages.

The persuasive impact of a public figure's image varies from audience to audience.

If a public realizes it has been fooled by misleading image building, the reaction is usually swift, and disastrous for those involved.

We accept persuasive messages from some sources because they have professional credentials which we respect.

Much of a person's ethos is created by how he talks and acts in our presence.

A message source creates a credible image to a large extent by nonverbal communication suggesting he is interested in the listener, expert in the subject, and admirable as a person.

Funny guys are not listened to on serious matters, but a judicious use of humor in a speech increases a speaker's crediblity as a human being.

incident in a way that demonstrates that you are wise, sympathetic, strong emotionally, understanding, dependable, friendly— whatever characteristic you feel will enhance your ethos with your intended audience. You should use the most effective verbal and nonverbal communication you can. Your purpose is not to entertain, however, you should select the experience and develop it in such a way that will make the audience accept you as a credible message source on some undisclosed topic. After you have finished giving your narrative, tell the class what persuasive topic you have in mind, and explain how you believe the personal experience narrative you have just related to the class would serve to enhance your persuasive position if you were to develop the whole topic on another occasion. Here is a brief example of what this exercise could be like, beginning with the personal narrative: "I had always been a loner, and I am very interested in science and technology. I was put in charge of our high-school Ecology Day and had to learn how to organize student committees and work with others. I discovered I enjoyed it. We had poster exhibits and class discussions and films; we also had a big all-school program in the auditorium. I introduced our visiting speaker. Unfortunately, I had worked so late every night all week making sure everything was ready, I was exhausted, and I fell asleep while the speaker was talking." I would tell this incident in a speech to students asking them to vote for me for student senate. I would hope to show them, with this story, that I am a person who becomes very committed to a job and works very hard at it, but that I am also human, have a sense of humor, and can tell a story about myself in which I am the butt of the joke.

3 Attend a speech given by some prominent individual. Write a paragraph about the speaker *before* attending the speech, analyzing what you think of the speaker and deciding how credible a message source the speaker is for you. Keep notes on important comments relating to the speaker's ethos that occur *during* the speech. *After* you have heard the speaker, write another paragraph describing any changes in credibility that resulted from the speech itself. Write a third paragraph explaining these changes in terms of things the speaker said or did during the speech — how his personality influenced your judgment of his credibility.

SUGGESTED READINGS

Andersen, Kenneth, and Theodore Clevenger, Jr. "A Summary of Experimental Research in Ethos," *Speech Monographs*, 30 (1963), 59–78.

McCroskey, James C., Carl E. Larson, and Mark L. Knapp. *An Introduction to Interpersonal Communication.* Englewood Cliffs, N.J.: Prentice-Hall, 1971. "The Source-Sender," pp. 78–92.

Chapter 12

PERSUASION, PROPAGANDA, AND MASS COMMUNICATION

Persuasion and Propaganda

PROPAGANDA AS A GOVERNMENT TOOL, 1935–1945

In the years before and during World War II, Germany, Italy, and Russia used communication as a weapon in a ruthless psychological war against their enemies both within as well as outside of their borders. The Nazis established a ministry devoted to propaganda warfare, under the direction of Joseph Goebbels. He and Hitler left documented evidence of their cynical and unscrupulous manipulation of the masses by the restriction of speech and the studied application of techniques of propaganda.

Similar tactics had been used during World War I, and the period between the two great wars had seen the rise of radio and the growing preoccupation of scholars with mass persuasion and propaganda. In 1935, for example, an advisory committee on pressure groups and propaganda of the Social Science Research Council published an annotated bibliography on propaganda which contained several thousand items.[1] Still, the propaganda efforts associated with the period from 1935 to 1945 came to characterize the nature and methods of the practice. Some people use *propaganda* and *persuasion* as synonyms, and they contrast *bad* and *good* propaganda to show that it is not always undesirable. Since the time of Goebbels and Hitler, however, the term *propaganda* has had a generally undesirable connotation, and when the United States government, in 1942, established an agency for war propaganda, it was named the Office of War Information.

Lasswell, in an essay on propaganda which introduced the Social Science Research Council bibliography, described propaganda as follows:

> Not bombs nor bread, but words, pictures, songs, parades, and many similar devices are the typical means of making propaganda. Not the purpose but the method distinguishes propaganda from the management of men by violence, boycott, bribery, and similar means of social control. Propaganda relies on symbols to attain its end: the manipulation of collective attitudes.[2]

Lasswell characterized propaganda as a process which transmits attitudes that members of a given community recognize as controversial, as opposed to education, which is a process of transmitting skills and accepted attitudes. Lasswell also distinguished propaganda from news. News is a presentation of events which reaches a large public and which interests many people. Some news, thus, may be propaganda, but not all propaganda is news, nor is all news propaganda.

Propaganda is usually a large-scale effort. During the war, a good many Allied social scientists were employed to analyze the propaganda of the enemy. One particularly interesting study was devoted to the home radio broadcasts of German radio.[3] Similar studies of newspapers, speeches, whispering and rumor campaigns, films, and other media of communication were conducted. The point is that a propaganda campaign usually involves many different media of communication and continues for a significant period of time.

Propaganda on behalf of a government "tries to strengthen the authority of the government among the governed, so that the governed will like to do what the government wants them

[1] Harold D. Lasswell, Ralph D. Casey, and Bruce Lannes Smith, *Propaganda and Promotional Activities: An Annotated Bibliography*, 1935; reprint ed., Chicago: University of Chicago Press, 1969.

[2] Ibid., p. 3.

[3] Ernst Kris and Hans Speier, *German Radio Propaganda: Report on Home Broadcasts During the War*, New York: Oxford University Press, 1944.

to do, and dislike doing what the government wants to be left undone."[4] The propagandists of World War II were often engaged in mobilizing public opinion on behalf of the war effort of their particular government, be they British, German, or American. The propagandist on behalf of a government has an easy job of it when there are good things to report. In the case of Nazi Germany, the propagandist had a relatively easy time of it when there were victories. Bad news poses greater problems for the propagandists. They may sometimes choose to report the news with considerable accuracy, because they feel the public is loyal enough in their support to allow the government to endure, or because more accurate reports will spread through other channels and injure the prestige of the propagandists as information sources. Despite this need to report events accurately at least from time to time, a study of Nazi propaganda revealed that "to a varying degree, the propagandist is constantly tempted to make use of one or several of the many forms of deception: slanting news by selection and emphasis, boasting, empty promises, flattery, the pretense of righteousness, studied enthusiasm, straight-forward lies, inventions, etc."[5]

The relationship of propaganda to coercion and violence is an interesting one. In some respects, propaganda is an alternative to violence. As Kris and Speir point out:

> Words may achieve what bullets do not accomplish, because words do not kill. A ruthless and powerful man would be foolish if he killed opponents he could use for his own purposes. The dead can neither fight nor work. . . . Political propaganda in Nazi Germany is a form of coercion: while it lacks the bluntness and irrevocability of physical violence, it derives its ultimate efficacy from the power of those who may, at any moment, cease talking and start killing. . . . National Socialist propaganda, however, cannot be understood if its relation to National Socialist terror is overlooked. Goebbels at home would be ineffectual without Himmler, and Goebbels addressing foreign audiences would be a comical figure were it not for Germany's armed might.[6]

PROPAGANDA IN DICTATORSHIPS AND DEMOCRACIES
In their study of Nazi propaganda, Kris and Speier pose the question "Does domestic propaganda in Nazi Germany differ from propaganda in other countries at war?" Their answer: "The difference is as great as that between dictatorship and

[4] Ibid., p. 4.
[5] Ibid., pp. 4–5.
[6] Ibid., p. 3.

democracy."[7] Certainly, as we have seen throughout this book, cultural differences are important in all aspects of the study of communication. Certainly, too, totalitarian countries can exercise stronger censorship, and propagandists who control a country's media, particularly radio and television, can manage the symbols of the populace much more efficiently than can propagandists in a democracy.

Recently, we were visitors in the capital city of a country whose government feels it is under threat from opposing ideologists. Looking for a museum which houses priceless artifacts from the country's ancient past, we walked by mistake past the media center, and were quickly but courteously questioned by a plainclothesman who spoke some English. There were uniformed men carrying machine guns stationed in front of the media building. After a short walk, we came to the building we wanted: The museum door was open; no one was in sight, as the attendant was out back having a cup of tea. The country's real priorities were made clear to us very dramatically in those few hours. They could exist without their artifacts, but they knew they must maintain control of their channels of communication.

All modern democracies, however, including the United States, have propagandists mounting and managing full-scale campaigns, for secret purposes as well as for public ends, and they utilize all of the means of contemporary mass persuasion that they can afford or finagle. Certainly many observers have accused presidential administrations since the Second World War of trying to propagandize on behalf of the administration's policies. They accused the Kennedy administration of news management, the Johnson administration of creating a "credibility gap" by suppression of information and distortion and lies, and the Nixon administration of the cover-up of Watergate, of secrecy, and of lying. The press secretaries of the Ford administration have had a difficult time as well.

OTHER USES OF PROPAGANDA

Propaganda campaigns are not dedicated solely to the support of an existing government. Propagandists also attempt to achieve social change, political reform, and revolution. They develop campaigns to support organizations, institutions, and business corporations. They create public personalities in all fields of endeavor, including the theatre, films, painting, music, sculpture, television, labor unions, and education.

[7] Ibid., p. 7.

Finally, propagandists are generally employed in political campaigns.

The professions of publicity agent, advertising specialist, fund raiser, campaign manager, ghost writer, and media adviser evolved slowly over the first half of the twentieth century. In the nineteenth century many causes and educational institutions employed agents whose job it was to raise money for a cause or institution and to give speeches, lobby, and otherwise promote the cause.[8] But by the 1920s, the professionals who emerged had a communication style which was quite different from past efforts at persuasion, enough so that practitioners could write books about it. The new style was mature enough to describe in detail, as did Edward L. Bernays, a leading public relations counsel, who wrote *Crystallizing Public Opinion* in 1923.[9]

Propaganda is communication with an ax to grind. Propaganda is organized, systematic communication which involves the use of all available channels of communication. Generally, successful propaganda is the product of professionals or of inspired amateurs who spend a good deal of time laying out campaign strategy and tactics; selecting symbols, slogans, and dramas to support the leading themes of the campaign; collecting financial and other resources; selecting channels (television, radio, print, billboards, speeches, rallies, word of mouth, and so forth); and deciding upon the timing of the various messages. In some instances, specialists running a propaganda campaign have sufficient financial resources to buy time on television or advertising space in newspapers, thus assuring that their message is transmitted with high fidelity.

HOW PROPAGANDISTS MANIPULATE THE MEDIA

Some campaigns, however, rely more heavily upon the ingenuity of the propagandist to manipulate the media through dramatic skill. Some years ago, a specialist in media manipulation with time on his hands decided, for the fun of it, to see how much publicity he could get on national media. He founded a dummy organization, called press conferences, finagled interviews on radio and television talk shows, and caught the attention of the general public. His gimmick was that his

[8] For a discussion of abolition agents in the nineteenth century see Ernest G. Bormann "The Rhetoric of Abolition," in Ernest G. Bormann, ed., *Forerunners of Black Power: The Rhetoric of Abolition*, Englewood Cliffs, N.J.: Prentice-Hall, 1971, pp. 1–38.

[9] New York: Boni and Liveright, 1923.

organization was going to promote the modesty of dumb animals. He wanted to clothe the animals in zoos and on farms. His notion that nude elephants were obscene and that dairy herds were analogous to the centerfolds of "girlie" magazines, caught the attention of a number of news staff members at newspapers and radio and television stations, and they put the reports on as "human interest" stories. Large segments of the general public became intrigued by the idea and it began to snowball. Without spending very much money at all, the fellow was able to get national media coverage.

As we wrote this book, "Jaws," a film dealing with a rampaging shark which mutilates and sometimes kills swimmers, was enjoying a huge success. One critic of the film charged that the movie is a third-rate horror film which has been puffed into popularity and that a good many serious film critics have been taken in by the propaganda on behalf of the film. The critic argued that the publicity campaign for "Jaws" had begun even before the book upon which the film is based was written! He also claimed that the film had "the largest pre-release advertising budget for any movie in the history of Universal Studios." The result was a carefully planned publicity campaign which was conducted while the movie was being made, which was aided by the "lucky strike of a *Time* magazine cover story." The publicists peaked the campaign with a heavy saturation of television spot advertisements the week the film opened, and the entire campaign contributed to the film's making about $90,000,000 in its first two months.[10] Another result of the campaign, as reported on television and in newspapers, is that many bathers are reluctant to swim in many of the nation's beaches, apparently because the drama of the killer shark has caught their imagination.

Propagandists for social movements with low budgets can often gain media coverage by similar tactics. During the 1960s protesters burned draft cards, American flags, and draft records. They sometimes flew a North Vietnamese flag, staged a demonstration, held a rally, and battled police. During the period that such tactics were novel, the propagandists achieved wide media coverage. When they became more commonplace and began to lose their shock value, the propagandists were forced to search for other ways of gaining media access.

Propaganda consists, therefore, of both the controlled and managed persuasion for which the propagandist pays, and that

[10] Stephen Farber, "'Jaws': $8 Millions Worth of Shoddy Exploitation?" *Minneapolis Tribune*, August 31, 1975, p. D1.

managed persuasion which the propagandist places in the media by means of skillful manipulation of the managers of the news channels.

THE DIFFERENCE BETWEEN PROPAGANDA AND PERSUASION

We will use the term *propaganda* to refer only to the irresponsible and unethical use of persuasive communication techniques, in relatively long-term and large-scale campaigns of symbolic manipulation to achieve the persuader's goals. The unethical features of propaganda include intentional assertion of falsehoods and half-truths, misrepresentation of facts, and exploitation of the human tendency to act without thinking. Notice that propaganda reflects a communication theory and criticism which are frankly manipulative. Hitler, in *Mein Kampf,* outlines an approach to propaganda which reflects a

very Machiavellian attitude towards technique. Any number of handbooks on advertising and public relations reflect the same general approach.[11]

Persuasion refers to a wider range of communication styles than does *propaganda,* and in our study of persuasion we will include the theory of the public-speaking and message communication styles which emphasizes those situations in which the people who communicate through the mass media are truthful, represent facts fairly, assume that human beings are capable of reflective and creative thinking, and use the techniques of communication to work cooperatively for a common good. As a student of communication, you should become alert to the differences among communication styles within the mass media and be particularly alert for the propaganda communication style, with its manipulative and Machiavellian theory. Persuasion in all styles of communication will continue to influence you during the rest of your life. One always has to make choices about such little things as which toothpaste to buy or about such big things as which candidate to vote for. Although it is sometimes difficult, you must be able to recognize propaganda devices for what they are, so that you can make up your own mind whether or not you will be persuaded by less than the best arguments. If you are not consciously aware of propaganda devices, you will react to propaganda without thinking. That is just what the propagandists want. They have many good reasons for believing they can make you do what they want you to do.

Fantasy Themes and Rhetorical Visions

We come now to one of the most important ways in which propagandists, publicists, persuaders, and mass media programmers and writers create attitudes, beliefs, values, and change behaviors—namely, the communication processes which result in small group fantasy chains, fantasy types, and the emergence of rhetorical visions relating to important public questions. In earlier times word-of-mouth was the main medium for generating drama, excitement, vision, and common dreams for groups and communities. Today word-of-mouth remains important but it has been heavily supplemented by the dramatizations of the mass media. As a result, the

[11] See, for example, Edward L. Bernays, ed., *The Engineering of Consent,* Norman, Okla.: University of Oklahoma Press, 1955; Arthur E. Meyerhoff, *The Strategy of Persuasion,* New York: Berkeley Publishing, 1965.

communication processes which develop our views on public issues, our common hopes and aspirations are much more complex than they were in an earlier time. We will begin by explaining the basic terms for our analysis of the current persuasive and propaganda climate.

GROUP FANTASY CHAINS

The process which is the key to understanding contemporary persuasion is the *dynamic chaining of group fantasies.* Bales discovered group fantasy chains while making a study of the content of small group discussions. Bales and his associates were coding messages into a category system in order to make quantitative descriptions of the discussion process; they wanted to know exactly what the group talked about every minute. Over the years of studying groups the researchers discovered an important kind of message behavior which they labeled *dramatizes,* which consisted of any comment made in a group which told a story about people, real or fictitious, or about imaginary characters, in a dramatic situation. The characters were acting in a setting other than the *here-and-now* communication of the group. (The here-and-now is a concept used in the relationship style of communication particularly in sensitivity and encounter groups and refers to what is happening at the moment in the group.) If in the here-and-now two members of a group come into direct conflict, the situation is dramatic, but because the action is immediate and here-and-now, their behavior would not be coded as "dramatizes." However, if the group members begin talking about a conflict some of them had in the past or daydreaming out loud about something they might do in the future, the comments would be dramatizing messages.

When coding the dramatizing messages, the researchers discovered that some dramatizing seemed to fall on deaf ears; the group members did not pay much attention to the comments. Some of the dramatizing, however, caught the other group members' attention. These successful dramas began to chain out through the group, that is, they passed from one member to another, as in a chain. The tempo of conversation would pick up. Members grew excited, interrupted one another, laughed, showed some emotion, forgot their self-consciousness. The members participated in the story with the sorts of responses that were appropriate. If the person telling the story was trying to be funny, the others laughed; if the person was serious, the others' verbal comments and non-verbal responses would be of the suitable tone. The group obviously tuned in to the fantasy. (If a member tries to tell a funny story and some of the others groan and indicate that they do not like the story, the drama has not chained out.)[12]

FANTASY CHAINS AND GROUP CULTURE

When a dramatizing message in a small group conversation results in a group participation and chain, it is an example of the dynamic chaining of group fantasies. Once group members have participated in a number of group fantasy chains they create a greater sense of community and cohesiveness and come to share a common group culture. They have some common heroes and villians; they have sympathized and identified with dramatic characters in suspenseful situations; they have come to share the attitudes implied by the stories. Let us say that a group of students are in a meeting as part of a communication exercise for class. One of the students, a girl, is a bit late for the meeting and arrives out of breath and out of sorts. She apologizes for being late and explains her tardiness by dramatizing the two hours she has just spent prior to the meeting trying to get registered for the spring term. Her dramatizations might be satirical, ironic, or ridiculing. They might be melodramatic and emotional. If they were satirical, the proper response from the others would be laughter with a bitter edge to it. If the group begins to respond to her dramatizations with the proper emotional tone and if others begin to add dramatizations on the same theme, the result would be a fantasy chain. Suppose she dramatized her plight in a satirical manner and portrayed herself as a well-intentioned, sane individual caught up in a scene where other characters acted like they were unreasonable and in a situation or procedure which was insane. By exaggerating the

[12] For the process of group fantasy chaining see Robert F. Bales, *Personality and Interpersonal Behavior*, New York: Holt, Rinehart and Winston, 1970; see also Ernest G. Bormann, *Discussion and Group Methods*, 2nd ed., New York: Harper & Row, 1975. For some studies of nineteenth-century movements which revealed fantasy themes see Carl Wayne Hensley, "Rhetorical Vision and the Persuasion of a Historical Movement: The Disciples of Christ in Nineteenth Century American Culture," *The Quarterly Journal of Speech*, 61 (1975), 250–264; Gordon Alan Zimmerman, "A Comparative Rhetorical Analysis of the Nevada Constitutional Convention of 1864," Ph.D. dissertation, University of Minnesota, 1973. For fantasy theme analysis of mass media communication see John Francis Cragan, "The Cold War Rhetorical Vision 1946–1972," Ph.D. dissertation, University of Minnesota, 1972; Virginia Venable Kidd, "Happily Ever After and Other Relationship Styles: Advice on Interpersonal Relations in Popular Magazines, 1951–1973," *The Quarterly Journal of Speech*, 61 (1975), 31–39; John Cragan, "Rhetorical Strategy: A Dramatistic Interpretation and Application," *The Central States Speech Journal*, 26 (1975), 4–11; Charles R. Bantz, "Television News: Reality and Research," *Western Speech*, 39 (1975), 123–130.

ridiculous aspects of the procedure and dwelling on them she gains more response and laughter. Members chime in with comments like, "I know just what you mean." "That happened to me just the other day, too." "I always dread having to register." Another member begins to tell about a friend who has figured out a clever way to bypass all the red tape by neglecting ever to see his advisor and by a judicious amount of forgery. The group gets caught up in the dramatization as well and applauds the clever scoundrel, indicating in their response that insane regulations deserve to be avoided or evaded. The group has created some common ground and developed some common attitudes and values in the process of their fantasizing.

The group begins to create a common culture with even a brief episode of fantasy chaining such as that described above. Cohesiveness of a group can be aided by fantasy chaining. Using the example above, the group has sympathized with two people, their fellow group member who tried her best and was honest and honorable but still frustrated by the system, and the clever fellow the other member told them about, the one who broke the rules but got around the frustration. The group has demonstrated and come to share some attitudes towards elaborate and careful work procedures heavily dependent upon paper forms and a certain rigorous following of a step-by-step plan. When the time comes for them to develop their own work norms for their group effort (in the here-and-now) they will not be likely to create elaborate agendas, written on paper, and designed to lead them through their planning stages in a lock-step fashion. They have also developed some attitudes towards getting around certain requirements in their class that they find trivial or meaningless.

FANTASY THEMES AND TYPES

The content of a given group fantasy is a *fantasy theme*. A description of the fantasy themes in the example above would include the people who were involved (the students trying to register and the people they met in the process,) the dramatic situations (the incidents that occurred,) and the setting (the administration building, various offices, and so forth.)

When a number of similar scenarios or outlines of the plot of the fantasies including particulars of the scenes, characters, and situations have chained through a group or a larger community, they form a *fantasy type*. The *fantasy type* is a stock scenario repeated again and again by similar characters or the same cast of characters. In the example above, if after the member told of her clever friend who had bypassed registration procedures, another member had added a story about still another student who used a different technique but still managed to successfully bypass the official registration procedure, and then if still another member had told of a third student who had managed to register without going through the normal channels, we would have an example of a fantasy type. The stock scenario would consist of a clever student hero or heroine who skillfully figures out a plan to get around the ridiculous, confusing, and meaningless registration procedures.

In our example above, the fantasy themes consisted of real people and actual events. The members of the group were not making up the stories but were telling them about real people they knew and real acts they had performed. In much the same way, authentic news stories are fantasy themes and if groups of people respond to the news stories they may chain through the groups as fantasies. Notice, however, that a member of the group may dramatize a Walt Disney type story and it may result in a group fantasy. We cannot make the point too strongly, however, that you should not let this possible use of an imaginery and unreal story to create a group fantasy mislead you into thinking that is the only sort of drama which can result in fantasies. To be sure, one common everyday use of the term *fantasy* is to refer only to stories about imaginary and unreal characters in some never-neverland. For some reason the definition of fantasy as fairy story seems to be the one that often comes to mind when people hear the word: *fantasy*. Another common definition of fantasy, however is much closer to our technical use of the term here. Fantasy also refers to an individual's daydreams which influence his or her behavior and self-image. For example, male and female sexual fantasies influence real-life sexual practices. In much the same manner, group fantasies provide shared concerns and values for the participants. Rhetorical fantasies are usually concerned with people and events which are much more widespread and significant to all our daily lives and actions and which are often a part of the historical record or the breaking news. Fairy tales which deal with imaginary events and unreal situations play a very minor part in rhetorical fantasies.

RHETORICAL VISIONS

Fantasy chains are not confined to the communication in small formal and informal group contexts. Fantasies also chain through the mass media and come to grip large communities of people within a city, within a state, within the nation; and, on occasion, they may chain world-wide. When a number of fantasy themes have chained through the general public and they have begun to cluster into fantasy types the next step is the emerging of a rhetorical vision.[13] A *rhetorical vision* is a symbolic reality created by a number of fantasy types and it provides a coherent view of some public problem or issue. Often you can tell that a vision has emerged when slogans appear or when a brief label serves to indicate the cluster of meanings, motives, and emotional responses related to a set of fantasy types. Quite often some unifying analogy will pull the fantasy themes together and give them a structure. The rhetorical vision relating to the foreign policy of the United States after WWII began to emerge after Winston Churchill's speech at Fulton, Missouri in 1946 when he used the term "iron curtain" to describe the border between the communist zone of influence and the British, French, and American zones in Allied occupied Europe. The term had been used before but never before had it spread through the media and the public as it did after the speech in Fulton. The unifying analogy that emerged was that the United States was in a state analagous to war except that it was not involved in the "hot" variety, not actually firing weapons at the communists in organized fashion; we were, rather, in a "cold war" occupying war zones divided by an "iron curtain." Similarly, through the years, rhetorical visions have been indexed by such terms as "The New Deal," "The New Populism," "The New Frontier," "Black Power," "Red Power," "The Right to Life," "Death with Dignity," "Woman Suffrage," and "Women's Liberation." In his State of the Union message of 1976, President Ford tried out the slogan "The New Realism" but apparently the requisite number of fantasy themes had not yet chained through the American public for the slogan did not catch on. Undoubtedly as you read this there are new rhetorical visions emerging with their new labels.

RHETORICAL COMMUNITY

When a rhetorical vision emerges, the participants in the vision (those who have chained in on the fantasies in an appropriate way) come to form a *rhetorical community*. Members of a rhetorical community can arouse considerable emotional response in one another with messages which

[13] For a description of the relationship between fantasy themes and rhetorical vision, see Ernest G. Bormann, "Fantasy and Rhetorical Vision: The Rhetorical Criticism of Social Reality," *The Quarterly Journal of Speech*, 58 (1972), 396–407.

simply allude to fantasy themes which have previously chained through the community. The "inside joke" is an example of such a message which evokes appropriate responses from insiders by using a code word for the fantasy. Throughout this chapter when we refer to fantasy themes, types, and rhetorical visions, we are dealing with public dreams. You could have a private philosophy or world view which would differ in some important respects from the rhetorical visions and fantasies in which you also participate publicly. Your private fantasies only become important in a communication sense when you discuss and share them with others.

We will examine the concept of the *American dream* to illustrate how large communities of people within a culture may participate in a series of chaining fantasies until a fantasy type comes to play an important part in the development of their culture.[14] The American dream refers to the fantasy type which has as its stock scenario a poor but talented, deserving, and hardworking hero or heroine, who, starting from poor and humble beginnings, works hard and achieves success. The variations on the scenario in the 19th and early 20th century in American history are many: Abraham Lincoln, the poor farm boy who became president; Andrew Carnegie, the poor immigrant boy who became a millionaire and who gave away his money building libraries; Henry Ford, the poor mechanic who became the rich automobile builder; Booker T. Washington who became a leading educator; George Washington Carver who came out of slavery to become a leading inventor; Victoria Woodhull who came from humble beginnings to a seat on the stock exchange and who ran for president of the United States before women had the right to vote; Susan B. Anthony who became a leading reformer; Amelia Earhart who became a daring flyer.

Because they had chained into fantasy themes of the type of the American dream, many people came from foreign countries to the United States at great sacrifice and hardship, and when they arrived in the new country they worked hard, often under miserable conditions, to achieve the success they fantasized about.

Individuals may still participate in fantasies similar to the widely held dream of the nineteenth century. You may daydream that you are playing a hero's part and doing interesting and exciting things. All of us want our lives to matter. We want to be appreciated for what we are, for what we can do.

[14] See, for example, Walter R. Fisher, "Reaffirmation and Subversion of the American Dream," *The Quarterly Journal of Speech*, 59 (1973), 160–167.

The boy who dreams of being a big league pitcher and sees himself striking out the opponents in an all-star game may practice long hours and live only to achieve his dreams. All of us are aware of the strength of the self-fulfilling prophecy.

THE DISSEMINATION OF MASS FANTASIES

How is it that the fantasy chains in small groups can come to have an influence on mass media communication and, in turn, be influenced by it? First, small groups of people create fantasy chains as they work together planning persuasive campaigns in behalf of products, candidates, institutions, and causes. Second, the group's fantasies are then worked into the messages which they channel through the mass media to the general public. Third, the media messages impact on individuals but tend to be processed by groups with which these individuals live and work. Sometimes we have a too-simple view of how persuasion and propaganda work in the mass media. Early scholars of radio and television impact thought that mass persuasion flowed directly from the TV set to the viewer-listener. When the president went on television and talked directly to the American people, for example, scholars assumed that this had a direct and persuasive impact on the viewers. Subsequent research found that the one-step view of mass persuasion was too simple; it revealed that the persuasive impact of television occurs in at least two steps: the persuasion first affects and is mediated by opinion leaders, and then it is processed in small group conversations. This process is called two-step flow.[15]

You are most likely to feel the influence of television second-hand, then, as the ideas and fantasies suggested on TV are talked about in conversations with your family and friends. Again the process of fantasy chaining is most important. If the original fantasy produced by the first small group of publicists is transmitted in approximately the same way by the media, and the groups which discuss it chain in to the drama as did the original groups, the persuasive impact will be much like the one intended. However, if the media change the drama or if the small groups that discuss it chain in to a fantasy which ridicules or satirizes the original drama, the result may be very different from what the people planning the persuasive campaign intended.

The three basic steps by which a fantasy originates in a group of professional persuaders, is then fed through the mass

[15] See, for example, Elihu Katz, "The Two-Step Flow of Communication: An Up-to-Date Report on an Hypothesis," *Public Opinion Quarterly*, 30 (1970), 61–78.

media, and ends up with small groups of lay people chaining into the drama so that it becomes a community fantasy only partially explains how public fantasies come about. Fantasies may arise spontaneously. Some public fantasies begin in groups of people with like interests meeting together casually and with no intention of starting a persuasive campaign. They may create a fantasy chain which is so compelling that they repeat the story in other groups and if the appeal of the drama is strong enough, it catches on at a grass-roots level in many such groups. Gradually these spontaneous group fantasies are worked into the mass media, and are again processed and vitalized in other groups. In the early 1970s in a medium-sized city in an eastern coast state, small groups of people began to chain into a drama about a woman who had tried on a coat made in Hong Kong or Taiwan in a local discount store. She put her hand into the coat pocket and pricked her finger on a pin. When her hand began to swell and she became ill, further investigation turned up a small, somewhat poisonous baby snake in the lining of the coat pocket. A local newspaper columnist heard the story and worked it into the paper. Television news programs mentioned it as a human interest story. Attempts by the media reporters to run down the rumor and discover what had happened revealed that there was no such woman and no such snake, but the chaining fantasies had done considerable damage to the chain of stores named in the drama.

Sometimes breaking news stories begin to chain in unexpected ways through small groups of citizens and the chaining response of the public encourages additional media dramatizations of similar events. In the mid-1970s, the national media featured a story about the parents of a young woman long in a coma who had gone to court to force the doctors to cease the artificial support systems which were keeping their daughter alive. The drama of the young woman began to chain through the general public, some groups casting the parents as heroes and others portraying those who wished to keep the young woman alive as heroes. The media journalists, alert to the audience response and controversy, kept the story alive by giving it more air time and began to dramatize similar situations relating to other people from around the country until a fantasy type emerged. Thus the spontaneous chaining of a public fantasy can begin with the media dramatizing a news event as well as from a small group of professional persuaders whose intent is to create public response and from small groups of laymen with no persuasive intent at all who happen to chain into a fantasy that is, in turn, chained into by others.

How Fantasies Function to Persuade

The suggestion inherent in a small group fantasy is a powerful force of persuasion for all of us, in our many relatively private dreams that never reach the mass media as well as in those dreams we share with much of mankind. Much of our motivation to be and to do is contained within the dreams that become real and exciting to us. Our personal dreams often are shaped by the positive and negative suggestion inherent in the messages of the mass media; many of our dreams are these messages after they have been discussed, re-created, reshaped in our talk with other people we like and enjoy; some of our dreams are the product of fantasy chains made up by the groups we belong to, and we become part of a dream that others share.

We are not necessarily persuaded by reason. We are often persuaded by suggestion that ties in with our dreams. To limit a study of communication to factual information is to deny the powerful influence we all feel when those things we hold most dear, our innermost hopes and dreams, are involved.

Persuasive Elements of Fantasy Themes

An important principle of learning is that the more intense the emotional impression something makes on a person, the more effective his learning of that thing will be. If something hits us emotionally, we are more likely to recall it. Abstract messages full of statistics, general principles, and words we half understand do not arouse our feelings or emotions. But give us a human-interest story, tell us something about another person so we can sympathize with him, make us happy or sad for him, and we find ourselves reacting with friendly or unfriendly responses to these believable people presented in real-life dramas.

When a newspaper reports that unemployment has risen by several hundred thousand in the last month, we make a mental note that the rise in unemployment is bad. But what if we then see a television documentary about the unemployment in our own city or town? The program is organized around three families, each from a different section of the area, each from a different socioeconomic level in the community. We meet one of the jobless fathers; we see him in the living room of a neat home and hear him tell of his efforts to find employment and of his discouragement. We learn that his family may lose its home. We meet the mother, who is now working daily as a waitress from 4:00 PM until midnight to supplement her husband's unemployment compensation. The program narrator interviews the children. We become emotionally involved with the people and thus with the unemployment problem. The situation that makes us think, "There but for the grace of God go I," touches us.

CHARACTERS IN PUBLIC DRAMAS

Real people often make the best characters in the public dramas of propaganda and persuasion. Hitler and, later, Stalin were the villians in many of the international dramas in which the people of the United States participated in the 1930s, 1940s, and 1950s. The character of Hitler, in American and British propaganda and persuasion of the time, bore little resemblance to the real-life man, but that fact was irrelevant to the suggestion involved in the fantasies. People find it more difficult to hate Nazism than its personification, Adolf Hitler. For their political friends and enemies, American presidents often serve the same function as characters in morality plays. Heroes and villains in action and conflict arouse our love or hate, fear or joy, admiration or disgust.

Successful persuasion not only relies on real-life people, but also uses fictitious characters who serve as hypothetical examples and who have admirable or hateful characteristics. Superman brings certain qualities to mind. So does Casper Milquetoast. Finally, a persuasive speaker may use the figure of speech called *personification* to create emotional responses to abstract propositions. When a speaker uses personification, he endows an abstract idea, institution, or government with human characteristics, so it begins to act like a person in a drama. Mark Twain once suggested that a lie could travel around the world while the truth was still pulling on its boots. Suggesting that truth can pull on its boots gives truth the attributes of a person. In nineteenth-century oratory, the personification of such abstract notions as *truth, virtue, beauty,* and *eloquence* was common.

Persuasive messages may contain personifications of abstractions such as the United States of America in the form of Uncle Sam or of Great Britain in the person of John Bull. Political cartoonists, who often work with suggestion to achieve their persuasive impact, frequently personify John Q. Public or give the atomic bomb the characteristics of a human being.

THE IMPORTANCE OF SETTING

In addition to characters, a propaganda or persuasive campaign must provide a setting for the drama. Watch several television commercials or clip several advertisements from a magazine. Notice the scene or location of the action. Although only a small number of people still work as cowhands in our country, a high percentage of characters in advertising campaigns ride horses, wear large western hats, and herd and brand cattle. Many commercial advertisements are set in homes that are gorgeous, lovely, and in perfect order. Much political persuasion derives its impact from the particular setting in which the drama takes place. Cesar Chavez battles the grape growers in the fertile valleys of California. The John F. Kennedy drama of Camelot was played out at Hyannisport, Palm Springs, and the White House. Jesse Jackson's Operation Breadbasket is set in the black ghettos of Chicago. Skillful propagandists planning a dramatic action for symbolic effect take pains to select the proper scene for their drama. In the 1950s, foes of school integration in the South bombed black churches rather than schools. Friends of integration encouraged black students to enroll at the University of Alabama. In the 1960s, foes of capitalism bombed Bank of America branch offices. In the late 1970s, foes of school busing demonstrated around the schools.

THE DRAMATIC ACTION

Finally, the characters placed in a scene and situation must participate in a dramatic action that arouses our emotions and causes us to become involved imaginatively in what is happening. Persuaders often can take actual events and, with a bit of imagination, remake them into dramatic actions to fit their purposes. For example, in the time of racial strife in the late 1960s and early 1970s, the Black Panthers came into conflict with police in major American cities. In Chicago, several Panthers were killed during a police raid on the organization's headquarters. One group of persuaders cast the Panthers in the roles of heroes and the police as villains. According to their scenario, the innocent Panthers had been murdered under the pretense of a police raid, and the dramatic action was explained in terms of a conspiracy on the part of policemen and the United States Justice Department to eliminate the Panthers. Another group of persuaders cast the Panthers in the role of lawbreakers and the police as heroes. The dramatic events lent themselves to two interpretations.

THE PERSUADER AS DREAM MERCHANT

We all have individual dreams that shape our behavior and
drive us to certain actions, but we often share a dream with a
large group of people—along with the emotions, values, and
motives it evokes—because of the powerful suggestive force
inherent in a given drama. Persuaders and propagandists are
in an important sense dream merchants, and to the extent
that they can catch their audiences up in a dream, they can
persuade them to act and believe in certain ways. One legend
has it that in the early days of the automobile, the tendency
was to advertise cars in terms of engineering details and facts
about their performance. Then an advertising genius developed an ad consisting of a photograph of a handsome young
man in driving togs and goggles, his scarf flying in the wind, a
beautiful girl at his side, driving an open car on a road that led
across a green valley to the mountains beyond. When asked
what in the world he was trying to sell with such a layout, he
is alleged to have replied, "A dream"; and modern advertising
was on its way.

The heroes of our public dreams are likable and believable
and tend to have a good ethos for us. The villains of our

dramatizations of events can seldom persuade us. Thus the dramatic interpretation of events provides the audience with emotional involvement as well as with credible sources. The positive and negative suggestions inherent in an attractive drama presented as part of a persuasive or propaganda campaign are among the most powerful forces for changing attitudes and behavior.

FACT IN THE FANTASY THEME

Some of the dramatizations that compose persuasive campaigns are made up of fictitious materials. The characters are like those in novels or plays, and their actions are made up. The most persuasive dramatizations, however, have solid bases in facts. The persuasive account describes the facts accurately, and the suggestion is a function of how those facts are placed into a dramatic sequence and what characteristics and motives are suggested for the leading characters.

Several different persuasive themes can grow up around the same events, and can be quite truthful in their descriptions of the actual happenings. The dramas may nonetheless present diametrically opposed suggestions about what to do and believe as a result of the historical event.

THE EXAMPLE OF WATERGATE

An interesting case study of how different fantasies can arise to interpret the same event is provided by the illegal entry on June 17, 1972 of the offices of the Democratic National Committee in the Watergate buildings. Certain facts were agreed upon by everyone who dramatized the event. A building custodian discovered the break-in, and authorities arrested five men in the process of setting up electronic bugging equipment and taking photographs of documents.

One group of publicists dramatized the event as a "two-bit burglary," an essentially senseless, bungled effort by a group of weird people on the fringes of the Committee for the Re-election of the President. They portrayed the burglary as an isolated and trivial by-product of campaign enthusiasm, carried out by some ineffective people who had no connection whatever with the president and his advisers.

Another group of publicists dramatized the event as the sinister tip of an iceberg of espionage which characterized the Nixon campaign. According to these publicists, the criminal activity was masterminded by Nixon's closest advisers in the White House and conducted at his orders and with his complete compliance. A number of other fantasies more or less supportive of the Nixon administration also chained through substantial groups of people.

The Initial Lack of Public Reaction

The burglary took place in the summer, and as the campaign of 1972 increased in tempo and intensity, the charges and countercharges about Watergate were dramatized by persuaders from various positions and redramatized by the reporters and journalists of the mass media. Some who participated in a violently anti-Nixon rhetorical vision chained early and vigorously into the drama of Nixon as the mastermind of underhanded political espionage; however, Watergate did not chain out with much force in the American electorate during the campaign. By November of '72, Watergate seemed to be only a minor issue in the election. Something seemed inherently wrong about this to those who had seen the incident as a great opportunity to defeat Richard Nixon. They puzzled in print and on radio and television as to why the American electorate seemed bored by Watergate, or seemed to accept the dramatization that it was only a second-rate burglary and "just politics." The explanation is that during these months, the fantasy theme was ineffective as a drama. The cast of characters was large and changing and consisted of a number of people with no public visibility or name identification. The public did not know Barker, Gonzales, Martinez, Sturgis, McCord, Hunt, and Liddy. As the drama unfolded, journalists and publists for political parties and other pressure groups added other names that were equally confusing.

Meantime, one set of persuaders who were writing for the *Washington Post* began chaining into fantasies which shifted their vision from a conspiracy for espionage to subvert the democratic processes, to a more diabolical and evil conspiracy of sabotage, in which Richard Nixon and his henchmen systematically set out to destroy the campaigns of Edmund Muskie and other front-running candidates during the primary, to defuse the anti-war movement, and to suppress efforts by people like Daniel Ellsberg to tell the truth about the war in Vietnam.[16]

With the conviction of those pleading innocent to the charge of burglary on January 30, 1973, the general public seemed willing to forget the matter. By this time, however, a number of people had evolved a compelling rhetorical vision in which Nixon was the head conspirator, in which Hal-

[16] See, for example, Carl Bernstein and Bob Woodward, *All the President's Men*, New York: Warner, 1975.

persona *A character in a dramatic work; the public personality or mask that an individual uses to meet a public situation; a character in a fantasy theme. The commonly used term* image *is less satisfactory than* persona *because it has been used for so many different concepts.*

deman and Ehrlichman were the main operatives, and in which the scenario of action involved the most severe test for democratic institutions in our history. The people caught up in the anti-Nixon vision were highly motivated to continue digging out information in order to reveal the extent of the conspiracy. They continued to dramatize Watergate.

New Fantasies Begin to Chain
When new information came to light and one of the convicted conspirators, McCord, wrote a letter to the judge in the case, John J. Sirica, indicating that the White House was involved, the new fantasy theme of the White House connection began to chain out through the public. Instead of a diverse cast of characters, mostly unknowns, involved in a bizarre and apparently senseless break-in, the new drama cast as its villains people who were widely known and very close to the president. Most importantly, the **persona** of the president himself gradually emerged as the main villain of the drama. With one central villain, a powerful persona cloaked with all the status accorded the office of the president, and with a clear and plausible scenario in which the president, to save his own career and protect his henchmen, covered up the facts—that the break-in was ordered by high officials in the Committee for the Re-election of the President, and that equally high officials in the White House were informed about what was going on—the conspiracy fantasy themes chained through a much wider segment of the public. When the Ervin Committee dramatized the entire affair on television, the almost-daily new complications served to increase and continue public involvement.

The White House Rhetorical Strategy
The small group of people who were making major rhetorical decisions about Watergate in the Nixon White House held hours of discussions about the breaking news, and various fantasies relating to their here-and-now problems chained through their meetings, until they evolved a rhetorical vision which differed markedly from the visions of their opponents. On many occasions they discussed possible scenarios for public distribution that might get the American people to chain into fantasies that would counter the damaging dramas being spread by the news media and by their political enemies. The way they planned their scenarios demonstrates that sophisticated professionals have discovered the power of fantasy themes in the media. The scenarios which the White House strategists discussed also demonstrate how the same

events can be dramatized to suggest quite different persuasive appeals.

On April 14, 1973, President Richard Nixon met with his aides, John Ehrlichman and Bob Haldeman. April 14, according to the vision of the small group of strategists in the White House, was the day that President Nixon received a detailed report from John Ehrlichman which indicated that John Mitchell, former attorney general of the United States; John Dean, counsel to the president; and Jeb Magruder, deputy campaign director of the Committee for the Re-election of the President, were implicated in the Watergate burglary. Ehrlichman began a possible scenario with the statement, "I'm trying to write the news magazine story for next Monday." The president responded, "Right." Ehrlichman then spun out the drama:

> 'The White House may have its coverup finally collapse . . . when the Grand Jury indicted John Mitchell and Jeb Magruder. . . . Cracking the case was the testimony of a number of peripheral witnesses who, each of whom (sic) contributed to developing a cross triangulation and permitted the Grand Jury to analyze it and so on and so forth. The final straw that broke the camel's back was the investigators (sic) discovery of this and that and the other thing.' That's one set of facts. And then the tag on that, is 'White House Press Secretary Ron Ziegler said that the White House would have no comment.'[17]

Clearly, the fantasy theme of how a recalcitrant White House had dragged its feet until developments provided by peripheral witnesses caused the cover-up to unravel would be a bad one to allow to develop. Ehrlichman, however, had another fantasy which would create a more attractive persona of the president.

> The other one goes: "Events moved swiftly last week, after the President was presented with a report indicating for the first time that suspicion of John Mitchell and Jeb Magruder as ringleaders in the Watergate break-in were facts substantiated by considerable evidence. The President then dispatched so and so to do this and that and maybe to see Mitchell or something of that kind and these efforts resulted in Mitchell going to the U.S. Attorney's office on Monday morning at nine o'clock, asking to testify before the Grand Jury. Charges of cover-up by the White House were materially dispelled by the diligent efforts of the President and his aides in moving on evidence which came to their hands in the closing days of the previous week."[18]

---

17 *The White House Transcripts*, New York: Bantam, 1974, pp. 301–302.
18 Ibid.

Ehrlichman's fantasy theme portrays a decisive president acting quickly to deal with the conspiracy once the facts of such a White House connection came to his attention. The dramatization suggests that the president was not a co-conspirator, not trying to cover up, and was, moreover, willing to act as the chief law enforcement officer of the land even if it meant acting against a good friend like John Mitchell.

Despite the massive efforts by the White House rhetoricians to counter them, the fantasies which dramatized the Nixon cover-up by the ringleaders of the burglary were beyond stopping. By late April and early June, the fantasies seemed to achieve a momentum all their own, and publicists of all sorts found themselves in a maelstrom when they tried to hook into, modify, or stem the power of the chaining dramas to arouse the public. Although the fury had subsided somewhat by the time President Ford came into office, when he pardoned Richard Nixon after his resignation, the force of the backlash of public opinion against the pardon indicated the continuing power of the vision.

Why Fantasies Chain

Human beings in social interaction exhibit several tendencies which help explain why some fantasies chain through groups. We will consider three important tendencies of this type within listeners: (1) aping behavior, (2) following directions, and (3) accepting suggestions.

APING BEHAVIOR

People often do or believe something because other people around them are doing or believing it. If the others in a group are participating in a fantasy chain, adding new ideas to it, exclaiming about it, or responding to it nonverbally, there is a strong tendency for a person to join in. Follow-the-leader behavior is very common. We will call it *aping* behavior, because of the stereotype of an ape is that it will mimic behavior. If a person walking down a street stops and peers up toward the sky, some people may walk on past the sky-watcher, but several other people will stop to see what has caught his attention, and soon a knot of people will be standing, peering upward.

How often have you been a part of this next scene? A siren sounds in a quiet neighborhood. People go to their windows or doors or out on their porches to see what is happening. One person runs from a house and dashes up the street. Soon several more follow, and if enough of the watchers are pulled into the parade, the pressure for you to go along with them grows strong. You probably go, too.

When people communicate with one another in a small group for the first time, they develop ways of proceeding on the same follow-the-leader basis. Someone may say, "Let's introduce ourselves." Someone else says, "Okay. You go first." Suppose that the first person tells her name and then a good deal about her background and manages to convey to the others a good idea of the type of person she is: chatty, informal, and friendly. The group has a chance to laugh with her and relax a bit. Finally she says, "That's about it for me. How about you?" She looks with interest at the person next to her; she seems genuinely interested in what the others have to say. She has broken the ice. The next person then describes as interesting a version of "me" as he can, and as the introductions continue around the group, no one resents the time being taken, because each feels his turn will come; everyone begins to feel comfortable about the group, and each acquires a good notion of what the other members are like. But consider another group that does not get off to such a good start. One person says to another, "Why don't you tell us about yourself?" and the second person simply mumbles her name in an embarrassed way and seems to have nothing to add. She looks at the next person immediately, as though her name is all she need give, and so the next person gives his name, and so on, and the group members' first attempts to get acquainted are not notably successful. In both groups the results stem from aping behavior; what one person starts, the others follow.

Beliefs and ideas can develop in the same fashion. So can norms or ways of behaving. Laboratory studies have shown the extent to which the behavior of others persuades us to do things we otherwise would not do.[19] A candid film made in the 1960s included a scene in which, when actors planted in an employment-office waiting room began taking off their clothes in a matter-of-fact way, as though this were the usual procedure in that situation, a number of unsuspecting clients, after initial reactions of surprise and bewilderment, also began to remove their clothes.

[19] For a survey of studies, see Leon Festinger, Stanley Schachter, and Kurt Bach, "Operation of Group Standards," in Darwin Cartwright and Alvin Zander, eds., *Group Dynamics: Research and Theory*, 3rd ed., New York: Harper & Row, 1968. See also Elliot Aronson, *The Social Animal*, San Francisco: Freeman, 1972, pp. 13–45.

You are probably not enjoying this evidence of how often we simply ape others in how we behave, what we do, even what we think. Aping behavior smacks of *1984* and Big Brother and totalitarianism. But human beings *do* behave this way. Aping behavior is often harmless and normal. However, you should resist being manipulated by propaganda that is designed to induce you to ape behavior which, if you stopped to consider, you would *not* choose to copy. You should particularly watch for the propagandist's use of the so-called "bandwagon" technique, which asserts that "everybody is doing it, so come on along."

FOLLOWING DIRECTIONS

Another common human behavior pattern is to do and believe as we are told. Again, this is an immediate and natural response. If one person gives another directions about what to do or what to believe, the second person tends to do or believe as directed. Directed behavior occurs without thinking. If the sign says "STOP," you stop. Often people are hardly aware of what has taken place when they unthinkingly accept directions. As parents, you will tell your children what to do. As children, you were told by your parents what to do. Much of our educational process is a matter of following directions. Carried to extreme lengths, controlling people by telling them what to do and think is like pushing buttons to direct the movements of a mechanical toy. Under deep hypnosis, people blindly follow the directions of the hypnotist, reacting much as a machine would to programed instructions.

Even so-called "rational" man is surrounded by persuasive messages capitalizing upon this tendency to follow directions. Paraticularly on radio and television we are ordered to:

Buy Buick!
Buy bonds!
Elect John Doe!
Vote Republican!
Shop downtown!
Throw the rascals out!
Save today!

ACCEPTING SUGGESTIONS

Direct and Indirect Suggestions
Directions, as shown above, are clear, blunt, and unequivocal. You are given no option. Directions are phrased and delivered

as commands. Suggestions, on the other hand, recommend a belief or an action, but are phrased in such a way that they seem to leave the receiver an option, some choice about doing or not doing what is suggested. The direction, "Quit your job!" becomes the suggestion, "May I suggest that you consider resigning." Suggestion slips the idea into the mind more gently than the jarring direction, and although suggestions encourage the growth of the idea or action, they do so less directly.

The process of suggestion, however, like that of direction, involves getting the listener to accept without thinking an idea, belief, or action. Suggestion is one of the most commonly used persuasive techniques in advertising and propaganda. See if you can think up a strong suggestion in behalf of some service or product in 25 words or less. Can you better these paraphrases of Madison Avenue masterpieces? "Glamour toilet tissue is like facial tissue. It doesn't *feel* like toilet paper." "If she kisses you once, will she kiss you twice?" "Clean odor, the Cologne of Mouthwashes." One we have always liked is the brief persuasive spiel of the hawker selling cheap inflatable pillows to people attending the big show in the state fairground grandstand. "Four hours on a board," he drones. "Four hours on a board. May we suggest a pillow?" Many of the people who bought pillows after hearing about the four hours on a board probably never consciously reasoned through their decision logically. We have observed many student discussion groups trying to find a good topic to present as a group for a class discussion. One member suggests a topic, and immediately another makes a face showing his disgust with the idea and says, "Let's not do that. Let's do something new and interesting for a change." The first participant then has to present good reasons and make a big effort to overcome the effect of the second member's suggestion that the topic is trite and uninteresting.

Positive and Negative Suggestion

Directions and suggestions may be positive or negative. Positive persuasion results when a belief or a course of action is urged: for example, "Save today at the Daisy sale!" Negative direction and suggestion urges the listener not to believe, or not to do something, as in the slogan "If you smoke, stop! If you don't smoke, don't start!" Positive suggestion and strong direct urgings have persuasive impact. Negative suggestions or directions are often less effective than positive ones. Negative urgings call attention to the belief or action you do *not* want to encourage and, in so doing, may arouse a curiosity about the subject which had not been in the listener's mind before. There is a line from a Carl Sandburg poem we often quoted to one another when our children were toddlers. The line well describes the unwanted effects of negative suggestion. Paraphrased a little, it reads, "Why does the child put molasses on the cat when the one thing I told the child *not* to do was put molasses on the cat." The sign "Do Not Open This Door" often prompts more than one person to open the door simply out of curiosity. You would be wise to consider *all* possible results when you use negative suggestions in persuasive communication.

The board-and-pillow example mentioned two paragraphs above is of further interest because the hawker's spiel contains the two major kinds of suggestion used in persuasion, direct and indirect. The sentence, "May we suggest a pillow?" is *direct suggestion* telling the potential customer what the seller wants him to do. The phrase, "Four hours on a board," is *indirect suggestion* that the potential customer will be uncomfortable shortly if he does not buy the pillow and, moreover, will be quite confortable throughout the show if he does buy and use the pillow. When a speaker hints at a point without actually saying it, the suggestion he is using is indirect. The listener is led to discover the point rather than being told directly about it.

Technique of Indirect Suggestion

Indirect suggestion is an important technique of both propaganda and persuasion. If a propaganda campaign maintains a steady barrage of indirect suggestion over a long time, the listeners may gradually come to believe something or begin to form a new attitude almost without knowing what has been happening to them. When television was still advertising cigarettes, one brand was sold for some time as the cigarette for sophisticates. Its advertisements showed a woman dressed in the current high fashion, surrounded by luxurious furnishings, holding this particular brand in a long cigarette holder. Then the company decided to change the cigarette's image, and a whole new advertising campaign was launched. Sophistication was out, and the ads now showed virile he-men, working in oil fields, punching cattle, fighting forest fires, logging, or building huge bridges in high mountains. Gradually many viewers came to associate this brand of cigarettes with strong, young outdoorsmen. Little was said in either campaign about the cigarette's flavor or its nicotine content. Both advertising pitches were expensive campaigns of indirect suggestion designed to persuade people to smoke the brand if they, too, wanted to be, at first, sophisticated, and later, ruggedly masculine.

Direct suggestion tends to be explicit, simple, and repetitive. The propagandist who uses direct suggestion searches for suitable slogans and then repeats them endlessly. Hitler and Goebbels, in propaganda for the mass audience, often used slogans, repeated over and over again. Indirect suggestion, on the other hand, requires considerable more artistry and skill.

NAMING   One important persuasive tool for the person using indirect suggestion is the ability to select exactly the right suggestive word to name a thing or event or to describe its properties and relationships. Mark Twain is supposed to have said that the difference between the right word and the almost-right word is the difference between lightning and a lightning bug; certainly that is the case with indirect suggestion: It must be subtle enough to be indirect, yet obvious enough to make your point.

In Chapter 3 we examined the way language can be used to discuss our world. We divided words into form words and content words and pointed out how content words can name something and then discuss its properties or relationships. When you study indirect suggestion as a valuable tool of persuasion, you will use this knowledge about words in a practical way. Suppose people are talking about the same thing, but are using different names for it. Even with these different names, they may all understand what is being discussed. Say that several people are talking about a college. They might name it *the college, the old alma mater, the institution, the nut house, the playpen with ash trays, the ivory tower* or any one of the names by which this college is known to its many students and alumni. No matter which name the person in the group chooses for labeling the college, all the others present know it is *the college* he is talking about. What, then, do we learn from the different labels? By the selection of a particular label for a thing, the source of a message indicates a lot about how he feels about the thing or event in question.

If several men are discussing female acquaintances, a given woman might be referred to as *darling, honey, my old lady, the little woman, that broad, my chick, slut, real dog, a sow,* or whatever happen to be the current slang words for attractive and unattractive females. And of course, women have a comparable vocabulary to describe the males they know. The name selected for a woman or man is powerful indirect suggestion to all others present. The words we use are important parts of our indirect-suggestion persuasive messages.

Propagandists often use names that reflect attitudes. Two hostile bordering countries report an armed clash of their troops. Country number one calls the event "shameless naked aggression," while country number two calls the same event "a defensive retaliation." One country names the government of another "a totalitarian regime"; the latter government refers to itself as "a democratic peoples' republic." Some revolutionaries set off a bomb in a public building. Sympathizers with the revolution call the bombing "a courageous act by heroic freedom fighters." Those who oppose the revolutionaries and dislike the destruction of public buildings call the same bombing "a cowardly, criminal act by mindless anarchists."

DESCRIBING Selecting names heavily loaded with suggestion is but one way in which choice of words is important. The words a speaker uses to describe the properties or qualities of the things, events, or people designated by the names are equally important. One person says, "This cheese has a rich bouquet." Another remarks, "This cheese stinks to high heaven."

Compare the following ways of describing the qualities of a given individual, and see how words work to carry suggestion to the listener:

John is prudent.
    versus
John is a tightwad.

John is courageous.
    versus
John is reckless.

John is sensitive.
    versus
John is emotionally unstable.

We can also suggest attitudes by the words and phrases we use to describe relationships among things, people, and events. Consider these examples:

John was a love child.
    versus
John is a bastard.

John and Mary have a deep and satisfying personal relationship.
    versus
John and Mary are living together like a couple of alley cats.

In the last example we used a figure of speech to describe the relationship. Figures of speech are important techniques to suggest or state a comparison between two things. By associating a thing, person, or event with something pleasant, admirable, or good, we suggest that the thing itself is also desirable. By associating the thing with something unpleasant or bad, we make the opposite impression. Compare "This cigarette has a springlike freshness" with "This cigarette reeks like a dumpyard incinerator."

One important propaganda technique is to describe a person in terms of an adjective or noun that connotes a positive or negative attitude toward that individual. Much of what people do when they persuade is to attack or defend other people and their actions. We often say that a friend has good qualities and an enemy has bad character traits. When a propagandist uses words with negative connotations to describe an enemy, we call the technique *name calling*. A politician using the name-calling technique might refer to an opponent as a "political hack," a "crook," a "left-winger," or an "arch conservative."

ASCRIBING MOTIVES   In addition to calling good or bad names, a speaker can create much the same impression by providing what he says are motives for the individual's behavior. *Motives* are inner drives to action. *Motive* has the same Latin root as the word *motor*, and we can think of a motive as the energy source that causes an individual to move and do certain things. We see a person working hard to gain political office and ask, "What makes him tick? Why does he do that? Why does he put up with all the grief of campaigning?" Someone may explain the candidate's actions by supplying a motive; for example, "He is driven by the desire for power. He is power hungry and is compelled by mastery motivation." A clever person can find some inner drive to account for every behavior. We all play the role of amateur psychologist now and then. Sometimes different people assign different motives to account for the same act. If the question is "Why does John devote his whole life to making money?" various answers might be "John is motivated by the need for security, and money will provide him with security," "John is motivated by the need for prestige, and money will provide him with prestige," or "John craves power, and he gets power from his money."

Because we can explain the same actions by different motives, the skillful persuader searches for good motives to explain what he and his friends do, and for bad motives to explain the acts of his enemies. Most schemes to explain human behavior divide motives into higher and lower, good or bad, reasons for doing things.[20] The basic division reminds us of the old religious view that the choice between the drives of the flesh and the aspirations of the spirit is the basis for our going down to hell or up to heaven. Generally we consider people who are out for quick satisfaction of fleshly desires less commendable than people who work for some high spiritual ideal. A gourmet, who enjoys elegant food, delightfully prepared, is judged better than a glutton, who eats anything and everything put in front of him. The physical expression of a deep and lasting love is judged better than mere sexual lust. We generally feel that unselfish acts are better than selfish ones. The man who is driven to pile up money for the security of his family is a more commendable fellow than the man who wants the money for himself. The advocate of women's liberation who wants to be in the limelight and get a lot of publicity is not as commendable as the woman who is unselfishly dedicated to the cause of all womankind.

The friends of the evangelist say he does what he does for the purpose of saving human souls and that he works for God's kingdom. He sacrifices his health, they say, and his time, and his own pleasure in order to work for the good of others. The enemies of the evangelist explain his behavior by saying that he does it for money, which he uses to buy big cars, fine clothes, and other fleshly comforts. They say he does it to make a big name for himself or to gain power through his control over people. The point is that two people observing a third person's behavior can explain the behavior differently: One can cut the person down by saying his motive is a low, selfish one, and the other can build the person up by saying his motive is a good and unselfish one.

USING PEOPLE AS SYMBOLS Successful persuasive and propaganda battles among businesses, political parties, governmental agencies, and nations usually need to present the issues in terms of human beings. Real live persons often play an important part, much like actors in a movie, in persuasive campaigns to change our attitudes, beliefs, and actions. Persons can come to symbolize ideas or whole movements. Ralph Nader is pro-consumer and actively involved in organizing efforts to help the consumer. We talk of Naderism or

[20] A popular arrangement of motives into a "pyramid," with the lowest motives including physiological drives and "deficit" motives, is provided by Abraham Maslow, *Motivation and Personality*, 2nd ed. New York: Harper & Row, 1970.

Nader's raiders as representing the whole movement. In the 1950s, Senator Joseph McCarthy of Wisconsin was actively involved in attacking "communists" in the government. His tactics were crude and propagandistic. The attack on individuals as communists or pro-communists came to be called McCarthyism.

Why Certain Fantasies Appeal to Certain People

PERSONAL PSYCHOLOGICAL PROBLEMS

Although most of us are more or less susceptible to aping behavior, following directions, and to being suggestible, some dramatic situations appeal to certain people more than others. In a small group getting together for the first time, some members may chain into a fantasy while others seem to be "turned off" by it and find it distasteful, and the latter members feel uncomfortable as the others get excited about a particular scenario.

Individuals with a particular psychological problem or difficulty are more likely to get excited and to chain into one sort of fantasy than another. Very often people will chain into fantasies that touch on the areas which they are already sensitive about; for example, a student trying to break away from parental control may find a drama relating to rebellion against authority very attractive. On the other hand, if a fantasy comes too close to a problem which has become very personal and upsetting for a person, even handling the problem on the level of a fantasy may be too uncomfortable, and the person will not chain in. Sometimes people do not chain into fantasies because they do not have strong feelings one way or another about the drama put forth.

COMMON GROUND OR COMMUNITY PROBLEMS

When fantasy themes move into the mass media they tend to chain through some segments of the general public and not through others. Often the people who participate in the dramas are sharing a common here-and-now problem of importance. Young men who were liable to be drafted to serve in the Vietnam war were likely to chain into fantasy themes which reflected their common problem. College-educated people who cannot find a job of their choice are likely to chain into certain fantasies. Frequently the fact that a fantasy is starting to chain through important segments of the public comes as a surprise to professional propagandists and public-opinion experts. Often they do not search for the connection between what dramas portray or reflect and common here-and-now problems.

Frequently, movies that catch the imagination of the public are good indicators of the mood of large numbers of people. The way the dramatizations of intelligence gathering and espionage chained through the American public in the period from the 1950s to the 1970s provides an example of how fictitious fantasies can reflect a growing here-and-now problem.

Movies and television shows dealing with espionage and intelligence gathering in the 1950s were often serious melodramas in which Russian communists were the villains and heroic American (or British or French) agents risked their lives in a vicious, amoral undercover battle with the communist international intelligence service. One popular television series, called "I Led Three Lives," involved an undercover agent for the FBI. Based on a book by Herbert Philbrick, the series depicted the adventures of an American counteragent who foiled the espionage and sabotage of a vicious and violent group of communists in the United States.

The next development in the 1960s was a series of popular spy novels in which dogged and amoral agents on both sides slugged it out against one another in a grim, dull underground battle in which the line between the good guys and the bad guys was fainter than in the early 1950s. Representative of the novels was the work of John LeCarre, who wrote *The Spy Who Came in from the Cold*.

The next big fad in the 1960s was the James Bond stories, in which the dramatizations were much more stylized and much further removed from reality. James Bond was pitted against international conspiracies which were not clearly tied to Russian or Chinese communists. He lived in high style; violence was emphasized, exaggerated, and stylized.

Finally, in the late 1960s and early 1970s the espionage dramas on television and in novels moved to parody, burlesque, and satire. One television series involved an agent named Maxwell Smart, who was a master bungler out to do in an enemy that was depicted as an abstract conspiracy without any realistic base of operations, and which had the vague evil purpose of gaining control of the world.

When the espionage dramas lost their audiences and were dropped from television, nonfiction fantasies began to chain through the public. The espionage and sabotage efforts of the Nixon White House were dramatized as amoral, criminal, and

systems approach *A way of analyzing complex human and material events by breaking them down into subsystems; it is assumed these subsystems relate to one another in such a complex way that any change in any part of the system will result in dynamic changes in all other parts.*
closed system *A system which is sealed off from its environment so that it is uninfluenced by unexpected energy, matter, information, and so forth.*

reprehensible. These were followed by dramatizations of the Central Intelligence Agency (CIA) in which the agency was portrayed as a villainous group utilizing unsavory tactics to meddle in the internal affairs of other countries.

Here-and-now problems relating to foreign relations, peaceful coexistence, detente, the threat of international communism, and the role of the United States in the world were all in transition during the years from 1960 to 1970, and these common here-and-now problems were reflected in the kinds of dramatizations which were attractive to large segments of the public. As the Cold War thawed and the American people became disillusioned with Vietnam, the rationale for fantasies celebrating amoral espionage and sabotage weakened.

Mass Media Political Campaigns

When we adopt a **systems approach** to a communication context, we examine it in terms of its important subsystems (or parts), which interrelate and influence one another. A good way to understand persuasive campaigns utilizing the mass media in our country is to take a systems view of the complicated interrelationships among political persuaders, professional media personnel, and the general public.

An *open system* is one in which new energy, matter, or information can enter or leave the system freely. A political campaign is an open system, in the sense that messages enter the communication channels in the United States from uncontrolled, haphazard, random, and unexpected sources, as well as from those that are expected and controlled. An accidental fantasy chaining through a small group may be told and retold until it spreads through a large public as a rumor or a whispering campaign. Foreign governments and foreign citizens may introduce messages. A candidate may make a slip of the tongue and create an event which chains through the communication system. When we study a **closed system** we know the inputs and components, and are thus able to make a much better estimate of how the system will operate than with an open system, which is a good deal more unpredictable.

The open system of a national presidential campaign, for example, can be analyzed as consisting of several important subsystems. An important subsystem is that of the informal two-person and small group conversations in which people discuss the campaign face to face. Another subsystem is rally and auditorium speeches, whether by the candidate or a spokesman for the candidate or by an ostensibly objective analyst. Still another subsystem is the mass media machinery (print, radio, and television) for developing and channeling messages related to the campaign.

The subsystems can be analyzed in another way by dividing them into three major categories in terms of who has the power to shape and control messages. The first category consists of all the messages under the control of partisans for a campaign. The second consists of the messages controlled by professional journalists, commentators, and public-affairs broadcasters transmitting messages of an informative or "news" character about the campaign. The third consists of the autonomous conversations in which citizens discuss and process the messages inserted into the system by the campaigners and the professionals from the media.

During the campaign, small groups of policy makers and rhetorical strategists plan the main themes of the campaign; the platform, or what the candidate is to stand for; and the main arguments and dramatizations which will provide the rhetorical vision for their campaign. The strategists also plan for the timing of various messages, deciding when certain themes will be inserted and stressed. For instance, they may decide when the candidate will give a major speech on the problems of the cities, on foreign policy, on inflation, or on the farm problem. The strategists further decide when the campaign is to "peak" and when the frequency of the various messages is to rise, particularly on radio and television. They implement their strategy by purchasing time on various media channels, and they plan campaign tours for the candidate, with hand shaking, rally speeches, interviews with the press, and appearances on radio and television talk shows. When publicists buy access to the media, for spot announcement campaigns, for coverage of a rally, or for staged interviews, they can assure that their message is transmitted with little distortion. In terms of the message communication model, the noise is kept to a minimum. Once the messages of a given candidate have entered the system, however, they are liable to modification by media journalists and commentators. Not only are the original dramas of the candidates modified, but the professional media people often insert different dramas to compete with those of the candidate.

The messages which come to the public are thus a mixture of what the campaign organization desires to send and what is sent by the subsystems controlled by the media professionals. As we have seen, messages in the mass media do not strike all members of the public with equal impact. They tend to be filtered through opinion leaders who process the messages again in small face-to-face groups, where fantasy themes may start spontaneously and new messages may be inserted into the system.

The system is complex in that the throughput of messages is modified by inputs from every subsystem in every category. Should a professional commentator like Eric Sevareid or Walter Cronkite or Howard K. Smith begin to send forth messages that the candidate's rhetorical specialists find dangerous, they will modify their campaign strategy and try to combat the destructive vision of their candidate. Thus when some professional commentators began to suggest in 1972 that Senator McGovern was the Goldwater of the left and that, like Senator Goldwater in 1964, he would lose the election because he was too extreme to attract the voters of the center, the McGovern strategists began to draft messages to defuse the vision. As we saw in the case study of the Watergate controversy, when Nixon and his advisors decided that the fantasy of the cover-up was chaining through the public, they took steps to try to send out a new scenario which would counter the damaging one. Should public opinion polls reveal key strengths or weaknesses of the candidates, both the professional journalists and the campaign strategists are likely to modify future messages.

THE ADVERTISING CAMPAIGN

While the advertising campaign resembles the political campaign, the strategists promoting a product or an institution or corporation can often close off the system to a greater degree than political campaigners. Because an ad agency buys media time and advertising space, it can assure that most of the messages about its product are under its control. To be sure, sometimes the professional news people will enter the system with a story about how some ad campaign is unethical, inaccurate, laughable, or is under investigation by a governmental agency or by a consumer group; sometimes counteradvertising campaigns are mounted, as when an organization plans a campaign against smoking cigarettes and runs its messages in the same mass medium that carries advertisements promoting cigarettes; and on occasions, advertisers will compare their product with another name brand, rather than with "brand X." These are examples of counterfantasies within the system which keep the system from being entirely closed. The fantasy theme of the unhealthy-looking man whose efforts to win the girl are frustrated because he continually breaks into a wracking cough when he tries to whisper romantic words into her ear, and because his reeking breath causes her to turn away when he tries to kiss her—all as a result of smoking—appears in the same communication system with the theme of the handsome, sophisticated man who has a gorgeous woman on his arm and who is cooly smoking a cigarette. But such counteradvertising is the exception rather than the rule. Of course, people in informal groups may chain into fantasies which make the commercial dramas ridiculous, laughable, or irritating, and thus add an interpretation to them which undercuts their persuasive impact. For the most part, though, advertisers can control their messages and keep the system somewhat closed and therefore more predictable.

THE CAMPAIGN FOR REFORM OR CONSERVATISM
The campaign on behalf of radical or revolutionary reform or radical conservatism resembles both the political campaign and the advertising campaign, except that the publicists seldom have the monetary resources to buy media time and space. Thus, as a system, it can be thought of as being the most open of all three. The people who want to gain a following for a movement which has little money must often use press-agent gimmicks to gain the attention of the media. Because they depend on appearances in newscasts or human-interest specials, their messages are filtered continually through the interpretation of the media specialists.

The Importance of Public Fantasies

The chaining fantasies of Watergate and their impact upon rhetorical visions of the presidency, Richard Nixon, and politics in the United States, provide an illuminating case study of how agreed-upon events (facts) can be dramatized in different ways to create different sets of heroes and villains, different emotional evocations, and different impulses to action. Our dreams give our lives meaning and provide us with our goals. The fantasy themes which dramatize news events and political positions are related to voting behaviors and actual programs put forward by the officials whom we put in office. If we participate in a rhetorical vision in which we are in a cold war with ruthless international communism and if the

Propaganda is usually characterized by a large-scale campaign which involves many different media of communication and which continues for a significant period of time.

Propaganda is communication with an ax to grind which uses persuasion in irresponsible and unethical ways to achieve the persuaders' goals.

Propaganda as a communication style differs from the three important styles emphasized in this book in that it is frankly manipulative in its theory and criticism.

Persuasion refers to a wider range of communication styles of which the propaganda styles are but a part.

The dynamic chaining of group fantasies is the mechanism which creates the social reality of small groups and larger rhetorical communities.

Mass-media persuasion has its first impact on opinion leaders and, through them, influences the general public, by means of small group conversations.

The small group is not only a consumer of public dreams but also a generator of small group fantasy chains, which later become public dreams.

Real people often make the best characters

fantasy themes dramatize Russian atomic bombs exploding in our cities, evoking our fear and hatred, we build bomb shelters in our back yards, or stock our basements with food and water in case of attack, or volunteer to watch the skies for Red bombers. There was a time, not so long ago, when we did this. If we participate in a rhetorical vision in which the president of the United States is the main conspirator in a law-breaking cover-up of a felony, if the fantasy themes dramatize the secrecy and injustice of the conspiracy, and the vision evokes emotions of disgust and hatred of the villains, we urge impeachment and try to throw the rascals out.

in fantasy themes for propaganda and persuasion.

When a speaker uses the figure of speech called personification, he endows an abstract idea or institution with human characteristics.

Fantasy themes often gain part of their suggestive force from the location or setting of the drama.

Persuaders often use actual events as the basis for fantasy themes intended to change attitudes and behavior.

Persuaders are in an important sense dream merchants, in that they can propagate a certain dream and can sell products and ideas that promise to fulfill the dream.

Fantasy themes which interpret the same events can be quite different and still be quite truthful in their description of the agreed-upon facts.

The principle of aping behavior is simple: What one person starts, others tend to follow.

People tend to do and believe as they are told.

Suggestion plants positions or points in the mind so they are hard to attack logically.

Whereas direct suggestion tells the listener clearly what he may do or believe, indirect suggestion only hints at it.

Negative forms of persuasion sometimes backfire, because the listener may be tempted to do what he is told not to do.

Selecting names for people and events that carry positive or negative connotations is an important technique of persuasion and basic to creating heroes and villains in fantasy themes.

Because the same action can be explained by several different motives, a skillful persuader selects an explanation that suits his purpose for a given fantasy theme.

The protagonist in a fantasy theme with a given scenario can appear to be either a hero or a villain, depending upon the motive provided for his action.

Mass media communication in a highly developed country like the United States takes place in a complex, open communication system composed of a number of important subsystems which interrelate and influence one another.

Among the subsystems of a political campaign utilizing the mass media are those channels and messages which are controlled by the candidates, those which are controlled by the media professionals, and those which are open to inputs from others.

As consumers of persuasion, and as persuaders ourselves, we should be very aware of the importance of public fantasies in relation to positive and negative suggestion. We should learn to look for the dreams that seem to be operating in our culture (and in other cultures, if we hope to communicate successfully with people from those cultures), for these dreams change as events change and reshape our priorities. Much of the advertising and selling of political candidates is shaped by what the dream merchants think the public is buying this year.

This does not mean that dreams are all bad and that we

should always try to operate on a dry and discursive level, without drama. We need not try to rule out our feelings and only use reason to deal with data statistically. Our rhetorical visions are important and cannot be separated from our intellectual processing of information. Nor should you fear that you will always or even often be manipulated by others who will mold their sales pitch to your private dreams to make you do or believe something you really do not want to do or believe.[21] Even the most skillful dramatizers of persuasive messages cannot always predict the public's response to their campaigns. Even in the most totalitarian of countries, with highly sophisticated propaganda machines controlling many channels of communication, large segments of the public remain steadfastly immune to manipulation. Nevertheless, your best defense against propaganda is the knowledge and skill to analyze and criticize the messages of the persuaders.

SUGGESTED PROJECTS

1 Write a short paper in which you describe and discuss six techniques of indirect suggestion that you have noticed in current television ads or in magazines and newspapers.
2 Select a persuasive drama or public dream from a recent speech, magazine article, book, or television program. (If you wish to piece the drama together from several sources you may do so.) Write an analysis of the persuasive power of the fantasy theme. Who are the heroes and who are the villains? What rewards does the drama promise that will move people to action? How would you predict that people who chain into the fantasy would act in some given situations? Be specific.
3 Select a hypothetical target audience for a persuasive campaign using the mass media. Analyze the main rhetorical visions which the majority of the target audience will participate in relating to the topic of your campaign. Develop several scenarios (fantasy themes) which will tie in with the existing action lines and casts of heroes and villains in the main rhetorical visions. For example, take a campus issue such as grading practices or tuition costs. Assume the target audience includes students and faculty. What are the present rhetorical visions relating to grading?

[21] Periodically a book popularizing a vision in which a defenseless public is cynically manipulated by Machiavellian experts in mass persuasion becomes a best seller. See, for example, Vance Packard, *The Hidden Persuaders*, New York: McKay, 1957; and Joe McGinniss, *The Selling of the President, 1968*, New York: Simon & Schuster, 1970. Usually such books select only those campaigns which were dramatically successful and neglect those which were unsuccessful.

SUGGESTED READINGS

Bales, Robert F. *Personality and Interpersonal Behavior.* New York: Holt, Rinehart and Winston, 1970.

Brembeck, Winston, and William S. Howell. *Persuasion: A Means of Social Influence,* 2nd ed. Englewood Cliffs, N.J.: Prentice-Hall, 1976.

Cronkhite, Gary. *Persuasion: Speech and Behavioral Change.* Indianapolis: Bobbs-Merrill, 1966.

Larson, Charles U. *Persuasion: Reception and Responsibility.* Belmont, Calif.: Wadsworth, 1973.

Chapter 13

HOW TO CRITICIZE COMMUNICATION

As we saw in Chapter 2, a communication style consists of an interrelationship among a practice (communicating in observable ways), criticism (public discussion of the strengths and weaknesses of the practice), and theory (developing systematic comments of a general nature about communication).

After a style has matured, there will be a record of actual messages produced by communicators in the style. The record may be written transcripts of speeches, television programs, interviews, small group meetings, counseling sessions, conversations, and so forth. The record may be largely in the form of recollections handed on orally from person to person. The record may be preserved on video- or audiotape. Because of the importance of communication in all cultures and in all social arrangements, we have preserved an enormous body of messages. Some of these messages are viewed as classics, in the sense that they speak about important matters relating to the human condition in such a universal way that even though the people who originally produced the messages participated in very different communication styles and lived in a very different culture from our own, the messages are still meaningful. Some messages are transitory and trivial, because they speak of unimportant matters in such stylistic or culture-bound ways that only a student of the history of the time in which they were produced, or of communication in general would be interested in them. Some of the messages are important historically or represent significant landmarks in the study of communication.

Criticism of day-to-day communication contributes to theory, in that, after a time, the critics come to agree on standards to use in judging the communication in a given style, and these standards become part of textbooks or handbooks to help its practitioners. Again, the process of criticism may leave a record of critical comments which are important for the scholar interested in the history of communication.

Theorizing develops a systematic and consistent account of the nature and function of communication, as well as advice on how to produce good communication. A systematized discussion of communication becomes a communication theory. Each communication style has a communication theory associated with it which, because it deals with the same basic subject, will have some similarities to other communication theories. We have seen how the concept of speaker *ethos* in the public-speaking style resembles the concept of *source credibility* in the message communication style; how the concept of *feedback* in the message and the relationship styles compare to one another, as well as to the concept of *audience response* in the public-speaking style; and so forth. But because each communication style is distinctive and unique, the theory associated with each is different from all other theories in its overall shape and detail.

Criticism As Evaluation

The first important type of criticism of communication, therefore, involves becoming knowledgeable about the theory of a given style of communication. Once we know the theory, we can examine a given communication event in that style and apply the appropriate standards to it. You have now learned the basic model used to criticize communication in each of the three important communication styles.

SELECTING CRITERIA
Let us look at how you might criticize a communication event in terms of the public-speaking communication style.

The first step is to take from the theory of public speaking a manageable number of criteria to use in evaluating the speech. You might select a number of things. You could pick the skill with which the speaker analyzes the audience and adapts the ideas in the speech to the audience. You could pick the skill with which the speaker argues the case, the quality of the evidence, the plausibility and consistency of the reasoning. You could pick the skill with which the speaker develops a persuasive platform personality. You could pick the skill with which the speaker delivers the speech nonverbally by gestures, facial expressions, voice projection, articulation, and so forth. You could pick the skill with which the speaker dramatizes his or her avowed position and evokes emotions, creates positive and negative suggestions, gives directions, and arouses the listeners to action.

From our treatment of the theory of the public-speaking style, you can see that there are still a good many other criteria that can be used to criticize a specific communication event in the public-speaking style. We have not touched upon the skill with which the audience responds or listens, nor upon such matters as nonverbal monitoring to assure that the transactional context is appropriately controlled, nor upon the way the participants control the tempo and flow of meanings within the transaction. Usually we do not raise every possible critical issue that we can about every speech. For example, if your instructor gave you an assignment to give a public speech, he or she might emphasize the delivery or the organization or the persuasive content; when you delivered the speech, then, your classmates and instructor would look for the particular aspect assigned when evaluating the speech.

DESCRIBING A COMMUNICATION EVENT
The second step in criticizing communication is to use the criteria as guidelines in examining a communication event (as it unfolds or as it is represented in a recording) and describing its features. Let us say that an assignment emphasized making ideas clear, and you have selected the theory in Chapter 9 as the basis of your criticism. You would then look at the speech and ask such questions as "Did the speaker use definitions? If so, what kind of definitions did he use? Did the speaker use any of the techniques of explanation, such as listing parts and so forth? Did the speaker use any examples? If so, were they real or hypothetical examples?" On the basis of the criteria, you would then describe the techniques that the speaker used in the speech in some detail. You might

describe the technique as follows: "The speaker tried to clarify the point about how high unemployment and economic recession could be accompanied by a high rate of inflation with a hypothetical example about a dairy farm that was losing money, was not milking all of its cows, and was still charging more for its milk."

EVALUATING THE EVENT

The last step in the critical process is to make an evaluation of the speech according to the criteria. You might decide that the speaker did a poor job of clarifying the concept of recession and inflation because the example drawn from agriculture was poorly adapted to the audience, which was composed of students who were all from the core city areas of a large metropolitan center and were unfamiliar with some of the technical details of dairy farming. The same sort of critical judgments could be made of organizational skill: "excellent central idea, well-unified speech, clear transitions"; about delivery: "poor eye contact, mumbled, lots of fidgeting; I thought she was going to break her pencil in two at least five times during the speech"; about the audience: "The audience really sat there like a bunch of zombies; they did not respond at all"; and so forth.[1]

The same essential critical process is used in all communication styles. The critic evaluating a communication event in the message communication style might select such criteria as fidelity of information transmission and might make his evaluation by conducting a survey of how much information the employees of a company receive from messages that are sent downward through the organization's formal channels of communication. They might conclude, for instance, that employees comprehend or can recall only 25 percent of the information that upper management transmits down through channels to them. Another critic in the message communication style might examine the amount of information that a jury gets from the judge's charge by giving them a test of their comprehension of key ideas. The critic might also study videotapes of conversations or small group meetings for evidence of nonverbal feedback, which he could evaluate as to quantity and effectiveness.

The critic of the relationship style makes similar kinds of evaluations. Aronson provides an example of a critic func-

[1] For a discussion of the criticism within the theory of communication styles in the classroom, see Walter R. Fisher, "Rhetorical Criticism as Criticism," *Western Speech*, 38 (1974), 75–80.

tioning to evaluate a communication event in a sensitivity training group. Member A says to member B that he has been listening to member B for several meetings and has decided that member B is a phony. According to the standards of good communication in the relationship style, it is better to express your own feelings than to make evaluations of other people (which gets *at them*). The group leader steps in and asks member A if he has any feelings about member B. Member A answers that he "feels" member B is a phony. The leader notes that this is simply a word game and member A is still evaluating rather than expressing a feeling. The leader nonverbally implies a criticism of the message and asks again what member A feels, but member A answers that he still feels member B is a phony. The leader continues to criticize the communication and asks member A what the judgment that member B is a phony does to him. Member A answers that it irritates him. This is a better communication. Irritation is a feeling, and member A's comment now expresses a feeling. Another member asks member A what member B has done to cause the feeling of irritation. After some further questioning by other members, member A discloses that he felt annoyed whenever member B showed affection for some of the women in the group, and upon further probing, member A reveals that he thinks member B is very successful with women and that he thinks of himself as very unsuccessful. In short, member A reveals that what he really feels toward member B is envy and that he had been playing games when he accused member B of being a phony. The critic comments on the communication as follows:

> Although his behavior [the charge that the other member was a phoney] was successful as an ego-protecting device, it didn't contribute to Sam's understanding of his own feelings and of the kinds of events that caused those feelings; and it certainly didn't contribute to Sam's understanding of Harry or to Harry's understanding of Sam (or, for that matter, to Harry's understanding of himself). In short, Sam was communicating ineffectively. As an ego-defensive measure, his behavior was adaptive; as a form of communication, it was extremely maladaptive.[2]

The honest expression of envy, on the other hand, was evaluated by the critic as opening the door to further communication and as helping member A and member B to understand one another.

All three major communication styles require the critical

[2] Elliot Aronson, *The Social Animal*, San Francisco: Freeman, 1972, p. 249.

process in order to exist and continue. Evaluative criticism is necessary for the practice of any art. Without criticism of cooking the art of the gourmet would be impossible. Without criticism of nonrepresentational painting, the style would be impossible, and without criticism to aid in teaching us to participate in a communication style, we would be unable to communicate in that style. In the sensitivity training group, after all the participants have learned the theory and how to criticize communication, member A can say to member B, "I think you are a phony," and the group can then try to get him to express his real feelings for an hour or more, if need be. They can do this without coming to blows or getting into a shouting match, because they have learned how to communicate within the relationship style. If member A made a similar comment in a message-communication-style committee meeting called to decide whether or not the company should market a new product, the results would be much different.

DAY-TO-DAY CRITICISM

We all evaluate communication events. Communication is such a vital activity that we all discuss our successful and unsuccessful communication attempts informally, just as we discuss films, plays, novels, and other artistic works if they are important to us. Our discussion may be of the basic I-like-it or I-don't-like-it variety. "I hate it when he asks me questions in class." "I just can't talk to my mother." "We had a great discussion in the dorm last night." "Can't you get something else on television? Politics is so boring." Or, as we become more sophisticated about our communication and receive some training in the theory related to a given style, we may provide more specific and detailed explanations of our evaluations: "I hate it when he asks me questions in class. Nonverbally he comes across to me as saying he is better than I am, like he is continually evaluating what I say. He also strikes me as manipulating me—trying to use me to make a point with the class. I get very defensive, but I'm in a one-down position, and if I told him what I really think he'd probably cut my grade." Or we may say about the politician on television, "Man, is he boring! His language is so abstract and filled with cliches. He never dramatizes. His organization is clear enough; fact is, it's so simple and he keeps repeating the points so often I begin to get the feeling he thinks I have the mind of a twelve-year-old. For a politician in national office, that man has got to have the most monotonous voice of anyone in Washington in the last twenty years. It's a real chore to keep your attention on what he's saying."

SCHOLARLY CRITICISM

Scholars who are theorizers of communication write essays of criticism which are essentially the same as the day-to-day criticism of people who are teaching and learning communication styles, which includes everyone from parents to peers to formal instructors. Scholarly criticism, however, tends more to be an act of appreciation; that is, scholars of any art form have become connoisseurs, and they enjoy discussing examples of the art in terms of fine points. Scholarly critics of communication frequently use the critical process of establishing criteria from within a given communication style and then examine the record of one or more communication events very carefully in terms of the criteria. They appreciate the artistic skills involved in a communication, as well as indicate the shortcomings.

Scholars in the public-speaking style of communication have written extensive handbooks and many essays on how to criticize a speech.[3] They have also written a large number of scholarly essays which establish criteria from the public-speaking style first and then go on to analyze an important speech, a series of speeches, or the entire speaking career of a given speaker.[4]

A number of scholars in the newly emerging style of media campaigns have studied the communication of campaigns and movements.[5] The style has not yet matured, so many of the essays are related to theoretical matters, and scholars often put forward their ideas as to the nature of the new style, its basic theory, and the criteria that should be used to criticize

[3] For some typical articles see Robert L. Scott and Bernard L. Brock, *Methods of Rhetorical Criticism: A Twentieth Century Perspective*, New York: Harper & Row, 1972.

[4] Each year a number of such studies are published in such journals as *Speech Monographs, The Quarterly Journal of Speech, Today's Speech, The Central States Speech Journal, The Southern Speech Journal*, and *Western Speech*.

[5] See, for example, the essays published in *The Quarterly Journal of Speech*, 59 (April 1973), relating to the political campaign of 1972. They consist of Edwin Black, "Electing Time," 125–129; David L. Swanson, "Political Information, Influence, and Judgment in the 1972 Presidential Campaign," 130–142; Ernest G. Bormann, "The Eagleton Affair: A Fantasy Theme Analysis," 143–159; Walter R. Fisher, "Reaffirmation and Subversion of the American Dream," 160–167; and Herbert W. Simons, James W. Chesebro, and C. Jack Orr, "A Movement Perspective on the 1972 Presidential Campaign," 168–179.

the communication events associated with a campaign or a movement.[6]

Scholars in the message communication style have tended to criticize communication events by examining them directly in field study situations. We have already alluded to surveys of information flow and loss in formal channels within organizations. When a critic asks the question "How accurate is the information transmission in this communication system?" he is using the criterion of high-fidelity communication as a standard of good communication. When a scholar discovers that there is a great loss of information between input into the system and output, the judgment is generally that the communication is not good. In some Machiavellian communication styles, a critic might judge that loss of information is good, and that the manipulators of the organization have skillfully confused the employees about what they are up to and have succeeded in having their way at the expense of the employees; but in the message communication style, loss of information is undesirable. Some scholars have examined the distribution of information through various channels or media. They have asked how information about some event such as an assassination reaches the general public.[7] A description of the information flow through channels fulfills the first two steps of the critical process in that it selects criteria from the ideal model of communication (namely, a description of message flow through channels) and describes what happens in a communication event. To complete the critical act, a scholar would go on to evaluate the flow of information as to accuracy (fidelity of information transmission) and effect on attitudes or behavior.

Scholars in the relationship style have recorded and criticized such communication events as therapy sessions, sensitivity training meetings, encounter groups, and so forth, and then selected certain criteria for evaluation. Watzlawick, Beavin, and Jackson do a considerable amount of communication criticism in their book, which is an important theoretical statement of the relationship communication style. Partly they use the criticism to teach the reader how to

[6] See, for example, Herbert W. Simons, "Requirements, Problems, and Strategies: A Theory of Persuasion for Social Movements," *The Quarterly Journal of Speech*, 56 (1970), 1–11; Dan F. Hahn and Ruth M. Gonchar, "Studying Social Movements: A Rhetorical Methodology," *Speech Teacher*, 20 (1971), 44–52.

[7] See, for example, Thomas M. Steinfatt, Walter Gantz, David R. Seibold, and Larry D. Miller, "News Diffusion of the George Wallace Shooting: The Apparent Lack of Interpersonal Communication as an Artifact of Delayed Measurement," *The Quarterly Journal of Speech*, 59 (1973), 401–412.

communicate in the style. They analyze several therapy sessions, but one of their more interesting communication criticisms is of the play "Who's Afraid of Virginia Woolf?" They begin their analysis by examining the way communication builds and sustains relationships; they use the notions of complementary and symmetrical messages. A symmetrical relationship is one where the communicators tend to respond to each message with a similar message. Complementary relationships, on the other hand, tend to dovetail. If two people both wanted to control or boss a situation, then their one-upmanship would put them in a symmetrical relationship. If one wanted to control, however, and the other wanted to be controlled, their relationship would then be complementary. Using these concepts, the critics looked at the dialogue of the play, which consists largely of bitter personal insults and arguments. They noted such things as that when the topic of conversation changed to the wife's drinking habits, the argument between husband and wife escalated until it became bitter and led to a power struggle over the issue of who was going to answer the doorbell. The critics imply that such escalations of power struggles are bad communication.[8]

Communication Criticism as Social Correction

The criticism of communication events which teaches people to participate in a given communication style is basic and pervasive. We have probably had such criticism since human beings first began to communicate. Scholars of communication, however, have not only used criticism to teach and evaluate the art of communication; they also critically evaluate politicians, political parties, social conditions, cultural practices, the ideas and programs of leaders of movements and campaigns, and of defenders of the status quo. By entering into debates about public issues through the use of communication criticism, you can expose the shoddy argument, manipulative practices, and propaganda techniques of your opponents or of communication in general which you find demeaning or destructive.

Usually the criticism of society comes under the general label of *rhetorical criticism*. Unfortunately, that label is also used for scholarly criticism within a given communication

[8] Paul Watzlawick, Janet H. Beavin, and Don D. Jackson, *Pragmatics of Human Communication: A Study of Interactional Patterns, Pathologies, and Paradoxes*, New York: Norton, 1967, pp. 161–163.

theory, as well as for another kind of critical activity which we will discuss later in the chapter. We saw the same kind of confusion in the way the term *communication theory* is used, in Chapter 2. Rhetorical criticism which is used by the critic to fight for his own position in a political or cultural or social controversy, operates in a much different way than the criticism which helps a person understand and practice a certain communication style.

TECHNIQUES OF RHETORICAL CRITICISM

Evaluating the Messages of a Leading Spokesman

Rhetorical criticism of society begins with selection of a set of messages to evaluate. The critic generally selects messages attributed to an important persona in an ongoing conflict in society. That is, if the country is in the midst of a political campaign, the critic may select the speeches attributed to a candidate for the presidency for evaluation. The critic selects the persona with care, because, as a persuader taking part in the ongoing controversy, the critic will be dramatizing the communication situation and must select the right cast of characters to make a persuasive case for or against the position under consideration. The critic will usually select a leading spokesman who symbolizes either the position of the critic's enemies or the critic's own personal position on a contemporary issue. If you look through some recent issues of the leading scholarly journals in speech communication, you will see a number of studies of presidents Truman, Johnson, Kennedy, and Nixon. In the 1940s and 1950s, many scholars criticized the speeches of Franklin Roosevelt. In the 1960s, many critics studied black speakers such as Martin Luther King, Jr., and Stokely Carmichael. In the 1970s many scholars studied leading female speakers and symbols of the women's rights movement. Indeed, a survey of topics studied by master's theses and doctoral dissertations in speech communication over the years gives a good indication of the political and social issues which have preoccupied the American public in the last forty years.

Usually when the critic selects individuals whom he or she admires, the critical strategy is to cast these personae as heroes. The critic describes the excellence of their communication and lauds the admirable ethos of the speakers and the soundness of their ideas. The critics who select people they detest will usually deplore the character of the communicators, point out the demagoguery of their communication practices, and detail the propagandistic nature of their messages.[9]

The use of communication criticism to enter current debates about change and continuity in society is an important function of citizenship. We all have the right and responsibility to take a public position and argue for its acceptance by a wider audience. One way to make our point is to dramatize the high quality of communication of a persona who symbolizes our position. Another way is to attack the shoddy quality of the communication of a persona who symbolizes our opponents in the controversy.[10] Such criticism not only helps clarify public debates on important issues, a process vital in an open society, but it also has the useful by-product of submitting the communication of pressure groups to careful, systematic, and professional scrutiny according to the standards of the predominant communication styles of a community. When reporters and journalists began to discuss a *credibility gap* between the Johnson administration and the American public caused by the low quality of official pronouncements, professional critics with scholarly credentials could and did submit the messages to evaluation by trained intelligences.

Attempting to Improve Communication in General
Some critics of communication with a desire to improve society make the function of criticizing the quality of public communication a primary one rather than a by-product. Their aim is to strive for a more objective stance and submit the communication of all sides of a controversy to careful criticism. They would not only study an administration's communication for explanations of the credibility gap, but would probably go on to study the communication of the reporters and journalists who made the accusation as well. They take the "guardian" role, that of keeping a critical eye on the quality of communication in society, and they strike out at what they see as shoddy communication practices no matter where they find them. They may ridicule the gobbledygook of bureaucratic communication in one essay, and in another attack the murky, jargon-ridden style of academic writers. They may discuss the decline in the quality of imagination and dramatization resulting from television commercials in one

[9] See, for example, Karlyn Kohrs Campbell, *Critiques of Contemporary Rhetoric*, Belmont, Calif.: Wadsworth, 1972.

[10] A number of essays criticizing the speechmaking of Richard Nixon have appeared in speech communication journals in the years from 1952 to the present, and most of them have been statements criticizing the rhetoric as undesirable and portraying Nixon as an evil persona.

essay, and in another the dull English created by ghost writers for the television broadcasts of a leading politician.[11]

Examining the Adverse Social Effects of Communication

Another technique for taking an "advocate's" position by means of communication criticism is to examine how communication contributes to an undesirable condition in society. Critics might examine how the language of the mass media or the dramatizations of the media give an undesirable impression of a particular ethnic or minority group. In this regard, a critic might analyze the negative connotations of the terms associated with darkness or blackness (e.g. black-hearted) and argue that black people are victims of the language of a racist society.[12] Or a critic might argue that Polish jokes reflect an innate prejudice against Polish people. Or the critic might argue that the commercials on television present male parents as simple-minded dolts who are continually duped by their spouses and children. Or the critic might argue that girls are dramatized in the mass media magazines as nurturing, selfless, soft, and defenseless, while boys are portrayed as assertive, tough, and selfish. Or the critic might argue that sexist bias is built into the language in that all terms for positions of power are associated with the male gender—*chairman*, for example. (Under the impact of the latter sort of criticism, at our schools we now have *chair-persons* and *chair-ones*. One of our daughters recently received a letter from a college she was considering attending addressed to "Dear Freshperson.") Or the critic might argue that the very structure of the language of important communications emphasizes the one-up relationship of the capitalists over the working class.

Criticism intended to change or resist change in society is important and should be practiced continually, but you should be able to distinguish such criticism from the critical activity associated with practicing a given style of communication. In addition, such criticism is likely to lose its usefulness when the issue which brought it into being fades from the scene. Today we find only minor historical interest in the essay in rhetorical criticism which dramatizes a heroic Harry Truman fighting against overwhelming odds to defeat the candidate of Republicanism and entrenched interests,

[11] See, for example, Ernest G. Bormann, "Ghostwriting and the Rhetorical Critic," *The Quarterly Journal of Speech*, 46 (1960), 284–288.
[12] See, for example, Haig Bosmajian, "The Language of White Racism," in Haig Bosmajian, ed., *Readings in Speech*, 2nd ed., New York: Harper & Row, 1971, pp. 202–215.

Thomas E. Dewey of New York, in a courageous whistle-stop campaign, while even the leaders of his own party were giving him only lukewarm support.[13] Thirty years from now we will have a similar minor historical interest in critical essays which dramatize how an evil Richard Nixon took to television in 1952 to manipulate the American public in order to stay on the ticket as a vice-presidential candidate by talking about his wife's coat and his dog Checkers.

Rhetorical Criticism as an Avenue to Knowledge

The final kind of rhetorical criticism aims at discovering knowledge about human communication which transcends communication styles and contexts and transitory issues currently under contention. Scholars criticizing public communication in this third way are trying to understand human communication in all its varied forms, but particularly as it is used in a rhetorical way. Rhetorical criticism thus takes its place as a liberal and humanizing art, a scholarly endeavor which aims to illuminate the human condition. It is particularly concerned with human symbolizing, which works to divide and integrate human social arrangements, to interpret human problems and enable cooperative efforts to be made to solve them, to provide self and group concepts for human beings searching for meaning in their existence and endeavors. In Karlyn Campbell's words, "The academic critic explores and analyzes whatever acts will aid in explicating the essential process of human symbolization."[14]

How does the rhetorical critic searching to illuminate human symbolizing proceed? In the first place, the critic does not ask questions such as, "Is this a good example of communication in the public-speaking style?" (or the message communication style, or the relationship style). Nor does the critic ask questions such as, "In what ways are my opponents in this controversy guilty of unethical, inadequate, or shoddy communication?" Rather, the critic asks questions such as, "How does communication function to divide individual from individual, group from group, and community from community? How does communication function to create a sense of community and integrate individuals and groups into

[13] See, for example, Cole S. Brembeck, "Harry Truman at the Whistle Stops," *Quarterly Journal of Speech*, 38 (1952), 42–50.

[14] Karlyn Kohrs Campbell, "Criticism: Ephemeral and Enduring," *Speech Teacher*, 23 (1974), 9–14.

larger cooperative units? How does communication function to interpret 'reality' for symbol-using human beings? How does it function to provide for social change and continuity?"

Having asked general questions about rhetorical purposes such as celebrating community, organizing social collectives, dealing with facts, and so forth, the critic may next ask, "Are there recurring patterns of symbolization which appear across styles, cultures, and situations? What are the similarities and differences across styles and cultures? Can we discover basic patterns which transcend styles? If basic patterns are found, how do they work rhetorically?"

Some critics have discovered patterns which they argue are widely employed and perhaps universal. A number of scholars have studied varied kinds of communication to see if they can discover the same basic patterns that critic Kenneth Burke discovered in a series of critical analyses. Burke found such patterns as the one consisting of the erecting of hierarchy, the search for perfection, the arousal of guilt, and the development of mystery. He also found patterns to purge guilt, such as scapegoating.[15] Critics following the lead of Burke continue to search for such patterning, because they want to see if it is universal and how it illuminates the human condition.[16]

We will explain in some detail one approach to rhetorical criticism which aims to discover knowledge about the human condition. You should understand that the approach which we outline is but one of several; academic critics have used a number of other methods to make important contributions to our understanding of human communication. Since you are being introduced to the study of speech communication, you do not have time to go into all of the intricate details of these major approaches to criticism, but you should understand the method of rhetorical criticism and how it illuminates the study of persuasion.

We will explain one dramatistic approach to the study of human communication. Burke uses a dramatistic framework to examine symbolization. A number of sociologists and students of literary and dramatic criticism also use dramatistic approaches to the study of symbolization.[17] The fruitfulness

[15] See, for example, Kenneth Burke, "The Rhetoric of Hitler's 'Battle,'" *Philosophy of Literary Form*, Baton Rouge, La.: Louisiana State University Press, 1967, pp. 191–220.

[16] The bibliography of critical studies indebted to Burke's recurring patterns is very large; see for example, Robert L. Ivie, "Presidential Motives for War," *The Quarterly Journal of Speech*, 60 (1974), 337–345.

[17] For an interesting dramatistic approach from a sociological viewpoint, see Erving Goffman, *The Presentation of Self in Everyday Life*, Garden City, N.Y.: Doubleday, 1959.

of the critical endeavors which employ a dramatistic frame-work testifies to its importance. The method we will use is simple enough that you can try your hand at criticizing discourse after you finish reading this chapter. Since we have discussed in previous chapters many of the discoveries which stem from scholarly criticism using this approach, you already know some of the key concepts.

FANTASY THEME ANALYSIS
We call the approach a *fantasy theme analysis of rhetorical visions* and use the method to explore the social reality of a group of people who share a rhetorical vision. From our discussion of fantasy themes and rhetorical vision in Chapter 12, you know that a fantasy theme is a dramatizing message, which contains characters (personae) in a dramatic situation acting out a scenario. Dramatizing messages occur in our talking to ourselves (our personal fantasies); they occur in two-person conversations; they occur in small groups; they occur in radio and television commercials; they occur in public speeches; they occur in radio and television talk

shows, public affairs broadcasts, and newscasts; and they occur in newspapers and magazines. In short, dramatic narratives are part of messages in all contexts. Dramatizing messages occur in all cultures and in all communication styles.

The important feature of dramatizing messages for the rhetorical critic is the fact that some dramatizing catches people's attention. They come to identify with the "good people," to root for their welfare, and to hope they will win out in the struggle; and they come to dislike the "bad people," to feel suspense as the forces of evil threaten to overwhelm the forces of good. They begin to feel fear, hatred, or disgust for the evil ones and begin to experience the emotions of the good people with whom they identify: When the heroine cries, they cry; when the heroine laughs with joy, they laugh; when the heroine jumps in fear, they jump and feel fear. A critic can document the chaining of a dramatization through groups of people by finding evidence that a given response to it is repeated in different contexts. Such evidence is available in written records as well as in audio- and videotapes.

The critic who discovers fantasies that chain through a small group or a community has evidence that the people have established the first bonds of a rhetorical community. When a group of people come to share a common cast of heroes and villains they have a common symbolism that serves to tie them together.

Why Do Certain Fantasies Chain?

Sometimes, however, the critic looks not only to the dramas which have chained but also to those dramatizations which were presented in messages for the community, but which for some reason failed to spark interest and did not chain in any appreciable fashion. The critic may ask why some dramas catch on when others do not and try to discover something about the symbolic climate which encourages some fantasies and discourages others.

For example, during the 1830s in the United States, there was a great impulse to do something about slavery. One set of fantasy themes dramatized the Constitution of the United States as a proslavery document created by a cast of hypocritical, evil men who knew they were fastening slavery on the country permanently. The conclusion of those who shared this fantasy theme was that the Constitution itself should be destroyed and the Union broken up. Another set of fantasy themes dramatized the Constitution of the United States as an anti-slavery document created by a cast of heroic founders who returned home to their individual states and began working for the elimination of slavery. They dreamed of purging the sin of slavery from the land and restoring the country to its original basis. The latter set of fantasy themes chained through the public in the North much more widely than the former.

For another example, in the 1930s there was a great impulse for economic reform, prompted by the here-and-now crisis of the Depression. One set of fantasy themes dramatized the capitalist system in the United States as the basic cause of the country's difficulty. The fantasy themes saw the capitalist crisis as inevitable and portrayed it as leading to a violent revolution of the proletariat which would destroy capitalism and create a socialist utopia. Another set of fantasy themes, dramatized by one individual, the colorful southern senator Huey P. Long of Louisiana, in a series of national radio broadcasts, portrayed the capitalist system as essentially all right. Every person ought to have a chance to be a millionaire, according to Long; the problem was that some people were becoming multimillionaires and billionaires because of inherited wealth and because of conspiratorial manipulations of the economic system by the very wealthy. The answer, he said, was a system which would put a ceiling of several millions on individual fortunes and would tax the excess wealth and distribute it to the poor people. Long's dream of sharing wealth—which he characterized as not being socialism, fascism, communism, anarchism, or any other of the "'isms' that they have over in Europe," but rather as "Americanism"—chained through the radio audience until millions of listeners wrote Long in support of the idea. Yet fantasies about destroying capitalism and creating a socialist utopia have never brought more than a million votes for socialist and communist presidential candidates. A rhetorical critic might study the question of why, in a given culture, certain fantasies chain when others do not, or why certain ones seem to chain more widely than others.

Recurrent Fantasy Types

Rhetorical critics have raised another important set of questions which ask whether or not some fantasy types—that is, scenarios that are used over and over again—are so universally appealing that they can be called rhetorical myths. The prototype myths were the Greeks' fantasy themes about the gods and their actions, which provided an explanation for human experience. To be a candidate for a cultural myth, a fantasy type must be of a universal and sweeping nature similar to the Greek myths. If a small number of myths comprise the most important, universal, and basic rhetorical transactions, such a discovery would be very important knowledge about the symbol-using behavior of human beings in social transactions. The discovery that important, basic myths are cross-cultural, for example, would be an important contribution to the study of cross-cultural communication. Should the critics discover that rhetorical myths are culture-bound, that, too, would be an important discovery.

A number of rhetorical fantasy types have recurred in the history of mass persuasion (public address) in the United States, and critics have suggested they may be of mythic proportion. We have already alluded to one important pattern, that of erection of a hierarchy, search for perfection, fall, guilt, mystery, purge, and salvation discovered by Kenneth Burke, and the efforts of other critics to see if the pattern is repeated in other bodies of discourse. In addition, a number of critics have discovered the rhetorical fantasy of the conspiracy drama in all historical periods and in the communication of all sorts of political and social movements — right-wing, left-wing, and middle-of-the-road.[18] Other critics have discovered the American dream — the scenario of a poor but dedicated hero who works hard and achieves great success.[19] Still other critics have discovered the scenario of an American Eden, or paradise, saved by God for the second coming of Christ, and the perfection of society to bring about the millenium in America.[20] Whether the rhetorical patterns that Burke discovered are universal or culture-bound is, as yet, unclear, although Burke discovered the scapegoat pattern in Hitler's *Mein Kampf*.[21] Whether the conspiracy fantasy type is cross-cultural is also a question for which we have not enough evidence. The two fantasies about America as an open society in which an individual can achieve success no matter what the conditions of his birth, and of America as the paradise saved by God for the millenium, are undoubtedly culture-bound myths. Nonetheless, the critic, by taking them apart and discovering how they work, rhetorically — by finding out, for example, how the American dream worked to build a sense of community and shape the American character — can make a contribution to our knowledge about American society, as well as help us learn more about how symbols work.

[18] See, for example, John F. Cragan, "Rhetorical Strategy: A Dramatistic Interpretation and Application," *Central States Speech Journal*, 26 (1975), 4–11.
[19] See Fisher, "Reaffirmation and Subversion of the American Dream."
[20] Carl Wayne Hensley, "Rhetorical Vision and the Persuasion of a Historical Movement: The Disciples of Christ in Nineteenth Century American Culture," *The Quarterly Journal of Speech*, 61 (1975), 250–264.
[21] See Burke, "The Rhetoric of Hitler's 'Battle.'"

Some critics have asked whether there are certain basic human conditions which restrict the options of communicators. If so, scholars may discover these options and outline the basic ways individuals can deal with them symbolically. Are there, for example, certain basic rhetorical patterns used by the person who, say, must defend himself or herself publicly? Is there a rhetoric of apology that individuals use when, like Richard Nixon, they are charged with crimes and misdemeanors or with having an illegal campaign fund, or, like Edward Kennedy, with complicity in a homicide?[22]

Some critics have looked to dramatic scenarios based upon metaphor or analogy. They have asked whether certain basic metaphors are associated with common rhetorical situations. Is the metaphor of cancer, as an often ungovernable destructive growth, characteristic of groups and individuals who wish to guard present conditions against the forces of change?[23] Is the dramatic scene of light after darkness a universal and important recurring pattern?[24] Is the comparison of society to an organism or to a machine an important metaphor?

Critics who ask such questions make discoveries about communication which transcend the criticism involved in the theory and practice of a style, and their discoveries have a permanent value, even when the communication they criticize is no longer important as a style.

How to Make a Fantasy Theme Analysis

You begin a fantasy theme analysis by selecting a general topic area that you would like to investigate. Perhaps you are interested in political campaigning or you enjoy ridiculing television commercials; you may be intrigued by the process of religious conversion, by the communication associated with transcendental meditation, by the communication within a large corporation, designed to increase employee morale, or by the communication of some pressure group or social reform movement. The communication you study need not be in the mass media; it can be messages produced by a

[22] See, for example, David A. Ling, "A Pentadic Analysis of Senator Edward Kennedy's Address to the People of Massachusetts, July 25, 1969," *Central States Speech Journal*, 21 (1970), 81–86.

[23] Edwin Black, "The Second Persona," *The Quarterly Journal of Speech*, 56 (1970), 109–119.

[24] Michael Osborn, "Archetypal Metaphor in Rhetoric: The Light-Dark Family," *The Quarterly Journal of Speech*, 53 (1967), 115–126.

discussion group or the conversations of two or three persons.

Once you have selected an area of study you begin to collect evidence relating to the content of the communication. You can use video- or audiotapes, or your own direct observation. Often you can find written transcripts or records of important public messages. You should try to restrict the scope of your topic of criticism, so that you can deal with it in considerable detail in the time you have for your study. Our advice on analyzing a topic for a public speech, in Chapter 7, will be useful to you.

DISCOVERING FANTASY THEMES

You should next go through the communication and note each dramatic incident in the messages you have collected. When you have gathered a number of dramatic incidents, try to sort them into fantasy types. Is the same story repeated over and over again, with slightly different characters and minor variations? Put all instances of that story together. You have now discovered a fantasy type. The discovery of a fantasy type is evidence that similar fantasy themes are chaining through in important community of people and that they are coming to share a common rhetorical vision. A rhetorical fantasy type is like the fantasy types used in television dramas. You may, for instance, find a dramatic series on one television network which features two or three policemen who deal competently with a series of incidents of a diverse nature, with some humor but with considerable seriousness. If you then find similar series on other networks, you can lump them together as police-action fantasy types, and examine all of the programs as a group.

Once you have a collection of basic fantasy types, you can begin to search the discourse again to see if the communicators themselves use fantasy types in their messages. If you find such use of fantasy types, it is further evidence that the fantasies have chained. A speaker can only use fantasy types in a message successfully if the listeners have previously chained into a number of similar fantasy themes. For example, a political pamphlet for a senatorial candidate may contain a statement something like the following: "Senator James Early Courageous was the first to speak out against the corruption in the state capital. He was the first to take the unpopular stand of raising taxes. He was the first to demand greater participation on the part of the poor people in local welfare programs. He was the first to . . ." etc., etc. The statement is essentially a fantasy type, and by alluding to but not developing the fantasies relating to each drama when Senator Courageous took an early and unpopular stand which later proved to be the right one, the overall type emerges. Namely, Senator James Early Courageous is an individual who characteristically sees the right thing to do before anyone else in government; he characteristically takes a stand for the right thing; and then, characteristically, those who are too selfish or too stupid to understand his farseeing statesmanship come forward to harass and attack him. Senator Courageous, however, stands firm for what is right and takes the blows and risks his career for these far-sighted programs.

RECONSTRUCTING A RHETORICAL VISION

Once you have discovered the basic fantasy types, you can reconstruct the vision of the people who have chained into the fantasies which formed the fantasy types. You can look for patterns of characteristics: Do the same people keep cropping up as villains?[25] Are the same people generally praised and identified with as heroes? You can look also for similar scenarios: Do you find the same stories told over and over, or very similar ones? You can look to the setting of the dramas.

Once you can describe the general vision of the communicators, you can ask more specific questions about various elements of the rhetoric. How concrete and detailed are the characterizations of the heroes and villains? What motives are attributed to the bad guys and to the good guys? (Often those participating in the vision will try to act for the same motives that they identify in their heroes.) How are the members of the rhetorical community characterized? ("We Americans are always. . . ;" "The farmer is. . ." ; "Black people are basically. . ." ; "Those of us interested in the ecology movement. . .") For what are the members of the community praised? For what are the enemies castigated? When you have made such an analysis of the heroes and villains, you can decide what values are implied in the rhetorical vision. Are the heroes active and involved in the general welfare? If so, then the value of active involvement for others is implied; and so forth.

Where are the fantasy themes set? In the wilderness? In the urban ghetto? On the campus? In the classroom? In an automobile? Often the place of the drama becomes an important territory and serves to establish home turf. People searching

[25] For an interesting analysis of villains in fantasies, see Bonnie McD. Johnson, "Image of the Enemy in Intergroup Conflict," *Central States Speech Journal*, 26 (1975), 84–92.

for rhetorical community often find a symbolic ground useful as a unifying symbol.

What are the typical scenarios? What actions take place? What do the good people do? Do they demonstrate in the streets? Vote? Plant bombs? Go to jail and resist the oppressive system? Stay home and tend to their personal affairs? What do the bad people do? Conspire to exploit the innocent? Hypocritically mouth platitudes about freedom while acting in oppressive ways? Use violence to coerce the good people? What actions are celebrated and what actions are censored? What life styles are celebrated as praiseworthy?

What meanings are inherent in the dramas? Where does the participant in the vision fit into the nature of things? Where does the community fit into the rest of the culture? into the scheme of history? What emotions are aroused by the typical fantasy types that you discover? Does hate predominate? rage? pity? love? indignation? resignation? What motives are embedded in the vision? Would those committed to it work for or resist legal action if necessary? violence? One industrial psychologist has developed a system of analyzing motives in fantasy themes which can be used to discover if a given drama reflects an affiliation motive (a love story), an achievement motivation (the Horatio Alger fantasy type), or mastery motivation (how the hero clawed his way to the top).[26]

You can examine how the rhetorical vision deals with facts or the breaking news; you can discover the kinds of argumentation that are implied by the vision. For example, some visions dramatize a written text as the ultimate legitimizer of argument. Certain religions' rhetorical visions portray the Bible (or some other sacred text) as the repository of knowledge, and the participants' reasoning and argument consist of providing a conclusion and quotations from the Bible which support the conclusion. Some rhetorical visions celebrate observations of facts as the ultimate legitimizer of argument, and participants tend to argue from data gathered in scientific studies, census surveys, and other systematic observations. Some rhetorical visions dramatize precedent, or previous human experience, as the ultimate legitimizer of argument, and the participants submit prior instances and the way these instances were handled as argument in behalf of a certain conclusion.

You need not, and often a brief rhetorical criticism cannot, raise all of the above questions about a given speech or series

---

[26] See David C. McClelland, "Methods of Measuring Human Motivation," in John W. Atkinson, ed., *Motives in Fantasy, Action, and Society: A Method of Assessment and Study*, New York: Van Nostrand, 1958, pp. 7–42.

The first important type of criticism of communication involves becoming knowledgeable about the theory and practice of a given style of communication.

The critical process within a communication style involves selecting criteria, describing the communication in light of the criteria, and evaluating the communication as good or bad.

Without criticism to aid in teaching others to participate in a communication style, we would be unable to communicate.

A second important way people use communication criticism is to enter debates about change and continuity in society.

One technique of using rhetorical criticism in an ongoing dialogue is to select a speaker who symbolizes our position and praise his communication; another is to pick an enemy and attack his communication.

Another technique of using rhetorical criticism in an ongoing dialogue is to try to remedy poor communication in general.

of messages, but for an in-depth study of a single message, a critic might ask more of the questions and search for more details.

Once you have analyzed some of the major features of a rhetorical vision in terms of the questions posed above, you can answer some more general rhetorical questions. You can learn of the hopes and fears, the emotional tone, and the inner life of a group by examining how it deals with basic, universal rhetorical problems. Such insight flows from answers to questions such as these: How well did the communication deal with the problem of creating and celebrating a sense of community? Did it help generate a group and individual self-image which was strong, confident, and resilient? How did the rhetoric aid or hinder the community in its adaptation to its physical environment? How did the communicators deal with the rhetorical problem of creating a social reality which provides norms for community behavior in terms of the level

A final technique of using rhetorical criticism in an ongoing dialogue is to examine how communication contributes to undesirable conditions in society.

By practicing criticism within the assumptions of a style, you can learn to appreciate good communication, and you can improve your own practice as well as that of others.

By entering into debates about public issues you can expose shoddy argument, propaganda techniques, and other unethical practices of your opponent, or communication practices which you find generally destructive or demeaning.

The third important kind of rhetorical criticism aims at understanding human communication in all its varied forms; it seeks knowledge which will transcend communication styles, contexts, and cultural influences.

Some rhetorical critics have found patterns of symbolization which are widely and perhaps universally employed.

One important scholarly viewpoint in rhetorical criticism takes a dramatistic approach to the study of symbolization.

One approach to dramatistic analysis of rhetoric is to study the fantasy themes which have chained through a group or community of people.

When a number of similar fantasy themes have chained, they form a fantasy type.

Out of the basic fantasy types a critic can reconstruct the rhetorical vision of a community.

By examining all or part of a rhetorical vision, a critic can discover important meanings, emotional evocations, and motives which characterize the people participating in the vision.

Critics may also examine rhetorical visions and ask more general rhetorical questions, such as how the vision generates a sense of community, converts others to join, and deals with argumentation.

of violence, exploitation, dominance, and injustice? Did the communication create a drama for the members to participate in which served such mythic functions as providing them with an account of the world, the gods, and fate which gave meaning to their community and themselves? How did the rhetoric meet the problems of celebrating the community's values? How well did it initiate and dedicate new generations who inherited the vision to the values of the community? How well did the communicator meet the needs for change within the community? How well did the style work to convert new members to the community? How well did the vision aid the people who participated in it to live with people who participated in different rhetorical visions?[27]

[27] For a brief analysis which answers some of these questions about the puritan rhetorical vision see Ernest G. Bormann, "Fantasy and Rhetorical Vision: The Rhetorical Criticism of Social Reality," *The Quarterly Journal of Speech*, 58 (1972), 396–407.

Once we participate through criticism in the rhetorical vision of a community or movement, we have come to experience vicariously the inner symbolic world of its participants and to experience a way to life that would otherwise be less accessible to us; we have enlarged our awareness and become more fully human.

SUGGESTED PROJECTS

1 Your instructor will assign a speech in the public-speaking communication style. You are to set up some criteria for evaluation from the chapters in this book which deal with the public-speaking style and write a brief criticism of the speech of one of your classmates, using the criteria you have selected. Remember that you must both describe the communication technique your classmate used, and then make a critical evaluation of it.
2 Your instructor will assign an exercise in the message communication style. You are to set up some criteria for evaluation from the chapters in this book which deal with the message communication style and write a brief criticism of the communication exercises of some of your classmates.
3 Your instructor will assign an exercise in the relationship communication style. You are to set up some criteria for evaluation from the chapters in this book which deal with the relationship communication style and write a brief criticism of the communication exercise in which you participated.
4 Select some communication relating to a public issue about which you are, preferably, excited or disturbed — or at least pretty interested. Make a criticism of the communication which serves to express your position in the controversy. You may select a public figure whose ideas and speaking you particularly abhor or one you particularly admire for the focus of your criticism. Your instructor may have you deliver the criticism orally or write a paper about it.
5 Select a number of messages for which you can get good records and which you believe represent a rhethorical community. Make a fantasy theme analysis of the rhetorical vision of the community.

SUGGESTED READINGS

Ernest G. Bormann. "Fantasy and Rhetorical Vision: The Rhetorical Criticism of Social Reality." *Quarterly Journal of Speech*, 58 (1972), 396–407.
Karlyn Kohrs Campbell. "Criticism: Ephemeral and Enduring." *Speech Teacher*, 23 (1974), 9–14.
Robert Cathcart. *Post Communication: Criticism and Evaluation.* Indianapolis: Bobbs-Merrill, 1966.

William A. Linsley, ed. *Speech Criticism: Methods and Materials.* Dubuque, Iowa: Brown, 1968.

Robert L. Scott and Bernard L. Brock. *Methods of Rhetorical Criticism: A Twentieth Century Perspective.* New York: Harper & Row, 1972.

Chapter 14

HOW TO TALK
TO ANOTHER PERSON

In Chapter 2 we presented the three basic styles of communication in contemporary society. Two of these styles relate to the situations in which you talk with another person. We will consider initially the two-person communication that is designed to achieve some common goal or task, such as the interview for information, the job interview, the conference between superior and subordinate, the planning session, and the instructional conference. These meetings are conducted in the message communication style.

How to Talk to Another Person
in the Message Communication Style

Our discussion will deal mainly with those instances when the basic criteria of the message communication model are fulfilled. On occasion, however, messages are encoded in a way that closely approximates the model, but they do not fulfill all the key parts of the process. For instance, in Chapter 8 we noted the situation in which one individual begins a conversation with the intention of playing the role of message source, but the other person does not play the role of receiver. Here we must point out another situation which fails to fulfill the assumptions of the model.

THE DIFFERENCE BETWEEN
SELF-EXPRESSION AND COMMUNICATION

When an individual *expresses* himself or herself, the communication is not in the message style. When a person says something in the presence of another, it is usually because of some want or impulse within himself or herself. If the person wants to tell another person something about the world, about the speaker, or about the listener we have the possibility of discussion, feedback, and communication. If, on the other hand, the person has an impulse to express his or her emotions, with no desire to tell anything to the other person, we have an instance of personal expression. When a source encodes a message to communicate, he aims to achieve some level of common meanings, denotative or connotative, between himself and his listener. When a person expresses himself, he gives vent to feelings and ideas, for example, with a grunt or a shout, by crying, or even by forming words into sentences. The person expressing himself has no interest in arousing common meanings. The attention of others, either positive or negative, often satisfies the impulse. A child in a temper tantrum is not communicating; he is expressing him-

self. When the parent asks, "What's the matter? What's wrong?" the child continues to kick, scream, and roll on the floor, yelling, "No, no, no." The parent may read some meaning into the tantrum and try to explain it; the child, however, makes no attempt to tell the parent what is troubling him. The act of giving vent to his personal feelings is his goal. Some problems in getting along with one another could be avoided if people could preface all self-expressive messages with, "I just need to hear myself talk. Don't pay any attention to me. I'm riled up and boiling over. Just plug up your ears." The trouble is, of course, that when we are emotionally upset, we are often least able to preface an outburst with such a reasonable explanation.

Consider the nonrepresentational painter; he does not care what the viewer thinks of his picture as long as it means something to him. He is expressing himself. The student protester who makes nonnegotiable demands and does not care to talk about them is expressing himself rather than communicating. Self-expression is neither good nor bad; often it is valuable, fun, and necessary. We must, however, be clear about the differences between self-expression and communication and understand that while self-expression may be artless, communication always requires artistry. We must work at effective human communication and learn the craft if we hope to succeed consistently.

WHAT IS MEANING

In two-person conversation in the message style, the source encodes a message in words and nonverbal codes. As he talks, he can watch for the response of the other person. The receiver provides the speaker with continuous feedback as the message unfolds. Since the channels in a face-to-face conversation include both sight and hearing, the speaker can get a reading on his listener's responses throughout, *at the same time* he is speaking, from the nonverbal feedback cues of the listener. We cannot stress too strongly that two-person communication provides ideal conditions for close-range continuous feedback. In many communication situations, such as when you are writing a letter, memorandum, or report, or are watching television or listening to the radio, such efficient feedback is missing. The opportunity for high-fidelity communication is greatest in the two-person situation.

As you listen to a message unfold, you do not simply absorb the other's meanings. You interpret the message by calling up meanings from your experience and fitting them

into the forms suggested by the structure of the message. We come, therefore, to the important question "What are *meanings?*" Philosophers, psychologists, and linguists have puzzled about the meaning of meanings and discovered that the definition is much more difficult than might at first be supposed. For the student of communication who wishes to improve his daily conversations with other people, however, the basic question has been answered.

When two people talk to each other, the meanings aroused by their interaction are within them. When you talk with another person, what you derive from the talk is something within your consciousness, and what the other person derives from the talk is something individual and personal for him. We are islands of consciousness and cannot break out of the boundaries of self to experience directly another person's interior life. For example, when you see a color and call it "red," you have learned from experience that when other people talk with you about flowers of that hue, they call them red. You thus come to call flowers of a similar color red. When a man gives his date flowers and says, "these red roses mean something special," she accepts his characterization of the roses as red; whereas had he labeled roses everyone has learned to name *yellow* with the word *red*, she would have corrected him. You know what the word *red* means, in the sense that you agree with others in the presence of a particular flower that it has the property "red." Such agreement is the basis for much common meaning when we communicate with one another.

However, even after you agree with another person that a rose is red, you have no way of knowing if the red you see is anything at all like the red the other person sees. Logically we have no evidence that when Mr. A talks with Mr. B, they may not have radically different worlds of color, sound, taste, and feeling. Mr. A's world may be full of bright and garish colors, while Mr. B's is full of muted tones. Mr. A's world may be a noisy, raucous one, full of violent and clashing sounds, while Mr. B's world is muffled and quiet. Mr. A and Mr. B may agree that the rose is red or that the musician is playing a Beethoven sonata, but in an important sense, neither one can know what the color red means to the other or what the music sounds like or means to the other. The point is made by an old unanswerable question, "How do you tell a color-blind person what 'red' means?"

ENCODING MEANING

Within his island of meanings, the source discovers a desire to tell another person about something. He encodes a verbal message and supports the *meaning* with nonverbal intonations and body language. Quite often the speaker finds that for what he wants to say, his tools are clumsy. He struggles to find the right names and right properties and relations. He casts about to form the words into the right kinds of sentences. Still he cannot put everything he wishes into his message. His island of meanings is too complicated; the ideas are so complex. He tries to pattern a message that reflects the complexity and the subtle richness of his ideas. The task is difficult. The world within the message source is changing, shifting, dynamic; the language he encodes is frozen once it leaves his lips. The sentences are set, static. He resembles the painter who tries to put a great idea and deep feeling into a series of static forms on a flat canvas. How can he catch the motion, the shifting relationships? The answer is, of course, that he cannot do so completely. The source approximates his ideas and meanings in the form of the verbal and nonverbal message codes.

Some sources encode messages better than others. The encoding of messages is an art that can be learned. Language is limited, but most natural languages are flexible and have great communicative power when handled by a well-trained and talented speaker. English is a particularly rich and powerful tool of communication. The source's language facility, the size of his vocabulary, the rules of his dialect, his creative ability to combine words into novel patterns and to associate ideas and make new meanings by coining figures of speech all affect the kind of verbal message he encodes. Also, some people use nonverbal communication better than others. The source who has a flexible voice and an expressive face, and who uses appropriate gestures naturally, enhances the effectiveness of his communication.

All of us when talking with another encode our messages from within our islands of meanings. We have biases, interests, prejudices, needs, and wants, all of which affect the way we encode messages. If we are trained as policemen or medical doctors or legal secretaries or automobile mechanics, our training and the kind of work we do begin to enlarge certain areas of our vocabulary, and that part of our internal world likewise grows in size and complexity, while the areas we seldom think about or discuss gradually dwindle in our perception. Our ability to talk technically and with understanding and complexity about the things we do most often increases, as our ability to talk about those things we seldom do or think about decreases.

All of us have to accept our ignorance as we communicate with someone else. I know little or nothing of you until you tell me. You are ignorant about me, also. Ignorance is simply what we do not yet know. You are bound to know a great deal about something I know nothing about. If I pretend I am not ignorant about something, I mislead you. We can expect communication problems. We have to learn to broadcast our ignorance on occasion and not try to conceal it. Only when we admit ignorance can someone else begin to tell us about what we do not know. Admitting ignorance is a vital key to providing feedback to improve communication.

INTERPRETING MEANING

The source's problems of finding the right message to communicate his meanings are mirrored to some extent in the receiver. The receiver of any message also has a personal island of meanings. The receiver has a certain language facility, a certain dialect, certain biases, interests, and prejudices. The listener tends to read into the messages those meanings associated with his personal biases and interests.

The receiver finds some parts of the message easy to associate with a denotative meaning. Generally, if a name is specific, such as, "My dog, Rover, sitting over there by the chair," the listener associates a part of his perceptual world quickly and easily, and both the speaker and the listener know what is being discussed. The receiver feels confident that he understands the message, and he may nod his head to indicate understanding. Problems arise because some words are abstract and difficult to associate with a denotative meaning. Messages that are not firmly anchored to clear denotative meanings may trigger a large pool of meanings and their emotional associations in the listener. The source may say, "I've just come from a long talk with my personal God. Are you a born-again Christian?" and the receiver may respond with a recollection of his evangelist father and call up his meanings for *born-again Christian*, which may be personal and quite different from those the speaker was trying to communicate. Another source may say, "The communists really hate democracy and all it stands for." The listener associates his own meanings for *communists* and for *democracy*, and the potential for misunderstanding is great.

Just as the speaker finds his verbal and nonverbal codes clumsy for the task of encoding messages, so the receiver finds the interpretation of messages difficult, but it is through this interpretation that human understanding can come about. Perhaps the listener interprets a nonverbal gesture as a clue to some deep and important idea within the consciousness of the speaker. The excitement of discovery regarding a fellow human being begins. The listener strains to find a verbal key to the idea. He asks for more messages. He strives to interpret these and seeks additional comments. He thinks he sees the shape of the idea; he gets a glimmer of the feeling within the source. Somehow he manages some contact through the self-protective walls of biases, dialect, background, interests, and motives. The interchange has proceeded until the two people feel they have achieved genuine understanding. Both are excited, moved, touched by the experience. They have glimpsed the interior island of another person's meanings.

Such high moments of high fidelity transmission of meaning come too seldom for most of us, and little wonder, considering the difficulty of the task and the fact that we often take the skills required for granted. When they come in the message communication style they resemble the ideal of the relationship style.

How to Talk to Another Person in the Relationship Style

How many times have you heard someone mutter when he is called to by another person, "What does he want *now*?" The tone indicates that previous messages from that particular source have been unpleasant and that the intended listener is not willing to enter into a communicating relationship because of too many bad experiences. Homeostasis is the tendency to preserve things as they are if we are comfortable, and to struggle to get things back into a comfortable state when we are uncomfortable. If you irritate a person, he usually tries to get away from the irritation. All communication in the relationship style is potentially irritating, and sometimes punishing. Communication often upsets the status quo, asks us to rethink our pet ideas and prejudices, challenges our self-image, and questions our habits.

BLOCKS TO COMMUNICATION

Defensiveness

To some extent, all of us adopt a self-protective, wary attitude as we begin to talk with other people. We develop a protective filter through which we hear everything said to us and which strains out meanings that would be too painful for us to admit to our inner selves. The thickness and complexity of the protective filter varies from person to person. Someone who has a good, comfortable feeling about his worth as a person has a relatively large-screen filter. A person whose self-image has been damaged by the problems of life has a fine-screen filter. Rarely is a person so mature and clear-eyed in his self-awareness that he is able to tell you what all his filters are. Most of us have some degree of self-knowledge, but most of us need to work at becoming more aware of the way we distort our interpretations of messages because of such protective devices. As instructors in colleges and universities who try to tell students about their various inadequacies in communication skills so that they can begin to improve themselves, we have had abundant opportunities to watch the fascinating operation of protective filters and the defensive communication that results. An instructor criticizes a student's speech in the public-speaking style, first pointing out that certain aspects were good. The student accepts this praise without flinching. Next the instructor criticizes the content and organization of the speech and the articulation of the student. The student immediately says he was nervous, that he was well prepared and had much good information, but forgot it because he was nervous.

If the student was well prepared, he should not have forgotten, the instructor persists. The student then says he is working 20 hours a week, had to stay up until three o'clock in the morning to get the speech ready, and was therefore tired and could not do a good job. No matter how the instructor tries to convey the idea that the student has certain inadequacies in his ability to communicate that can be overcome by coaching and practice, the student meets each attempt with an excuse or an explanation that blames the problem on something other than his own inabilities. More than likely as he leaves the conference, the student thinks to himself, "That instructor just does not like me. Why do I always end up with instructors who pick on me because they do not like me?"

Self-Centeredness

Everyone has a sense of self. Our image of ourselves is important to our mental and emotional health. Our self-image is modified as we go through life, certainly, but it can change somewhat even from hour to hour, depending on our experiences. As you will learn in the next two chapters about small group interaction, a person's behavior is always affected to some extent by those with whom he happens to be. This is just as true in two-person interpersonal communication as it is in groups.

Some students become upset because when they learn to be more analytical about their communicating behavior, they discover that they communicate differently with different people; they wonder, "When am I acting, and when am I the real me?" The answer is that two-person interaction is dynamic. Communication involves two complex human beings and you are a different person, to some degree, when you interact with a different listener. This is not hypocrisy, as some students fear; it is simply normal human adjustment to a complex part of human behavior. It is still valid taking into consideration the many variations we all experience, to call that general feeling we have about ourselves our self-image.

We all search messages to determine what they mean in terms of our self-image. Because of this natural protective response, when interpreting a message, the listener often reads into the words meanings that have to do with himself as a person. Is the other person saying or implying something about me? Is he saying that he likes me? That he dislikes me? That he respects me? Values my work? Thinks my work is mediocre? Thinks that I'm attractive? That he wants to know me better? A lot of questions about *me as a person* intrude into my interpretation of the other person's words.

The communicator is often as preoccupied with himself as the listener is with himself, and therefore the speaker puts his own excuses, explanations, interests, biases, and prejudices into the message. The speaker may be wondering about the impression his communication is making. Does the listener find me attractive, interesting, and competent? Does he see the depth of my feeling? The great humor in my personality? Little wonder that the moments of glimpsing the other person's inner self in the course of our conversations come as seldom as they do. Learning to be meaning-centered is a first step beyond the natural self-centeredness we all bring to communication interaction. Learning further to be listener-centered is an art requiring constant awareness and practice on the part of any person communicating in the relationship style.

The Eight Images in a Two-Person Conversation

In a given communication event involving two people, the way they perceive one another is as important in their conversation as the way they see themselves. Let us take a situation in which John is talking with Mary. John has an image of himself which influences his manner and approach to the communication; John also has an image of Mary; John further has a dream image of the way he wishes Mary would see him; and finally, John has an estimate of the way Mary really does view him. Mary, likewise, has a set of images which mirror those of John. She has a self-image, an image of John, an image of herself which she wishes John to have, and an estimate of the way John does view her. Each person, thus, has four images of important selves involved in the conversation. If the four images of John and the four of Mary are more or less alike, they can talk in a relaxed and trustful way. You might call this an ideal basis for good two-person communication.

Much communication takes place, however, with one or more of the images in conflict. We will illustrate several possibilities leading to conflict—there are many more, of course—and suggest that you try to see what other images might be out of phase and what other communication difficulties are likely to follow. When John's self-image is much less attractive than the impression he wants Mary to have of him, he may overdo everything because he feels inadequate. He may talk too much, drive his car too fast, and generally come across as overbearing. If John thinks Mary has an attractive image of him as a handsome, brilliant, witty fellow, whereas she really thinks he is plain, dumb, and boring, John will have trouble talking with Mary. Mary's internal response may be, "Brother, does he think *he's* God's gift to women!"

IMPROVING COMMUNICATION
IN THE RELATIONSHIP STYLE

Most freshmen and sophomores in college are, according to one thoughtful war-veteran student, at about the worst time of life in regard to knowing who they are, what kind of a person they hope to be, what their self-image really is. "When I was 16 I had all the answers," he went on to say. "When I was 18 I had a different bunch of answers. Now I've been around the world and back, I'm 21 years old, and I know less now than I used to, about me, other people, life, you name it." To ask you, particularly if you are in the usual age group of college freshmen and sophomores, to try to figure out what your self-image is and to keep it in mind when communicating with others, is a big order. Learning to know yourself is a lifetime job, but there is no better place than college to start a more sophisticated, systematic examination of yourself and the way you respond. Many college courses have the examination of one's self as the not-so-hidden item on their agenda. Certainly any course in interpersonal communication must include this probing of one's own basic reactions to life, to situations, and most of all, to people.

Self-Disclosure

One way to improve the agreement among the various images involved in a conversation is to open oneself up to the other person. We call the revealing of self the process of *self-disclosure*. We know certain things about ourselves, and sometimes we disclose some of these things to another, and sometimes we decide to hide them. Often we hide the unpleasant truths about ourselves to protect the image we want the other person to have of us. We fear the truth will keep us from gaining the liking and respect of the listener. Oddly enough, there are some things about ourselves that we do not know. We may not know, for example, about our little nonverbal mannerisms that disturb other people when we speak. We often do not know what someone else may have told the listener about us.

When two people talk with each other, therefore, they both know some things about each other. When they share much the same information about themselves and one another, their communication is easier and their talk tends to be free and less protective. Communication becomes protective and less open when one person knows something about the other that is unknown to him, or when one person knows something about himself that is unknown to the other. Take the first instance: Bill knows that Harry has damaged his knee

cartilage to the extent that he will never be able to play football again, but Harry does not know his injury is permanent
and will partially disable him for life. What Bill knows and
Harry does not know makes it difficult for the two of them to
have a free and open talk about Harry's future as a professional athlete. Take the second instance: Mary knows something about herself that Ann does not know. Mary knows she
is an alcoholic who has controlled her drinking problem
through membership in Alcoholics Anonymous. As Mary and
Ann discuss plans for a party, the hidden fact of Mary's al-
coholism means her communication is always, to some extent, protective.

When a high level of communication is desirable between
two people, the goal of both should be the widening of the
area of what they both know about one another. Self-
disclosure is the technique for such widening or sharing of
inner experiences.

Supportiveness

How does one go about creating a communication climate in
which self-disclosure is possible, even encouraged? Psychologist Carl Rogers, working as a clinical therapist with patients
who had mental and emotional problems, developed a technique of counseling which he called nondirective. He did not
lead or direct the patients in their conversations with him;
rather, he encouraged them to pour out things in a free, uncri-
tical, nonjudgmental atmosphere. He learned how to build
trust between the patient and himself so that the patient
came to know he could say anything he wished and not be
punished for saying it. What Rogers began as a therapy technique, he and others have now modified into a general
technique for working with normal people to improve communication. The heart of the humanistic approach in psychology is to release the human potential within individuals by
eliminating the threatening, critical, evaluative communication which brings out a listener's protective filters and
produces defensive or counter-threatening messages, and by
using, instead, supportive comments to encourage honest discussion.

Because of the manner in which many Americans have
come to communicate with one another, we can say that
most of us need to develop skills in being consciously supportive of others in those moments of deep and serious talk that
are so important to us. We tend to leave things unsaid, to drift
through our conversations leaving many loose ends. Through
sheer bad habit we often knock the props out from under one

another without meaning to do so and sometimes without even knowing that we have done so. One of our friends who lived in the Middle East for a decade commented, upon returning to live in the United States, that she was more than ever impressed with the coldness and reserve with which we interact socially. "We touch so seldom," she said. "We seem to fear getting personal when people don't want us to, so we stop talking just when people in the Middle East would begin to open up and really help one another. When something really bothers Americans, we tend to clam up." Her comments apply more to the Scandinavian, North European heritage of many people in the Upper Midwest where the authors now live, than to many other groups of people in our complex, pluralistic society; nevertheless, what she said is true of many subcultures in our country.

The feeling of estrangement which our neighbor found inhibiting upon her return to the United States is sometimes called *alienation*. Today many people feel alienated. All of us are handling more sensory stimuli, in the form of messages, sounds, and emotional assaults, every single day, than our ancestors had to handle in a week or more. Much of our interaction grows impersonal because we simply cannot devote our full attention to every new person we meet, every conversation we take part in, and every message we hear on radio or see on television.

Our feeling of alienation is increased by the impersonality of urban life. When several generations of a large family live together or nearby, as they may in a small town and as they did a generation ago in the inner-city ethnic communities, there is a feeling of belonging, of having many people who care how you are, how you behave, what you do, and what happens to you. Today, our mobility from place to place, class to class, group to group has resulted in a loss of the feeling of community. The burden of providing the feeling of closeness and belonging has been placed on the nuclear family. One father and one mother are supposed to give each other and their children all the warmth, support, love, and care each needs. The rising divorce rate is one result. When, for any number of reasons, the family is not able to fill our need for close and important human relationships, we go out into the world somewhat crippled in our ability to interact and communicate with others. We fail to be warm and supportive; others, in turn, fail to be warm and supportive to us. People close emotional doors, begin to turn away, and do not care about one another.

Mutually supportive communication between two people

is extremely difficult; certainly the degree of maturity each has attained influences its success. The strain caused by the demand that all the supportive human interaction each of us craves must come from just one other person has led to the development of life styles other than the traditional nuclear family. These experimental communes, trial marriages, and multimarriages attest to the difficulties involved when two people interact; many of these experimental life styles are attempts to broaden the bases for supportive communication, or in the case of the trial marriage, to acknowledge the possible difficulty of developing a continuing relationship and to give both parties an option to stop it without the traditional proceedings of divorce. Despite the development of these new life styles, the majority of Americans plan to marry, and the requirements for sustaining a supportive dyadic (two-person) relationship are important for most of us. And to a lesser degree than is necessary in marriage, all of us are involved in two-person relationships with family members, good friends, and co-workers.

If we can learn to communicate accurately and meaningfully with those around us, we will find that our skill in human relations is greatly improved. Much of what people feel about us is related to the way we communicate with them. People who make us feel good, we tend to like. People who make us angry or depressed, we tend to avoid. The more genuinely supportive communication we learn to give to others, the more we are liked. If we remember that the other fellow wants to be talked to as a worthwhile person, we are more likely to be successful communicators. Even if the other person misunderstands us, if we have made clear, verbally and nonverbally, that he is a person we value, he is more likely to mention his confusion, to voice his doubts, and generally to disclose his real response to us, often leading to better understanding. Once trust has been established, even unpleasant communication can take place—not without discomfort, of course, but with a feeling of mutual respect.

We believe that good communication must be based on trust—which is not to be confused with liking, necessarily. Initially we all learn basic communication habits from our own families. If the early examples we use as communication models are good, our chances of being effective communicators are increased. If our parents relate well verbally with each other, they also probably communicated pretty well with us. When the person you should be able to trust most of all, your parent, or if you are married, your wife or husband, lets you down, the experience is a terrible instance of taking an important risk and being punished because of it. If for no other reason than to learn what is supportive and what is damaging in the interpersonal communication within your immediate family and circle of friends, you should begin to build a good understanding of healthy communication and learn how to create good interpersonal relationships with free and open discussions. In his play *Hamlet*, Shakespeare urged actors to suit their actions to the words of a play. The advice is good for real-life interpersonal communication as well as for successful acting. If you say one thing and do another, you set up contradictory responses that cause misunderstandings. If you say yes and then do as you say you will, you build trust. If you say "love" and act "hate," you set up discord. In Chapter 4 we saw the potential for psychological damage in the two-edged message.

Exposing the Hidden Agenda

Some communication problems come about simply because people avoid talking about what really bothers them. In these instances, people often pretend that when they talk with one another, they are primarily interested in discussing facts, events, and "business." Suppose a teacher and a student have arranged a conference to talk over the student's courses for the coming term. The stated object of the talk is to find out about hours, requirements, and scheduling. To be sure, the topics are important and of concern to both teacher and student. Of equal importance to both, however, are some questions about *self*, and these questions have not been stated. The student may feel isolated and alone in the new environment of the college. He may have liked the teacher's course he took the previous term, and he may have found the teacher an interesting, reassuring person. A personal problem is troubling him greatly: His father has always wanted him to become a lawyer, and he has now decided he does not want to study law. He would like to talk to the teacher about this.

The instructor also has some personal interests he would like to talk about with the student. He has taught the course the student has just completed in a different way, and he would like to have the student's opinion of the course. He has some new projects in mind and would like to ask the student's opinion about them.

Because the stated object of the meeting is to talk about the student's next-term courses, both the student and the instructor feel a certain pressure to stick to the stated business. The conference could very well end with neither of them discussing their more important concerns. We speak of the stated business of a conference (interview, meeting, committee session) as the *agenda*. The agenda of the student and teacher we have been discussing concerns what courses the student should take next term. When people talk, they often have hidden items on their agendas. In this example, the student's hidden item was his career problem, and the instructor's hidden item was the student's reaction to the course just finished. Often, bringing what speech people usually call the *hidden agenda* into the open through the process of self-disclosure is a good way to improve communication. The responsibility of centering communication interaction on the subject you really want to talk about is *yours*. If you wonder why the other person is acting and talking in unexpected ways, and you sense some hidden agenda item, our advice is simple: *Ask*.

Providing Feedback

Much talking that passes for communication is merely people talking *at* other people, because the speaker and the listener demand neither feedback nor clarification. One of the surprising discoveries of people who study communication in the relationship style is that so many people are so poor at providing and interpreting feedback to aid understanding.

Several important factors operate in two-person communication to keep people from providing the essential feedback. One is the mistaken notion that talking with another person is a simple matter. After all, we reason, we have proba-

bly spent more of our total communication time in such two-person talks than in any other form of communication. We ought to be good at it by now, we tell ourselves. Besides the fact that we take such interaction for granted, the situation itself is often informal and relaxed and makes talking seem much less difficult than giving a good formal speech to an auditorium full of people. When we do misunderstand something in an informal conversation, we often blame our failure to find out more on some inherent trait of the other person or some factor beyond our control: "I guess George didn't hear me," or "We were interrupted about then, and I guess it wasn't clear," or, "I don't know what it is about Lorraine, but she just never can get anything straight."

Another factor that operates to prevent feedback is our assumption that our first attempt to tell another person something has succeeded. We often interpret silence as understanding and acceptance. We even interpret mumbling or other unclear answers as acceptance. Actually, our first attempt to communicate is *likely to fail*. The more completely we have failed, the more likely it is that the listener will greet the communication with silence. Silence itself often should be interpreted as feedback indicating not that the other person understands or agrees with you, but rather that he is confused. If you give a directive to someone else, particularly if you are in a position of authority, you should be as suspicious of a simple yes answer as you are of silence. When a policeman has been called to an apartment because of a domestic argument and he "lays down the law" to the couple and then demands of them, "Now, is that clear?" what can their answer be but, "Yes." As one young policeman said in class, "And then I had to go back five nights later and spell it out again." He was disgusted, until he realized that he had left little opening for the couple to express their real failure to understand his advice and their refusal to appreciate the need for working out their problems in some way that would not disturb their neighbors at four o'clock in the morning.

An additional factor in poor feedback is concern for protecting the self. We have discussed protective and defensive communication at length. One of the important effects of the need to defend self is unwillingness to reveal lack of information, know-how, understanding, or skill by providing feedback. We have to learn to be comfortable admitting what we do not know in any situation.

A final factor in poor feedback in the relationship style is lack of skill. Watch a television play or go to the theater, and watch the actors who are *not* speaking at any given moment.

The good performers are acting every minute, reacting to what the speaker is saying, responding nonverbally, *communicating* to the audience what they understand and how they feel about what another character is saying or doing. A good communicator does much the same thing when listening to another person; he responds in such a way that the speaker can see and hear and understand his response.

The Importance of Privacy
We have stressed throughout this chapter the need for self-disclosure to build trust, because too often, the importance of the *relationship* between two people trying to talk with one another is overlooked. The need for openness and trust is, without question, great. We do not want to leave the impression, however, that maximum self-disclosure, honesty, and openness are desirable at all times and under all circumstances in every communication situation and in every style. The thrust toward instant trust is, we feel, being misunderstood and misused by many people. There *are* limits to what we need to tell others about ourselves. Psychiatrists trying to help mentally ill people rebuild a good enough self-image to get by in the world day by day, find themselves not only allowing people to keep certain inhibitions, certain established ways of responding to life, but encouraging them to rebuild many of the defenses they found fairly useful before becoming ill. While not all the defenses these people had constructed could be considered good or even desirable, some of the defenses enabled the people to get along. To some extent, all of us have built into our personality structure defenses which enable us to face life. These defenses are there for a reason, and anyone working to break them down had best be prepared to provide replacements or face trouble.

Many people do not care to go about belaboring the world with their innermost thoughts and feelings, and these people should have the right to keep whatever they want to themselves. Few of us who have passed through adolescence do not remember at least one painful truth session with "a good friend," who, after telling us all our faults, assured us that "it was for our own good," and left us hanging emotionally, wondering if that was what all our friends thought of us!

Good communication in the relationship style, we feel, requires restraints and respect, as well as, on occasion, self-disclosure. Part of the trust needed in supportive communication comes from knowing that when we are interacting with a person, he will *stop short of hitting below the belt*. He knows the limits of privacy set by me, and he

When a person expresses himself he gives vent to feelings or ideas and has no interest in arousing common meanings in listeners.

While self-expression may be artless, communication always requires some artistry.

Two-person communication in the message communication style provides ideal conditions for close-range, continuous feedback.

The opportunity for high-fidelity communication in the message style is greatest in the two-person situation.

We are islands of consciousness and cannot really break out of the boundaries of self to experience directly another person's meanings.

Our interior world is changing, shifting, dynamic; the language we use to encode our meanings, however, is static.

The encoding of messages is an art that can be learned.

The English language is a particularly rich and powerful tool for communication.

Admitting ignorance is a vital key to pro-

respects them. The wife who tells her husband's secret worry to outsiders is headed for real trouble; so is the husband who repeatedly reminds his wife about her worst habit. This sort of communication hurts and is extremely destructive to the relationship between two people. There are limits in good interpersonal communication, and they are drawn just at that point where we take a swipe at the underpinnings of the personality of the other person.

Differences must be talked out, and verbal battles are useful when they serve the purpose of clearing the air. Verbal battles fought within agreed-upon limits can be useful, even fun, when they help dissipate the natural hostilities generated in any close relationship. Nonetheless, when two people want to maintain good communication, they both have to know where to draw the line. Naturally, as a relationship deepens,

viding feedback for improved communication.

Listeners often read into messages the meanings that fit their personal biases and interests.

Communication in the relationship style is potentially irritating and sometimes punishing.

We all search messages with an eye to what they mean to us personally and, particularly, what they mean in terms of our self-image.

The way two people see one another is as important to their conversation as the way they see themselves.

Self-disclosure increases what two people know about one another and thus increases the possibility of high-level communication.

Threatening, critical, evaluative communication brings out a person's protective filters and produces defensive communication.

Deep and serious talk in the relationship style requires consciously supportive communication.

Through bad communication habits we often knock the props out from under one another without meaning to.

Once trust has been established between two people, even unpleasant things can be discussed openly—not without discomfort, but with a feeling of mutual respect.

Some communication problems come about simply because people avoid talking about what really bothers them.

Often bringing the hidden agenda of a conference into the open through self-disclosure is a good way to improve communication.

Many people are unskilled at providing or interpreting feedback in the relationship style.

Our first attempt to communicate with another person is likely to fail.

Silence should usually be interpreted as feedback telling the speaker the other person is confused.

Maximum self-disclosure, honesty, and openness are not desirable at all times and under all circumstances.

Each of us has limits of privacy which no other human being should ever cross.

each can push the line back a little from time to time, but no matter how close any two people become, each has privacy limits across which no other human should ever intrude.

Airing Grievances
Within a personal relationship with any other person, however, while respecting the limits which he or she places on inner privacy, it is still important to express your feelings openly, to be honest about the times when you are hurt or angry. When even the smallest grievance is swallowed, one swallowed word may be added to another, until after a while, the load becomes too heavy. Then, when you simply cannot carry those unsaid words around any longer, you will find them tumbling out for almost no reason whatsoever, accusation upon accusation, explosive emotional charges that will

strain any relationship. Keeping things to oneself causes inner tension, and when things are left unsaid between two people, at least one of those people is aware of it, if not both. Moreover, the person who is the object of a grudge often fears unspoken words far more than he or she should, imagining them to be far worse than they actually are.

When one of your authors was teaching interpersonal communication for the first time, one of our teen-agers picked up the textbook she was using. She seized the notion of "gunny-sacking" (carrying all your grudges around with you until you unload them on someone inappropriately) and delighted in accusing her mother of doing just that "all the time!" "But that's the point," her mother said. "Since I do it all the time, that's not gunny-sacking." "Yeah," our daughter replied, momentarily resigned, since there had just been one of those mother-daughter "and another thing . . . " sessions; "I guess what you always do to me is more like sand-bagging."

Relationship communication must be based on openness, trust, a sharing of authentic selves, enough empathy so that you withhold judgment when another person is expressing his feelings, even if they upset you, an ability to allow other people to grow and mature even if you feel them slipping ahead of you. We wear the lightest reins most easily. If you have sufficient maturity to let those with whom you communicate in close relationships grow, then you will grow with them. Respecting the self you also want respected, you work all the time to keep the channels of communication open between you and those you care most about.

Not too long ago there was a movie with a line that was often repeated; it upset us that it seemed to catch the fancy of so many. It was "Love means never having to say you're sorry." We would rewrite that line in terms of relationship communication, which is, at many different levels, a close and loving, supportive bond: "Love means always being able to say, and mean, 'I'm sorry.'" Better yet, a truly supportive communication relation between two people can tolerate success and share joy. If the best thing life has to offer is a truly delightful relationship with another human being—and we believe it is—relationship-style communication skills are very worthwhile indeed.

SUGGESTED PROJECTS

1 This is a job interview project. The instructor may have interviewers come from companies in the community and conduct simulated job interviews with some or all of the students individually in front of the class. (Many businesses consider a request for

an interviewer excellent public relations. If local businessmen are not available, a fairly realistic situation can be created if the college's personnel officer will interview for student employment, or if the school newspaper editor will interview prospective reporters, ad solicitors, or business managers.) If no outside interviewers are available, the class can be divided into pairs, with one student playing the role of interviewer while the other presents himself or herself as the job applicant. Roles can then be reversed. Our students often make the simulated job one they are actually hoping to qualify for in the future, so that the role they play is meaningful and a rehearsal of things to come. If possible, the interviewers should be video- or audio-taped, so that each student can evaluate his or her own communication skill as a job applicant. If the instructor and the viewing class members write critiques of the interview while it is taking place, the student can compare his own appraisal, which he makes from the tape recording, with the comments of his peers and instructor, and write a short paper evaluating his performance.

2 The class is divided into pairs. One person in each pair selects an important idea or process to explain to the other. The idea should be something that the first person knows from a course he has taken or from a personal experience he has had but the second person has not. The first person acts as a message source and tries to explain the idea or process to the other. The second person concentrates on providing feedback, both verbal and nonverbal, to the first. The second person can only ask these three questions: "What do you mean?" "How do you know?" and "So what?" at the appropriate times.

3 Write a brief paper describing an instance when you became thoroughly angry with someone and could not communicate your anger to him. What happened? Why couldn't you communicate it? (Was the person someone you feared or someone who had some power over you that you feared?) Do you think that if you could have communicated your anger and brought it out into the open it would have helped? How?

SUGGESTED READINGS

Giffin, Kim, and Bobby R. Patton. *Basic Readings in Interpersonal Communication*. New York: Harper & Row, 1971.

Goffman, Erving. *The Presentation of Self in Everyday Life*. Garden City, N.Y.: Doubleday (Anchor Books), 1959.

Jourard, Sidney M. *The Transparent Self*. New York: Van Nostrand, 1967.

Keltner, John W. *Interpersonal Speech-Communication: Elements and Structures*. Belmont, Calif.: Wadsworth, 1970.

Matson, Floyd W., and Ashley Montague (eds.). *The Human Dialogue: Perspectives on Communication*. New York: Free Press, 1967.

Rogers, Carl. *On Becoming a Person*. Boston: Houghton Mifflin, 1961.

Chapter 15

HOW TO COMMUNICATE IN GROUP DISCUSSIONS

Both the relationship communication style and the message communication style occur in group sessions. Sensitivity training groups and encounter groups require the presence of a facilitator to teach appropriate styles of communication to the participants. Aside from the general theoretical discussion that you have found throughout the book, there is little more that can be said about group communication in the relationship style in an introductory way. You will need the training that comes from participation in a given group under the coaching of a trainer to understand the fine points of the style. Even then, details vary from group to group, and from trainer to trainer.

Our emphasis in this chapter and the next will be upon the task-oriented small group, which is conducted for the most part in our culture in the message communication style. As a student, you probably attend many message-communication group meetings in our society. A student may be a member of an athletic team or club, a neighborhood or street gang, a fraternity or sorority, a Young Americans for Freedom club, a student socialist group, a departmental association, or a student cooperative. A student may attend meetings of committees for student government, dormitory groups, student unions, religious foundations, and increasingly, of special groups to prepare projects for class.

In addition to performing duties for an immediate work group on the job, a person who works for a store, a factory, a service industry, or a government agency such as a police force or fire department, attends committee meetings, union meetings, and work group sessions. Off the job, a typical citizen takes part in religious groups, political organizations, or groups for other community and voluntary purposes.

Every project to get things done requires working with small groups in the message communication style. If we wish to change our neighborhoods and organize for community power or political power at another level, we must work productively with others in groups.

Despite the importance of working with small groups, most of us take our role in a discussion for granted. Few people have a chance to study group discussion or drill in the techniques of group work in order to become professional communicators in the message communication style in the small group setting. However, one of the best ways to ensure that the group meetings you attend in the future will be useful and that you will feel satisfied about your contribution to them is to study small group communication and evaluate critically the dynamics of the meetings you attend.

Group Discussion

Group discussion refers to one or more meetings of a small number of people who communicate face to face in order to fulfill a common purpose and achieve a common goal.

The small group is an identifiable social entity. Authorities differ on details relating to the size of a small group, but the general features are agreed upon. The communication networks and personal relationships that develop while people hold a discussion change when the size of a group is increased, and these changes can be used to describe the "small" group. When a third person is added to a two-person interview, the nature of the working relationships and the flow of communication change; thus a small group is composed of at least three people. The upper size limit of the small group is more difficult to specify. However, when the

group becomes so large that it begins to change its patterns of communication, it should no longer be considered a small group. In groups of five or less, all members speak to one another. Even those who speak little talk to all the others. In groups of seven or more, the quiet members often cease to talk to any but the top people in the group. As groups become even larger, the talk centralizes more and more around a few people; group interaction falls off. In groups of thirteen or more, from five to seven people hold the discussion while the others watch and listen.

The best size for a group discussion is probably five. Members of groups with fewer than five people complain that their groups are too small and suffer from a lack of diversity of opinion and skill. Groups composed of even numbers of people tend to be less stable and rewarding than groups of odd numbers. A group of five or seven works better than a group of four, six, or eight. On learning this, many people have said, when analyzing unproductive groups they have been in, "Well, that was our first mistake! There were ten of us."

FUNCTIONS OF WORK GROUPS

A discussion group in our culture is a special transactional form of the work group. Work groups use several different sorts of meetings. If the members come to the meeting with the wrong idea about what the meeting is for and what it will be like, they may be frustrated. For example, if the meeting is just a ceremony to rubber-stamp decisions already made and a member comes expecting to change the decision, he feels cheated.

Every organization has some meetings that are rituals. A ritual is a set ceremony that has come to be expected at certain times to celebrate an organization or group. In a meeting that is a ritual people may say one thing and mean another. Some religious rituals contain prayers which the worshipers repeat over and over again, and the meaning of the prayers as expressed in the words is not as important to the worshipers or to the ritual as the act of saying the words over and over again. The ritual meetings of an organization may aid its cohesiveness, or ability to stick together, and ensure that people in authority are recognized. For example, the department heads of a business organization may make an oral presentation of their yearly budgets at a meeting of all the vice-presidents. The meeting is really meant only to rubber-stamp decisions already made. Yet the meeting is important to the others in the business. The newcomer who says that the meeting accomplishes nothing and is therefore a waste of time is judging it on the wrong grounds.

Another kind of meeting is the briefing session, used to give members information they need to carry through on plans already made. The objective of the group is clear: The members know what they want to do and need only find out who is to do what, when, and where.

A group discussion may also have the purpose of instructing participants in some concepts or skills they can use in the future. Teachers may use small discussion groups to teach a course in English literature, for example, by dividing up the class and having each group discuss a novel.

A small discussion group may meet to advise the person or persons empowered to make decisions. The person in charge consults or asks the advice of the people in the meeting. A department head at a college or university might ask a committee of students and faculty about changes in course requirements. If the meeting is consultative, the department chairman does not promise to abide by their advice, but does ask for and consider it. The danger in an advice-giving discussion is that if the people who attend may not understand its purposes; they may expect their advice to be accepted and feel cheated when it is not. "We spent all that time making that decision, and then they ignored it."

Finally, an extremely important kind of meeting is one called actually to make the decision. Members of decision-making groups often are more fully committed to their decisions and usually work harder to implement them than do the participants in other kinds of groups. One of the most important functions of small groups in many organizations is to provide a way for people to participate in management decisions and to exercise some of the power relating to the use of the organization's resources.

Characteristics of the One-time Meeting

Students of small group communication must understand not only that a discussion meeting may serve different functions

but also that groups differ in other significant ways. In a group that meets only once, the dynamics of the communication are quite different from those that operate in a group that meets several times. Groups also differ depending on how closely they relate to an organization. A group of students from a speech-communication class is different from a standing committee of the speech department composed of students, teaching assistants, and faculty members.

The one-time discussion group is such an important communication event that it deserves some special attention. The people in a one-time discussion group have not worked together before and are not likely to do so again for the purposes under discussion. Some may have worked with others in similar groups and some may know one another socially, but the particular grouping of these five or six people for this particular purpose has not happened before.

CONTRASTS BETWEEN ONE-TIME AND *AD HOC* GROUPS

The one-time discussion meeting is different from an *ad hoc* committee. *Ad hoc* is a Latin term meaning "for this special purpose." An *ad hoc* committee thus is formed for a special purpose important enough to cause the group to meet for several sessions over a period of weeks or months before it makes its final report. An *ad hoc* committee is also different from the standing (permanent) committees of an organization, which continue for as long as the organization exists. For example, if a political action group has a standing committee for public education, that committee will function as long as the group continues. However, a group of people organize a committee to meet and work for several months for the specific purpose of freeing a political activist who has been jailed, that committee is *ad hoc*.

The one-time meeting is held by people who expect to achieve their purposes in a single meeting. Since its composition is unique, the discussion group has no history, and the people who come to the meeting cannot be guided by past experience with one another in such a discussion. The group holding a one-time meeting has no team spirit, no usual way of doing things, no idea about how the communication and social interaction will proceed.

The first meeting of an *ad hoc* committee is like the one-time meeting in that its members have not previously met together for this particular purpose. But although the *ad hoc* committee has no history, it does have a future. The members will be meeting together for a considerable period of time, and the influence of the future expectations produces some important differences between the first session of an *ad hoc* committee and a one-time meeting.

The group without a history but with a future is under pressure to test potential leaders and other possibly important members, to develop a common way of doing things, to take nothing at face value, and to check reputations, formal status, and assigned structures before accepting them.

One of the most important things about the one-time meeting is the willingness of the participants to accept leadership. Whether the person calling the meeting is a self-appointed moderator or has been assigned to lead the meeting by some organizational unit, the members are likely to accept and appreciate guidance from that individual. The group needs quick help in getting started. Members realize they have little time to waste and tend to accept with little argument the leader's description of goals and his method of getting on with the meeting.

Participants in one-time meetings tend to use any information they have to help form an impression of their fellow committee members. If students in a speech-communication class meet to plan something and discover that one member is majoring in elementary education, another is the president of the freshman class, a third was a beauty contest winner, and so on, they use such information to help them structure their meeting.

Once the discussion is under way, those members who do not hold positions of stature, or who are not known by reputation, tend to be quickly stereotyped. The stereotyping that takes place in the one-time meeting comes from first impressions. Each person makes a quick judgment about every other member and, thus, a person who does not speak for 15 or 20 minutes may be stereotyped as quiet, shy, apathetic, or uninterested and be dismissed as unimportant. Another, who speaks loudly, expresses strong opinions, and makes flat judgments may be stereotyped as bossy or pushy.

The people in a one-time meeting take shortcuts to structure their group into a pecking order, so they can get on with the business at hand. They are willing to risk getting a wrong impression because they are pressed for time and often because they think the purpose of the one-time meeting is less important than that of a discussion group that meets repeatedly.

Members of one-time meetings tend to accept a stereotyped picture of how a meeting should be run. A newly formed group that plans to meet for many sessions works out its own unique ways of getting the job done, but the one-time meeting does not allow enough time to do this. The accepted picture of how a small group meeting should be conducted—the transactional norms which most North Americans come to accept by the time they reach college—includes the idea that there should be a moderator, leader, or (depending upon how authoritarian the leadership style is to be) and a secretary or recorder.

The moderator, leader, or presiding officer of a one-time meeting is expected to attend to the administrative details of setting up the meeting place, planning the agenda, sending out preliminary information, and scheduling the meeting.

Planning the One-time Meeting

If you are assigned the duty of moderating, leading, or chairing a one-time meeting, you ought to do the following things in the planning stage:

1 Determine the purpose of the meeting. Every one-time meeting should have a clear and specific purpose. Make sure the other members know the purpose of the meeting either before it starts or early in the session. You should also make the type of meeting clear to the members: Is the meeting for briefing, instructing, consulting, or decision making?

2 Plan the meeting to achieve the purpose. You should ask such questions as: Where is the best place to hold the meeting? What format will best achieve the purpose? Who should take part in the meeting? Should people with special knowledge be invited? Should some high-status people be invited?

3 Plan the little details. A successful one-time meeting requires time and effort in the planning stages. Do not neglect the small details. If you do, you may save a bit of your own time, but wasting the time of your colleagues in a useless meeting is not wise. Little things such as providing pads and pencils, refreshments, properly arranged (and enough) seating all contribute to the success of the meeting. When minor details of administration are handled smoothly, people feel the meeting is important and is going to do significant work.

4 Specify the outcomes of the meeting. Making the outcomes clear is not the same as deciding on the purposes. If plans are to be made, how will they be developed? In detail?

In general outline? Decide what decisions can be made in such a meeting and in what form they should be made.

5 Utilize the results of the meeting. What can be done to follow up and apply the results? Do not let important leads drop at the end of the meeting.

Leading the One-time Meeting

During the course of the meeting the assigned (or elected) chairman is expected to lead the discussion. The chairman's duties are commonly understood to include the following:

A. Chairman's duties in regard to the task
1. Start the meeting
2. Act as pilot to keep the group on course, remind members of the discussion outline, cut short those who wander too far from the outline
3. Help the group arrive at decisions (take votes when necessary)
4. Provide transitions from topic to topic
5. Summarize what the group has accomplished
6. Control the channels of communication to ensure that everybody has a chance to talk and that all sides get a fair hearing; encourage the quiet members to take part and discourage the too-talkative ones
B. Chairman's duties in regard to human relations
1. Introduce members to one another
2. Help break the ice at the start and relax people so they can get down to business
3. Release tensions and bad feelings that come from disagreements and conflicts of personality or opinion

TECHNIQUES FOR LEADING THE ONE-TIME MEETING
Assuming the willingness of participants to follow his or her direction, the leader still needs certain basic skills to conduct an efficient meeting. The three basic techniques for this purpose are the question, the summary, and the directive. Summaries are always useful to indicate progress and to orient the group. The democratic style requires more questions than directives; the authoritarian style, more directives than questions.

The first task is to get the group down to business. A certain amount of time should be devoted to getting acquainted, but then the group must go to work. Questions are useful, especially open-ended questions asked in such a way that they cannot be answered with a simple yes or no. An open-ended question can get things started. Early in the meeting, the leader should set the mood for short, to-the-point comments. If the first comment runs too long, the leader may have to interrupt with a question directed to someone else.

The leader needs to watch carefully and make running choices about the drift of the discussion. Is it part of the necessary kicking around of an idea? He or she should not take the easy way out and make the choice strictly according to the agenda. When he decides the discussion is wasting time, he should bring the meeting back to the agenda. Questions are most useful for this: "Can we tie this in with the point about rules in the student union?" "Just a minute; how does this relate to grading procedures?" Summaries can give an overview of the past few minutes of the meeting and bring the group back to the agenda. Finally, a leader may simply assert that the discussion off the track and direct that the group get back: "We seem to be getting off the subject. Let's get back to Bill's point."

The moderator should not push the group too fast; on the other hand, devoting 20 minutes to material that deserves only 5 produces restlessness and frustration. The leader should watch for signs that a topic has been exhausted. If members begin to repeat themselves, fidget, pause for lack of something to say, the leader should move to the next item. The summary is the best way to do so. A summary rounds off the discussion of one point and leads naturally to a new one. It also gives the group a feeling of accomplishment.

From time to time the group needs to make decisions. The leader can help by stepping in at those times and asking, "Are we in substantial agreement on this point?" If the question is important, he or she may call for a vote.

Often some tension-producing behavior creates an awkward moment for the leader and the participants. What we offer here are some hints about how to handle the awkward situation immediately when it crops up in a meeting. One common difficulty for the moderator is the member who talks too much. The leader may break into a long comment by an overtalkative person with a yes-no question and then quickly direct another question to someone else:

LEADER: *Just a minute, Joe; would you be willing to drop that course from the requirements for a major?*

JOE: *Now, I didn't say . . .*

LEADER: *I just want to be clear on this. Would you be in favor of that?*

JOE: *Well, no, but . . .*

LEADER: *Bill, I wonder how you feel about this?*

Sometimes the leader can stop the talkative member by asking for specific information. Interrupting him for a summary is another technique. He or she can conclude the summary by directing a question to someone else. People usually sit back for a summary. Sometimes the leader simply has to say, "I'm going to ask you to stop there for a minute and hold your next comment. Everyone has not had a chance to be heard on this point."

The member who is too quiet also poses problems. The leader should use questions to draw out the quiet members. He or she should ask the nonparticipating person a direct open-ended question, addressing him by name, so that only he can answer. Do not ask a question that can be answered with a yes or no, and, of course, do not ask a question that he might be unable to answer for lack of information. Once he answers, encourage him to elaborate.

Participating in the One-time Meeting

The transactional norms of a one-time meeting do not assign specific roles to any group member except the chairman. All leadership functions are assigned to the moderator, and other members are expected to follow his lead and accept his directions. When the chairman recognizes a person, the others are supposed to respect that decision and not interrupt. When the chairman cuts off discussion on a topic, the others are supposed to accept that decision.

The duties of the participant include the following:

A. Participant's duties in regard to the task
   1. Enter into the discussion with enthusiasm
   2. Have an open-minded, objective attitude
   3. Keep contributions short and to the point
   4. Talk enough but not too much
   5. Speak clearly and listen carefully
B. Participant's duties in regard to social and human relations
   1. Respect the other person
   2. Be well mannered

3. Try to understand the other person's position
4. Do not manipulate or exploit the other person

Of course, the model of how a good one-time meeting should proceed differs considerably from the realities of even a short session. Participants do not all willingly follow the assigned moderator even when they know they should. They are, however, much more likely to do so in a one-time meeting than in the first session of a group that will meet a number of times. People in the more permanent group move strongly in the first meeting to test the assigned leader's abilities.

Even in a short meeting, role differences become apparent. A few people speak more than the others, despite the best efforts of the chairman. Some people are silent. Others are humorous and friendly. The generalized picture of a meeting composed of a chairman and a group of indistinguishable followers soon changes under the pressure of discussion with a common purpose.

The group discussion, even a short one-time meeting, is an extremely complicated event. The addition of a third person (or several more) to the two-person communication situation adds a good deal more than one-third in additional complexity. The general discussion above of how to prepare for, moderate, and participate in the discussion should be viewed in terms of our knowledge of group dynamics.

If, indeed, a small group meeting is such a complicated thing, why do most people think it is easy to assemble a few people, and, in the course of an hour or two, discuss a series of important topics, make a couple of vital decisions, and adjourn in time for the next class?

The main reason for our too-simple approach to groups is that we have a rather clear idea of what we think a meeting ought to be like, and this clouds our perception of what a group, in fact, *can* be like. Many people think a business or committee meeting should be an efficient, no-nonsense affair. The meeting should be well planned. The discussion should follow the agenda. Everybody should say about the same amount and everything they say should be to the point and helpful. The members ought to be involved, eager to participate, good listeners and speakers.

The ideal discussion is largely a fiction seldom encountered in real life. Lest you think our treatment of the one-time discussion reflects only the common stereotype of an ideal discussion, we hasten below to set the record straight. What we have described above are the expectations people commonly have about what moderators and participants should do in preparation for and during a discussion. Below, we describe what, in fact, tends to happen in a discussion.

A Realistic Picture of Small-group Communication

What is a realistic picture of how a good group communicates? Good group communication takes time. Given the complicated communication network that must be developed in a work meeting, we should not expect a group to cover more topics in a two-hour meeting than one person could study and decide about in an hour if he were working alone. Yet we often expect a group to cover as much work in a few hours as one person would be hard put to accomplish in a day. When we ask a group to do more than it can, it either gets bogged down on the first part of the agenda and leaves some business undone or races through the meeting without dealing adequately with anything. As a result, the people who attend come away feeling the meeting was a failure.

THE LIMITED ATTENTION SPAN OF A GROUP

Also unrealistic is the notion that a group can organize its discussion so it keeps to the main ideas and moves in a logical, step-by-step way through a series of topics. Individuals have attention spans measured in minutes, and sometimes in seconds. When we listen, read, or think about something in a logical, step-by-step way, we often find our attention wandering. You may read a paragraph and understand it quite well; then halfway down the next page you realize that while your eyes are moving, your thoughts are on getting a drink or on the date you are going out with later. People who listen to a speech may attend closely to the speaker for a minute or so and then begin to daydream about something else. Even when people puzzle about an important problem or decision, they often find their attention drifting to other subjects.

Groups, like individuals, have short attention spans. Most groups cannot talk about a topic for much more than a minute before someone changes the subject. Sometimes the group wants to change the subject, because it has finished talking about one topic and should move on to another, but quite often the person who changes the topic does so while others still want to consider the original subject. Sometimes the new topic is not relevant to the matter under discussion.

A short attention span for a group meeting is natural and inevitable, and we must work within the limitations it imposes.

Most of what we have said about a group's short attention span comes from research on what members say during meetings. Investigators have studied a group's communication and noted when the group changed topics. Of course, during any given period of time during the meeting, people may or may not be listening to what is being said. Thus the job of holding everybody's attention is probably even more difficult than the evidence, gathered by looking at the content of the messages, indicates.[1]

When several people are fighting for control of the channels of communication or trying to take over the meeting as message sources, they often do not listen to others. Early in a meeting whose participants do not know each other well, a member who wants to make a good impression may try to make a brilliant comment or say something funny. When he has to move out of the limelight, he often does not listen to the next person but thinks about what he will say next.

Clearly, people in small groups have difficulty keeping their attention on an idea so they all can understand it and give their opinions about it. They have trouble chaining together several ideas to get the big picture or see how things relate to one another. Yet if the meeting has work to do, they feel pressure to get on with the job. Participants in a discussion with a purpose do not like the aimless skipping from idea to idea that is common in social conversations. If the group has an outline or an agenda for the meeting, the members will keep looking at the plan, using it to measure how well they are doing. When the discussion leaves the agenda, they often comment that the group is getting off the topic or that much still should be done.

BALANCING FREEDOM AND STRUCTURE

People vary as to how much fooling around they can stand in a meeting. Some are uncomfortable unless the point of the

---

[1] David M. Berg, "A Descriptive Analysis of the Distribution and Duration of Themes Discussed by the Task-oriented Small Group," Ph.D. dissertation, University of Minnesota, 1963; Irene Faffler, "A Cross-Cultural Study of the Task-oriented Small Group in the Middle East," Ph.D. dissertation, University of Minnesota, 1971; Charles U. Larson, "Leadership Emergence and Attention Span: A Content Analysis of the Time Devoted to Themes Discussed in the Task-oriented Small Group," Ph.D. dissertation, University of Minnesota, 1968; Lillian Ryberg, "A Comparative Study of Small Group Discussion in the Native and Target Languages," Ph.D. dissertation, University of Minnesota, 1974.

THE KEY IDEAS

Every organized attempt to get things done in our society requires working with discussion groups.

The small group is an identifiable social entity with its own patterns of interaction.

The best size for a group discussion is probably five members.

Groups composed of even numbers of people tend to be less stable and rewarding than groups of odd numbers.

Every organization has some meetings that are rituals.

Discussions may be used to brief or instruct the participants.

Some group meetings advise the person or persons with the authority to make decisions.

An extremely important kind of meeting is one called actually to make a decision.

People in a group which has no history but which is expected to meet again size each other up very carefully.

meeting is clear and the outline of topics is specific. They want the group to stick to business. Others feel hemmed in by a sticking-to-business approach. They have what seems to them an important or exciting comment, and they want to say it even if it does not relate directly to the topic under discussion.

How does a person organize a discussion in a realistic and yet productive way? At times participants want and need the freedom to suggest ideas and mull them over without worrying too much about how they hang together or how they fit into the agenda. At other times, a group needs and wants to get on with the job and to get things organized. At this point, group members seem to feel they know what they want to do and they are tired of rehashing things that are clear or decided. A leader should be alert to the alternate needs for freewheeling and for structure. Most groups develop a rhythm in regard to when they want to be loose and easy and when they want to get things organized. Careful attention to verbal

The participants in a one-time meeting, with no history and no future, are generally willing to accept assigned leadership.

The people in a one-time meeting take shortcuts to structure their group so they can get on with business.

The moderator of a one-time meeting is expected to attend to the administrative details of setting up the discussion.

During the course of a one-time discussion the moderator is expected to start the meeting, make transitions, summarize, take votes, and generally guide the group.

The participant in a one-time discussion is expected to follow the moderator's lead, enter into the discussion with enthusiasm, and stick to the point.

The main reason many people get upset with meetings is that they have a clear, simple, and impossible ideal for a good discussion.

The ideal discussion is seldom encountered in real life.

Groups, like individuals, have short attention spans.

When several people are fighting for control of the channels of communication, they often do not listen to one another.

Members in discussions have trouble chaining ideas together and getting an overall picture of the topic they are discussing.

People vary as to how much fooling around they can tolerate in a meeting.

At times, particularly early in a discussion, participants want and need the freedom to introduce ideas and mull them over without worrying too much about sticking to an agenda.

Later in a discussion, participants want some structure to organize their work.

Decisions tend to emerge from group discussions rather than being carefully discussed, and voted upon.

and nonverbal cues can help the leader decide about any given group. For example, members of a group may display frustration when the chairman reminds them their discussion is off the topic. A person may accept the suggestion that his comment is out of order in a grumpy fashion, sitting back in his chair and frowning. Another person may say, "I don't want to make a motion or ask for a decision, but I would like to throw out a few ideas and see what you think of them before we get down to business." When, as a leader, you see gestures or hear comments expressing the desire for less concern with the agenda or with structure, you should go along with the group members and give them a chance to kick ideas around.

Other verbal and nonverbal cues indicate that the group wants more structure. A member may look at his watch, shift in his seat, and let his attention wander. When several people seem to be saying, "Let's cut out the talk and get down to business," or "What should we do to get rolling?" the chairman or someone else in the meeting may suggest that they follow an outline, and the group will accept the suggestion and stay with an outline. When they wish to have a more tightly organized meeting, their attention span will continue to be short, but they will welcome attempts to get them back to the business at hand and willingly follow such suggestions.

A realistic picture of how groups work includes the notion that groups do not systematically pick the best solution from a carefully drawn list of possible solutions; rather, they tend to throw out the worst, the not so good, and the fair, until they are left with several good answers which they mull over until the final decision emerges. The group circles problems rather than dealing with them in a straight line. Thus, a sensible agenda might well suggest running over topics A, B, and C in about 30 minutes and then returning to the total agenda for a more penetrating discussion. The group needs to find the areas of quick agreement and the points of minor and of serious conflict.

Groups tend to approach the total problem, grabbing hold of it almost any place in order to get started. Their first pass at the topic results in a rather simple approach. They return again, dig more deeply, and begin to cut closer to the important difficulties. When people start to argue and disagree they feel social tension and become uncomfortable, so they pull back and turn to less painful matters. After a time they return to the central issue and drive still closer to a solution. The approach-withdrawal action is typical of groups making tough decisions.

A group often appreciates a relatively free and unstructured period early in the meeting to allow a quick survey of all the business and get some idea of how people feel about things. Some members will need to prod the others to get down to the important arguments, because groups do not like to discuss touchy subjects. If you watch for the tendency to take flight, you as leader can often help the group by pushing for a discussion of the tough issues.

Once a decision has emerged, the group ought to state formally, confirm, and plan details to implement the decision. At the point of getting things in order to carry out a decision, the members are usually pleased to have an outline or an agenda, and they work through these items with fewer digressions during the last stages of the problem-solving process.[2]

[2] For a survey of the research and an expansion of this account of group problem-solving and decision-making, see Ernest G. Bormann, *Discussion and Group Methods: Theory and Practice*, 2nd ed., New York: Harper & Row, 1975, pp. 280–309.

SPEECH
COMMUNICATION:
A COMPREHENSIVE
APPROACH

SUGGESTED PROJECTS

1 The class is divided into one-time-meeting discussion groups of five or six, and the instructor provides each group with a timely community or campus topic to discuss. A moderator is appointed, and the group plans a brief agenda. The group tries to have a good discussion and, at the same time, to let everybody participate equally. To aid in this equal participation, each group member is given the same number of poker chips or tokens of some sort. Each time a member speaks, he has to "spend" a token. When all his tokens are spent, he can no longer participate. Each group should devote 10 minutes after the discussion to evaluating the effect of striving for absolutely equal participation during the meeting.

2 Attend a one-time meeting of a real-life campus group. Write a short paper describing and evaluating the leadership of the meeting. List the specific techniques used by the leader to keep the discussion moving, on the track, with maximum involvement of the group members.

3 Find three real examples that have occurred in the last month in your community of each of the following kinds of group discussion meetings: (1) ritualistic, (2) briefing sessions, (3) instructional meeting, (4) consultative meeting, (5) decision-making meeting.

SUGGESTED READINGS

Bormann, Ernest G., and Nancy C. Bormann. *Effective Small Group Communication*, 2nd ed. Minneapolis: Burgess, 1976.

Brilhart, John K. *Effective Group Discussion*, 2nd ed. Dubuque, Iowa: Brown, 1974.

Phillips, Gerald M. *Communication and the Small Group*, 2nd ed. Indianapolis: Bobbs-Merrill, 1972.

Chapter 16

WORK GROUPS AND ORGANIZATIONAL COMMUNICATION

Small task-oriented groups and organizations use communication as a way to accomplish common tasks. Most organizational communication within and among the work groups which compose the structure are in the message communication style. One way to view an organization is as an information-processing structure. The organizing behavior of the people who at any moment participate in a formal institution is largely accomplished by verbal and nonverbal communication transactions. Again, a great deal of the communication takes place within formal and informal small groups as people go about their daily organizational tasks.

Many of the same basic communication skills that are important in the one-time meeting can be used in communicating in continuing groups. The essential difference between the one-time meeting and the meetings of groups that work together over a period of time is twofold: The work group's history influences the participants' thoughts about the future; and the group's future hopes and plans influence their present behavior. A basketball player can learn some important skills in a pick-up game, with two or three other players on a side, using half a basketball court. You can learn important communication skills in a one-time meeting in much the same way as the player learns in the simpler game situation. When a basketball player takes part in a full-dress game, however, with five players on each side and the entire court in use, he acquires a whole new set of skills relating to teamwork, the potential for more complicated plays, and the psychological momentum of the real game. In this chapter we will take the principles and skills of the one-time meeting and build upon that foundation the small-group theory that has to do with continuing groups. We will start with the *ad hoc*, or standing, committee and then examine the effect of an organizational structure on the work groups that do the organization's tasks.

Characteristics of a Good Work Group

The work group is a social event. When several people share ideas or produce a product, a social dimension emerges. The first question in the mind of every person in a new work group is "How do I relate to these other people as a human being?" Every member wants this question answered, and he wants it answered early. Even after he has been in the group for months or years, he wants the answer repeated from time to time.

If a person feels that the others like, admire, and respect him, enjoy his company, and consider his ideas important, he can relax and turn his full attention to doing the job. Such an

atmosphere of trust and understanding should be the goal of every participant, and *particularly* of every manager, chairperson, moderator, or leader of a work group.

We are discussing only those groups that have a job to do. Inevitably, the members expect, and usually want, to concentrate on the job. If the group is a discussion meeting or conference, they want to start talking about the agenda. If the group is working in an office, the members want to start reading the mail, filing papers, drafting letters, holding conferences. If it is a production group, the workers need to get the machines rolling. The family too is a working group; its job is to maintain the living arrangements of its members and manage their day-to-day existence. Many studies have been made on "the family as a group." The group's work is hampered by poor plans, misunderstandings, faulty reasoning, inadequate concepts, bad information, and most importantly, the way directions and orders are given and received. *A whole book could be devoted to the subject of giving and receiving orders.* Orders must be given, but when you give another person an order, the social and task dimensions of your interaction may come into conflict. If the group member thinks the direction indicates that the leader feels superior to him or is using the group for his own purposes, the order may be misunderstood or disobeyed even though it is a good order.

MORALE AND PRODUCTIVITY

A good work group has high morale. The members are happy with the group; they enjoy working with the others on the job and are pleased with their place in the group. They receive a sense of belonging and a feeling of personal satisfaction from their role.

A good group gets things done. It reaches its goals with a minimum of wasted motion. It turns out a large quantity of a high-quality product, wins games, solves problems, or makes good decisions.

Some people think productivity is all that counts, but the individual should gain a sense of satisfaction and worth from his participation in the group. We do not believe that the individual exists solely for the group. The group has certain duties and responsibilities to the individual.

COHESIVENESS

Cohesiveness is the key to successful work groups. *Cohesiveness* refers to the ability of the group to stick together. Another term for the same quality is *group loyalty*.

A highly cohesive group is one in which the members work for the good of the group. They form a tightly knit unit, and they help one another. They exhibit team spirit. They reflect the motto of Alexander Dumas's *Three Musketeers:* "All for one and one for all."

Cohesiveness encourages increased and improved communication, morale, and productivity. Cohesive groups do more work, because members take the *initiative* and help one another. They distribute the work load among themselves, and take up the slack in times of stress. People in groups with little cohesiveness tend to stand around and wait for assignments. They do what they are told to do and no more. They do not care about the work of others. While members of cohesive groups volunteer to help one another, people in groups with little cohesiveness look out primarily for themselves.

The more cohesive the group, the more efficient the communication within the group. Cohesiveness encourages disagreement and questions. Both are necessary to communication. Highly cohesive groups disagree among themselves. A member of such a group cannot stand by and watch the others do a shoddy job or make a wrong decision. His group is at stake. He must speak up and do what he can to assure its success. Such disagreements improve the quality and quantity of the work by assuring a high level of communication. Cohesiveness encourages questions, because in the cohesive group, every member knows his place and is secure. His position is not threatened if he admits he does not know something. Indeed, the welfare of the group requires that each member have adequate information. The group rewards questions that help it achieve its goals. Likewise, the important member does not feel insulted when people demand more information. He is more interested in the welfare of the group than in his own personal feelings. Since the group succeeds or fails largely depending upon the efficiency of its communication, the cohesive group encourages its members to work cooperatively to achieve understanding.

To build cohesiveness in your group, you need to know some of the dynamics of group process. Every member of the work group is constantly experiencing pushes into and pulls away from the group. The cohesiveness of the group changes from day to day. A unit that is highly cohesive this year—an effective, hard-hitting group—may next year suffer a series of reverses or a change of personnel that causes it to lose cohesiveness and be less effective. If the group comes into competition with similar groups, cohesiveness is usually increased. Athletic teams develop high levels of team spirit and will to win because they compete with other teams in a win-or-lose situation. Coaches know the importance of cohesiveness and how to build it.

On the other hand, a *competing* group may try to lure a member away from his group and thus decrease his feeling of commitment. If you wish to examine the cohesiveness of your group, you must look to the other groups that are competing for the loyalty of the members. The attractiveness of his group for a given member is partly dependent on the character of the other groups he could join. If another group becomes more attractive, a person may leave his original group.

If you want to know how attractive your group is to a member, total the rewards it furnishes him and subtract the costs; the remainder is an index of group attractiveness. At any given moment, an individual feels the pull of his group because it satisfies one or more of his basic needs.

If you understand how a group can satisfy the needs of its members, you are well on the way to understanding how to make a group more cohesive. A group can provide its members with material rewards such as money, with social rewards such as the sense of belonging, with prestige rewards that come from being part of a respected group, with an opportunity to do good work and to achieve, with the chance to fight for a good cause, and with a sense of individual significance and worth. Think of a group you are working with and ask yourself of each member: What is this person getting out of the group? Run down the list. Does the group give the person material rewards, or does it cost him money to belong? Does the group give the person social rewards? If you wish to improve the group, the next step is to see if changes can increase the rewards the group furnishes for the individuals who are not committed to the group.

Building a Positive Social Climate

One way to increase the attractiveness of a group is to build a social climate that is rewarding and fun for all members. When the members of a new work group meet for the first time they begin to interact socially. They nod or talk to one another. They smile, frown, and laugh. All these things help build a climate that is pleasant, congenial, and relaxed; or one that is stiff and tense. A positive social climate makes the group attractive, builds cohesiveness, and encourages people to speak up and say what they really mean.

Investigations of the social dimension of groups indicate three kinds of verbal and nonverbal communication that build good social feelings among group members, and three that build a stiff and negative social setting. The positive communications are shows of solidarity, of tension release, and of agreement. The negative messages are shows of antagonism, of tension, and of disagreement.[1]

SHOWING SOLIDARITY
Any action or statement you make that indicates to the others that the new group is important to you is a show of

[1] Our discussion of a positive social climate is organized around the category system originally developed by Bales. (See Robert F. Bales, *Interaction Process Analysis: A Method for the Study of Small Groups*, Reading, Mass.: Addison-Wesley, 1950.) The concepts come from Bales's categories, but we have modified them as a result of using them to teach small group communication and as a result of further research at the University of Minnesota. (See Ernest G. Bormann, *Discussion and Group Methods: Theory and Practice*, 2nd ed., New York: Harper & Row, 1975, pp. 176–197.) In 1970 Bales published a revision of his original category system which included changing the category of "Shows Solidarity" to "Seems Friendly" and the category of "Shows Antagonism" to "Seems Unfriendly." Most importantly he changed the original category of "Shows Tension Release" to "Dramatizes." We have discussed in previous chapters the importance of dramatizing communication, in regard to fantasy theme chaining. For pedagogical purposes, however, we continue to find the original categories more useful than the revision. (For the revisions see Robert F. Bales, *Personality and Interpersonal Behavior*, New York: Holt, Rinehart and Winston, 1970.)

solidarity. Raising another's status, offering to help do something for the group, volunteering, or indicating that you are willing to make a personal sacrifice for the group shows solidarity.

SHOWING ANTAGONISM

The opposite of showing solidarity is showing antagonism to the group or to another person. While shows of solidarity build a pleasant spirit and rapport, shows of antagonism make the others uncomfortable.

RELEASING TENSION

People in new groups always feel a certain amount of tension. Embarrassment, shyness, and uneasiness when meeting with strangers are shows of social tension. When a discussion group first meets, everyone experiences *primary* tensions. They feel ill at ease. They do not know what to say or how to begin. The first meeting is tense and cold and must be warmed up. When groups experience primary tension, the people speak softly; they sigh, and they are polite. They seem bored and uninterested. No person is really bored when he has an opportunity to speak up and make a name for himself. Every individual, however, gambles a great deal by plunging into the meeting, by taking an active part and trying to make a good showing. A person who has had success in similar situations in the past may be more willing than others to take this chance. The others may be impressed by his ability and decide they like him as a person; on the other hand, they may be irritated by him, decide he is stupid and uninformed, reject him. This gamble makes a person feel nervous and tense, and he may take flight from the situation by pretending he is not interested. Do not be misled. The person who seems bored and uninterested is really tense and most interested, particularly in the social setting of the group. If the meeting never releases primary tension, the whole style of future meetings may be set in this uncomfortable mold. It is vital that the primary tension be released early! Tension is released through indications of pleasure, such as smiles, chuckles, and laughs. Members of a new group should spend some time joking and socializing before getting down to business. Judiciously used, socializing is time wisely spent. Once the primary tension is released, however, the group should go to work.

Once people relax and get down to work, new and different social tensions are generated by disagreements over ideas and by personality conflicts. *Secondary* tensions are louder than primary ones. People speak rapidly, interrupt one another, are impatient to get the floor and have their say; they may get up and pace the room or pound the table. When secondary tensions reach a certain level, the group finds it difficult to concentrate on its job. When that point is reached, the tensions should be released by humor, direct comment, or conciliation. Secondary tensions are more difficult to bleed off than primary ones. There are no easy solutions, but the tensions should not be ignored. They should be brought out into the open and talked over.

COPING WITH DISAGREEMENTS

Agreement is one of the basic social rewards. When the group members agree with a person, they say, "We value you." When others agree with us, we lose our primary tension; we loosen up; we get excited; we take a more active part in the meeting. The more people agree, the more they communicate with one another.

Disagreements serve as negative-climate builders. When people disagree, they grow cautious and tense. *Disagreements are socially punishing but absolutely essential to good group work.* They are double-edged. They are necessary to sound thinking. Yet disagreements always contain an element of personal attack. The person who finds his ideas subjected to rigorous testing and disagreement feels as though he is being shot down.

One of the reasons that the number of disagreements increases with a rise in cohesiveness is that groups must develop enough cohesiveness to afford disagreements and still not break up. The rate of disagreements is often highest in the family—the most cohesive unit in our society. How often someone complains, "You're so much nicer with strangers than with the members of your own family!"

Some people try to cushion the hurt in a disagreement by saying things such as, "That's a good idea, *but* . . ." or "That's right. I agree with you, *but*. . . ." Eventually the others discover that these prefatory agreements or compliments are just ways of setting them up for the knife. They begin to cringe as the ". . . *but* I think we ought to look at the other side of it" hits them. The fact is, disagreements must be understood to mean, "Stop, this will not do." When they are thus understood, no amount of kind words of introduction serves to sugar-coat them.

An important way to resolve conflicts is to build group

cohesiveness. It helps to do things to knit the group back together after a period of heavy disagreement. Often disagreements increase as a group moves toward a decision. Good groups use positive-climate builders after the decision is reached. They joke and laugh. They show solidarity. They say, "It was a good meeting." "It accomplished something." "Let's all get behind this decision." They compliment the persons who advocated the rejected plan. They tell them they are needed, that the group cannot succeed without their help.

Another technique sometimes used by successful work groups is to allow one person to become the "disagreer." He tests most of the ideas and the group expects him to do so. Whenever they feel the need for disagreements they turn to him. They reward him by giving him a nickname or by joshing him about how disagreeable he is. Since he plays the role of critical thinker, other members are less hurt by his criticisms, because, "After all, he disagrees with everybody."

Group Roles

In Chapter 15 we described the one-time meeting. Here we analyze the dynamics of an *ad hoc* group, that starts without a history but continues to meet over a period of time until it develops a group culture and the members get to know one another well enough to form friendships, animosities, and opinions of one another.

The first important discovery from research into zero-history groups is that after several hours the members begin to specialize.[2] That is, not every member does an equal amount of the same thing. If we analyze the content of the typical group's communication, we find that some members talk more than others and that members tend to say different kinds of things. Some give more information along the lines discussed in Chapter 9; some talk more about personal characteristics and social relationships; some make more suggestions about doing the work of the group.

When it becomes clear to a person that he is specializing and when the group discovers he is doing so, he takes a *place* in the group. He has his particular *role*. Individuals change "personality" as they go from group to group. The buxom college woman who has such a sparkling personality in class and enjoys flirting with the men may be quiet, devout, and reserved with her church circle. She may be ill-tempered and

[2] Bormann, ibid., pp. 198–219.

bossy with her family. Think of yourself. In one group you may be a take-charge person who gets things rolling. In another you may be likable, joshing, and fun-loving, but not a leader at all. In a third group you may be quiet, steady, and a responsible worker.

PRINCIPLES OF ROLE EMERGENCE

A member's role is worked out jointly by the person and the group. This is the basic principle. We should not blame the group's problems on innate unchangeable personality traits inherent in a troublesome person. Groups can be more neurotic than individuals, and they love to blame their troubles on one member—make him the scapegoat for their failure. If we understand the nature of roles, we will no longer make that mistake. Instead of wishing we could get rid of Bill so we could have a productive group, we ask what the group may be doing to Bill to make him act as he does.

Once everyone has found a place, a second important thing happens. The group judges the relative worth of each role. It gives the roles it judges more valuable a higher status than the others. After a group has been working together for several hours, a trained observer can arrange a status ladder by watching the way the members talk and act. They talk directly and more often to the people they consider important. High-status people talk more to the entire group. The high-status people receive more consideration from the others: The others listen to what a high-status individual says; they often stop what they are doing to come to him; they stop talking to hear him, and they agree more, and more emphatically, with him. The group tends to ignore and cut off comments by low-status members.

Since rewards of much esteem and prestige are given to high-status members, several people usually compete for the top positions. In this competition they come into conflict; there are disagreements. The group's energy is directed to the question of who will win, and attention is drawn away from the work. In extreme cases the struggles become heated, and the group gets bogged down. Every new group must go through a "shakedown cruise," during which the members test roles and find out who is top dog, who is best liked, and so forth. During the shakedown cruise, secondary tensions mount, and people who are contending for leadership come into conflict.

Each contender for a high-status role is led to specialize, through both his own efforts and the group's encouragement.

The group agrees with him when he does what it wants him to and disagrees when he does not; it thus discourages him from a role it considers unnecessary or unacceptable. A given person does not have a monopoly on the role assigned him in this way, but he fulfills most of that role's functions in the group.

Group stability and communication increase side by side. When a group achieves a stable role structure and a high level of cohesiveness, an increase in feedback usually follows. A person who is strongly attracted to the group and wishes it well wants to maximize communication. He knows the group will do a better job if each member is thoroughly briefed. Therefore, if he does not know something, he is likely to ask. In addition, if he has a stable place in the group, admitting his ignorance does not hurt his reputation. Sometimes bad habits that developed during role struggles carry over, and groups continue to function without adequate feedback. The group should make periodic evaluations of the level of feedback and make conscious plans to encourage it as needed.

Just as the need to appear more knowledgeable disappears with stable structure, so does the need to show off. A person can relax and be honest in a group with a high level of cohesiveness, and the change in attitude allows greater concentration on listening to messages. When roles stabilize, the members no longer feel the need to view each message in personal terms. They no longer think, "Does this message mean so-and-so is leadership material? that he likes me? that he doesn't like me?" Members can become more message-centered, which is the first step to improved listening.

The members of an organization vary as to their skills in the art of communication. Some may have trouble holding long chains of argument in mind. Achieving effective communication takes considerable time and tension-producing effort. Communication is hard work. Groups should establish the rule that enough time will be allocated and spent (not wasted) to ensure that the proper level of understanding is reached during the meeting.

The presence in a meeting of a person with high formal status in a community or organization immediately inhibits the free flow of communication and feedback. People wait for the high-status person to take the lead; they wait for cues from him about the proper tone of response. They tend to tell the high-status person only what they think he would like to hear. If a feeling of cohesiveness is generated within the work group, the dampening effect of the high-status person can be overcome to some extent. If the others discover he is sincerely interested in the good of the group, tolerates disagreements, and recognizes the necessity of sound communication, a productive meeting should follow.

THE LEADERSHIP ROLE

Of all the roles that emerge in a work group, none has fascinated the philosophers, writers, social scientists, and man in the street more than the high-status, influential role of leadership.[3]

In our country we are of two minds about leadership. If a member of a new group suggests that another person would be a good leader, that person's response typically is, "Oh, no! Not me. Someone else could do a better job." Despite such protests, nearly every member of every group would like to lead. We would like right now to dispel that old saying that some people are born leaders and others born followers. This just is not so. All people would like to be leaders and usually are, if not in one group, in some other group. Some people have more skills in the leadership area and become leaders in more groups. But never underestimate the desire of every member of any group to take over the leadership role. Publicly, people sometimes do not admit this, but privately they usually do.

Why this ambivalence? On the one hand, our democratic traditions suggest that all men are created equal and that nobody is better than anybody else. We maintain a belief in a classless society. Many groups in the 1960s made a strong commitment to not striving for leadership and tried hard to do away with the leadership concept in their group work because they found it distasteful. They preferred the idea of working in a commune or cooperative rather than in a corporation and tried to arrange their groups so there would be no "leaders." But even the people dedicated to denying leadership—because it meant power, which they viewed as evil—discovered that their groups needed structure to survive and that structure implied leadership.

The most satisfactory explanation of leadership is that it is a result of the individual's traits (inherited characteristics plus training), the purposes of the group, the pressures put on the group from the outside, and the way the persons in the group talk, work, and relate with one another.

Such a contextual explanation provides a more complete

[3] For a survey and bibliography which gives some indication of the extensive investigation of leadership, see Ralph M. Stogdill, *Handbook of Leadership: A Survey of Theory and Research*, New York: Free Press, 1974.

view of leadership than other approaches. It includes the idea that leaders are to some extent "born," but it also suggests that potential leaders can achieve skills and improve talents. The contextual approach (the consideration of the total context, or all components, of each group) explains why someone who emerges as leader in one group may fail to emerge as the leader of a second, apparently similar, group.

The members of a group spend time and energy on selecting leadership because it is so important to the success of the group. We are touchy about the people who boss us around. We do not like to take orders. If we have to, we prefer a leader who gives wise orders in a way we can tolerate. The leader makes crucial suggestions and decisions about the way the work will be divided and the way the material resources of the group will be distributed. In the end, the group rejects potential leaders until they are left with the person who seems best able to lead *for the good of all.*

Sometimes the struggle for leadership is never resolved. Groups in which this happens become invalids. The members spend their time in backbiting and getting back at internal enemies. If, after working together for some time, a group is left with two or three potential leaders, each having substantial handicaps, the leadership question may not be resolved.

Central Persons

Some people are so dominant in their verbal and nonverbal communications in a new work group that they fascinate the others. They may be positive or negative people; we shall call them *central* persons. A central person may be a *star:* He may be unusually capable and a potential asset to the group's productivity, or he may be exceptionally skillful at human relations and unusually charming. A central person may be one who seems extremely hostile to the group and its purposes, who downgrades the work, or who makes it plain he feels the other members are incapable. Such a person is a potential threat to the group. A central person may even be someone who is unusually apathetic and uninvolved and simply refuses to take part in the group. All these people are central because they distract the group's attention from its tasks.

A common threatening central person is the *manipulator.* He comes to the group with the intention of exploiting it for his own ends. He intends to take it over and run it. Manipulators tend to be either *hard sell* or *soft sell.* The hard-sell manipulator usually comes on strong. He talks a great deal and takes charge immediately with a strong hand: "Let's get down to business. Now here's what we will do." When the group resists his leadership, he tries to argue and browbeat the others into line. When someone resists him, the others swing to support the contender, and the hard-sell manipulator then stands alone against the group, trying hard to talk everyone down. Sometimes, the hard-sell manipulator is not immediately challenged and is then certain he has succeeded in taking over. When he gives orders, however, they are not followed. People continually misunderstand or fail to follow through. He decides he has not been working hard enough at his leading, so he begins to give his orders slowly, carefully, in simple English, as though he were talking to morons. This arouses even greater resentment and gold-bricking. He decides the group members are all lazy and irresponsible. Inevitably, another contender emerges and becomes leader. The manipulator is now extremely frustrated. His self-image is badly dented. He came into the group confident of his superiority and his ability to run the group his way, and the group has rejected him. He seldom examines where he has failed. Usually he turns on the group members: They are ignorant and stupid. If he remains in the group, he is often a troublemaker. Finding him an acceptable role takes ingenuity.

The soft-sell manipulator is often much more successful in his second phase. He often emerges for a time as the leader. He has many tricks and formulas of human relations at his command. He is friendly and congenial. He seems less bossy and more democratic. He sizes up the group to see who can be conned and who will be troublesome. He does more work outside the group's formal meetings, such as chatting with this or that member over coffee. He is a politician. After several weeks of working with him however, the others find him out. They discover that he is getting his way and that under his apparently congenial and democratic facade, he is using the group for his personal ends. When the soft-sell manipulator is found out, a challenger comes forward, and the group reshuffles roles until a new leader emerges.

Changing Membership

A change in group personnel is always unsettling. If a new person is added, this person brings with him certain skills and talents, and a role has to be found for him. All the roles have to be reshuffled to free enough duties to provide the new man with a job. When a member is removed, a role struggle again results. The remaining members must take on the tasks that the former member used to do. If he had important duties, the members who stand to gain by climbing upward on the status ladder may come into conflict. When a member is replaced, the new man does not simply take over his predecessor's role; reshuffling of all roles is necessary. The importance of realizing that any change in a group's personnel causes problems cannot be overstated. This knowledge will help you to help any group in which you are a member through the inevitable reshuffling of roles.

The effect of changing personnel by adding, removing, or replacing individuals is a repeat of the shakedown cruise. The typical result is a period of role instability and struggle that surprises and frustrates the members. People often do not understand what is going on and why it must go on. They respond by blaming the new member: "Everything was fine until he came." Or they bemoan the loss of a member: "Before John left, everything went along fine; we sure miss John."

Formal Leadership

Many of the groups to which we belong are neither one-time discussions nor *ad hoc* committees. Many groups are not composed completely of peers, and everyone does not start out equal. Many work groups function within a *formal* organization. The salesman works *under* a sales manager within a corporation. The teacher supervises a group within the framework of the class. The executive committee of the fraternity chapter functions within the larger organization. People come to such work groups with different status. Sometimes the status is internal to the organization, as when the dean meets with a group of students. Although status differences introduce complications, the basic process of group development can be adjusted to take these into account.

In our consulting with many real-life organizations and businesses, we have found the principles of *ad hoc* group process transfer readily and facilitate understanding of the workings of so-called structured, as well as unstructured, groups. To illustrate, we will show how leadership is related to the management of organizational work groups.

The formal structure of an organization is static. The organization's informal work groups, which develop and change with a turnover in personnal and with fluctuating working conditions, are dynamic. They change constantly, a little or a lot. Frequently the power structure of the informal organization differs from what the formal organization would indicate. The organizational chart no longer reflects the realities. You cannot figure out a man's power and esteem by finding out whether he is a supervisor, a vice-president, or an engineer. The real boss may not be the man with the title. What then?

POWER STRUGGLES WITHIN AN ORGANIZATION

The role struggle between a man with the power of a formal position (the formal leader) and a man with the esteem and power furnished by his standing with the members (the natural leader) can be long and bloody. Let us say that a person in a position of formal leadership leaves the organization and a new man takes his place. Assume that the replacement is a stranger to the members in the work group. The entire group is subjected to a shakedown cruise. The new manager must assume certain leadership functions for the work group because the formal position guide says he must. He is expected by top management and by the organization to lead his group immediately. He is not, however, accepted as the natural leader of the group without a period of testing. He must find his role in the informal groups within his department according to the basic principles of group process. When he finally assumes his role, it is slightly different from that of the former manager, and the whole group experiences a reshuffling of roles.

The new manager does have certain standard levers furnished him by the organization to help him emerge as leader. These may include the right to increase salaries, give bonuses, promote, assign jobs and vacations, and punish tardiness, malingering, and poor work. You may think these levers give the new man an insurmountable advantage. Wisely used by a person who understands the dynamics of small groups, they may. Sometimes, however, the authority to punish and reward members turns out to be a handicap rather than a help.

Here is how this might happen. The new manager, whoever he is, is a marked man! His boss is watching him closely to see how he will work out. He tries to do an exceptionally good job. The members of the group watch him carefully. Will he turn out to be a man they can follow? If he begins with strong and decisive leadership moves, he can expect some resistance. He may find he is misunderstood: Misunderstanding directions is a common way of resisting an order. To

Chapter 16

THE KEY IDEAS

When people must work together, a social dimension results from their communication.

When someone structures a group's work, the social and task dimensions come into conflict, because giving and taking orders causes social tension.

Good work groups have good morale and get things done.

A highly cohesive group is one in which the members work for the good of the group.

The more cohesive the group, the better the communication, because cohesiveness encourages disagreements and questions.

At any given moment a person feels attracted to a group if it satisfies one or more of his basic needs.

People in new groups always feel some social tension, because they are unsure how the others will react to them as people.

The person who seems bored and uninterested at a first meeting of a group is proba-

a man on trial, eager to prove his efficiency, such response may lead to frustration and anger.

If so, the new manager has come to a crucial point. If he controls his anger and asks, "What have I done wrong?" he may be able to mend his fences and start to build a role of leadership within the group. If he understands the way people emerge as natural leaders, he may win the power and esteem that the authority and prestige of his job deserve, and without which he must remain ineffective and unsatisfied to some extent. If he lashes back and pulls the levers by which he can force members to obey, he will start a spiral that results in malingering, more crises, less production, and trouble with upper management. If he panics and decides he has not been firm enough, he may wildly put pressures on his men. He will lay down the law, read off the lazy workers, make sure his directions are crystal clear, and supervise the most minute debly tense and most interested, particularly in how the others would view him if he spoke up.

Agreement is one of the basic social rewards in our society. Disagreements are socially punishing but absolutely necessary to good group work.

One important fact of group dynamics is that members tend to specialize in doing certain tasks over a period of time.

When all members have a common expectation about how a person will behave, that individual has a role in the group.

A member's role is worked out jointly by the person and the group.

Members award a higher status to those roles they judge more valuable to the group.

Feedback is related to role stability and cohesiveness because a person can ask questions with less fear of losing status in a cohesive and stable group.

The presence in a meeting of a person with formal status within a community or an organization poses a barrier to successful communication.

The leadership role is the one most fascinating to both the general public and the experts.

In our culture we both deplore leadership as an undesirable feature of a classless democracy and applaud the successful person who rises to a position of power.

The members of a group spend much time and energy on the leadership question because it is so important to the successful achievement of group goals.

A change in group personnel is always unsettling.

Many work groups function within a formal organization, which, in turn, exercises a controlling influence on certain factors of communication.

When the power structure of the informal organization differs from the formal structure, one can predict communication problems.

tails of the work. The members of his unit will then reject him as their leader, and someone else will emerge as the natural leader—the one to whom they all go with their gripes. Such groups disturb their members. Morale declines. Members have difficulty talking about anything but their troubles. They vent their spleen on "him" and on any members who have sold out to "him." They plot and plan ways to get back at "him."

Although our example applies the knowledge about the work group to a hypothetical business organization, the same principles apply to the newly elected club, sorority, or fraternity president, or to the Student Union Board members, the Black Student Union officers, the American Indian Movement, the YMCA board members, or any of the dozens of organizations, large or small, to which you belong now and to which you will belong in your lifetime.

SUGGESTED PROJECTS

1 Divide the class into groups of five. For each group, have five common group roles printed on slips of paper that are folded up and picked blindly by the group members. No one discloses the role he has drawn. Discuss some perennial problem (for example, the need for more individual student-teacher time in most college courses) and stay in the role you have drawn throughout the discussion. After 5 minutes, stop the discussion and have each member write down the roles he thinks the *others* have taken. After this, compare notes and discuss roles in groups. If you drew a role very unusual for you, explain the difficulties you found trying to stay in character. As you continued to play the assigned role, did you begin to feel more natural in it as time went on?

2 Students are placed in leaderless groups of five or six. Each group is furnished with a tape recorder and spends one or two class meetings, which the group records, preparing a panel discussion program on some important public issue to present to the class. The group selects a moderator for the program and after discussing the topic in front of the class for 30 minutes, throws the discussion open for audience participation. Each member of the group listens to one of the tapes taken during the planning meetings and writes a short paper evaluating the role emergence that takes place during the planning sessions and the actual presentation.

3 Select a small group that you work with on a regular basis. This group could be part of an office or business organization, a committee of students working on a long-term project, a church or social action group—any task-oriented small group. Keep a journal of your experiences in the group. Describe the group's cohesiveness, role structure, and leadership. Where do you fit into the group's role structure?

SUGGESTED READINGS

Bormann, Ernest G. *Discussion and Group Methods,* 2nd ed. New York: Harper & Row, 1975.

Bormann, Ernest G., and Nancy C. Bormann. *Effective Small Group Communication.* 2nd ed. Minneapolis: Burgess, 1976.

Fisher, B. Aubrey. *Small Group Decision Making: Communication and the Group Process.* New York: McGraw-Hill, 1974.

Gouran, Dennis S. *Discussion: The Process of Group Decision-Making.* New York: Harper & Row, 1974.

INDEX OF NAMES

Mills, Glen E., 277
Mitchell, John, 322, 323
Monroe, Alan H., 198n, 203
Montague, Ashley, 389
Mortensen, C. David., 28n, 49n, 102n, 248
Moyer, J. R., 279n
Mueller, Ronald A., 226n
Muskie, Edmund, 320

Nader, Ralph, 331
Newman, Dale R., 277
Newman, Robert P., 277
Nichols, Ralph G., 20, 223
Nilsen, Thomas R., 248n, 276n, 277
Nixon, Richard M., 302, 319, 320, 322, 323, 333, 336, 337, 352n, 354, 360
Nofsinger, Robert E., Jr., 128n
Nunnally, J. C., 27n

O'Keefe, Daniel J., 280n
Olbright, Thomas, 245
Orr, C. Jack, 348n
Osborn, Michael, 360n
Osgood, Charles E., 268n

Packard, Vance, 340n
Parrish, Wayland, 27n
Patton, Bobby R., 389
Pearce, W. Barnett, 281n, 283n
Peterson, Owen, 178, 203, 245
Philbrick, Herbert, 333
Phillips, Gerald M., 407
Postman, Leo, 265n
Press, Allan N., 280n

Rarig, Frank M., 103n
Raven, I. McDavid, Jr., 76n

Reid, Ronald F., 20
Renshaw, Steve, 250
Robb, Mary Margaret, 103n
Rogers, Carl R., 220, 221n, 379, 389
Roosevelt, Franklin D., 351
Rubenstein, Aniela, 10
Rubenstein, Arthur, 10
Ruesch, Jurgen, 115n, 148
Ryberg, Lillian, 403n

Sartre, Jean Paul, 50
Schachter, Stanley, 324n
Schelling, Thomas C., 250
Scheidel, Thomas M., 287n
Schramm, Wilbur L., 34
Scott, Robert L., 277, 348n, 367
Seibold, David R., 349n
Sereno, Kenneth K., 49n
Sevareid, Eric, 336
Shakespeare, William, 382
Shannon, Claude, 34
Shapiro, George L., 20
Sheflen, Albert E., 115n, 116n, 119n, 121n, 131n, 135n, 138n, 148, 152
Sheflen, Alice, 115n, 116n, 119n, 121n, 131n, 138n, 148, 152
Shulman, Gary M., 135
Shuy, Roger W., 87
Sieburg, Evelyn, 292n
Simons, Herbert W., 279, 348n, 349n
Sirica, John J., 321
Smith, Bruce Lannes, 300n
Smith, David H., 250n
Smith, Donald K., 103n
Smith, Howard K., 336
Smith, Ralph R., Jr., 124n, 148
Smith, Raymond G., 279n

Speier, Hans, 300n, 301
Stalin, Joseph, 316
Steinfatt, Thomas M., 349n
Stevens, Leonard, 223
Stewart, John, 57, 121n, 225n
Stogdill, Ralph M., 419n
Swanson, David L., 348n

Tannenbaum, Percy H., 268n
Taylor, Orlando, 77n
Tolela, Michele, 292n
Tracy, Joseph, 198n
Truman, Harry S., 351, 353
Tubbs, Stewart L., 250
Tuppen, Christopher J. S., 279n
Twain, Mark, 316, 328

Wallace, Karl, 30, 103n
Wallas, Graham, 185n
Walster, Elaine, 292n
Walter, Otis M., 277
Washington, Booker T., 312
Watzlawick, Paul, 48n, 57, 131, 350n
Weaver, Andrew T., 198n
Weaver, Warren, 34
Weiss, Walter, 279
White, Eugene, 26n
Whitehead, Jack C., Jr., 280n
Wiener, Norbert, 44n, 46, 57, 61
Williams, M., 284n
Williams, M. Lee, 250n
Winans, James A., 31, 57
Woolbert, Charles W., 198n
Woodhull, Victoria, 312
Woodward, Bob, 320n

Zander, Alvin, 324n
Ziegler, Ron, 322
Zimmerman, Gordon A., 308n

INDEX OF SUBJECTS

two-person communication and, 370–372
verbal, 216
Fidelity of information transmission, 37, 120, 374
Forensic speech, 252
Form words, 63–64

Gay Liberation, 17
General American Dialect. *See* Dialect
Gestures
in public speaking, 142–143
Ghostwriters, 14
Grammar, 80, 83
Groups
ad hoc, 395–397
attention span of, 402–403
cohesiveness of, 410–413
evaluation of, 409–413
functions of, 393–394
morale of, 410
one-time meeting of, 394–395
size of, 391–392
social climate of, 413–414
Group discussion, 391–393

Habitual pitch level, 107–108
Hamlet, 382
Hearsay evidence, 265
Hidden agenda, 382–383
Human-potential movement, 12
Humor, 295–296

"I Lead Three Lives," 333
Illumination phase in creativity, 187
Image
building of, 289–290
dynamic nature of, 287–289
limits of building, 290–291
role-related, 291–292
Impromptu speech, 194–195
Incubation phase in creativity, 186–187
Information, 224–225, 228
Informative speaking
causal explanations, 232–233
classification, 233–234
definitions, 229–230
descriptions, 231–232
examples, use of, 235–238

hypothetical examples, 234–235
literal analogy, 238–239
narrative as explanation, 233
real examples, 234–235
Intelligibility, 95
Intercultural communication, 126–128
International Phonetic Alphabet, 93
International Phonetic Association, 93
Interpersonal communication, 30. *See also* Relationship communication style
Introduction
of public speech, 191
speech of, 169–170

John Birch Society, 288

Kinesics, 121–122

Language
aspects of, 65
consonants, 93, 94–96
content words, 64–65
form words, 63–64
grammar, 80, 83
phoneme, 93, 96–97
property terms, 64–65
relation terms, 64–65
rules of, 79–81
vowels, 92–93
Leadership
emergence in small groups, 419–420
formal organizational, 422–423
one-time group meeting and, 396, 398–400
Lecture 162–163
Listening
actively, 220–222
critically, 210–212
defensive communication and, 218–220
fantasy themes and, 211–212
feedback and, 212–213, 215–216
likability and, 283
message communication style and, 212–216
nonverbal communication and, 212–213
public-speaking communication style and, 205–212

relationship communication style and, 216–218
supportive, 218–220
Logic of argument, 268–270
Loudness, 99
Lyceum, 150–151

Machiavellianism
and persuasion, 249–250
Manipulative communication styles, 249–252
Manipulator
and persuasion, 284
in small groups, 420–421
Mass media political campaigns, 334–336
Massachusetts Institute of Technology, 34
Mathematical Theory of Communication, The, 34
Mean. *See* Statistics
Meaning
connotative, 68–70, 73, 103, 369
decoding, 44, 58, 95, 373–374
defined, 370–372
denotative, 65–68, 103, 369
encoding, 44, 58, 93, 372–373
interpreting, 373–374
Measurement, 257–258
Median. *See* Statistics
"Meet the Press," 15
Mein Kampf, 359
Message, 40
basic unit in public speaking, 241–244
double-edged, 129–131
sturcture of, 66–68
Message communication style, 6–7, 29, 34–47, 49
channels in, 40
consistency hypotheses and, 275–277
criticism of, 345, 349
encoding in, 44
decoding in, 44
entropy in, 44, 46
feedback in, 35–37, 40
fidelity in, 37
human element in, 41–44
information processing and, 224–226
listening in, 212–216
message in, 40
model of, 34–40
monitoring behavior in, 137–138

76 77 78 79 80 9 8 7 6 5 4 3 2 1

LIBRARY
L. S. U. IN SHREVEPORT